BILL CLINTON

In 1993, William J. Clinton began his eight-year stint as the forty-second President of the United States. A key figure of change in the Democratic Party, Clinton's political and personal actions ensured his lasting status as an important if controversial leader at a critical moment in recent American history. In *Bill Clinton: Building a Bridge to the New Millennium*, David H. Bennett traces the life of Clinton from childhood through his two terms in the White House. From his earliest years to college, from state government to the executive branch and after, Bennett provides a concise and readable biography that places Clinton's achievements, problems, and legacy in historical context.

Situating the former President in the trajectory of twentieth-century liberalism, the author draws on Clinton's life to illuminate the political landscape of America in the 1990s, and the role of the United States in a global context of the post-Cold War world. Combining keen scholarship with accessible prose, this book will be an essential resource for all those interested in understanding the recent history of the United States.

David H. Bennett is Meredith Professor of History in the Maxwell School at Syracuse University. He is the author of *Demagogues in the Depression: American Radicals and the Union Party, 1932–1936* and *The Party of Fear: The American Far Right from Nativism to the Militia Movement*.

ROUTLEDGE HISTORICAL AMERICANS

SERIES EDITOR: PAUL FINKELMAN, ALBANY LAW SCHOOL

Routledge Historical Americans is a series of short, vibrant biographies that illuminate the lives of Americans who have had an impact on the world. Each book includes a short overview of the person's life and puts that person into historical context through essential primary documents, written both by the subjects and about them. A series website supports the books, containing extra images and documents, links to further research, and, where possible, multimedia sources on the subjects. Perfect for including in any course on American History, the books in the Routledge Historical Americans series show the impact that everyday people can have on the course of history.

Woody Guthrie: Writing America's Songs
Ronald D. Cohen

Frederick Douglass: Reformer and Statesman
L. Diane Barnes

*Thurgood Marshall: Race, Rights, and the Struggle for a
More Perfect Union*
Charles L. Zelden

Harry S. Truman: The Coming of the Cold War
Nicole L. Anslover

John Winthrop: Founding the City upon a Hill
Michael Parker

John F. Kennedy: The Spirit of Cold War Liberalism
Jason K. Duncan

Bill Clinton: Building a Bridge to the New Millennium
David H. Bennett

Forthcoming:

Laura Ingalls Wilder: American Writer on the Prairie
Sallie Ketcham

Ronald Reagan: Champion of Conservative America
James Broussard

BILL CLINTON
BUILDING A BRIDGE TO THE NEW MILLENNIUM

DAVID H. BENNETT

Routledge
Taylor & Francis Group

NEW YORK AND LONDON

www.routledge.com/cw/HistoricalAmericans

First published 2014
by Routledge
711 Third Avenue, New York, NY 10017

and by Routledge
2 Park Square, Milton Park, Abingdon, Oxon OX14 4RN

Routledge is an imprint of the Taylor & Francis Group,
an informa business

Library of Congress Cataloging-in-Publication Data
Bennett, David Harry, 1935–
Bill Clinton : building a bridge to the new millennium / David H. Bennett.
    pages cm. — (Routledge historical Americans)
    Includes bibliographical references and index.
  1. Clinton, Bill, 1946– 2. Presidents—United States—Biography. 3. United
States—Politics and government—1993–2001. I. Title.
    E886.B45 2014
    973.929092—dc23
    [B]   2013027219

ISBN: 978-0-415-89466-1 (hbk)
ISBN: 978-0-415-89468-5 (pbk)
ISBN: 978-0-203-08158-7 (ebk)

Typeset in Minion Pro
by Apex CoVantage, LLC

Printed and bound in the United States of America by Publishers Graphics,
LLC on sustainably sourced paper.

For Jake and Ethan
For Sophie and Audrey
And for Gerda

CONTENTS

ACKNOWLEDGMENTS

Any study of a President less than two decades out of office, and still active in a remarkable post–White House career, has to be seen as but a first draft of history. Of course, this was never planned as a definitive treatment of the life and presidency of Bill Clinton. But so important has been Clinton's role in modern American history, so dramatic and event-filled his years in the Oval Office, so rich the available literature on this period, and so fresh the memories of many who helped him shape this history that when asked if I would offer this perspective of his life and work, I was happy to say yes.

Many have been helpful in this project. First, thanks go to my friend Paul Finkelman, the accomplished and prolific scholar who agreed to edit a series of works on "notable historical Americans" and invited me to do this book on Bill Clinton. Paul has been a shrewd reader of the manuscript and I have profited by his suggestions for additions or corrections.

I am also in debt to others who have read all or parts of the manuscript. Roger Sharp, my close friend and colleague in the Department of History in the Maxwell School at Syracuse University, provided many helpful comments on the text as well as encouragement throughout the project.

My sons, as usual, have been enormously supportive. Matthew Bennett, who served in the Clinton White House, first as assistant counsel and trip director for Vice President Gore and later as Deputy Director for Intergovernmental Affairs (before becoming a founder and Senior Vice President of Third Way), offered invaluable insights. So, too, did Steven Bennett, formerly Executive Director of the Global Fairness Initiative and now Vice President and Chief Operating Officer at the Brookings Institution.

I was fortunate that several distinguished figures who served in major posts in the Clinton administration generously took time from their busy schedules to respond to my questions: John Podesta, Chief of Staff; Sandy Berger, National Security Director; Paul Begala, political consultant and strategist; Strobe Talbott, Deputy Secretary of State (and now president of

Brookings); James Steinberg, Deputy National Security Director (and now dean of the Maxwell School) all offered invaluable help.

I presented an early assessment of this Clinton project to the seminar of the History Department at Syracuse. Thanks go to my colleagues in the department for their questions and comments, and special thanks to Department Chair Carol Faulkner. Senior Associate Dean of the Maxwell School Michael Wayselenko has been encouraging and provided needed funds to help defray expenses for a trip to the William J. Clinton Presidential Library in Little Rock.

Librarians in the Bird Library at Syracuse University were helpful during research, as was the staff at the Clinton Library, particularly archivist Whitney Ross.

Paul Arras, a senior graduate student in History at Syracuse University, and a very gifted teaching assistant in my courses, read the manuscript with great care and helped as well in selecting the pictures that accompany the book.

As always, I am most indebted, for everything, to Gerda.

PROLOGUE
INAUGURATION 1993

It was the largest crowd in the history of presidential inaugurations. There were 800,000 people filling the expansive grounds of the United States Capitol Building and stretching down the National Mall toward the Lincoln Memorial. They had assembled under a brilliant blue January sky to see Bill Clinton take the oath of office and deliver his first speech as President of the United States.

All such ceremonies represent a changing of the guard, but this one had a special resonance. The tall, youthful new President, wearing a dark blue suit but no top coat on this bitterly cold midwinter day, was 46 years old. George H. W. Bush, the man he had defeated in November, sitting stoically to the side during the speech, had been a heroic naval airman in World War II. Ronald Reagan, Bush's predecessor, was in his mid-70s when he left office in 1989. For forty years, America's leaders had been influenced by the tumultuous events of the Great Depression, World War II, and the booming prosperity that had followed. Clinton, the first member of the postwar baby boom to reside in the White House, represented a new generation, shaped by the social and political upheavals of the Sixties, the bitter debates over Vietnam, the economic defeats of the Seventies.

It seemed, to so many observers, remarkable that he was there at all. Eighteen months earlier, Clinton was little known across the land, the long-time governor of a small southern state that was among the poorest in the Union. President Bush, his opponent, had a soaring national public approval rating of over 80 percent, reflecting America's victory in the first Gulf War. But a wrenching recession had turned the political world upside down.

Now Bill Clinton, in a compact, fourteen-minute inaugural address, the third shortest in history, told the huge crowd in front of him and the millions watching on television that "we inherit an economy that is still the world's strongest but is weakened by business failures, stagnant wages, increasing inequality, and deep divisions among our people." He then issued a call for renewal: "Thomas Jefferson believed that to preserve the very foundations of our nation, we would need dramatic change from time to time. Well my fellow citizens, this is our time. Let us embrace it." And echoing John F. Kennedy's first inaugural, Clinton exclaimed that although "we have drifted, and that drifting has eroded our resources, fractured our economy and shaken our confidence . . . there is nothing wrong with America that cannot be cured by what is right with America."[1]

It had been a festive few days of inaugural activities. On Monday, an enormous "Call for Reunion" on the Mall had attracted almost a million people, tents stretching from the Capitol to the Washington Monument. The massive, happy throng enjoyed a free outdoor concert featuring a variety of celebrity singers for every taste: Bob Dylan and Diana Ross, Tony Bennett, LL Cool J, and others.

On Tuesday, when the official ceremonies were complete, when Bill Clinton, placing his hand on his mother's King James Bible, had taken the solemn oath to uphold the US Constitution, when Maya Angelou had recited her memorable poem and Aretha Franklin had sung (and the nuclear codes were silently transferred from the outgoing President's aide to the new), Clinton took the traditional ride down Pennsylvania Avenue to view the inaugural parade. But now the new chief executive and his family, responding to crowds along the route chanting "Walk, walk," got out of their armor-plated Cadillac and, to rolling cheers, walked the last few blocks to the reviewing stand in front of the White House.

That night, there were fourteen official inaugural balls and many unofficial ones. At one, sponsored by MTV and called "Inaugural Ball for the Not Well Connected," Bill Clinton told the crowd of rock-and-roll fans that "everybody here knows that MTV had a lot to do with the Clinton–Gore victory." (The reference was to Senator Al Gore, the Vice President-elect.) At the ball filled with fellow Arkansans, after he introduced his mother to Barbra Streisand, the President borrowed a saxophone and played a solo; he finished his impromptu speech with the University of Arkansas football chant: "Soooooeeee Razorbacks." Rahm Emanuel, Clinton's tough 32-year-old campaign finance director, had raised the money for all of these inaugural events: "It is going to be something different," he said. "We want to give voice to the diversity of America."[2]

During the campaign, conducted during a time of deep economic anxiety in this last decade of the twentieth century, candidate Bill Clinton had said that he wanted to "build a bridge to a new millennium." Now, he would have the opportunity.

NOTES

1. First Inaugural Address of William J. Clinton; January 20, 1993, http://avalon.law.yale.edu/20th_century/clinton1.asp
2. *New York Times*, January 21, 1993.

PART I

BILL CLINTON

CHAPTER 1

THE BOY FROM HOPE BECOMES
THE MAN FROM HOPE

Once Bill Clinton had secured enough delegates to ensure the nomination, his team discussed ways to reintroduce the candidate at the Democratic National Convention. He had been a Rhodes Scholar, a graduate of a top-tier college and a famous Ivy League law school. It was easy for foes to characterize him as just another member of the elite. But while the nominee often would make reference to the iconic figures in his party—Thomas Jefferson, Franklin D. Roosevelt, John F. Kennedy—all of them born to wealth and privilege, Clinton himself had a very different life story. So his friends Harry and Linda Bloodworth Thomason, Hollywood producers (and Arkansas natives), were asked to create a seventeen-minute film to be shown to the nation before the nominating acceptance speech. It would describe Bill Clinton's remarkable road toward the pinnacle of power. And it took its theme of hope and change from the name of the candidate's hometown. It was called *The Man from Hope.*

Bill Clinton was born on August 19, 1946, in Hope, Arkansas, a town of about six thousand near the southwestern corner of the state, just over thirty miles east of the Texas border at Texarkana. His mother named him William Jefferson Blythe III after his father, William Jefferson Blythe Jr., one of nine children of a poor Texas farmer. But Bill Clinton never knew his birth father. Bill Blythe had married his young wife, Virginia, only two months after they met in 1943 and then left for wartime service in Italy. He had returned after the war and gotten back his old job as an equipment salesman in Chicago. He had purchased a small house and was en route to Hope to pick up his pregnant wife and bring her back to Chicago when, at 28, he was killed in a car accident in May. He was driving fast and a tire had blown out on a wet road in Missouri.

Bill Clinton never knew much about Bill Blythe, described by his family as a handsome, charming, fun-loving man. It was only after Clinton was in the White House, in 1993, that he would learn from investigative newspaper reports that his father—a mysterious figure, one biographer noted, who constantly reinvented himself—had been married three times before he met his mother, who was unaware of these marriages, and had at least two other children. (The President later reached out to try to meet these half-siblings.)[1]

And so Bill Clinton's early years would be in Hope. At first, he would live with his mother in the home of his maternal grandparents, Edith and Eldridge Cassidy, whom he would call Mammaw and Papaw. It was a comfortable, two-and-a-half-story white wood-frame house that had been in the family since 1938, although it occasionally shook from trains coming by on the nearby tracks. Edith, 45, a strong, volatile personality and a respected private nurse in the community, was the dominant figure in the household. Her worst trait was her temper, her daughter would recall. "She had hell-fire in her, but she was a good woman," one friend said. Her good-natured husband, a former iceman but now a grocery store proprietor, often was the object of her angry outbursts. But both of them were devoted to their grandson, and Edith was teaching little Bill—who was extraordinarily precocious from the start—to read while he was still in a high chair. (He was reading numerous books by age 3.) They would be the primary caregivers when his mother left for New Orleans for a year, to be trained in a hospital as a nurse anesthetist.[2]

When Virginia Blythe returned to Hope, she soon announced she would marry Roger Clinton, a car dealer with the Buick franchise in town. Clinton had a reputation as a drinker, a womanizer, and a party-lover. Edith Cassidy disliked him, even threatened to seek custody of Virginia's son, and refused to attend the marriage ceremony. But Bill Blythe, age 4, moved into his new home, a one-story wooden cottage in a postwar Boomer neighborhood of large families and children, with the newlyweds. He soon began to call his stepfather Daddy and not long afterward began calling himself Bill Clinton. He would later make the name change official.

When young Bill was finished with first grade, he would leave Hope, Arkansas. Roger had decided to return to his hometown, neighboring Hot Springs. He sold the dealership and moved the family to a farm near town. (Bill Clinton later found it politically useful to recall his days living on a farm with an outhouse.) But after a year, Roger Clinton disposed of the farm and took a job in the city, working for his affluent brother Raymond, the prosperous regional Buick dealer.

The family soon moved into a large, two-story frame house on a hill—rented from Uncle Raymond—in a community so much different than little

Hope. Hot Springs, an aging but prosperous resort town of 35,000, was a tourist center located adjacent to a national park, with large hotels and numerous bath houses. It had a colorful history as a haven for illegal gambling and prostitution; in the Twenties and Thirties, Al Capone and other mobsters had visited often. Now, it housed a multiracial, multiethnic population. Bill was sent to a Catholic grade school at first, but then went on to public schools, where, not for the last time, he would be a star student.[3]

Virginia Clinton's relationship with her second husband (whose youthful nickname was "Dude") was stormy from the start. He was not only a serial adulterer, but an alcoholic and violently abusive when drunk. He beat his wife. During one angry, drunken outburst, when Bill was 5, he pulled a gun and fired in her direction; the police took him to jail. Later, when Bill was 14 and he was in the house with his 4 year old half-brother Roger (named after his dad), Roger Clinton again began screaming and hitting his wife. Now grown larger than his stepfather, Bill Clinton grabbed a golf club and threatened to beat the man he called "Daddy" if he did not stop; the drunken man collapsed.

This story of Bill Clinton's intervention to protect his mother was featured in the film at the convention, *The Man from Hope*. When it was shown, several of his friends told reporters that they never knew about the troubled household in which the candidate was raised, never knew of the violence and alcoholic rampages. Clinton would later write that these were family secrets; they were a normal part of his life. He never talked about them with anyone: a friend, a neighbor, a teacher, a pastor, a counselor. And then he noted that while we all have them, some secrets "can be an awful burden to bear, especially if some sense of shame is attached to them . . . or the allure of our secrets can be too strong, strong enough to make us feel we can't live without them, that we wouldn't be who we are without them."[4]

The year after the golf club confrontation, when Roger was drinking again, Virginia Clinton moved her sons into a new house and soon filed for divorce. Bill was 16 when the divorce was granted. But a desperate and remorseful Roger Clinton begged to be taken back, and his former wife finally agreed. It was then that Bill Clinton went to the courthouse and officially changed his last name. He never rejected his stepfather: "a combustible mix of fears, insecurities and psychological vulnerabilities . . . but a fundamentally good person." The renewed relationship between the Clintons would hardly go smoothly and there would be ugly episodes to come. But soon Bill Clinton would be out of that household and off to college.[5]

Still, during his school years, in Hope and Hot Springs, the boy living in a home with such an explosive marriage, the child of an alcoholic, seemed to flourish. His mother adored him and was deeply supportive—as were his grandparents—and he was an exceptionally bright and gregarious youngster. He made close friends and nurtured these relationships across the years. In Hope, two of these boyhood pals—Vince Foster, neighbor from next door, and Mack McLarty, a fellow kindergartener—would later have notable careers; they would be asked to accompany the new President to the White House, one as Counselor, the other as Chief of Staff. They were, perhaps, the charter members of the FOB, the "Friends of Bill," Clinton's extraordinarily large and devoted circle of friends.

Clinton described himself in junior high as "fat, uncool, and hardly popular with the girls." But he was smart, articulate, and always interested in politics and public life. Back when he was a child, at age 10, he watched—entranced—the national Democratic political convention on the family's first television set. He had friends across the color line and, even as a boy, rejected the racist policies of Governor Orville Faubus and some other home-state politicians. As a teenager, he cried, sitting alone, watching Martin Luther King's famous "I Have a Dream" speech at the Lincoln Memorial.

While big for his age and rather clumsy, certainly not a gifted athlete, he did make his mark right through high school as a musician. He loved music: classical, jazz, Elvis Presley. His instrument was saxophone and he was in the high school concert and marching bands as well as a jazz trio. For seven summers, he attended band camp at the University of Arkansas.

Bill Clinton, always gregarious, became immensely popular. Later, he would call high school a "great ride." He was elected president of the junior class, winner of so many awards that he was kept from running for student council or senior class president only by a school rule restricting students from too many activities. But in the summer of his junior year he did become a representative at the annual American Legion Boys State program, where kids from all across the state engaged in model government exercises. He excelled in the debates and in the political maneuvering. He won election as one of the two coveted Arkansas "senators," which meant he would go to Boys Nation, at the University of Maryland, adjacent to the capital. In Washington, he would be introduced to the powerful members of the Arkansas congressional delegation, including Senator J. William Fulbright. Of course, he would be first in line to shake the hand of John F. Kennedy, when the President greeted the Boys Nation delegates in the White House Rose Garden. Clinton had been a passionate supporter of JFK; the picture of the handshake would become famous.

Bill Clinton was entranced by Washington. He wrote later that "I knew I could be great in public service. I was fascinated by people, politics, and policy, and I thought I could make it without family wealth, or connections or establishment southern positions on race." So against the advice of school counselors, family, and friends, he applied to only one college: Georgetown. He thought he could get in; he had been fourth in a class of

327 students, had been a National Merit semifinalist, and his board scores were good. Coming from Arkansas was an advantage (as it would be in the Rhodes Scholar competition) because a national university wanted representation from across the nation. It was pricey, even in the mid-Sixties, but his parents encouraged him to try and he knew he could work while at school and maybe get scholarship aid. And so in the fall of 1964, at the height of a critical presidential election between Lyndon Johnson and Barry Goldwater, he arrived—escorted by his mother—at his freshman dorm on the Georgetown campus.[6]

Clinton was enrolled in the School of Foreign Service. In 1964, Georgetown's college of arts and sciences—blocks away in "the Yard"—was 100 percent male and 95 percent Catholic, but the foreign service school was much more eclectic; there were Protestants, Jews, Hindus, Buddhists (although few Southern Baptists like Clinton), and there were women. Bill Clinton lost no time making friends and contacts across campus. He ran and won the election as president of the freshman class that fall; he later called it "one of my better campaigns, waged to an electorate dominated by Irish and Italian Catholics from the East." He would be reelected as sophomore class president. He had a remarkable capacity to meet, make, and keep new friends and to enlist some of them to work for him in his campaigns.

He had enormous energy and seemed to operate on less sleep than almost anyone else. And he excelled in class. Later, he would recall almost all the courses he took, particularly in the first two years, and the teaching styles of the instructors. He even saved notes taken in these classes and he certainly made a point of getting to know the faculty, which probably irritated some fellow class members. Students who were in study groups with him were struck by his easy mastery of the material.

Clinton was especially influenced by the required freshman course "Development of Civilizations," taught by a legendary teacher, Professor Carroll Quigley. He recalled Quigley's view that "the future can be better than the past, and each individual has a personal, moral obligation to make it so." He wrote later that "from the 1992 campaign through my two terms in office, I quoted Professor Quigley's line often, hoping it would spur my fellow Americans and me to practice what he preached." One fellow Georgetown undergraduate said when he first heard the song "Don't Stop Thinking About Tomorrow" at the 1992 Democratic Convention, the song which would serve as the Clinton campaign anthem, "that was pure Quigley." (And it was Quigley who once remarked to a class that great men and women who make a mark on their times operate on less sleep.)[7]

In the summer between his second and third years, Bill's uncle Raymond helped him get a job working on the campaign of Judge Frank Holt, a candidate for the Arkansas Democratic gubernatorial nomination. He helped to hand out brochures and organize rallies, but when the judge had to miss one speaking engagement, Clinton was asked to speak in this place; he did well enough to become a stand-in at some subsequent smaller rallies. This was his earliest lesson in "retail politics," reaching directly out to voters at fairs and pie suppers, answering their questions, touching their hands. "That's how I learned politics," he would recall. "It works better than TV wars. You had to talk but you had to listen, too." You could take a shot at your opponent but could not "hide behind some bogus committee that hoped to make a killing from your time in office if its (televised advertising) attacks destroyed the other candidate."[8]

Frank Holt narrowly lost the primary to "Justice Jim" Johnson. A right-wing racist politician who would become an enemy of Clinton's in succeeding years, Johnson was defeated by Winthrop Rockefeller in the general election. Later, he was a source for some of the "Clinton scandal" stories written by major national newspaper reporters in the Nineties.

But Bill Clinton's experience that summer proved critical to his future. Judge Holt's brother, another experienced Arkansas political figure, wrote to J. William Fulbright, chairman of the Senate Foreign Relations Committee, recommending him for a job. Clinton had written Fulbright earlier but had been told there were no openings. Now he would be offered a part-time position as assistant clerk on the Foreign Relations Committee. It paid enough to cover tuition and expenses without any help from his family. Because Roger Clinton was now struggling with terminal cancer, and the medical bills were mounting, Clinton feared he would soon have to leave Georgetown and come home, where college was much less expensive. The call from Fulbright's office changed his life.

Working for the committee between 1966 and 1968 was a rare opportunity. It was at the height of the Vietnam War, in the midst of intense debate over the wisdom of America's involvement and the shaping of a powerful antiwar movement spreading across the campuses of the nation. Chairman Fulbright, the author of *The Arrogance of Power*, had been one of President Lyndon Johnson's senatorial supporters, but now he had turned against the war. Not only did this committee assignment give Bill Clinton new insights into the workings of Congress and the character of key players on Capitol Hill, but it helped inform his own views about the Vietnam War.

Clinton opposed the war. But in the context of those days, he was a moderate activist, like the delegates at the National Students Association (NSA) convention he attended in summer 1967. He was not a firebrand and not a member of Students for a Democratic Society—an antiwar liberal but certainly not a radical. "Though I was sympathetic to the zeitgeist, I didn't embrace the lifestyle or the radical rhetoric. My hair was short, I didn't even drink and some of the music was too loud and harsh for my taste." In a time when some protesters in front of the White House (and not far from his Georgetown campus) were shouting bitter and lurid slogans like "Lee Harvey Oswald, where are you now when we really need you," Clinton said, "I didn't hate LBJ; I just wanted to end the war, and I was afraid the culture clashes would undermine, not advance, the cause."[9]

When the charismatic Allard Lowenstein addressed that NSA meeting, he called for an effort to defeat Lyndon Johnson for the Democratic nomination in 1968. But when he persuaded Senator Eugene McCarthy to run for his Coalition for a Democratic Alternative in the primaries, Clinton was not committed to this new "McCarthy movement." Yet, after McCarthy did well in the New Hampshire primary and Robert F. Kennedy, who initially had rejected Lowenstein's appeal to run, decided to enter the race—creating two antiwar candidates—Clinton did become an RFK supporter. He was persuaded that Bobby Kennedy would be a much better President. It was not only foreign policy. Later, he would observe that "Bobby Kennedy became the first New Democrat . . . before the Democratic Leadership Council, which I helped to start in 1985, and before my campaign in 1992. He believed in civil rights for all and special privileges for none, in giving poor people a hand up rather than a handout: Work was better than welfare. He understood in a visceral way that progressive politics requires the advocacy of both new policies and fundamental values, both far-reaching change and social stability."[10]

His smart and articulate girlfriend at the time, fellow Georgetown undergraduate Ann Markusen, was a passionate McCarthy supporter. She did not agree. Like so many others in the McCarthy camp, she was furious at Kennedy, feeling he was opportunistically trying to steal the nomination that belonged to their man.

Bill Clinton, handsome, bushy-haired, tall (6 feet, 3 inches), charming, a major figure on campus with an astonishingly wide circle of friends and an interesting job on the Hill, was now the very opposite of his junior high persona: "fat, uncool and unpopular with the girls." (He would have several striking girlfriends across his Georgetown and Oxford years; but while no monk, he wasn't really a ladies' man in the usual and assumed sense.) Yet in spring 1967, at the end of his junior year, he made one of the few miscalculations of his political life when he decided to run for president of the student council. He had been spending too much time away from campus and, for once, was outmaneuvered and out-organized and lost the race.

It was a minor setback. Late 1967 and spring 1968 would be a time of tumult and heartbreak in America. There was the massive antiwar March on Washington in the fall and then the bitter, historic Democratic primary campaign across the winter and spring. In April came the assassination of Martin Luther King Jr., followed by upheavals in inner cities across

America, particularly in Washington, D.C. And then there was the murder of Robert F. Kennedy in June. Bill Clinton, living, studying, and working in Washington, planning a career in politics and public service, was profoundly affected by these events, maybe even more so than some others, and particularly by the death of two of his heroes. Yet in the midst of such shattering developments, there was one piece of spectacularly good news for him. Clinton won a Rhodes Scholarship.

The Rhodes can be a golden passport. In 1968, it was given to only thirty-two men. Those who were nominated and then survived the rigid state and regional competitions—marked by grueling interviews with committees composed, for the most part, of former Rhodes winners—headed off to Oxford University in Britain for graduate school. Much more important, they were anointed as being among the few and the very few, the most brilliant and accomplished young people of their time.

Clinton's academic and extracurricular credentials were outstanding and he had strong support from faculty and administrators who had come to know him well. But perhaps most important in propelling him to the regional interview stage in a competition traditionally dominated by Ivy League graduates was a letter from the famous Senator Fulbright, a former Rhodes winner and president of the University of Arkansas, the man who proposed the Fulbright Scholarships. Not surprisingly, Bill Clinton did well enough in the interview stage to be selected.

With the Rhodes in hand, Clinton spent the summer of 1968 working for the reelection of Fulbright, who was being challenged in the primary by "Justice Jim" Johnson. He even served briefly as the senator's driver (at which he did not excel) during campaign swings across Arkansas. But at the beginning of October, in the middle of an extraordinary election campaign featuring Richard Nixon, Hubert Humphrey, and George Wallace, Clinton would be in New York City, boarding the liner *United States* for the journey to Oxford.

On the voyage to England, he bonded with the other Rhodes Scholars on board. Many became lifelong friends. He demonstrated once again his remarkable capacity to relate to people. As always, he was warm and generous and understanding. (One acquaintance remarked that he "had a way of making you feel you were the most important friend in his life and what happened to you was the most important thing that ever happened.") Later, when he was elected in 1992, some of his Rhodes friends would be given key posts in his administration or would be named to important judicial positions. And at the time, near the end of the voyage, there was some chatter among the new Rhodes about how extraordinary a politician—in the best sense—was their new friend Bill Clinton, and how he might be president some day.[11]

In the first few months, he was particularly close to Robert Reich, a mul-titalented, dynamic, and confident Dartmouth graduate. Reich was less than five feet tall, the result of a rare genetic illness, and walking with the lanky southerner through the ancient colleges, they seemed an odd pair. Reich's razor-sharp intellect focused on political and economic issues; he was a facile and prolific writer and would be named Secretary of Labor in the Clinton cabinet. The two later would have serious disagreements about the nature and shape of policy; Reich would publish a work titled *Locked in the Cabinet.*

In that book, Reich recalled Clinton from their student days at Oxford and, later, at law school: "the good natured prankster, the fun-loving sto-ryteller, the fellow who could spend hour after hour telling jokes, play-ing cards, gossiping about politicians, taking delight in himself and those around him," a man with a capacity for "sheer, exuberant joy." But he had a serious side; politics were serious, race relations, the Vietnam War. "I never considered him a close friend," Reich wrote, "in the sense of someone who shared with me and with whom I shared the most intimate thoughts and feelings. I don't know how many close friends Bill has. I have very few.... As his friend I never assumed I was a member of an exclusive club."

Another Oxford friend was Strobe Talbott, former editor of *Yale Daily News*, a brilliant young Russian scholar who would be a housemate of Clin-ton's during his second year in Britain. And they would be close friends—as would their wives—across the years ahead. At Oxford, Talbott was work-ing on the secretly recorded memoirs of Nikita S. Khrushchev and would publish the critically important book *Khrushchev Remembers.* He would become Deputy Secretary of State in the Clinton administration and the President's special adviser on Russia.

Clinton chose to study for a B.Phil. in Politics at Oxford. His tutor in the first year described him as not the ablest American he had taught—"at least not in a purely academic sense"—but a young man with a "sharp analytic mind and an impressive power to master and synthesize complex mate-rial . . . the mind of a politician, trying to figure things out, rather than the patience of an academic," but "an effective arguer, on paper and verbally." Clinton was not as committed as some of his fellow Rhodes Scholars to pursuing a degree program and producing publishable work; he traveled as widely as possible and took advantage of this new world.[12]

But like all the Rhodes Scholars, he was fixated on the Vietnam War and the likelihood of being drafted to fight. For all of them, it was the continu-ous subject of conversation, beginning on the voyage to England. For Bill Clinton, it was a particularly complicated matter. He opposed American involvement in Vietnam, certain—like his old boss Senator Fulbright—that the war was a disastrous error. But he was planning a political career and did not want to threaten his viability for future candidacies. Perhaps more important was his knowledge of the sacrifices made by so many others on the battlefield, for he had received news of the death or injury of friends from home and college. Could he refuse to serve if so many others had been put in harm's way? It was an agonizing issue.

He was not alone. Frank Aller, a young, gifted China expert who despised the war, a "good middle-class boy who loved his country," Bill Clinton would remember, the Rhodes who would share a house with him and Talbott the next year, made the fateful decision to become a draft resister. Bill Clinton tried to console him, and Aller in turn said that Clinton had the "desire and ability to make a difference in politics and it would be wrong" to throw away his opportunities by resisting the draft. "His generosity only made me feel more guilty, as the angst-ridden pages of my diary showed." Clinton's letters home were filled with his tortured ruminations on the matter. But when he received his draft notice and then passed the physical, he headed home for the summer sure that he would not be back for a second year at Oxford.

When he arrived in Arkansas, he had about a month before reporting for induction and was free to make other military arrangements. There were no available slots in the National Guard or the reserves. His vision would not qualify him for flight and so the Air Force was out. He failed a physical for a naval officer program, because of poor hearing. He thought the last best option was enrollment in law school and joining the Army Reserve Officers' Training Corps at the University of Arkansas. He was accepted at the law school and into this program—probably with the help of recommendations from those he had worked with in Washington. But because his acceptance had come too late for the mandated summer camp before starting ROTC classes, he could return to Oxford for a second year, starting at the university in Fayetteville, Arkansas, following the next summer's camp. Then, after the three years in law school, he would have a two-year service obligation as an officer.[13]

But back in Oxford, in October, he had second thoughts. He said later that despite his opposition to the war, he did not believe in deferments and decided "I cannot do this ROTC." He wrote home and asked to be put back in the draft, and on October 30, the draft board reclassified him 1-A. Because President Nixon had just ordered a change in the Selective Service policy, allowing graduate students to finish the entire school year before they were inducted, he knew he could not be called until July. And within two months, a new policy calling for a draft lottery was put into effect. On December 1, Bill Clinton's birthday was picked 311th, a lucky number, virtually assuring that he would never be called to serve. Not only that, Nixon already had revealed what he had characterized in the campaign as his secret plan for the war. It was "Vietnamization": the United States would steadily reduce its troop commitments to the conflict and depend on its Vietnamese allies to fight the war. And so it was now clear to Clinton and others in his age cohort that draft calls in the United States would be steadily reduced.

Clinton's draft saga became an incendiary political issue when he ran for office. It was alleged that he used influential contacts to gain access to the Arkansas ROTC program under false pretenses and then switched to the draft when it seemed likely he would never have to serve, allowing him to finish at Oxford and then go on to a more prestigious law school.

The stories of this supposedly sophisticated draft dodging were circulated in 1992 by Cliff Jackson, an Arkansas native who knew Clinton as a student at Oxford (but he was not a Rhodes, he was there on Fulbright scholarship). Jackson implied that he had played a role in helping Clinton. They were supported in a statement by Colonel Eugene Holmes, the head of the Arkansas ROTC program during the war years, to whom Clinton had written a very long, agonized letter trying to explain why he had asked to be released from the program and re-enter the draft. But Jackson, a conservative figure in Arkansas Republican circles, now had become a bitter political enemy of Bill Clinton and had attacked him on other issues. And the statement by Holmes in 1992—implying that Clinton had deceived him—was prepared with the aid of his daughter, a Republican activist, and released with the help of a GOP congressman, after having been reviewed by the "opposition research" team of the Bush presidential campaign. In fact, Holmes had discussed the Clinton matter in very different terms in earlier years.[14]

It is clear that Bill Clinton opposed the war and was deeply ambivalent about military service in Vietnam. He would pay a political price for this ambivalence. But the allegations of "draft dodging" were unfounded. It was not unusual for many graduate and professional students—and particularly for Rhodes Scholars—to be allowed by their draft boards to complete their studies; others found acceptance in ROTC programs. And in Clinton's case, with U.S. war policy changing dramatically in 1969 and 1970, this meant it was not unusual for such students to avoid service in the war. In the years after Clinton's presidency, with questions raised about the controversial actions of his successor, George W. Bush—a strong supporter of the war who found service (perhaps with the aid of his famous relatives) in an Air National Guard unit in the American south that it was clear would never be sent to Vietnam—the issue was forgotten.

Clinton's second year at Oxford was marked by further travel across Europe, including a long journey to the Soviet Union. He was reading widely—major works of fiction as well as political theory and history—but he did not focus on finishing requirements for his degree. And he elected to forgo the optional third year and return to the United States. Many of his friends already assumed he was headed for a political career that would lead to fame and high position. And now he had won admission to Yale Law School; he was, after all, a Rhodes Scholar and also had high board scores. It was one of the most selective institutions in the world. But it was a place where young members of the political elite gathered; it was a center of activist, liberal politics. And it was another sterling credential.

Even before starting at Yale, Clinton spent the early summer at work on a political campaign in Washington. It was named Project Purse Strings, a citizens lobby calling for the passage of an amendment cutting off funding for the Vietnam War. He went from there to work on a primary campaign in Connecticut, where Joe Duffey, an antiwar activist (and president of the liberal Americans for Democratic Action), was running for Senate, with the support of an extraordinary array of celebrities, writers, and historians. By fall, it was time to begin law school, but Duffey had won the primary and Clinton was asked to coordinate the Third Congressional District (which included New Haven, site of Yale) for the general election. He took the job.

It was possible to do that because of the way Yale Law School operated in these years and the way Bill Clinton worked. With grades virtually eliminated and the pass-fail system in operation, Yale was not a buttoned-up place where it was expected that a group of academic high achievers would compete for perfect averages, positions on the law review, key judicial clerkships, and ultimately invitations to join white shoe law firms on Wall Street, guaranteeing them lives of affluence and power. Some might be doing that, but others used the relaxed atmosphere to focus on interests beyond their classes. The faculty had many notable figures of different ideological persuasions, from the deeply conservative Robert Bork to Charles Reich, author of the counterculture best seller *The Greening of America*; both of them were Clinton's teachers. But Bill Clinton, a remarkably quick study who had always performed well in courses, was more interested in politics. He focused the first semester on his campaign efforts for Duffey, missed many classes, borrowed other students' notes before exams, and still did well in his courses.

Across his years at Yale, he demonstrated once more his ability to read and comprehend difficult material with astonishing speed, to master complex issues on little sleep, and to do so seemingly without effort or anxiety. A fellow student, convinced that Clinton must be cramming, found him deep in a book late at night before an exam, but he was reading Proust. One faculty member, baffled as to how Clinton could do so well on a test when he had seemed so disinterested in the class and had started the exam thirty minutes late, asked for an explanation: "Corporate law is a lot like politics and I understand politics. It is just a case of making sure each employer gets something out of it."[15]

But Clinton, who could focus more directly on school after the congressional campaign was over in fall 1970, was not only distracted by politics but by the need to support himself. Even with a scholarship, he had two jobs, one as a researcher in a local law office, the other teaching in a law-enforcement program at a neighboring college.

In spring 1971, his life would change when he saw a woman in the Yale law library that he just had to get to know better. She was a most unusual figure, a Wellesley College graduate already featured in national news. As president of the student government, she had been asked to address her graduation commencement. Rejecting the views of the regular guest speaker, Senator Brooke of Massachusetts, who had not mentioned civil rights or Vietnam, she asserted "the indispensable task of criticizing and constructive protest." It was an eloquent, moving, and controversial response. She would soon appear in *Life* magazine and on television in Chicago.

In fact, Clinton had seen her on his very first day at Yale, when he was having lunch with Robert Reich, his Rhodes Scholar friend—and now law school classmate. Bob Reich had known the woman since he was an undergraduate, when, as president of his sophomore class at Dartmouth, he was paired up with her—the freshman class president at Wellesley—at a "presidential summit meeting." At lunch, she had stopped by to say hi to Bob and he introduced her to Bill. Sometime later, in the library, they became reacquainted. She recalled that after the tall young man with a "curly mane of hair and reddish brown beard" and Elvis sideburns stared at her, she went over to him: "If you are going to keep looking at me and I am going to keep looking back, we might as well be introduced. I am Hillary Rodham."[16]

Bill Clinton was smitten. This blond young woman with eyeglasses and no makeup "conveyed a sense of strength and self-possession I had rarely seen in anyone." The exceptionally brilliant student was, he discovered, "a formidable presence in law school, a big fish in our small but highly competitive pond." And the attraction was mutual. An interviewer later asked Hillary what attracted her to Bill Clinton: "He wasn't afraid of me," was the response. "But I was afraid of us, I tell you that," Clinton would admit.

A few days after their law library encounter, he sought her out and there followed an intense period of walking, talking, and learning about each other. She had grown up in an upper-middle-class suburb north of Chicago, part of a relatively conservative family, her father a Republican businessman. She had led the Young Republicans in her early days at college, but the civil rights movement, the Vietnam War, and the dramatic cultural developments during the tumultuous Sixties had changed her views.

Within a month, they seemed inseparable. Clinton's work in the Duffey congressional effort had so impressed Gary Hart, the campaign manager working for the presidential nomination of Senator George McGovern, that he asked the Yale student to spend the summer as coordinator of the McGovern effort in the south in the run-up to the primaries. It was an exceptional opportunity for a young man with a passion for politics and plans for his own career. But when Clinton found out that Rodham had accepted a summer internship with a law firm in Oakland, California, he decided that if they were separated for months he might lose her. He asked if he could escort her to California. He told Hart (later a famous Colorado senator with his own presidential aspirations)—who found the refusal astonishing—that he could not take the job. They were together that summer in the Bay area and when they returned, rented a place together in New Haven.[17]

Bill and Hillary made an extraordinary pair. Among other things, they competed as a team in the Barristers Union competition at Yale. It was no ordinary student mock exercise; the judge at the Prize Trial was a former Supreme Court justice. They made it to the finals. The next summer, Rodham went to Washington to work for Marian Wright Edelman, at what soon would be called the Children's Defense Fund, investigating all-white southern academies established in response to court-ordered public school integration.

Around this time, Strobe Talbott called with the terrible news that their friend, Frank Aller, had committed suicide. Aller had decided that he could not avoid the war by staying outside the country and had returned to his Spokane home to "face the draft music." As a resister, he was arrested, arraigned, and then released pending trial, but now a psychiatric exam found him depressed and unfit for military service; after his draft physical, he was declared 1-Y, draftable only in national emergency. He had been offered a job working in the Saigon bureau of the *Los Angeles Times*, but before leaving, had taken his own life. Clinton felt both grief and anger, wondering if he could have done something to prevent it. It would not be the last time a good friend would kill himself.

But now Bill Clinton was called back to a key role in the McGovern campaign. On his own, he had opened a McGovern office near campus during the school year and won over the Democratic organization in town. He was rewarded by being asked to join the campaign's national staff at the Democratic National Convention. He worked with the Arkansas and South Carolina delegations, learning more about party politics in those states and adding to his growing list of contacts in the region.

After McGovern won the nomination, he was given a major role, asked to co-chair the candidate's campaign in Texas. Hillary would join him late in the race—which would end on election day in November with a disastrous two-to-one defeat in the state. But George McGovern's chances of winning Texas always had been hopeless; the campaign organizers would not be blamed. And Clinton was impressive even in this moment. Samuel

"Sandy" Berger, a speechwriter for the candidate and later a member of Bill Clinton's White House team, recalled their first meeting, during a McGovern airport campaign stop in San Antonio: "This tall, energetic, charismatic young guy in a white suit bounded up the plane's steps to brief us . . . it is not that I knew he would be President someday, but I was not surprised he would head back to Arkansas for a political career—and that he would be heard from."

Following the election and a brief vacation, Bill and Hillary returned to law school. Despite their long absence from classes, they got through their exams in good shape.

Next semester, as they prepared for graduation, they considered their next moves. Both of them had the credentials that would have brought them to lucrative jobs in New York. But Hillary Rodham decided to work full-time in Cambridge, Massachusetts, at the Children's Defense Fund. And Clinton had other plans. He always knew he would return home to begin his own political career. Now, with strong recommendations from some of the distinguished members of the Yale law faculty, he secured a position as assistant professor at the University of Arkansas Law School.

After receiving their degrees but before starting these new jobs, Bill Clinton took Hillary to Europe, showing her his old haunts at Oxford. Then they traveled to Arkansas and she met his mother. Hillary and Virginia were two strong women with very different styles. At first it would be a cold relationship, but Bill Clinton warned his mother to be more receptive, telling her that "for me, it's Hillary or it's nobody." As with Bill Clinton and Hillary Rodham's father, Hugh, it would take a while before the two women appreciated each other. In England, Clinton had asked Hillary to marry him. Her response: "No, not now." He would wait her out.[18]

As the newcomer on the law faculty at Arkansas, he would have preferred his first teaching assignments in constitutional or criminal law but he was given instead courses in agency and trade regulation. He turned discussion in the agency class to the contemporary Watergate crisis, asking students if the people who were involved were agents of the President. When given a course in constitutional law, he also focused on pressing political questions, spending much time on the critical abortion case, *Roe v. Wade*.

Known for being slow in marking exams, he was unconventional in other ways. He rejected the Socratic method, spoke without written notes, lectured in a conversational tone, stimulated free-flowing discussion. African American students found him particularly sympathetic. The law school's first black students had appeared twenty-five years earlier, but only now were a substantial number beginning to enter school. Many were not well prepared, often coming from poor, segregated institutions. Clinton set up tutoring sessions for some, recognizing that they were bright and able individuals with a particularly high mountain to climb. Many went on to distinguished careers as lawyers and judges. They called him "wonder boy," one black student remembered; "he would not let race treat you different from anyone else."[19]

In Washington—and across America—the Watergate crisis had been the central development of the day. And while Hillary was in from Boston, visiting him in Fayetteville, Clinton had been called by John Doar, who had been named head of the House Judiciary Committee impeachment inquiry. Doar, a key member of the Kennedy Justice Department, knew them both from Yale; he had served as a judge in a moot court competition and recognized their talents. Now he asked Clinton to join his staff investigating the case for the impeachment of President Richard Nixon. And he noted that Hillary Rodham was also on his list to call. Hillary accepted, and flew east for the move to Washington. Clinton declined; he had decided to run for Congress. It was a long shot, but he got approval of the dean to make the race, promising to keep up with his classes and make time for his students.

To gain the Democratic nomination, Bill Clinton first had to run against two opponents in a primary. And it would be Bill Clinton running. When his first press release referred to William J. Clinton, one salty, tough local party regular, restaurant owner Billie Schneider, shouted at him: "What is this William J. Clinton? You are back in Arkansas now and this is not Oxford or Yale!" She told the young professor: "You're gonna run as Bill Clinton." He borrowed money for the effort, mobilized friends and family, toured the district, attended rallies and pie suppers, outworked and out-organized his foes, but still needed a runoff election to secure the nomination.[20]

He was not entirely successful in meeting all his academic obligations. He took his exams in one course in his car with him while campaigning, "graded as we rode or at night," and somehow, during the travel, lost five of the exams. He made arrangements for the students to take the exam again or get full credit without a specific grade. But one very strong student was particularly upset because she probably would have made an A. She "was a good Republican" who had worked for the very congressman, John Paul Hammerschmidt, Clinton would now oppose in the general election. Later, she became a federal judge, Susan Webber Wright. She would be the presiding judge—a quarter of a century later—in the Paula Jones case, the critical step on the way to Clinton's own impeachment crisis. The message for all faculty members: Don't procrastinate when grading and don't ever lose an exam.

Bill Clinton took a leave of absence from the law school for the fall election. He promoted an ambitious agenda of change: a fair tax system, national health insurance, public funding of presidential elections, more federal education dollars. And while campaigning, he sometimes had Hillary at his side.

When the House impeached Nixon in August 1974, she was suddenly out of a job. She had taken the Arkansas bar exam, just in case, and now called the dean of the law school, who earlier had offered her a position. It was still open if she could start within a month. Of course, it was obvious she had a wide choice of interesting career opportunities at that moment. One friend thought her out of her mind: "Why would you throw away your future?" But in September 1974 she started teaching at the law school. In November, Bill Clinton lost narrowly in his race for Congress, 52 to 48 percent. He was deeply in debt from the campaign and would now not go to Washington. Yet, as he later reflected, if he had won, he would not have had "eighteen wonderful years in Arkansas." And he might not have become President of the United States.[21]

Back to teaching in January 1975, he stayed active in state Democratic politics, touring Arkansas as head of a committee on affirmative action. He worked hard eliminating his campaign debt with the help of fund-raisers and contributions from some large donors. He taught both semesters of summer school and put the down payment on a house that he and Hillary had both admired. It cost $17,000, a small but handsome Tudor with one bedroom, close to campus. Now he asked her once again to marry him and this time she agreed. They were married in the living room of the little brown brick house in October.

But he was already planning a new campaign. After taking another leave from the law school that spring, he entered the primary race for Attorney General. He opened an office in the state capitol at Little Rock. He had the support of his growing legion of friends, including Mack McLarty and Vince Foster from boyhood days. Always the indefatigable campaigner and fund-raiser, he defeated two opponents. As he would throughout his political career, he seemed to have limitless energy, meeting and talking with strangers, reaching out to everyone in the shops, restaurants, and public places he visited. Later, some writers would say that like many other politicians, he had a visceral need for these transactional encounters and for the affection of the crowd. But it was more than that; he not only loved politics but he was devoted to the process.

He traveled to parts of the state where he had little chance—but even there he would make his mark. One night in unfriendly territory he entered a bar in a tiny town; one of the domino players told him, "Kid, we are going to kill you up here. . . . You're a long-haired professor from the University. For all we know, you're a Communist. But I'll tell you one thing. Anybody who would campaign at a beer joint in Joiner at midnight on Saturday night deserves to carry one box. . . . You'll win here."[22]

On election night, he had an overwhelming margin in the congressional district in which he had run a year and half earlier, strong support among

African Americans, and big turnouts in his hometowns of Hope and Hot Springs, as well as throughout southern Arkansas. Moreover, the Republicans had decided not to field a candidate in the general election, and so victory in the primary meant he would win the race.

He and Hillary celebrated. They took a brief summer vacation in Spain before returning to campus, where he completed his final teaching assignment that fall. He had taught eight courses in five semesters and summer session, but now he would leave the law school. At the beginning of 1977—age 30—he moved to Little Rock to begin his term as Attorney General of Arkansas.

In office, he shaped a reputation as a supporter of consumers' interests, attacking utility companies, creating a division of energy conservation and rate advocacy with a much larger litigation staff than had existed previously. He traveled across Arkansas discussing the state code and commenting on policy questions. But he also had to block efforts by social conservatives, inspired by the religious right's new Moral Majority organization, to try to legislate morality. One bill in the Arkansas House would have made it illegal to show X-rated films even to adults; Clinton had to maneuver carefully to avoid headlines: "Attorney General Comes Out for Dirty Movies." On another occasion, he had to help head off a bill placing a large tax on every Arkansas couple who lived together without benefit of wedlock; he avoided the headline "Clinton Comes Out for Living in Sin."

As he moved back and forth across the state, he deepened his ties to different constituencies, speaking before Rotary Clubs and at churches and picnics. He attended many events in the black community and got to know influential black preachers. And he established close ties to white Christian Pentecostals. Even as he did his job as Attorney General, he was making his name known and building contacts for the next race.

In only his second year in office, he briefly considered running for the open U.S. Senate seat in 1978. He decided instead to run for governor. Retiring Senator McClellan told him that was a bad idea: "All you do in the governor's office is make people mad. . . . [I]n the Senate you could do big things for the state and the nation. . . . [T]he governor's office is a trip to the political graveyard." But Bill Clinton knew better.[23]

While the Democratic primary for the Arkansas senatorial nomination that year was a nail-biter, with three prominent figures, including the outgoing governor, almost equally splitting the vote, Clinton had a much easier time in the gubernatorial primary. It was a four-way race, including one conservative evangelical Christian—the favorite of the Moral Majority—but with no other political stars. And Bill Clinton, who had brought in a young, aggressive political pollster and consultant from New York, Dick Morris, to help him, was ahead from the very start.

Once again, he demonstrated his exceptional energy and appetite for campaigning. In one town, he participated in a tug-of-war with burly loggers, in another county he was a contestant in a tomato eating contest (at the annual Pink Tomato Festival). On election day, he got 60 percent of the vote, carrying seventy-one of seventy-five counties. In the fall campaign, he defeated his opponent, a cattleman and the state Republican Party chair, with little trouble, winning with 63 percent of the vote, carrying all but six counties in the state. At 32, he was governor of Arkansas.

He and Hillary moved into the Governor's Mansion in Little Rock, a massive, 10,000 square foot tan brick Georgian Colonial with a dramatic pillared entrance, flanked by two smaller structures, a guest house and a headquarters for the state troopers who watched over the complex. The troopers were tasked with protecting the chief executive, and Clinton found it hard to get used to their following him everywhere in an unmarked car.

When they first had moved from the university to the capital, his wife had joined the Rose law firm downtown, which called itself the oldest large legal office west of Mississippi. Vince Foster, Bill's old friend, was a partner at Rose, which handled law business for some of Arkansas' biggest companies, including Wal-Mart and Tyson Foods. She worked on some difficult and challenging cases and by 1979 became the first woman to be made partner.

Hillary Rodham, who had not taken her husband's last name, soon was earning more than her husband. And she was demonstrating her business skills—perhaps a heritage from her businessman father—by also making money speculating in the commodities market. Encouraged by a partner in the firm who had developed a system for trading, she took risks in the world of cattle futures and margin calls, where it is possible to make or lose large amounts quickly. It was not long before, as she put it, "I lost my nerve for gambling." But she made $100,000 before "walking away from the table."

She and her husband would be less successful in another business venture. Jim McDougal, a veteran state politico, approached them with a "sure-fire deal," a plan to buy 230 undeveloped acres on the bank of the White River in North Arkansas and develop the land for vacation houses. Affluent second home buyers from Chicago and Detroit should be interested; they would sell the lots for a profit. Bill Clinton had met McDougal in 1968 (when he was 21) working on the Fulbright reelection campaign. In the end, the deal for this property (which the Clintons would never visit) created the Whitewater Development Company. It would become a financial loser and a political disaster for Bill and Hillary Clinton. It was an albatross that would trouble them for years when they were in the White House, the source of seemingly endless rumors and investigations of wrongdoing.

But at this time Bill and Hillary were also planning a family. In February 1980, the governor's wife gave birth to a baby girl. Chelsea Clinton was named after Joni Mitchell's song "Chelsea Morning." Bill and Hillary liked Judy Collins' version of the song, and walking through Chelsea in London during their Christmas vacation in 1978, Bill Clinton had said, "If we ever have a daughter, we should name her Chelsea." And he started singing the song.[24]

In office, Bill Clinton resolved to focus first on education and highway construction. Arkansas ranked last among all states in per capita education spending, and Clinton pushed through legislation calling for a 40 percent increase in funding over the next two years, and his was a two-year term. Included: a significant increase in teacher pay, special education spending, and textbook expenditures.

The state's highways, county roads, and city streets were in lamentable shape. There had not been a substantial road program in years. Clinton called for increasing taxes to fund improvements, but erred seriously in rejecting a gas-tax increase in favor of a substantial hike in fees for car registration tags. He was outmaneuvered when he attempted to limit the burden on the less affluent owners of older cars, and the ensuing legislation hit them hardest. Later he would write: "It was the single dumbest mistake I ever made in politics until 1994, when I agreed to ask for a special prosecutor in the Whitewater case when there was not a shred of evidence to justify one."[25]

The car tag issue would haunt him across his gubernatorial term and play a key role in his defeat in 1980. He had won the rural districts in the election, but now these voters—poorer farmers and small businesspeople certain that this legislation was aimed at them—would punish him in the next race. Suddenly, he seemed to many of them only a youthful egghead from the university, unaware of the hardships of real life. He looked younger than his 32 years. Wags called him "Baby." A well-known newspaper cartoonist portrayed him as Attorney General in a baby carriage; as governor, he was shown on a tricycle.

But it was not only the car tag issue that would doom his reelection effort. Even as he worked hard on energy and economic development efforts (including the first Arkansas trade missions to the Far East), he had to deal with a foreign policy crisis that impacted his state. In the spring of 1980, Fidel Castro deported 120,000 Cuban political prisoners and other "undesirables," many with criminal records, to the United States. Sailing to Florida seeking asylum, they created a massive problem for the administration of President Jimmy Carter. Against Clinton's strong advice (he favored using the U.S. Guantanamo base on the Cuban island), the White House sent over 20,000 Cubans to Fort Chafee, a large military installation near Fort Smith on the Oklahoma border. (It had been used as a relocation center for Vietnamese refugees earlier in the decade.)

Fort Smith was a conservative town and residents were apprehensive. When many young, restless Cubans, tired of being fenced in, created disturbances, broke out of the base, and poured into the surrounding area, frightened and angry residents armed themselves and prepared to defend their homes. It was an explosive situation. Things settled down only after Washington, on Clinton's insistent urging, sent instructions to maintain order and keep the Cubans on the base. It was too late.

Fueled by anger over the car tags and the Cuban debacle, running on a ticket headed by the unpopular Carter—himself en route to a massive defeat at the hands of Ronald Reagan—Clinton carried only twenty-four counties, many with heavy black populations. On election night, he thanked the staff at the Governor's Mansion. He was devastated by the outcome. But now he and Hillary would have to find a new home. (It would be a small house but in a good neighborhood, the Heights, filled with upper-middle-class and bohemian residents.)

Out of work for the first time in his adult life, his growing legion of influential friends suggested a wide range of attractive possibilities. One offered to nominate him for a major university presidency in Kentucky. The newly elected governor of California asked him to become his chief of staff. He was urged to consider the chairmanship of a famous Washington-based national environmental organization or the leadership of a new and notable liberal activist group—People for the American Way—organized to combat the social conservatives of the Moral Majority. But perhaps most interesting was the notion of running for the chairmanship of the Democratic Party. After all, by the time of the Democratic Convention the previous fall, he had become chairman of the Democratic Governors Association.

He considered all these choices but decided to accept the one hard job offer available, a position to be "of counsel" at Wright, Lindsey & Jennings, another big Little Rock law firm. He had to stay in the state if he was to revive his political career. He had grappled for weeks with why he had lost reelection and concluded that the real reasons were more than "car tags and Cubans"; people "thought I had gotten too big for my britches, too obsessed with what I wanted to do and too oblivious to what they wanted me to do." One friend, a hardware store owner in the hill country, told him, "Bill, the people thought you were an asshole!" His conclusion: "It was a near-death experience" and "invaluable for the future." It "forced me to be more sensitive to the political problems inherent in progressive politics: the system can absorb only so much change at once; no one can beat all the entrenched interests at the same time, and if people think you've stop listening, you're sunk."[26]

Bored by his new work in the law firm (where his $33,000 salary was barely two-thirds of his wife's at the larger Rose office) he yearned to get back in the political arena. And the two-year term for Arkansas chief executives at the time made it possible for Clinton to immediately plan another race, which Hillary strongly supported. While there was no precedent for a beaten governor to return to power in this state, Bill Clinton saw an opening. The new governor, Republican Frank Wright, a conservative savings and loan executive, was an uninspiring figure prone to political gaffes. He had become an object of ridicule by yielding to the pressure of fundamentalist religious groups and supporting a creation science bill, requiring every school in the state to teach the "theory of creation" along with the theory of evolution. He allowed appointees to the public service commission to be vetted by the managers of Arkansas Power and Light, the powerful private company responsible for massively unpopular increases in utilities rates. Inept and inarticulate, he was the perfect target for the man who would be known, in later years and in a different context, as "the comeback kid."

Still, Clinton again would have to face a bruising primary—this time against two opponents—to gain the nomination. And again he used the services of the abrasive Dick Morris. But a much more important counsel was Betsey Wright, a shrewd political operative he had first met back as a Yale student working on the McGovern campaign in Texas. Wright, with Hillary strongly endorsing the move, had come to Little Rock and, not for the last time, would help Clinton shape a winning campaign strategy.

He overcame attack ads—placed by his most formidable opponent—reminding voters of the car tag issue and made it into a runoff. (He had met one old-timer who told him that eleven members of his family had voted against Clinton because he had raised their car license fees; when the candidate asked if they might consider ever voting for him again, the answer was, "Sure, we've already gotten even on that." He then called Hillary and said, "I think we have a chance here.")

But late polls indicated he was on the brink of defeat, one that would have strangled his political career, when Frank White blundered into the race with an anti-Clinton television ad. A last-minute radio advertising effort saved Clinton: If the Republican was intervening in a Democratic primary, he must want Bill Clinton beaten because he knew he would win against the other candidate. The next day, Clinton won the runoff with 54 percent.

He had fun in the fall campaign against White, who struggled with a weakened economy. On November 2, he won fifty-six of the seventy-five counties, particularly pleased that even the white rural counties came back to him. He was governor again. He would run three more times and never be defeated. He would enter the White House from the Governor's Mansion.

Back in power, he appointed Betsey Wright as manager of the governor's office. One writer suggested that the two had an unusual relationship—she was like a tough but caring big sister, deeply protective of Clinton, with whom she would, on occasion, have shouting disagreements. The governor also built a strong education team, with his former world history teacher, Paul Root, playing a key role.

He traveled the state but made sure to be home at night so "I could be there when Chelsea woke up" (she was 2 when he started his second term) and he could breakfast with his young daughter and wife. No one ever suggested that Bill Clinton was not a devoted father and committed to his family. Hillary, persuaded by friends and advisers that keeping her maiden name might have been damaging in his campaigns, now officially changed her name to Hillary Rodham Clinton. She later wrote that the famous African American political luminary (and FOB) Vernon Jordan, visiting town for a speech, had made this suggestion. "The only person who didn't ask me or even talk to me about my name was my husband. He said my name was my business."[27]

In office, Betsey Wright helped him schedule his time differently from his first term, when he had been perceived as inaccessible because of the numerous speaking engagements out of state he could not refuse. He would now focus again on education—also a priority when he was first governor—and on jobs. The new education agenda was both ambitious and chancy, for he would have to raise taxes and take on the powerful teachers union, the Arkansas Education Association.

Inspired by the publication of the National Commission on Excellence in Education's report, *A Nation at Risk*, which had detailed how America was slipping behind other industrialized nations in an increasingly competitive world where education was the key to prosperity, Clinton went on television to propose a bold program of reform. He called for state standards requiring maximum class size; uniform testing of all students; mandatory retention of those who fail an eighth-grade test; more math, science, and foreign language courses; a required core curriculum; and—most controversially—a mandatory national teacher exam. The proposals, which went beyond those in the *Nation at Risk* report, were the product of a fifteen-member education standards committee he had appointed, chaired by Hillary Rodham Clinton. The changes would be paid for by an increase in the state sales tax and a hike in natural gas taxes.[28]

Over intense opposition, particularly about the teachers' test, Clinton prevailed. Arkansas soon got positive national coverage for these reforms. In the next years, state teachers' pay went up fastest in the nation and student test scores rose above the regional average.

His popularity rising, Clinton won an easy victory in November 1984, carrying 63 percent of the vote. And this was the year that the Democrat on the top of his ticket, presidential candidate Walter Mondale, was trounced in Arkansas by the incumbent, Ronald Reagan, who had 62 percent of the vote.

In his new term, he would defend his educational reforms and work to save and create jobs in his state. He traveled widely to persuade company executives in New York and elsewhere not to act on announced plans to close Arkansas plants. His efforts helped to save a paper mill that had been operating since the Twenties, a shoe plant, and a Van Heusen shirt factory. He flew to Osaka, Japan, to see the president of Sanyo, a man who had become a friend in earlier years, suggesting that if Sanyo's large television-assembly plant stayed open, he would ask Arkansas-based Wal-Mart to sell Sanyo's sets. It worked.

He sponsored trade missions to Europe and Asia, helped finance high-tech ventures involving the universities in the state, and took some credit for the expansion of successful plants, such as the steel tube factory in Pine Bluff. He considered his "biggest coup" getting Nucor Steel to come to northwestern Arkansas.[29]

Bill Clinton, now with his state in the top ten in new-job growth as a percentage of total employment, would have no problem in his next reelection race in 1986. Arkansas had changed the terms for governor, and now he would be running for a four-year stay in the Mansion. In the Democratic primary, he easily trounced Orville Faubus, the aging former governor, best known for his notoriously ugly racist effort to block school integration in Little Rock back in 1957. Then he smashed his old foe Frank White in the general election. He won almost two-thirds of the statewide vote and a stunning 75 percent in Little Rock. (A desperate White had mounted a nasty television advertising campaign, which included an attack on Hillary; Clinton responded by asking if White wanted to run for first lady and issued bumper stickers and buttons saying "Frank for First Lady.")

It was 1987 and Bill Clinton—riding a tide of success—was becoming a national political figure. The previous August, he had become chairman of the National Governors Association and celebrated his fortieth birthday. Now he accepted more than two dozen invitations, in fifteen states, and began to consider a race for the Democratic presidential nomination the next year.

As he traveled across the state and the nation, he not only spread his message of "good schools and good jobs," but began to advocate reform of the welfare system. He asked the Arkansas legislature to require recipients with children 3 years or older to sign a contract committing themselves to a course of independence, through literacy and job training. He went to Washington and testified before the House Ways and Means Committee, calling for tools to "promote work, not welfare—independence, not dependence." Here was the origin not only of his controversial effort, when in the

White House, to promote changes leading "from welfare to work," but of what he began to call his "New Democrat" philosophy.

He was interested in the presidential race not only because he lamented problems in the economy in the Reagan years—the decline in American manufacturing, the escalating budget deficit, and the fact that 40 percent of the population had suffered a reduction in their real income in the previous decade—but also because he thought his strong record on education, welfare reform, and fiscal responsibility positioned him well: "Republicans could not paint me as an ultra-liberal Democrat who didn't embrace mainstream values." That, he felt, was "the box Republicans had put us in" since 1968.

But soon he decided that 1988 was not the year he should run. It would be a difficult primary contest against many contenders, although other key figures, like New York governor Mario Cuomo, had decided not to run. He would enter late and need to raise large amounts of money.

Still, it was a close call. Sandy Berger and a few other Washington policy experts, who had come to know Bill Clinton better during the Arkansas governor's visits to D.C., flew to Little Rock to be present if there was to be a race. They were downstairs in the executive mansion and Bill and Hillary were upstairs making the final decision. Hillary felt it unlikely that a Democrat could win; the "Reagan Revolution" had proven popular at the polls, and the sitting Vice President, George H. W. Bush, would be too formidable a foe. Moreover, Clinton still had an agenda to defend in Arkansas. The major newspaper in the state, the *Arkansas Gazette*, a supporter in every campaign, editorialized: "Bill Clinton is not ready to be President; Governor Clinton is needed in Arkansas." So now he announced he would not run in 1988.[30]

Of the prominent figures seeking the nomination, including Senators Al Gore and Joe Biden as well as African American leader, the Reverend Jesse Jackson, Clinton favored Governor Michael Dukakis of Massachusetts. They had become friendly at meetings of state chief executives, and Clinton felt that Dukakis was presiding over a successful high-tech economy, governing as a fellow New Democrat. Mike Dukakis, hearing that Clinton had taken himself out of the contest, had given him an early birthday present, a T-shirt inscribed: "Happy 41st. Clinton in '96. You'll only be 49."

When Dukakis secured the nomination, he asked Bill Clinton to present the nominating speech. Governor Clinton had made the exclusive list of speakers at the two previous national conventions, but his role had been a minor one. This was a coveted prime-time television opportunity for a potential future presidential candidate. It turned out to be a disaster. He worked hard on the address and had it cleared by the Dukakis team. But it proved much too long, over thirty minutes, and observers found it tedious;

two networks cut away after twenty minutes, the third showed a red light flashing on the podium, a signal for Clinton to stop. People were heard shouting, "Get the hook!" Television anchors mercilessly roasted Clinton. The next day, the *Washington Post* headlined its coverage of the speech "The Numb and the Restless"; its columnist called it "Windy Clinty's Classic Clinker."[31]

How to recover? His friend the TV producer Harry Thomason said he could capitalize on this humiliating flop but only if he acted quickly. He suggested an appearance on the *Tonight Show*, the late-night comedy and interview program hosted by the hugely popular Johnny Carson. The famous Carson had been using Clinton as a laugh line repeatedly in his nightly monologue, saying, "This speech went over about as well as a Velcro condom." Yet, with Thomason's urging, Carson agreed to have the governor come by as a guest, telling his audience that night, "Don't worry, we've got plenty of coffee and extra cots in the lobby."

But Clinton proved equal to the challenge. His self-deprecating humor hit a responsive chord: "I wanted to make Mike Dukakis [not known as an orator] look good, and I succeeded beyond my wildest imagination." In fact, he said, Dukakis "liked the speech so much he wanted me to go to the Republican convention and nominate Vice President Bush, too." He traded one-liners with the legendary Carson, got laughs from the studio audience, played his saxophone with the *Tonight Show* band. The same columnist who had called him a loser the previous week now wrote, "Clinton recovered miraculously." When he arrived back in the capital, the hometown crowd cheered him.[32]

Dukakis, of course, would be defeated in the 1988 election. He proved a weak and inept candidate, unable to effectively respond to a brutal TV campaign assault characterizing him as unpatriotic and un-American, a governor who had released a vicious convict—a black man's image filling the screen—to kill and rape again. (Ronald Reagan, as governor, had done something similar and Dukakis never used this information in an ad of his own. Later, as President, Bill Clinton would learn never to be used as a punching bag.)

Clinton could not prevent his party's crushing loss, but he had his own state agenda to address. He continued to focus on education, calling for a massive effort to obliterate adult illiteracy and asking for state takeover of failing school districts. With state unemployment better than the national average and state taxes still relatively low, he called for a modest increase in taxes to pay for his education and new health care initiatives. The legislature passed some of his reform plans but this time would not raise the taxes needed to fund the more expensive efforts, including teacher salary increases and early childhood education.

In late 1989 and into early 1990, he continued to speak to audiences across America, played a central role in the Governor's Task Force on Education, and joined President Bush in a White House summit meeting on education. But he had to decide whether or not to run for a fifth term as governor in the fall. Three well-known state Democrats were preparing to run, as were two formidable former Democrats seeking the GOP nomination. There was press speculation that Hillary, who had played such an important role in the Clinton education effort, would run if he did not.

By March 1, he announced he would be a candidate again for reelection. There were three other Democratic aspirants. Two withdrew: Attorney General Steve Clark and Jim Guy Tucker, an old foe and rival, who declared for lieutenant governor. The third, Tom McRae, the president of the Rockefeller Foundation, a man whose grandfather had been governor, stayed in the race with the support of the AFL-CIO state leaders, who refused for the first time to endorse Bill Clinton because he was not liberal *enough*. Clinton would later write that they made the classic error of liberals, "making the perfect the enemy of the good." But eighteen local unions defied the leaders and Clinton easily won nomination.

In the general election, Clinton had to face Sheffield Nelson, former president of the Arkansas-Louisiana Gas Company. He had supported— back when he was a Democrat—Senator Edward Kennedy against Jimmy Carter. But now he had moved dramatically to the right. He assailed Clinton's "tax and spend" record, called for a reduction in welfare benefits to "illegitimate children," and assailed Clinton for blocking the National Rifle Association's efforts to prohibit local governments from any restrictions on firearms. Perhaps most damaging, his campaign helped to spread rumors about Clinton's alleged extramarital sex life.[33]

The stories had been first circulated by Larry Nichols, a former employee of the state Development Finance Authority, who had been fired by Governor Clinton after making more than 120 phone calls from his office to right-wing supporters of the Nicaraguan Contras. Of course, these "Contras" would be at the heart of the infamous Iran-Contra scandal, but at this time their cause was being strongly backed by national Republicans. Immediately after his dismissal, Nichols called a press conference and accused the governor of using finance authority funds to carry on affairs with five women. Clinton asked journalists to call the women. They all denied the story. One of them, Gennifer Flowers, threatened to sue Nichols if he did not stop. The charges did no harm to the campaign; Clinton was overwhelmingly reelected on election day 1990, 57 to 43 percent.

Still, rumors about Clinton's extramarital activities had been heard in Little Rock for some time. There were stories of sexual liaisons with a variety of women. Later, Betsey Wright told an interviewer that she was convinced there was truth to the stories; she strongly suggested to Clinton that he not get into the 1988 race because of how they might be used against him. Friends and acquaintances knew that this famous, charismatic man, an extraordinarily outgoing, charming, larger-than-life-personality, an "inveterate flatterer and flirt," as one writer put it, was in love with his wife and devoted to her. But, like his father, stepfather, and even grandfather, he had an eye for other women. The Nichols-Sheffield stories in the campaign might lack substance, but the issue was there nonetheless, and of course it would not go away.[34]

After delivering yet another inaugural address in January 1991, Clinton readdressed his reform agenda for the state. This time, after an intense ten-week effort in which he personally lobbied key legislators, attending their committee meetings, "cornering them in halls, cloakrooms, and nighttime events," the governor prevailed. He ranged across the Arkansas State Capitol building (built eighty years earlier as a nearly exact, smaller replica of the U.S. Capitol) to seek out critical votes, and the legislature passed his program, including health insurance for pregnant women and children. One veteran political columnist noted: "For education, it was arguably the best legislative session in the state's history."[35]

Now he turned back to the national scene, traveling the country as spokesman and chair of the Democratic Leadership Conference. He spent time in California with major figures in the entertainment industry and leaders of the Business Roundtable. He presided over the DLC convention in Cleveland in the spring, which attracted many prominent party figures, including prospective presidential candidates Senators Al Gore, John Glenn, Joe Lieberman, and Chuck Robb, as well as former senator Paul Tsongas of Massachusetts and former governor Douglas Wilder of Virginia, both soon to announce their candidacies.

By June, when he returned to Arkansas, he knew he would have to make his own decision. He had promised during the gubernatorial race to finish out his term, and polls indicated that state constituents did not want him to run for President. President Bush looked unbeatable to many observers. And Bill Clinton, despite his speech-making in many states and his national work with the Democratic National Committee and the DLC, remained a virtual unknown to most Americans. Polls conducted between January and June had him thirteenth among possible Democratic choices, at a tiny 1.7 percent; his name recognition was merely 30 percent. (Even by December, he would be polling only 8.3 percent, with name recognition still under 50 percent.)[36]

But after discussions with Hillary and their key political advisers, he edged closer to a decision to run. A National Rifle Association lobbyist had come to Arkansas and, referring to Clinton's action on gun control, threatened that the NRA would "beat your brains out in Texas" if he ran. Not liking to be threatened, Clinton responded: "We'll saddle up and meet in Texas." Similarly, when Roger Porter, a Rhodes Scholar the year after Clinton and now a domestic counselor in the Bush White House, warned that if he ran in 1992 and did not wait until 1996, the Bush team would destroy him personally: "We'll spend whatever we have to spend and get whoever we have to say whatever they have to say to take you out," it only redoubled Clinton's growing resolve.[37]

Now, key Arkansas political leaders—including both senators—encouraged him to say yes. He received word that Al Gore had dropped out of the race, a big break for him. He set up an exploratory committee and started touring the state, asking constituents if they would release him from his pledge not to run if his decision was to go. He hired a fund-raiser and a new pollster (Morris had become too involved with Republicans and was compromised in the eyes of other Democrats). He traveled to the key Midwestern states that would have important primary contests. It was late summer. His mother told him she was strongly in favor of him taking the plunge. Finally, Hillary said she thought he should run. He made the formal announcement in October.

Many friends were not surprised. Shortly after the Dukakis defeat, Robert Reich, in an annual letter in the *American Oxonian*, and noting that Strobe Talbott agreed, wrote: "America will survive the next four years the same way it survived the last 20 since we set sail for England; waiting for Clinton to become President."[38]

Nine months after his announcement, at the Democratic Convention, he would conclude his acceptance speech, which had been introduced with the Thomasons' film *The Man from Hope*, exclaiming, "My fellow Americans, I end tonight where it all began for me. I still believe in a place called Hope."

NOTES

1. Bill Clinton, *My Life* (New York: Alfred A. Knopf, 2004), pp. 4–7.
2. Ibid., pp. 8–16; David Maraniss, *First in His Class: A Biography of Bill Clinton* (New York: Simon and Schuster, 1995), pp. 20–31; John D. Gartner, *In Search of Bill Clinton* (New York: St. Martin's Press, 2008), p. 81; Virginia Kelly, with James Morgan, *Leading With My Heart* (New York: Simon and Schuster, 1994), pp. 19–24; Michael Takiff, *A Complicated Man: The Life of Bill Clinton as Told by Those Who Know Him* (New Haven: Yale University Press, 2010), p. 12.
3. Clinton, *My Life*, pp. 12–34.
4. Ibid., pp. 41–47; Takiff, pp. 15–16, 21–22.
5. Clinton, *My Life*, p. 51.
6. Ibid., pp. 37, 43, 55, 59–68; Maraniss, pp. 50–61.
7. Clinton, *My Life*, pp. 76–81; Takiff, pp. 32–36.
8. Clinton, *My Life*, pp. 87–91.
9. Ibid., pp. 101–110, 116–118.
10. Ibid., pp. 121–123.

11. Ibid., pp. 114–117, 135–145; Takiff, pp. 37–38; William H. Chafe, *Bill and Hillary: The Politics of the Personal* (New York: Farrar, Straus and Giroux, 2012), pp. 27–32.
12. Maraniss, pp. 122–146; Robert B. Reich, *Locked in the Cabinet* (New York: Vintage Books, 1998), pp. 84–85.
13. Clinton, *My Life*, pp. 143–157; Maraniss, pp. 149–178.
14. Ibid., pp. 178–205; Takiff, pp. 39–41; Clinton, *My Life*, pp. 148–16l; James Carville and Mary Matalin, *All's Fair: Love, War, and Running for President* (New York: Random House, 1995), pp. 132–134.
15. Clinton, *My Life*, pp. 174–180; Maraniss, pp. 225–244.
16. Hillary Rodham Clinton, *Living History* (New York: Scribner, 2003), pp. 38–52.
17. Ibid., pp. 53–57; Maraniss, pp. 246–264; Gail Sheehy, *Hillary's Choice* (New York: Random House, 1999), pp. 74–91; Clinton, *My Life*, pp. 181–185.
18. Ibid., pp. 179, 187–201; interview with Samuel "Sandy" Berger, July 25, 2012; Hillary Rodham Clinton, pp. 60–61; Chafe, pp. 81–82; Kelly, p. 192.
19. Clinton, *My Life*, pp. 198–206; Maraniss, pp. 291–294.
20. Ibid., pp. 304–305.
21. Clinton, *My Life*, pp. 218–228.
22. Ibid., p. 240.
23. Ibid., p. 246.
24. Ibid., p. 255.
25. Hillary Rodham Clinton, pp. 84–88; Clinton, *My Life*, pp. 584–585; Maraniss, pp. 369–375.
26. Clinton, *My Life*, p. 265.
27. Takiff, pp. 57–61; Clinton, *My Life*, pp. 274–287; Sheehy, pp. 134–149.
28. Hillary Rodham Clinton, p. 93.
29. Clinton, *My Life*, pp. 291–323.
30. Interview with Sandy Berger, July 25, 2012; Clinton, *My Life*, pp. 330–331.
31. Ibid., pp. 332–341.
32. Maraniss, pp. 445–447; Clinton, *My Life*, pp. 342–344.
33. Ibid., pp. 357–358.
34. Takiff, pp. 87–60; Maraniss, pp. 456–458; Sheehy, pp. 157–158, 173–179; Clinton, *My Life*, pp. 340–342, 358–360.
35. Ibid., p. 362.
36. Nate Silver, "A Brief History of Primary Polling," *New York Times*, April 4, 2011.
37. Clinton, *My Life*, pp. 363, 368–369.
38. Maraniss, p. 448.

CHAPTER 2

TO THE WHITE HOUSE

Now in the race, Bill Clinton's first task was to assemble a team that could carry him to victory in a long series of bruising primary contests, and then, if successful, against the incumbent president in the general election.

He had been preparing for this moment for decades. Only 45, he had been involved in national politics since his college and law school years. From Georgetown and Oxford, from Yale Law and across his Arkansas years, he had attracted more and more FOBs ("Friends of Bill") who would support and counsel him. In fact, everywhere he had gone, in every campaign he had worked, in every organization he had led, addressed, or helped, he had met activists, officeholders, and political strategists. He had an uncanny memory for names, family details, and anecdotes connected to so many of these figures. He would put all of this to good use in shaping his campaign organization.

He asked Eli Segal, a wise and warm friend he had first met in the McGovern effort, to help with the selections. Segal agreed with his choice of a young congressional staffer, George Stephanopoulos, as a team member. Stephanopoulos had worked for Democratic majority leader Dick Gephardt; he was a smart, shrewd former Rhodes Scholar with a talent for quick responses to political attacks and an ability to reach out to members of the national press corps. Another former Rhodes, Bruce Reed, came to the campaign from the Democratic Leadership Council.

Two young Chicagoans were recruited. David Wilhelm, a political operative particularly gifted in the all-important struggle for winning convention delegates, signed on as campaign manager. Rahm Emanuel, a tough, intense individual who had worked on the successful campaigns of Mayor Richard J. Daley and was a master fund-raiser, became finance director. And from Bill Clinton's old Arkansas contacts emerged a number of new staffers. Notable in this group: Bruce Lindsey from Little Rock, a close friend since the National Students Association meeting back in the Georgetown days, the lawyer who had given Clinton a job after his defeat in 1980, an adviser and confidant during the gubernatorial years.

What was needed, however, were experienced political pros, consultants who had successfully run campaigns and could play the central role in shaping the Clinton campaign strategy and tactics. Two hot political properties, in demand during this presidential cycle, were James Carville and his younger partner, Paul Begala. They had recently helped elect Senator Harris Wofford of Pennsylvania. Both of them had southern roots: Carville a Louisiana Cajun and ex-Marine, Begala a shrewd Catholic populist from Sugar Land, Texas. They both understood, as Hillary put it, that presidential politics was a contact sport.[1]

Clinton arranged to meet them in Washington. In this case it was the would-be client trying to entice the potential employees. They expected that Bill Clinton, already famous as the consummate politician, a man who studied polls and had a sophisticated understanding of fund-raising and endorsements, would wow them with his insider's understanding of the political climate. Instead, Clinton talked at length about the crisis facing the nation.

Begala recalled the occasion: "James and my first meeting with Governor Clinton was love at first sight. We met in the lobby bar of the Powers Court hotel in Washington. I'd never before (or since) met anyone who so masterfully synthesized policy and politics; a big brain with a good heart. What specifically got to me was that he treated Carville and me not like mere campaign strategists, but rather like citizens. He spoke about ideas and issues and where he wanted the country to be when his daughter was grown up. He did not simply go through strategy (e.g., I can win in the South and my wife is from Illinois . . .). The only question we had as we walked out the door was whether this guy was too good to be true. Turns out he was the real thing."[2]

Putting the political organization together was one critical matter. But more important: having a persuasive message that informed the campaign, an articulated vision that the candidate would bring to the White House, the very reason why Bill Clinton thought he could make a difference as President of the United States.

Clinton laid out his vision in a remarkable series of presentations—the "Covenant Speeches"—that he delivered at his alma mater, Georgetown University, in October, November, and December 1991.

He began the first speech, "The New Covenant: Responsibility and Rebuilding the American Community," by telling the students and faculty that while his years as a Georgetown undergraduate were eventful times, marked by the social upheavals of the Sixties and the agony of Vietnam, this moment in history was "truly revolutionary." The last three years had seen the Berlin Wall come down, Germany reunify, all of Eastern Europe abandon Communism, the Soviet Union itself disintegrate, as well as the liberation of the Baltic and other former Soviet republics. And as the Cold War ended, Nelson Mandela walked out of jail in South Africa, another sign of how "all around the world, the American dream is ascendant."

And yet America was not celebrating in fall 1991. There was deep anxiety in the land, and many feared that the American dream, reigning supreme abroad, might be dying here at home.

People who once looked to the President and Congress to bring them together and solve problems now were disillusioned and "our government stands discredited." The Reagan–Bush years had "exalted private gain over public obligation, special interest over the common good, wealth and fame over work and family. The 1980s ushered in a gilded age of greed and self-ishness, of irresponsibility and excess, and of neglect."

While taxes were lowered on the wealthiest, poverty rose and inner-city streets were taken over by crime and drugs, "welfare and despair." And millions of decent, ordinary people who worked hard and played by the rules were "falling more and more behind." For twelve years "these forgotten middle-class Americans" had watched their economic interests ignored. It was time now, he exclaimed, "to forge a new covenant," to repair the damaged bond between "the people and their government." The covenant would require "change in my party" and "change in our leadership." And that "is why I am running for President."

The change in his party, Bill Clinton suggested, involved less emphasis on big government activism as well as reduced focus on help for groups victimized and marginalized in the past. This was a more moderate message, centering on personal responsibility, government efficiency, and a commitment to "honor middle-class values." There will "never be a government program for every problem," he exclaimed. "People no longer want a top-down bureaucracy telling them what to do."

This new covenant, he said, "can break the cycle of welfare," for "welfare should be a second chance, not a way of life. In my administration we're going to put an end to welfare as we have come to know it." It would help people "to help themselves" through education, job training, child care, and medical coverage; it would "give them all the help they need on public assistance for up to two years, but after that people who are able to work will have to go to work."

He skewered the leaders of American business for allowing hugely excessive executive compensation: the CEOs at major American corporations were being paid 100 times what the average worker earned, compared with twenty-three to one in Germany and seventeen to one in Japan. And he attacked the Reagan and Bush administrations for rewarding companies that transferred jobs abroad, for "pitting rich against poor, playing for the emotions of the middle class, white against black, women against men, fostering an atmosphere of blame and denial." Thus he endorsed the enduring themes of Democratic liberals and generously quoted FDR. But he was also signaling a change in emphasis in Democratic politics.[3]

Clinton continued to shape this message the next month in his November address, "A New Covenant for Economic Change." Here he began by focusing on the Republicans' "failed experiment in supply-side economics," which rewarded the rich with huge tax cuts but did not produce either growth or upward mobility. He borrowed from JFK, saying that we needed a President who would "get this country moving again."

He promised to reverse the "twelve years of Reagan–Bush" policies, which had led to the brutal recession ravaging the country, with a series of bold steps: He would push for a "middle-class tax cut" but an increase in taxes on the rich, a massive highway bill to add thousands of jobs in construction, and restrictions on ruinous interest rates that banks were charging credit card holders. There was no reason why America should be defeated in marketplaces of the world. "I believe we can win again in the global economy of the 1990s."

As he did in Arkansas, Clinton insisted that "education is a key to economic development," and for the United States be a high-wage, high-growth country, investment in education was essential. He pledged to fully fund Head Start for poor preschool children and to institute a national examination system to push all students to meet "world-class standards." He proposed a "domestic GI Bill," which would offer middle-class as well as low-income Americans a college education if only they either paid back the tuition (at low interest rates) or committed themselves to two years of national service, "as teachers, police officers, child care workers." The cost would be financed in part with a portion of the "peace dividend," made possible by the end of the Cold War and thus the reduction of huge defense expenditures.

So there would be big government efforts in a Clinton administration. And this was made even clearer when he turned to health care in America, noting that we are "losing jobs because health care costs are 30 percent more than [in] any other country." If we have "the courage to demand insurance reform and slash health care bureaucracies," he said, there could be improvement in health care without reducing quality. "And no nation has ever done this without a national government which took the lead in controlling costs and providing health care for all. In the first year of the Clinton administration, I will deliver quality, affordable health care for all Americans."

But not all new initiatives would involve new government programs. The tax code could be used to achieve liberal goals with conservative means; he offered poor Americans a massive expansion of the Earned Income Tax Credit, which would reward the working poor.

Moreover, government need not grow with this new effort for economic transformation. He talked of "reinventing government, cutting administrative costs," eliminating unnecessary layers of management, "reducing bureaucracies," and spending less money.

He emphasized the need to unleash the American private sector to compete in an interdependent world marketplace. "The American people aren't protectionists," he insisted; the new covenant must include a new trade policy. Even though some of his party's strong union supporters did not share his views, he promised to work for a free trade agreement with Mexico and throughout North America. He endorsed a new trade policy across the globe that would stimulate U.S. exports as one key to growing prosperity.[4]

All of this, he insisted, would make possible "a renewal of America."

In his final address, "A New Covenant for American Security," he focused on foreign and military affairs. The Arkansas governor had help with this speech from some experienced foreign policy hands, notably old friend Sandy Berger, deputy director for policy planning in the State Department in the Carter years, and other Carter-era authorities. These figures had been recruited by Berger, who had introduced them to Clinton in earlier years: Anthony Lake, Richard Holbrooke, and Madeleine Albright, along with Middle East expert Martin Indyck. (All would be the important players in the Clinton administration foreign policy team.)

Now, he promised to take advantage of the post–Cold War era to save precious dollars on defense. He suggested shrinking the size of America's conventional forces and withdrawing many troops from a Europe no longer threatened by the Red Army. He spoke of cutting costly and needless weapons systems designed in the past for the bipolar nuclear standoff with the Soviet Union, like the B-2 strategic bomber and those wildly expensive (if futile) antiballistic missile programs that had been a fixation of the Reagan–Bush years. Pricey new Air Force fighters and Army armored systems should now be "redesigned to meet regional needs."

Indeed, our allies should be asked to do more in maintaining security. "Cost-sharing" should be a new priority, for we "need to shift the burden to a wider coalition of nations of which America will be part." All these changes would make a huge difference: "My plan would bring cumulative savings of about $100 billion beyond the current Bush plan."

Certainly, there would be daunting foreign policy challenges in the new post–Cold War environment. The United States must take a lead in responding "more forcefully" to one of the great security issues of this time: nuclear proliferation. This meant not only helping the Russians "destroy nuclear weapons," but aiding Ukraine (and other nations that had been part of the former USSR) to do likewise. It meant working to check the spread of weapons of mass destruction everywhere.

Bill Clinton warned of coming dangers in "the growing intensity of ethnic rivalry" and of "separatist violence inside the borders of the old Yugoslavia." He noted the continuing importance of finding a "broader policy toward the Middle East." And he returned once more to his advocacy of free trade abroad as essential in a time of growing global interdependence as well as being vital in the effort to create "more jobs at home." For "restoring America's economic leadership," he insisted, was inextricably linked to any foreign policy agenda.

As he completed the set of covenant addresses, he restated the central theme of his emerging campaign: the goal of reversing the economic stagnation that had weakened America for almost a quarter of a century. Achieving this would make it possible for the next President to be "not the last President of the twentieth century," but "the first President of the twenty-first century."[5]

The Covenant Speeches not only helped to formulate the message Bill Clinton would carry into the campaign of 1992. They represented a further refinement of the distinctive political position to which Clinton had been moving for many years. And this was the vision that would prove so controversial inside his Democratic Party.

In the late 1960s, as a college student, he had admired Robert F. Kennedy as "the first New Democrat." In 1986, now governor of Arkansas, he had begun to outline what he characterized as the "New Democrat philosophy." At a management meeting of the Gannett newspaper chain (which had just bought the leading paper in the state), he spoke of the need for constructive partnership between business and government, the importance of addressing waste in government as well as in the private sector, and the imperative of rebuilding a "resurgent sense of community."

By 1990 he was playing a central role in the Democratic Leadership Council. He was aware that the DLC now was being assailed by liberal critics as "Republican lite." But, as he told the Texas DLC chapter, we are "all good Democrats." The DLC, he insisted, stood for a "modern, mainstream agenda: the expansion of opportunity, not bureaucracy; choice in public schools and child care; responsibility and empowerment for poor people; reinventing government away from top-down bureaucracy."[6]

It was essential, he argued, that the DLC lead an effort to entice "mainstream, middle-class voters" back to the Democratic Party, for while the party's leading liberals, like Governor Mario Cuomo and the Reverend

Jesse Jackson—who said that DLC stood for "Democratic Leisure Class"—dismissed the organization as much too conservative, Clinton insisted it was the group that represented the essential modernization of the party.

The left wing of his party might call him a "closet Republican" and deride his advocacy of welfare reform, trade policy, and fiscal reform. But in fact, his big differences were with the Republicans: their unfair tax cuts, their big deficits, their opposition to health care and gun control, their failure to fund education, their unwillingness to protect the environment, and their anti-choice stand.

Still, these liberals, along with what he characterized as "members of the political press" and so many academic and public intellectuals, were unhappy with Bill Clinton and his allies in the DLC. They did not fit comfortably into what Clinton called those "little boxes" that left liberals had long tagged "Democrat" and "Republican." And so, as he would argue later, "They said we did not believe in anything."

Of course, that was not true. But it was the belief in these "ossified little boxes" that made it possible for Clinton's critics to miss the important new direction he was suggesting his party must take if it was to ever retake the White House. This was his "third way" vision. This was the New Democrat message that he offered in the speeches at Georgetown, in the campaign to follow, and into the White House.

In fact, this was now a hinge moment in modern American political history. For what candidate Bill Clinton was proposing was a significant change in the approach taken by the party of activist government. And his was an argument that went beyond the political debate in a critical election year. It was informed by a view of historical developments that had been in process for decades.

When the industrial revolution in the late nineteenth century transformed America into an urban-industrial society, with a growing gap between the rich and the rest, political debate in the United States was turned inside out. "Liberals" in the early part of the nineteenth century had argued, with Jefferson, that the "government that governs best governs least." But the enormous concentration of economic and political power in the hands of the very few, during the rise of the railroad barons, the steel and oil titans, the banking and finance moguls, and other leaders of big business, changed that. It led many to conclude that government must intervene to protect "the people" from the powerful men of great wealth, and from those politicians—mostly members of the dominant Republican Party—who served their interests.

The Progressive Era had begun with the work of journalists, academics, and state and local politicians during the days of the "robber barons" of the 1890s. The call for activist government—already a theme of the

Populist movement in the Nineties—reached the national stage with the administrations of Theodore Roosevelt and Woodrow Wilson. And when TR, a Republican, the accidental President brought to power by the assassination of his conservative predecessor, William McKinley, was so angered by the policies of his hand-picked successor, William Howard Taft, that he unwisely ran as a third-party candidate in 1912, this not only led to Democrat Wilson's victory, but was a critical step in shattering the fragile progressive wing of his party. In the future, the Democrats would be the party of activist government.

World War I marked the end of progressive dominance in Washington. But the return to power of Republican conservatives in the White House in the 1920s would have a short run when the Wall Street crash ushered in the Great Depression and provided the setting for the election of Franklin D. Roosevelt.

Herbert Hoover, the brilliant engineer and political neophyte who was in the White House for only a few months when disaster struck, had acted with greater vigor to address the problem than his deeply conservative predecessors, Warren Harding and Calvin Coolidge, would have shown if the Depression had happened on their watch. But Hoover was the self-made man. He believed he had been a product of the "American Dream," the individualist ethos that held that the United States was different than Europe or anyplace else in the world. For here, there was equality of opportunity and every American had the freedom to succeed or fail. So while his brand of government intervention in the Depression allowed for federal aid for banks and businesses (that might then employ people), he rejected direct federal relief to the victims of the crisis. If Uncle Sam provided such help, he feared, Americans would always expect aid, and this umbilical cord from the federal government would undermine the "American Way of Life" and destroy proud American individualism.

But as his efforts failed and the nation sank deeper into the economic abyss, his name became the ugly prefix on the symbols of despair: the shantytowns inhabited by the homeless were "Hoovervilles," broken-down cars were "Hoover Wagons," empty pockets turned inside out were "Hoover flags."

This all changed with the election of Franklin D. Roosevelt. The presidential election of 1932 was a referendum on the failure of anti–big government conservatism, and even some Republicans feared that the enormous collapse could bring on revolutionary violence if something was not done. And so this was to be a transforming election. FDR's New Deal ushered in thirty-six years of liberal dominance in American national politics. It became the period that Clinton's critics would remember so well and so fondly. They would attack Clinton for failing to promote similar big government programs and for abandoning some of the triumphant rhetoric of this liberal golden age.

The New Deal would not only immensely strengthen the regulatory role of the federal government begun in the days of Theodore Roosevelt and Woodrow Wilson, but address the desperate straits of the unemployed millions. It made Washington the employer of last resort, and emergency relief measures would be supplemented by Social Security, the essential building block of any permanent social safety net. There were a wide variety of other federal initiatives as this "age of Roosevelt" reasserted the role of activist government.

The Depression had lasted for almost four years before Roosevelt's first inaugural, making it possible for the brilliant master politician in the White House to pin the cause of all the suffering on the "economic royalists" and their Republican friends in Washington. In a series of elections, he would shape a "working majority" in Congress for his agenda. Not all issues on some liberal activists' wish lists were addressed: There was no civil rights legislation, no federal health program, and no federal help for impacted school systems across the land. Fearing that southerners in Congress would retaliate by blocking other New Deal initiatives, FDR even refused to support anti-lynching legislation.

Still, much was accomplished before war once more turned attention away from domestic reform. While it can be argued that the New Deal already had run its course even before the outbreak of World War II, the world crisis made it clear that "Dr. New Deal," as the President said, would have to step aside in favor of "Dr. Win the War."

Of course, it was the war that finally ended the economic downturn of the Thirties. Even at the high tide of the New Deal, in 1937, unemployment and gross national product data lagged behind the pre-Depression figures. But confronted by the threat of the Wehrmacht and the Imperial Japanese fleet and army, the dollar sign was eliminated; the war cost almost twice as much as everything spent by the federal government from the nation's founding right up to 1939, and this unprecedented example of federal investment, deficit financing on an unimagined scale, put every able-bodied American to work and washed away the last remnants of the depression. And all of it was managed by a presidential government that grew in size and strength across four remarkable years.

The huge effort provided the setting for the postwar boom. After years of depression and conflict, when people lacked money to buy consumer goods or the war made them unavailable, there was enormous pent-up demand. And at war's end, in the late Forties and Fifties, with the private sector producing good jobs at good wages, there would be little impulse for enlarged domestic programs.

After Roosevelt's death, Harry Truman talked of a "Fair Deal," which would address the hidden agenda left over from FDR's years. But there was no chance of congressional passage of such legislation. And grappling with foreign policy crises in the early Cold War era, shaping the "containment" vision with the Marshall Plan and other initiatives, Truman lacked the support to promote a dynamic domestic effort.

Still, while the liberal age of reform did not grow in these years, there was no real effort to return to conservative policies of the past. The Republican Party seemed to accept the inevitable triumph of the New Deal era. Confronted with a choice between a real economic conservative, Senator Robert Taft of Ohio, known as "Mr. Republican," and General Dwight David Eisenhower in 1952, the GOP chose Ike, the moderate, eastern liberal Republican. Like GOP choices Wendell Willkie in 1940 and New York governor Thomas E. Dewey in 1944 and 1948, Eisenhower was the Republican presidential candidate from a party that seemed to have learned its lesson after catastrophic defeats by right-wing choices in 1932 and 1936.

Eisenhower was not interested in quixotic efforts to repeal the New Deal. But with the significant exception of the Interstate Highway Act, a monument less to belief in big government than to federal help for the flourishing private culture of the Fifties, he just would not build upon it. And that is the way he governed until 1960.

That year, as freshman Bill Clinton began his college career at Georgetown, the Democrats nominated John F. Kennedy, a candidate who warned that economic growth was slowing in the late Fifties and promised to "get this country moving again." Kennedy offered a New Frontier agenda similar to Truman's, and in his brief thousand days in office, there were similar results: no health care, no federal education aid, no civil rights bills passed. Of course, JFK, the quintessential Cold Warrior, was more concerned with foreign policy challenges, speaking in his inaugural address of how "we are watchmen on the walls of world freedom." In fact, many on his team believed his domestic accomplishments could follow only after a 1964 reelection victory, which would give him stronger congressional support.

The Kennedy assassination, historic trauma that it was, served as prelude to a remarkable legislative run of victories for activist government. Memories of the fallen leader, who had strongly endorsed a powerful civil rights bill, may have aided its passage through Congress in 1964; indeed, memories of the martyred President may have helped JFK's successor win a spectacular election triumph later that year.

The Republicans also helped. They nominated Barry Goldwater, a disciple of Hooverian conservatism, an honest figure who candidly promised to repeal Social Security and rejected much of the New Deal agenda. The author of *The Conscience of a Conservative*, the man who told his convention that "extremism in the cause of liberty is no vice," he would lead his party to a historic defeat at the polls. Lyndon Johnson's landslide gave the Democrats a 155-seat majority in the House and a 68 to 32 margin in the Senate.

And LBJ was already the master legislative leader of his age, the man who "knew the deck on Capitol Hill." His political skills had been critical in the passage of the Civil Rights Act of 1964. His accomplishments in the next two years would rival FDR's. Liberal historians, politicians, and activists have harbored such hostility toward LBJ because of Vietnam that they often downplay the enormous impact of what he called The Great Society, his domestic agenda. Although persona non grata in the Democratic Party, his name never mentioned at national nominating conventions, he shaped the final, triumphant expansion of activist government.

The list is well known. For health: There was Medicare for the aging and Medicaid for the poor, as well as money for medical training and heart, cancer, and stroke centers nationwide. For education: The Higher Education Act provided millions with loans and grants in the next decades, and the Elementary and Secondary Education Act made federal dollars available to poorer school districts. For civil rights: the essential Voting Rights Act of 1965 supplemented the historic action the year earlier. Key legislative objectives never addressed by FDR, never successfully pursued by Truman or Kennedy, were enacted into law.

In addition, several new regulatory initiatives would protect workers, children, and consumers. There were a host of related efforts to address poverty, including Head Start, the Job Corps, Community Development, Volunteers in Service to America. The Urban Mass Transit Act brought rapid transit systems to Washington, Atlanta, the San Francisco Bay Area— the last time the federal government would boldly address infrastructure needs in the nation. The Clean Air, Water Quality, and Solid Waste Disposal Acts were only some of the Great Society's pioneering environmental efforts. The Corporation for Public Broadcasting, the National Endowment for the Arts, and the National Endowment for the Humanities helped fulfill LBJ's promise that his agenda would be about "the quality of our lives as well as the quantity of our goods."

Not all of these programs would work as planned or endure in the years ahead. Some would be canceled or starved by hostile future politicians, others put in the hands of administrators who sought to weaken them. But many would become essential parts of the national landscape, some considered "entitlement" programs with such widespread support that even enemies of government action feared to touch them.

Yet even as Johnson was succeeding in winning congressional approval for his multifaceted activist agenda, forces were at work that would end the era of liberal dominance.

One important factor, of course, was the President's fateful decision to send American combat troops into the Vietnam conflict. Intense opposition to the war would shatter the liberal political coalition. As important, the huge, hidden costs of the war would help overheat the economy, stimulating a ruinous inflation that brought the booming economic prosperity of the Sixties to an end. Americans would support an expansion of government programs, including ones helpful to the most vulnerable and victimized, when their own real wages were rising. That would no longer be the case.

But as important as Vietnam in ending the thirty-six-year-long age of Roosevelt through Johnson were the social upheavals of the Sixties, followed by the series of economic defeats in the Seventies. These developments helped produce a new group of political leaders, nongovernmental actors, and social movements, all of whom challenged the dominant liberal narrative. And they would be successful, creating the new world Bill Clinton observed during his gubernatorial years. It was this changed political environment that led him to seek a third way, and made a New Democrat.

Even as the civil rights movement achieved its goal of demolishing the system of legal segregation in the south, forces were at work creating new racial anxieties in the land: Martin Luther King Jr.'s failed crusade to bring integration to the north, the rise of Black Power, the urban riots spreading from Watts in 1965 to Detroit in 1967. While this tension was growing in relations between black and white, there were other problems between the young and old. The student rebellion at the University of California erupted in fall 1964 and soon the "student movement" was impacting campuses across America. Predating U.S. involvement in Vietnam combat operations, at the start this was a cultural upheaval, a rejection of the values of prosperous postwar America, derided by the Berkeley Rebellion's spokesman, Mario Savio, as a "moral and intellectual wasteland, a chrome-plated consumers' paradise." But as the abyss of Vietnam widened, the student movement became another element in the "antiwar movement," marked by enormous confrontations not only on campus but in the streets of Washington and other communities.

The heady, liberating themes of the booming Sixties, the age of civil rights successes and Great Society legislation, nourished as well the women's movement, Hispanic rights, Native American rights, and nascent gay rights efforts (although the critical Stonewall uprising for gay activism came only at decade's end). Moreover, this was the setting not only for a sexual revolution in the country of the young, but for the emergence of a new group of cultural rebels, the "hippies." Their styles of dress and music and endorsement of drug use served as the anthem of the age; it had wide impact.

Much of this was unconnected to the triumph of LBJ's activist government. Indeed, many of the participants in these different movements loathed the President and were indifferent to his programs. But all of them, including the war protestors, the student activists, the new feminists, the Black Power spokesmen, and affirmative action proponents, created anxiety in the ranks of those who embraced an earlier vision of America. This was that time, wrapped in myth and memory, of "traditional family values."

Among those responding so negatively to the Sixties upheavals were large numbers of white working-class men and their families, the very people who had become the backbone of the Roosevelt coalition. They had been the voters won over to the Democratic Party by the way the New Deal had brought them help in a desperate hour. They had turned away from Hoover's conservatism, his celebration of American "individualism" and contempt for big government, and enlisted in the party of reform. Truman had gone back to the Roosevelt coalition for his upset victory in 1948; Jack Kennedy and Lyndon Johnson could call on such voters for support in their victorious races.

Now that would begin to change. In the tumultuous 1968 election, after the assassinations in April and June of Rev. Martin Luther King Jr. and Senator Robert F. Kennedy, the Democratic Party imploded at its convention in Chicago in August. "The whole world is watching!" shouted thousands of protestors beaten in the streets of the city when assailing the war. Johnson had been forced out of the race for reelection, but with Robert Kennedy dead and the McCarthy movement a failure, the Democratic candidate, Vice President Hubert Humphrey, led a fractured party, torn apart by the war. But Humphrey was menaced as well by a formidable third-party candidate, George Wallace.

This rogue Democratic governor of Alabama now led a crusade not explicitly keyed to race hatred but to the cultural disaffection of members of the old Roosevelt coalition. He characterized his supporters as "my barbers and beauticians, the steel workers and auto workers, the policeman on the beat." These were the people who reviled the draft-card-burning students at elite schools, because their kids were being sent to fight and die in the war; they hated the "limousine liberals" in the leafy eastern suburbs, who asked working-class whites to integrate the very city schools their kids could avoid. His message: The Democratic Party had abandoned a key part of its constituency; vote for me.[7]

In the end, Wallace failed, carrying only five southern states—including Arkansas—and Humphrey lost to Richard Nixon by a hair-thin margin. But four years following the Democrats' huge victory in 1964, despite all those legislative accomplishments, it might as well have been a landslide. And the new president was already working the same side of the street as

Wallace. One writer described an "emerging Republican majority" built around angry former Democrats. Some of these new recruits were from the south, responding, as LBJ had predicted, to the civil rights bill and punishing their old party for pushing it through. But many more were from the north. These were the people, embracing a view first advanced by Wallace and now borrowed by Richard Nixon: The Democrats had become the party of the welfare constituency and the liberal elites.

The terrible economic travail of the Seventies only added to their distress. The great inflation continued even as the war in Vietnam was downsized; the Arab oil boycott in 1973 and the Iranian oil shock in 1979 massively escalated prices in an oil-fueled economy and made the situation worse. The oil crisis had led to disastrous declines in the auto and steel industries, leading to mass unemployment, ravaging cities in the Midwest and the Northeast (now called "the Rust Belt"), forcing wage, hour, and pension "givebacks" by proud union members, the elite workers of blue collar America.

Although a Republican was in office at the beginning of this debacle, the Democrats could not take much advantage, even though Richard Nixon's presidency was wrecked by the odious Watergate scandal, and Gerald Ford, his successor, proved unable to respond to the economic disaster. Jimmy Carter, the Democratic outsider who served one term after 1976, also was ineffectual in facing the great "stagflation," which was making the prosperous postwar era only a memory for millions.

In mid-decade, *The Economist* magazine announced "the end of the American century," predicting relative national decline and a future belonging to Asian rivals. It was a grim moment. And now new political voices were heard, pointing to Democratic liberals as the source of all the problems, adding new emphasis to the incendiary arguments first used by Wallace.

Even as Bill Clinton began his years as governor, the attack on activist government was taking a new turn. One new group included the spokespeople for a wave of fundamentalist Christian fervor sweeping the nation. These were the televangelists—Jerry Falwell, Pat Robertson, Jimmy Swaggart, and other shrewd, persuasive television preachers—rapidly building vast media audiences in the Seventies and Eighties for their sermons calling the flock back to fundamental Christian teachings. But they were not only endorsing biblical literalism. They insisted that religious belief be inextricably linked to a conservative political agenda, an assault on the destructive policies of liberal activists.

They insisted that liberals were responsible for the rise of homosexuality and abortion, for the Equal Rights Amendment, sex education, and secular humanism; liberals dominated schools, colleges and universities, television and radio, publishing, the film industry, and the judiciary. They were behind the "filth of hell running rampant over this nation," said Swaggart in one memorable televised sermon. Someone had to protect America. These televangelists were at the spear point of a new movement of "social conservatives."

It did not take long for activists from the more traditional political "hard right" to seek them out as allies in a joint assault on hated liberal policies. Paul Weyrich, who had been instrumental in the birth of an influential right-wing think tank, the Heritage Foundation; Richard Viguerie, the powerful conservative fund-raiser; and Terry Dolan, head of the Conservative Political Action Committee, were involved. These were people who loathed liberal policies and wanted to demolish big government programs, believed in free market economics and hated higher taxes for the rich, and derided the social safety net as un-American, European-style socialism. After meeting with the televangelists, together they formed the Moral Majority.[8]

Soon these economic and social conservatives would have additional support. A small coterie of former Democrats, many of them writers and intellectuals, virulently anti-Communist "hawks" advocating a muscular foreign policy and supporting the Vietnam War but now furious at the anti-war attitudes they found inside their old party, switched sides. At one time, they had been liberal supporters of Democrats' domestic agenda, but they abandoned those positions as well. These were the neo-conservatives. Now they would help shape an attack on federal social programs, calling them "beyond the state of the art," contemptuously insisting that we "declared a war on poverty but poverty won."

They shrewdly used their magazine and journal platforms to demean the achievements of activist politics and to demonize the very word "liberal." Somehow "liberal" now became connected to drug abuse, out-of-wedlock children, crime in the streets, flag burning, and other unpatriotic acts. Liberals were responsible for inflation, unemployment, the rising national debt, and, of course, any example of weakness in foreign or military policy. Most of this did not make any sense, but liberal politicians seemed unable or unwilling to defend themselves in rational discourse. By the Eighties, many were afraid to use the term; they now preferred "progressive."

In that decade, Ronald Reagan was President. Some had believed that the GOP long ago had acknowledged the dominance of the activist vision, with only the nomination of Goldwater in 1964 serving as the final, ritual rejection at the polls for the old conservatism of Hoover and his Gilded Age forebears. They were wrong. Reagan offered a return to the old rhetoric, his victory made possible by the economic distress of the Seventies, his ideology given force by that emerging set of new conservative voices. We must "get the government off our backs and out of our pockets," said this leader, the ex–movie star, former corporate pitchman, and pro-business lecturer now turned "great communicator" in the White House. He promised to lead a crusade against both government regulation and the taxation of the successful, people like Ronald Reagan himself and that band of self-made men in California who had encouraged him to enter politics.

The "age of Reagan" was a time of praise for the individualist ethos, personal responsibility, and the ideals of an older America. President Reagan (and his speechwriters) shrewdly shaped a message keyed to the feelings of that earlier age: the belief in federalism and states' rights, the importance of power being diffused, checked, and balanced to protect individual freedom. And Ronald Reagan not only attacked federal intervention in the private sector but celebrated religious and traditional values, as defined by the social conservatives, now one critical part of his base of support.

A new political reality had been created by recent events, and the Democrats seemed blind to it. The Democratic candidate in 1972, George McGovern, nominated in a chaotic convention dominated by the very forces easily caricatured by the new conservative actors, led the party to a crushing defeat; Bill Clinton was an eyewitness in Texas. In election after election after that, the party of Roosevelt seemed to lose its way. Certainly, it lost key elements of its traditional constituency. By the Eighties, many people (or their children) who had been part of the Roosevelt coalition had become "Reagan Democrats."

From the Governor's Mansion in Little Rock, Bill Clinton recognized what was happening. His leadership of the DLC, his New Democrat vision, and the programs he discussed in the Covenant Speeches all were responses to a new political environment long in gestation. He would pitch his appeal to the "forgotten middle class," hardworking Americans who had been left behind and left out. His campaign theme would be "Putting People First." But to do so, he would have to win the nomination and take back the presidency.

The campaign was under way throughout the fall and gained new intensity when Carville and Begala joined the team in December. The primary season would begin with the critical first election in New Hampshire in late February, but a crowded field of candidates would be tested long before that, in a series of debates and straw votes.

Of his numerous rivals, at first Clinton thought his strongest competitors in New Hampshire would be Iowa senator Tom Harkin, running as an unabashed old-line liberal, and Nebraska senator Bob Kerrey, Vietnam Medal of Honor winner, a personable man with high-powered consultants. But there were others. One was former governor Jerry Brown of California, a constant critic of Clinton's, a figure Carville later characterized as a "How Bad Everything Is Democrat," a pessimist who believed, the consultant said, that "nothing is ever going to be any good, everybody is rotten." Douglas Wilder of Virginia and former senator Paul Tsongas were also in the race, and before long Clinton would come to understand that Tsongas had been underestimated; from a neighboring state, he would be the man to beat in New Hampshire.[9]

The one formidable figure he would not have to worry about was Governor Mario Cuomo of New York. "Our party's finest orator" said Clinton, the liberal who had demeaned the DLC and Clinton, he took himself out of the race at the last moment, on December 20.

The first media event that attracted most of the candidates was the NBC debate on December 15. Brown, Tsongas, Harkin, Wilder, and Kerrey were there. Bill Clinton promoted a plan for a middle-class tax cut and talked of change and confidence in America's future, demonstrating to a national audience just how articulate and persuasive was this relatively little-known southern governor. The polls that followed said Clinton had won. That same day, he took the nonbinding Florida straw poll at the state Democratic convention with 54 percent of the delegates to 31 percent for Harkin and 10 for Kerrey. The media now anointed Bill Clinton as the emerging front runner for the nomination. Two days later, a fund-raiser in Arkansas netted $800,000, far more than any single event had produced in the state, and by mid-January the campaign had raised $3.3 million. Wilder withdrew from the race, reducing competition for African American voters, and Clinton moved ahead of Tsongas in the New Hampshire polls. Everything seemed to be on track.

But now there was the Gennifer Flowers episode. Rumors of past affairs between Clinton and various women had come up from time to time early in the campaign, appearing in tabloids but given little credence. Carville was unconcerned and he coined the "Smoking Bimbo" theory: No one ever came forward and said "we did it." Then a supermarket scandal paper, *The Star*, published an article alleging Ms. Flowers, who had been paid $100,000 for the piece, had a long-running affair with Governor Clinton. Gennifer Flowers, of course, was the same woman who had denied allegations of such an affair during the earlier gubernatorial campaign, threatening to sue an Arkansas radio station that had made such charges. But coming at a critical moment of a presidential race, this would be the second near-death experience of Bill Clinton's political career.[10]

Ms. Flowers gave a press conference and 350 journalists crowded the room. She claimed a twelve-year relationship with the governor and said she had ten tapes of phone conversations as evidence. It was a media firestorm. The stories obliterated all other coverage of the primary campaign. Clinton's New Hampshire poll numbers immediately sank. Many speculated he would be forced out of the race within days. The candidate phoned

Eli Segal and convinced him to come down to Little Rock as campaign chief of staff, a calming influence for his relatively young team; adult leadership was needed at this moment.

The campaign counterattacked. It was helped when a Los Angeles TV station hired an expert who characterized the tapes he heard as "selectively edited" and "suspect at best." Next, Bill and Hillary appeared together on *60 Minutes*, the most influential and widely watched news hour on American television. Steve Kroft, the investigative reporter, asked Clinton if the Flowers story was true. He responded that it was not. Of course, many years later, in his autobiography, Clinton would acknowledge that while there was no "twelve-year affair," he and Flowers did have "a relationship that I should not have had" in the 1970s. And when Kroft then asked if there had been other affairs, Clinton responded that he already had agreed that "I've caused pain in my marriage and everyone out there knows what I'm talking about." Bill Clinton's reckless womanizing was now threatening his political future.

But the candidate survived. For Kroft, looking at both Clintons, went on to assert: "Most Americans would agree that it's very admirable that you have stayed together . . . that you seem to have reached some sort of an understanding, an arrangement." An angry, but controlled, Bill Clinton replied: "Wait a minute. You're looking at two people who love each other. This is not an arrangement or an understanding. This is a marriage." Hillary added: "I'm sitting here because I love him and I respect him and I honor what he's been through and what we've been through together. And you know, if that's not enough for people, then heck, don't vote for him."[11]

After the program, an ABC poll showed that 80 percent of Americans felt Bill Clinton should stay in the race (and 70 percent thought the press should not report on the lives of public figures). One Arkansas political reporter observed that "Gennifer Flowers actually helped him in the short run. It made him a nationally known figure." With Hillary at his side, many Americans could understand what was happening in this now-famous marriage. The next New Hampshire poll showed that Tsongas had forged ahead, but Clinton was still a strong second. If it held, that would be good enough to move on to the southern primaries.[12]

But just before primary day, there was another trial to come. The *Wall Street Journal* ran a story on the candidate's draft experience. Soon ABC's *Nightline* announced that it had a copy of Clinton's letter sent to Colonel Holmes, the former head of the Arkansas ROTC, a man now being quoted as saying Clinton misled him to stay out of the draft. The newspaper article did not mention how the colonel had offered a different and benign view of Clinton in statements in the previous twenty-two years. Excerpts from the long letter seemed so damaging that the distressed press aide, George Stephanopoulos, asked if it was not time to think about withdrawing.

The "character issue," that media fixation that had almost sunk the campaign during the Flowers crisis, now took on a new and seemingly unstoppable momentum. The poll numbers again dropped, this time seemingly in free fall. And the pros at the Little Rock headquarters knew that if Clinton finished below second in New Hampshire, it would be all over. But James Carville suddenly insisted that "this letter is our friend, anyone who actually reads it will think he's got character." So an ad was taken out in New Hampshire's dominant newspaper containing the full text of the letter as well as the names and phone numbers of 600 Arkansans who asked New Hampshire Democrats to call them to find out the truth about their governor. Television time was purchased allowing voters to ask the candidate about the charges. And dozens of Arkansas friends and supporters—the FOBs—arrived in the state for a last-minute campaign blitz; they called themselves "The Arkansas Travelers."

Just before the election, Clinton concluded a speech to an enthusiastic crowd in Dover: "Character is an important issue in a presidential election," he said, and while specifically laying out what he would do if elected, stated after each item, "That's a character issue." He concluded: "You give [this election] to me, I'll never forget who gave me a second chance, and I'll be there for you 'til the last dog dies."[13]

"The last dog dies" became the campaign's rallying cry, and on election night, although Paul Tsongas won with 35 percent of the vote, Clinton was a strong second with 26 percent, far ahead of Kerrey, with 12 percent, and Brown and Harkin, who had even less. Paul Begala coined the phrase the media would soon embrace: Bill Clinton was "The Comeback Kid."[14]

The "character issue" had been checkmated for a while, but it would reappear throughout Bill Clinton's campaigns and across his White House years. "Slick Willie" was the insulting term his detractors liked to use. Paul Greenberg, an Arkansas political writer whose acid columns about Clinton over three decades were later made into a book, took credit for first using the phrase in the Eighties. It is a southern metaphor for someone you can't quite pin down, and James Carville noted that there was a chain of pool halls in the south by that name. Clinton's opponents did not like that he had an answer for everything and sometimes answers changed over time. You can't trust him, they insisted.[15]

He was not the first political figure to be attacked for being both articulate and adroit in sometimes adjusting his positions in light of changing realities. FDR, the heavyweight champion of liberal America, was called a "chameleon on plaid" even at the high tide of the New Deal in the Thirties. His critics charged: You can't tell where he stands, he changes his views more often than a chameleon changes its color. Of course, Roosevelt's supporters called him a "pragmatist," not a term of derision back then.

Still, in Clinton's case, his political style seemed to infuriate not only rivals—in his party and out—but many journalists. They accused him of dissembling, saying that he had assured them—and his staffers—that he had shared everything there was to know about his Vietnam era history, and then something else would turn up. (They were particularly irritated that in the middle of the New Hampshire primary, for some reason he had denied to reporters having received a draft notice or having sent the letter to the draft board renouncing his request for the ROTC appointment. One prominent Washington writer exclaimed, "That's bullshit. . . . This is a guy who reconstructs his own history to suit his needs.")

Later in the primary season, they had a field day when Clinton, during a televised candidates' forum, was asked if he had ever tried marijuana at Oxford. He replied, "I experimented with marijuana a time or two but I didn't like it. I didn't inhale and never tried it again." There he goes again, the pundits scathingly observed: Clinton trying to have it both ways, a man with a character flaw, who simply could not candidly tell the truth about anything.

But Clinton was telling the truth. He never smoked cigarettes and did not inhale the pipe he used on occasion at Oxford. Inhaling, for Clinton, like some others, made him cough or sneeze. (This child of an alcoholic was not a real drinker, and always opposed serious drug use.)[16]

Of course, while some political observers during this primary season focused on what they saw as character flaws, others noted how remarkable were the skills this southern governor was demonstrating as communicator and campaigner. There was his extraordinary mastery of the smallest details of a vast number of complex domestic and foreign policy questions and his astonishing ability to speak so persuasively about these matters in major addresses, in televised forums, in small group settings, or in person-to-person encounters on the campaign trail. He was brilliantly articulate without appearing condescending or pompous. Bill Clinton looked and spoke like someone who could do the enormous job he was trying to win, a person smart enough, strong enough, knowledgeable enough to be the President of the United States. More than anything else, for some potential voters, this was what separated him from the pack of contenders, all of whom had impressive career credentials. After listening to him address the large crowd on a quadrangle at the center of the Syracuse University campus during the New York primary contest in the spring, several faculty members, who had no intention of supporting this small-state southerner, told each other that they had become instant converts.

Bill Clinton was having a remarkable impact on people who had never seen or heard him before and not because he had "charisma of office." At this point, he did not have the great national office; he was just seeking it. But he seemed to have real charismatic authority, even in an age when that term (from Max Weber) seemingly had been devalued after being used by journalists and publicists about so many athletes, movie stars, and aspiring politicians. One shrewd professional in his campaign observed that he was "one of the very rare people who can walk in and change the chemistry of a room."

As impressive as was his understanding of the issues and his eloquence in addressing them, it was his talent and passion for campaigning that made him one of the great political figures of the age. He was warm, personable, and empathetic. He was terrific in town hall meetings, able to relate to individual life stories and deal with a range of questions. His critics liked to make fun of him: "I feel your pain," they had him saying. But he loved what he had called "retail politics," learned first as a very young man in small towns in Arkansas. When one woman, at a primary campaign event in New Hampshire, burst into tears while describing how her family was devastated by the declining economy, he came over to her, hugged her, and there were tears in his eyes. This was not a show. He had entered public life with a commitment to social justice.

He not only liked to talk to individuals; he was sure that if given enough time, he could not only learn from them but persuade them that he was a leader they should support. On that campus quadrangle, it took repeated efforts by his advance team to persuade him to leave when, animatedly talking to groups of two or three or—at the end—just one final student questioner, he did not want to move on to the next event, even though the speech was long over and the crowd, save for a few, had dispersed.

One of his advance men, who had served in the 1988 election and watched the earnest but awkward Michael Dukakis try to relate to crowds, marveled at this new presidential aspirant, who loved to work the rope lines, to talk to these total strangers. Clinton had to be pushed along by aides because he could not get enough. (Another staff member, noting that she had met—for the first time—an Arkansan in an airport who said she disliked Clinton, found the candidate asking for the person's number so he could phone her up and convert her to the cause.) The advance man called Clinton "a natural." That was the phrase Joe Klein would later use as the title of his book on the presidency of Bill Clinton.[17]

There would be a presidency only if he secured the nomination. But after the trials of New Hampshire, the momentum began to build. March would be a big month, and although Clinton managed only a virtual three-way tie (with Brown and Tsongas) in Colorado, he swept to victory in Georgia. Kerrey had said that voters would split Clinton open like a "soft peanut" in Georgia, but instead he took 57 percent of the vote and Bob Kerrey withdrew from the race. The following Saturday, the southern governor took his second southern state, winning South Carolina with 64 percent, and Tom

Harkin dropped out. It was only Tsongas, Jerry Brown, and Clinton left on Super Tuesday, with its eight primaries—and Clinton carried Texas, Florida, Louisiana, Mississippi, Oklahoma, and Tennessee (polling 66 percent of the vote in Texas, with the help of some of the friends he had made in the 1972 McGovern effort). He also triumphed in the caucuses (there were no primaries) in Hawaii and Missouri.

The next big tests were in two large Midwestern industrial states, Illinois and Michigan. Clinton had traveled there in earlier months and was a prohibitive favorite. They were critical battleground states, more for the general election than the primary. In fact, at one event in Macomb County, near Detroit, a "prototypical home of Reagan Democrats," with voters who had been lured away by Reagan's antigovernment, strong defense, tough-on-crime message, Clinton focused on how these voters thought that "Democrats no longer shared their values of work and family, and were too concerned with social programs, which they tended to see as taking their tax money and giving it to blacks and wasteful bureaucrats." In his speech, Clinton told the crowd he would give them a new Democratic Party, with economic and social policies "based on opportunity for and responsibility from all citizens."[18]

Just before primary day, in a televised debate in Chicago, a desperate Jerry Brown assailed Clinton and said he had steered state business to his wife's Rose law firm. This did not hurt Bill Clinton; he would sweep to victory with 52 percent to 25 percent for Tsongas and only 15 percent for Brown. And in Michigan, he took the state with 49 percent to 27 percent for Brown. Tsongas got only 18 percent and within a week withdrew from the campaign, citing financial problems. That left only Brown as a Clinton opponent.

But following the television debate, when reporters questioned Hillary Clinton about Brown's charges (while she was greeting voters in a downtown Chicago coffee shop), her lengthy response included: "You know, I suppose I could have stayed home and baked cookies and had teas, but what I decided to do was fulfill my profession." This became the news item of the day. GOP critics—Clinton called them "culture warriors"—immediately portrayed Hillary as a "militant feminist lawyer," the ideological leader of a "Clinton–Clinton administration" with a "radical feminist agenda." It was not the last time opponents would use this characterization.[19]

Still, Clinton was now firmly in command of the primary race. Many believed he could not be denied his party's nomination. Yet after a setback in Connecticut, it seemed essential that he take the New York primary in early April. And that state, with its strong unions, its active ethnic communities, and its enormous press corps (including the powerful presence of the nation's most influential newspaper, the *New York Times*), was a challenging environment. In fact, the *Times* used this race for its first series on the Whitewater matter. The investigative reporter was talking to Clinton critics in Arkansas; the clear innuendo was that the governor and his wife were guilty of shady dealings. Soon there would be other press reports, alleging that Governor Clinton had allowed the poultry industry in his state to pollute the waterways.

One famous radio talk-show host now called him a "redneck bozo," a columnist described him as "a fraud and a fake . . . vulgar, garish and, of course, a liar." On Phil Donahue's widely watched television show, he faced an endless series of questions about marital infidelity and finally refused to respond: "We're gonna sit here a long time in silence, Phil. I'm not gonna answer any more of these questions. . . . You are responsible for the cynicism in the country. You don't want to talk about the real issues." The audience cheered.[20]

He persevered, helpfully being booed at a Wall Street rally for referring to the Eighties as a decade of greed and opposing a cut in the capital gains tax. Jerry Brown was working hard and had African American leader Jesse Jackson's support. Brown had said that if nominated he would consider Jackson as a running mate for Vice President. But because Jackson had made some comments that New York Jews interpreted as anti-Semitic (he had referred to New York City as "Hymietown"), Jackson's support only depressed Brown's poll numbers. With Betsey Wright rejoining the campaign (as "director of damage control") and the whole Clinton team pouring into the state for the final push, with all the New York papers, including the *Times*, at last giving him their endorsement, Clinton took New York with 41 percent of the vote. (Tsongas, asking his supporters for a symbolic last gesture, got 29 percent and Brown 26.) The majority of African American voters went for Clinton.

The day he carried New York, he also won in Kansas, Minnesota, and Wisconsin. Later that month, he was the victor in Pennsylvania. In May, he easily triumphed in his home state and then, on June 2, won the primaries in New Mexico, Alabama, and Montana and the big state races in Ohio, New Jersey, and California, where he defeated former governor Brown 48 to 40 percent. He had clinched the nomination. He received more than 10.3 million votes, 52 percent of all cast—his lone surviving opponent, Jerry Brown, less than 4 million.

It had been a grueling, exhausting effort. Often he had shown the strain, and one writer described how aides had recoiled at his incendiary anger and bouts of self-pity. In the spring he had suffered from the flu, lost his voice, and could not sleep for more than an hour without waking to cough. He put on 30 pounds, keeping alert on adrenaline and donuts. His friend Harry Thomason bought him new suits "so I didn't look like a balloon about to burst."[21]

Nonetheless, he was the nominee. But now some wondered if that prize would prove an illusion. For while headlines announced "Clinton Set to Clinch Nomination," the second line was "All Eyes Are on Perot"; other papers announced: "Perot the Man to Watch." Even as Bill Clinton was shaping his remarkable series of primary successes, his presidential chances were threatened by a new contender. President George H. W. Bush's popularity might have plummeted because of the recession gripping the land, and the incumbent even had to fight off a threat to his own renomination in the form of right-wing isolationist Pat Buchanan. But seemingly out of nowhere had come a formidable third-party challenger, H. Ross Perot, a hugely wealthy and successful businessman with the personal resources to buy massive amounts of television time. He appeared on the scene as a "populist," and his poll support was skyrocketing. A Gallup poll taken just after the California primary had billionaire Perot leading the national race at 39 percent, with Bush 31 and Bill Clinton at a mere 25.

Clinton was aware of Perot, and he knew that the bruising primary fight had taken its toll. Yet now he had to solidify support and prepare for the nominating convention. The presumptive candidate was invited onto several late-night national TV shows. He brought his sax to one of them, wearing sunglasses and playing "Heartbreak Hotel," which had special meaning because his staff's nickname for Clinton was "Elvis."

But he also had to deal with the fallout from a comment he had made in a mid-June speech to Jesse Jackson's Rainbow Coalition. He had compared the popular rap singer Sister Souljah—who had addressed the group the night before Clinton's appearance—to the white racist extremist David Duke. A month earlier, Souljah had told a national newspaper, after the Los Angeles riots following the arrest and beating of a black motorist, Rodney King: "If black people kill black people every day, why not have a week and kill white people? So if you're a gang member and you would normally be killing somebody, why not kill a white person?"

Jackson felt Clinton had abused his hospitality to make "a demagogic pitch to white voters." He even threatened to support Perot. Some columnists thought it was just Slick Willie at work again, using the rapper as fall person for a politically motivated appeal to conservative swing voters. But Clinton and staff felt he could not ignore the incendiary nature of her remarks, and his comment certainly would separate him from the more radical McGovern wing of the party.[22]

The pressing business at this time was preparing for the nominating convention and selecting a vice-presidential running mate. He considered a wide range of choices, including Kerrey and several other key figures on Capitol Hill, but decided on Senator Al Gore of Tennessee. To some, it seemed a curious decision. Clinton was only 46 and Gore was even younger;

Gore was from a border state, adjacent to Arkansas and—like Clinton— identified with the New Democrat wing of the party. Where would be the "balance" in this ticket? But for Clinton, Gore's expertise on national security, arms control, information technology, and energy balanced his own mastery of a range of critical matters. And Al Gore was an acknowledged authority on the environment, author of the best-selling book *Earth in the Balance*. They had a good meeting in early July and then traveled together to their native states. In Gore's hometown, Clinton met his father, Al Gore Sr., a three-term senator who had lost his seat in 1970 because he had been a supporter of civil rights and an opponent of the Vietnam War.

The convention was in New York City. It was shrewdly orchestrated by Clinton and the DNC leaders to demonstrate the unity of the party. It would be much different than previous gatherings, like the bitter convention upheavals of 1972 or 1980. There were a series of rousing speeches, notably by Bob Kerrey, defeated rival now supporting the candidate; Ted Kennedy, liberal conscience of the party, the "lion of the Senate" and bearer of the Kennedy heritage; and Al Gore. The VP choice electrified the huge crowd by citing a series of failings of the Bush administration and, after each one, leading the audience—which took up the call—in the resounding shout: "It's time for them to go!" Mario Cuomo, the noted party orator, gave the nominating speech. The next night, the Thomasons' film brought on the candidate.

Clinton did not disappoint. "In the name of all those who do the work and pay the taxes, raise the kids and play by the rules, in the name of the hardworking Americans who make up our forgotten middle class, I proudly accept your nomination. I am a product of that middle class, and when I am President, you will be forgotten no more." He spoke of his wife and daughter, of his mother and grandmother, and said of his grandfather, the country storekeeper with a grade school education, that he had taught him more about "equality in the eyes of the Lord" than "all my professors at Georgetown," more about the "intrinsic worth of every individual" than "all the philosophers at Oxford," more about the need for equal justice under law than "all the jurists at Yale Law School." He said that "frankly I am fed up with politicians in Washington lecturing the rest of us about family values. Our families have values. But our government does not." He laid out his critique of the Bush record, reminding the nation that "we have gone from first to thirteenth in the world in wages since Reagan and Bush took office" and he referred in detail to his new covenant of opportunity, responsibility, and community. He described how he had been inspired as a teenager by John Kennedy's "summons to citizenship" and even quoted his old professor Carroll Quigley on how tomorrow could be better than today, but only if everyone took personal responsibility to make it so. The speech had run somewhat long, fifty-four minutes, but the candidate never lost his audience. And he ended with that reference to still believing "in a place called Hope." The crowd now was roaring, musicians filled the stage, and the whole hall sang "America the Beautiful." Post-convention polls had Clinton now in the lead.[23]

The next morning, Bill and Hillary Clinton and Al and Tipper Gore drove together to New Jersey to begin the campaign with a long bus tour. It was a 1,000-mile journey, filled with stump speeches and hand shaking, through Pennsylvania, West Virginia, Ohio, and other states to Illinois. The next month there would be four more bus tours. The general election was under way.

Back in Little Rock, the structure of the campaign was changing. The primary schedule from February to June had dictated efforts focusing on the states in play; now Clinton believed there was need for better coordination and a single strategic center. James Carville, at 48, much older than the young staff, became the critical leader. The vacated offices of a newspaper were the campaign headquarters, with all elements—press, politics, research—in one big open space in the old newsroom. Carville said that it was Hillary who named it "the War Room." And he put up a sign near his desk, composed of three lines: "Change vs. More of the Same," "It's The Economy, Stupid," and "Don't Forget Health Care."[24]

The War Room was active 24 hours a day. Carville wore a T-shirt with the inscription "Speed Kills . . . Bush." He created a rapid response team and had pins with that slogan given to the team members doing night and day duties. Carville, George Stephanopoulos, Mandy Grunwald, an important figure throughout the primary season, pollster Stan Greenberg, and Betsey Wright were key players in this headquarters, and the "Road Warriors"— including Paul Begala and Dee Dee Myers (who would be President Clinton's first press secretary)—were out on the hustings with the candidate.

One thing that had given the campaign a lift, and pushed Clinton into the lead in the polls, was Ross Perot's announcement—made just before the last day of the Democratic Convention—that he was dropping out of the presidential race.

Perot, a Naval Academy graduate whose meteoric rise in business was a national success story, was a bizarre figure on the political scene. A former salesman for IBM, he had founded a small data processing company, Electronic Data Systems, in 1962. When the U.S. government gave EDS immensely lucrative contracts to computerize Medicare records, he would be on the cover of *Fortune* by 1968, called the "richest Texan." Even before he sold the controlling interest in his company to General Motors for almost $2.5 billion in 1984, he had dabbled in politics, first calling for educational reforms in Texas, next assailing Presidents Reagan and Bush for alleged failures to secure the release of POWs left behind in Vietnam, and, finally, becoming a vociferous critic of the first Iraq war. Now he began to speak out against both political parties, insisting that they were partly responsible for the American decline. In late February 1992, on CNN's Larry King show, he announced his intention to run as an independent for President—but only if his supporters got his name on the ballot in all fifty states.

Candidate Perot's political positions placed him on both sides of the issues dividing the two major parties. He was for a balanced federal budget and expanding the war on drugs and was opposed to gun control. But he also supported the Environmental Protection Agency and was firmly pro-choice on abortion. He decried the outsourcing of American jobs, warning that if the North American Free Trade Agreement were passed, there would be a "giant sucking sound" from the jobs lost to Mexico. Many thought he was more comfortable with Republicans than Democrats, but it was hard to tell. He certainly demonstrated animus toward President Bush. And he hired two well-known figures from each camp as campaign managers, Democrat Hamilton Jordan, President Jimmy Carter's former chief of staff, and Republican Ed Rollins.

Perot's supporters were mesmerized by his folksy insistence that America needed new, tough, and candid leadership. Despite his wealth, he appealed to middle-class strivers. They liked his arrogant self-confidence, his insistence that the government was run by losers and lackeys and that it was time for a nonprofessional to take over, because "a chimpanzee" could do better than the mainstream politicians. But Jordan and Rollins found him uninterested in their advice. He insisted on full control of operations and even forced volunteers to sign loyalty oaths. With his poll numbers slipping in July, Jordan threatened to quit and Rollins did resign. It was at this time that Perot announced, again on the Larry King TV show, that he would not seek the presidency. His reason: He did not want the House of Representatives to decide the election if a three-way race caused a split in the electoral college. Later, he said the real reason was that he had received threats and feared that Republican operatives would sabotage his daughter's wedding with doctored photographs.

By September, Ross Perot had qualified for ballots in all fifty states and he changed his mind again, announcing on October 1 that he would reenter the race. He proceeded to spend almost $70 million (of his own money) on a series of half-hour infomercials on major television networks and managed to climb back into the race, qualifying for inclusion in the three critical television debates with Clinton and Bush. But his poll numbers would never again approach the level reached before his erratic behavior and the abrupt decision to leave the race in July.[25]

Inside the Clinton campaign, things were going well—with a twenty-point lead in the polls—when the Republicans opened their convention late in August. Speaker after speaker attacked Bill Clinton. Some called him a "draft dodger" and "skirt chaser"; famous televangelist Pat Robertson referred to him as "Slick Willie," a man with a radical plan to destroy the American family. George Bush, in his acceptance speech, admitted he had made a mistake in signing a bill with a gas-tax hike and promised to cut taxes if reelected.

Bush, of course, had been struggling with this issue for many months. He had promised in 1988 that he would not raise taxes, famously borrowing from a Clint Eastwood line: "Read my lips, no new taxes." In office, he had not only failed to fulfill this promise but infuriated people who celebrated Ronald Reagan, appearing to them a weakling on hard right issues, a feckless moderate who had announced that "our will is strong but our wallets are thin" when discussing the very social programs that the libertarian wing of his party found so offensive.

Now he tried to make amends to the Republican base. And he cleverly said that Clinton would give America "Elvis Economics" and take America to the "Heartbreak Hotel." By convention's end, the poll margin was at ten points or less.[26]

Throughout September, as Clinton, Gore, and surrogates crisscrossed the nation, reaching voters in every region, the gap slightly widened again. Some important Republicans, including thirty major figures in Silicon Valley's high technology industries, endorsed Bill Clinton. The two Democratic candidates, of course, kept focusing on the economy and the Bush administration's responsibility for the recession. And George H. W. Bush—intelligent, accomplished, with a lengthy record of public service—had never been a gifted campaigner; now he was up against a brilliant opponent. As his frustration grew, he angrily lashed out in private, calling Clinton a "bozo" and Gore "Ozone Man." Then television cameras at one campaign stop captured him looking bemused at a supermarket, where he seemingly had never before encountered a price scanner. He told the grocer he was "amazed by some of the technology." Journalists and millions of Americans could only conclude that here was someone who was not like them, who had led a privileged, insulated life.

But GOP activists were tough foes. They accused Clinton of raising taxes 128 times in Arkansas, although this charge did not stick when major national newspapers, including the Wall Street Journal, called the allegation misleading. The Bush team tried to raise the draft issue—even though Vice President Dan Quayle's lack of service in Vietnam had been widely noted. The War Room's rapid response group got help from Bob Kerrey in countering this attack, the Medal of Honor winner announcing that the draft should not be an issue, as well as from the endorsement of Admiral William Crowe, former chairman of the Joint Chiefs of Staff.

Republicans, growing desperate as poll numbers continued to show them trailing badly, also returned to Clinton's days at Oxford to charge that he had participated in antiwar rallies in London, and even sought evidence of un-American, antiwar activities during his trip to Russia. In fact, the Clinton team felt that their opponents were hitting below the belt on several occasions. Mary Matalin, a key GOP player—Clinton referred to her as the "pit bull" in the Bush organization—had called Bill Clinton a "sniveling hypocrite." Then she was quoted as saying he was "a philandering, pot-smoking draft dodger." Ms. Matalin was famously engaged to James Carville, and they would soon marry. Carville told the press: "You can hate the sin and love the sinner; she's an A plus operative who pulled a C minus stunt."[27]

Into October, Clinton maintained his lead. But now Perot reentered the contest and the three candidates finally agreed on three debates—and a single vice-presidential debate—all within nine days, between October 11 and 19. The first and third presidential debates would have members of the press asking questions, the traditional format. The second debate would be a town hall meeting with citizens asking the questions. The outcome of these encounters would be critical in determining whether Bill Clinton could maintain his momentum.

The first debate was in St. Louis, and both major party candidates went through elaborate preparations, including mock debates against politicians skilled at imitating the arguments and even the style of the two rivals. Clinton was under particular pressure because polls indicated that most Americans thought he would win. He did well enough, arguing that change was essential and focusing on the economy. But Perot helped himself with a relaxed performance. When President Bush accused him of having no experience, he replied: "I don't have any experience in running up a $4 trillion debt." A diminutive man with a crew cut and large jug ears, he insisted that we must collect taxes, "but if anyone has a better idea, I'm all ears." At debate's end, polls showed 60 percent of watchers had a more favorable opinion of Perot than before. For Clinton, that meant the race was still unpredictable.[28]

But the second debate played to Bill Clinton's greatest strengths. The town hall meeting format allowed him to demonstrate to a national audience his skill and sensitivity in dealing with citizen questions, the heart of "retail politics." And the President did not fare as well. He seemingly could not understand one woman's question about the impact of the recession, but Clinton grasped the moment, walking over to the questioner and describing the huge human toll of the recession in his own state, caused by "the failed economic theory of the administration." Meanwhile, George H. W.

Bush looked nervously at his watch. The cameras—and many pundits in the days following—fixed on this incident. The President, trailing going in, now again looked awkward and out of touch; the wealthy patrician in the White House uncomfortable with listening to stories of ordinary people's pain. In the CBS post-debate poll, 53 percent thought Clinton had won, to 25 percent for Bush and 21 percent for Perot. Another national poll, focusing on the election itself, had Clinton's lead back to 15 points over Bush, with Perot getting but 15 per cent.

George H. W. Bush did better in the third debate, but momentum now was clearly on Bill Clinton's side; three post-debate polls had him the winner to one calling it narrowly for Perot. The Bush team thought their man had done well, but then came the national polls: The President was behind by 18 points and now the election was only days away. Most observers felt it was all but over.

As is the case in many presidential contests, the gap narrowed just before the nation went to vote. As all the candidates and their running mates made one last frantic effort to campaign in critical battleground states, one poll suggested that Clinton's lead was down to two points, but most others still had the margin higher. And on election day, that is what it was: over 104 million votes were counted, Bill Clinton winning by 5.5 percent: 43 percent to 37 for Bush and 19 for Ross Perot. In the electoral college, the win was even more decisive: 370 (in thirty-two states) for Clinton to 168 (in eighteen states) for Bush.[29]

Perot carried no state. His presence on the ballot probably added to Clinton's margin in the electoral college. But it seems likely that in the popular tally, this third-party candidate took almost as many votes from Clinton as from Bush, as an analysis of exit poll data demonstrated. That was because Perot positioned himself as another advocate of "change" in the race, and so he would appeal to independents also attracted to Bill Clinton's New Democrat agenda. Other Perot voters might have abandoned Bush, because the populist conservative strongly supported balanced budgets and other Republican concerns.

In Little Rock on election night, Bill and Hillary Clinton and Al and Tipper Gore shared the stage at Clinton's favorite building, the stately white Old Court House, where years before he had been sworn in as Attorney General. In the huge, ecstatic audience, there were many friends and family members. "There were bands playing," old friend Carolyn Staley would recall, "because we had crowds thronging into the grounds from early in the afternoon and we had to keep them entertained. All the hotels had big satellite dishes on them and the lights—it was like something out of E.T. There was a choir that he loves, from Lone Oak, Arkansas, the Pentecostals." It was a chilly fall night. There was anticipation and, finally, "joy."

The President-elect told the big crowd and the millions watching on television that "this victory was more than a victory of party, it was a victory for those who work hard and play by the rules, a victory for people who felt left out and left behind and want to do better." He called on supporters of President Bush and Ross Perot to join him in creating a "re-United States."[30]

In his post-election reflections, Bill Clinton noted the very high support he had from minorities and from women. He would later write that he was the third youngest president in history and that he was "carrying more baggage than an ocean liner." How did he win? It was the economy that was by far the biggest issue—with "character" down the list behind health care and the deficit. The candidate, his running mate, and their gifted, disciplined campaign organization had kept the focus on this central question, the key to victory. But it was Clinton's persona and his talent on the campaign trail that was essential.

Now it was transition time, with less than eighty days to go before inauguration. He asked old friend Vernon Jordan to chair the transition board and Warren Christopher to be director. Christopher, prominent Los Angeles attorney, earlier had been helpful in the vice-presidential selection process. And, of course, Hillary Rodham Clinton, his closest confidante, would play an important role.

Clinton felt his first task was to choose a cabinet, and the economic team would have first priority.

He selected Lloyd Bentsen, chairman of the Senate Finance Committee, as Secretary of the Treasury. He had considered Robert Rubin, a major Wall Street insider, the vastly wealthy co-chairman of the world's leading investment bank, Goldman Sachs. But Bentsen, the VP nominee on the Dukakis ticket in 1988 who had campaigned with Clinton, was an attractive choice; he wanted the post and if it went to Rubin, the administration's economic agenda still would have to face Bentsen's committee. Rubin was named to lead an important new board overseeing all economic policy, the National Economic Council. Named Deputy Treasury Secretary was Roger Altman, an old Georgetown FOB and Assistant Treasury Secretary in the Carter years before he went on to make millions as a Wall Street investment banker.

Old friend and fellow Rhodes Bob Reich could not be named chair of the Council of Economic Advisors (CEA) because he was not a professional economist; he took Secretary of Labor, where he might put some of his well-published ideas into practice and serve as advocate for liberal policies in the administration. Laura Tyson, of the University of California at Berkeley, was named to the CEA, and Leon Panetta, chair of the House Budget Committee, became director of the Office of Management and Budget (OMB). Panetta, whom Clinton did not know, had criticized some of the candidate's arguments during the campaign. But the President-elect liked him when they met in Little Rock; Panetta announced that he was a "deficit hawk." Named as his deputy was the finalist for the OMB job, veteran economic analyst Alice Rivlin, another conservative figure on the deficit.[31]

In mid-December, a series of new cabinet appointments were announced, and Clinton noted that he was fulfilling his goal of naming the most diverse administration in history. Donna Shalala, chancellor of the University of Wisconsin, another old friend of Bill's and Hillary's, became Secretary of Health and Human Services. Carol Browner became director of the Environmental Protection Agency (she had been Florida's environmental director), and Hazel O'Leary, an African American executive from Minnesota, became Secretary of Energy. Henry Cisneros, mayor of San Antonio, an immensely popular Hispanic politician, became Secretary of Housing and Urban Development; Ron Brown, the African American leader of the DNC, Commerce Secretary.

Not all observers were impressed. One magazine complained that "rigging certain departments for a single gender or race, tracking down an individual not for her intrinsic talent but for her ethnic makeup, is an insult to minorities and a depressing sign of the cultural balkanization of our politics." But, on balance, it was a successful process; Clinton's appointees would be part of the longest serving cabinet in history.

On Christmas Eve, Bill Clinton announced more cabinet appointees, including Zoe Baird, the 40-year-old general counsel for Aetna Life, as the first female Attorney General. But within three weeks, it was revealed that Ms. Baird had not paid the employer's portion of Social Security taxes for two undocumented immigrants she had hired as household help. This became a focus of intense media attention and a major problem for an administration that had not yet taken office.

Before Christmas, the entire National Security team had been announced. And while the end of the Cold War had thrust domestic affairs to the forefront, particularly in a time of recession, State and Defense traditionally were the most prestigious of all cabinet positions. Clinton did select well-known foreign policy figures for these posts. But was he making the right choices? Warren Christopher was named Secretary of State. He had credentials, as Deputy Secretary of State in the Carter administration and a major player in negotiating the release of American hostages from Iran. But he had a quiet, restrained persona, the skilled lawyer's habit of seeing all sides of a problem. Would he be aggressive and tough enough for this job? (Madeleine Albright, who later would make a mark as Secretary, was asked to be Ambassador to the United Nations, elevated by Clinton to a cabinet-level appointment.) Les Aspin, chair of the House committee on military affairs, was named Secretary of Defense, when Sam Nunn, the powerful chairman of the Senate Armed Services Committee, declined the post. As with Christopher, observers questioned whether Aspin, for all his knowledge of the Pentagon, was the right person for a job that needed an assertive, authoritative figure.

For the less high profile positions, Clinton named individuals whom he had known and trusted as his foreign policy experts throughout the campaign. Anthony Lake and old friend Samuel "Sandy" Berger would be National Security Adviser and Deputy NSA, respectively. James Woolsey went to the CIA.

Years later, reflecting on the transition, Bill Clinton would regret spending so much time on the cabinet (where he felt he erred in failing to appoint at least one Republican) and not enough time on the White House staff. He had pressed his oldest friend, Thomas "Mack" McLarty, to become chief of staff. McLarty, although serving earlier on two federal commissions, had little Washington experience. Clinton asked Stephanopoulos to continue on as his communications director. James Carville, like Vernon Jordan, rejected any role in the new administration, telling reporters, "I wouldn't live in a country whose government would hire me."[32]

The staff was filled with young, bright, talented, and energetic individuals who had come out of the campaign or Arkansas. But they did not know the Washington political culture and were inexperienced in administrative matters at the federal level. Sometimes they demonstrated a lack of sensitivity in dealing with press and politicians in a city of entrenched interests and large egos, where great attention was paid to relative status. In their dress and demeanor in the White House, they would be faulted for lacking the gravitas their roles demanded.

Some would be accused of self-serving leaks to the press or of being responsible for more than the expected infighting. But most important, as Clinton later observed, they failed to understand the importance of messaging. That had been a strong point during the campaign, but now, all too often, the narrative was lost. The policy message—on important issues—was not delivered; print and electronic news outlets became filled with minor but damaging matters, like Zoe Baird's tax problems with undocumented employees. The young team had to learn on the job. People who perform well in a campaign do not always work well in the White House. It made for a very rough beginning.

Later, it would be said that Bill Clinton lacked discipline during the transition, that he became overwhelmed with the process, took too much time making decisions, conducted endless debates about policy choices. One writer insisted that the "degree of squabbling was poisonous"; another called it the "worst transition in modern history." Rambling late-night sessions, overeating, failure to arrive on time for meetings were all old Clinton habits. Was this essential time before taking office affected by such short-comings? That seems unfair. On the big issue, setting the economic agenda, Clinton was on the mark. He had promised that he would "focus like a laser beam" on the economy. And that became the critical issue during the transition.

At the beginning of December, he invited Alan Greenspan, chairman of the Federal Reserve Board, to come to Little Rock. They had a one-on-one meeting at the Governor's Mansion. Greenspan was an immensely influential figure, a conservative Republican who had served in the Ford administration and was appointed chair of the Federal Reserve System by President Reagan and reappointed by George H. W. Bush, his pronouncements and congressional testimony carrying great weight with the press and the public. The Fed controlled short-term interest rates (which affected long-term rates impacting businesses and consumers). Greenspan was deeply concerned with the escalating federal deficit. If he raised rates to address this issue, there would be no way the Clinton administration could succeed in creating a booming economy.

Greenspan, who had dealt with four presidents, was impressed by Bill Clinton, a bright, sophisticated thinker who, one writer noted, did not need a chief of staff to understand the complex issues at hand. Now he was told that Clinton shared his concerns about the deficit. And Clinton was relieved that this famous libertarian, disciple of Ayn Rand, devoted to the free market, distrustful of state power and always opposed to taxes on economic winners, was so concerned about the deficit that he would not oppose Clinton's plan for a tax hike on the rich.[33]

In succeeding weeks, there were spirited debates inside the transition about the Clinton economic agenda. Liberals like Reich, who argued that "the peace dividend must not be squandered on consumption but directed at public and private investment," pollster Stan Greenberg, campaign stalwarts Paul Begala, Mandy Grunwald, and others feared that more conservative economists, Wall Street regulars, and Washington insiders—people who had not been involved in the campaign—would shape policies that abandoned the heart of Clinton's "Putting People First" plan. They were concerned about the fate of the candidate's promise to help middle-class America while shielding the most vulnerable from the effects of 7 percent unemployment and the punishing recession.

The climactic meeting, chaired by Rubin, came on January 6, two weeks before inauguration. The Bush administration's OMB director had just announced that the coming year's budget deficit would be many billions higher than previously estimated. The irritated Clinton team was sure that this bad news had been delayed until after the election, but now the deficit problem loomed even larger. Liberal economist Alan Blinder, OMB deputy director designate, was asked to assess the impact of strong deficit-reduction packages on future growth. It was essential to keep the Federal Reserve from raising interest rates, which would have a devastating effect on the bond market. "You mean to tell me," Clinton was quoted as saying, "that the success of the program and my reelection hinges on the Federal Reserve and a bunch of fucking thirty year old bond traders?" There was no dissent to that statement.[34]

How to balance competing claims? To address the deficit meant less government spending or higher taxes or some combination of the two. Clinton had promised a middle-class tax cut during the campaign, and while his more liberal advisers were concerned, that was now off the table. And plans for investment in education, training, and nondefense research, along with efforts to address joblessness and declining incomes through stimulus spending, would have to be reduced. As Clinton later wrote of this economic summit, "I decided the deficit hawks were right."[35]

There would be a tax hike for the wealthiest. He would consider finding new income sources through cutting cost-of-living allowances for Social Security (with Hillary Clinton warning of the price paid by the elderly poor if this happened) and/or following Al Gore's proposal for a broad-based energy tax (BTU), which could raise revenue while helping the environment. And while he would not abandon plans to help less affluent working families with the Earned Income Tax Credit and would still back billions in new spending, the emphasis had to be on the deficit or all hopes for a future economic boom would be dashed.

The time of transition was over. As Bill Clinton and family left for Washington on January 16, a major news poll gave the President-elect a 60 percent favorable rating. Earlier, *Time* magazine had named him Man of the Year, saying he had been given the opportunity to "preside over one of the periodic reinventions of the country."

The inaugural events filled the next days and when the inauguration balls were concluded, it was 2 A.M. before Bill and Hillary Clinton returned to the White House. It was a full house. The President's mother and brother were there, his wife's parents and siblings, Chelsea's friends from home, and other FOBs. Bill Clinton did not retire immediately. Of course, he had been there before, but now he had to look around at his new home. The next day would begin a new chapter in his life.

Clinton's presidency would be a crowded time. THE BUCK STOPS HERE was the famous sign on President Harry Truman's desk: domestic, foreign, and military policies, and political crises often all had to be addressed at the same time in the Oval Office. But while noting the impact of all these matters in dealing with the presidential years ahead, it is best that we consider such important developments separately. Bill Clinton had promised to focus on his domestic agenda, and that is what we will address in Chapter Three. Chapter Four will consider foreign/military policy challenges in the post–Cold War era. And in Chapter Five, we will look at the politics of scandal across the presidential years and the impeachment crisis during Bill Clinton's second term.

NOTES

1. Clinton, *My Life* (New York: Alfred A. Knopf, 2004), pp. 375–377; Hillary Rodham Clinton, *Living History* (New York: Scribner, 2003), p. 103; Martin Walker, *President We Deserve* (New York: Random House, 1996), pp. 5–6.
2. John Harris, *The Survivor* (New York: Random House, 2005), pp. xi–xii; James Carville and Mary Matalin, *All's Fair: Love, War, and Running for President* (New York: Random House, 1995), pp. 83–85; interview with Paul Begala, October 3, 2012.
3. Governor Bill Clinton, "The New Covenant: Responsibility and Rebuilding the American Community," Georgetown University, October 23, 1991 (The Third Way, Key Documents) DLC dlc.org/ndol
4. Governor Bill Clinton, "A New Covenant for Economic Change," Georgetown University, November 20, 1991 (The Third Way, Key Documents) DLC dlc.org/ndol
5. Governor Bill Clinton, "A New Covenant for American Security," Georgetown University, December 12, 1991 (The Third Way, Key Documents) DLC dlc.org/ndol; interview with Sandy Berger, July 25, 2012; Clinton, *My Life*, p. 383.
6. Ibid., p. 361.
7. David H. Bennett, *The Party of Fear: The American Far Right from Nativism to the Militia Movement* (New York: Vintage Books, Random House, 1995), pp. 334–337.
8. Ibid., pp. 375–408.
9. Clinton, *My Life*, pp. 380–382; Carville and Matalin, p. 89.
10. Ibid., p. 101.
11. Clinton, *My Life*, pp. 384–388; Hillary Rodham Clinton, pp. 106–108.
12. Takiff, p. 111.
13. Ibid., pp. 114–115; Clinton, *My Life*, p. 391.
14. Carville and Matalin, pp. 112–114, 131–142.
15. Ibid., p. 121; Paul Greenberg, "The History of Slick Willie—from the Coiner of the Moniker." http://www.jewishworldreview.com/cols/greenberg062504.asp
16. Clinton, *My Life*, pp. 404–405; Harris, pp. xxii–xxiii; Carville and Matalin, pp. 167–168; William H. Chafe, *Bill and Hillary: The Politics of the Personal* (New York: Farrar, Straus and Giroux, 2012), pp. 145–146. On the marijuana quote: see Walker, p. 65, and Paul Begala in Michael Takiff, *A Complicated Man: The Life of Bill Clinton as Told by Those Who Know Him* (New Haven: Yale University Press, 2010), p. 126.
17. Joe Klein, *The Natural* (New York: Random House, 2002).
18. Clinton, *My Life*, pp. 392–396.
19. Hillary Rodham Clinton, pp. 109–110.
20. Walker, pp. 134–136; Clinton, *My Life*, pp. 399–403.
21. Ibid., pp. 406–408; Carville and Matalin, pp. 170–171.
22. Clinton, *My Life*, pp. 409–412; Walker, pp. 143–144; Carville and Matalin, pp. 214–216.
23. Ibid., pp. 239–240; Clinton, *My Life*, pp. 413–421.
24. Carville and Matalin, pp. 243–258
25. *New York Times*, July 16, September 19, October 2, October 26, 1992; Carvillle and Matalin, pp. 147–150; "Ross Perot," *Time* (May 25, 1992); Gerald Posner, *Citizen Perot* (New York: Random House, 1996).

26. Clinton, *My Life*, pp. 426–428.
27. Ibid., pp. 428–430; Carville and Matalin, pp. 281–288.
28. Clinton, *My Life*, pp. 432–435.
29. Ibid., pp. 435–444; Walker, pp. 156–158.
30. Takiff, p. 144; Clinton, *My Life*, pp. 443–446.
31. Ibid., pp. 447–452; Bob Woodward, *The Agenda: Inside the Clinton White House* (New York: Simon and Schuster, 1994), pp. 59–63.
32. Ibid., pp. 80–81; Takiff, pp. 147–148; Harris, p. xxvii; Clinton, *My Life*, pp. 448, 454–457, 467–468; interview with John Podesta, July 24, 2012; Kurt M. Campbell and James B. Steinberg, *Difficult Transitions* (Washington: Brookings Institution Press, 2008), pp. 80–82.
33. Clinton, *My Life*, p. 451; Woodward, *The Agenda*, pp. 68–71; Chafe, pp. 154–161.
34. Clinton, *My Life*, pp. 458–463; Woodward, *The Agenda*, pp. 72–98; memo from Robert Reich, NEC Economic Conference 1992, Box 37 (1), William J. Clinton Presidential Library, Little Rock, Arkansas.
35. Clinton, *My Life*, p. 461.

CHAPTER **3**

BUILDING THE BRIDGE

CLINTON'S DOMESTIC AGENDA

It was an ambitious agenda that Bill Clinton and his team brought to the White House on January 20, 1993. But they would face formidable obstacles. Early in the administration, there would be a signal success in passing the critically important budget bill—if by a hair-thin margin and only after significant revisions. It was a major step in reviving the economy and building that bridge to the new millennium. And there would be another legislative victory in the trade bills Clinton championed—like the budget bill, controversial but essential action in stimulating the coming economic boom. But both would play a central role in the political defeats of 1994.

Certainly, there were major setbacks in these first two years. The failure to pass health care was the biggest disappointment. This bold and complex effort to bring medical coverage to almost all Americans—spearheaded by Hillary Rodham Clinton—was beaten after a long and bitter battle; it was a deflating defeat.

Yet there were several small but significant initiatives taken at the very outset of the new administration. In his first week in office, Bill Clinton acted on campaign pledges and issued executive orders ending the Reagan–Bush ban on fetal-tissue research and abolishing the prohibitions placed on federal aid to international family planning agencies. He also canceled the Bush-era "gag rule" barring abortion counseling at family planning clinics receiving federal funds. A few days later, he signed his first bill into law, the Family and Medical Leave Act, which made it possible to do what 150 other nations had in guaranteeing workers time off when a baby is born or a member of the family is sick. President Bush had twice vetoed such legislation, saying it was burdensome for business. But this major initiative would prove a boon to millions of Americans in succeeding years. And then he signed the "motor voter" law, making voter registration easier.[1]

As Bill Clinton attempted to shape his domestic agenda, focusing on how to deal with the economic downturn and bring prosperity and job growth to the United States in this last decade of the twentieth century, he could not avoid international developments. Crises in Somalia, Haiti, Bosnia, and elsewhere demanded the attention of the leader of the world's strongest power, and most would stir opposition to the President's actions. And even as he addressed these complicated matters, he found himself the object of incessant attacks by political enemies.

In one sense, the Clinton administration had a very difficult time in its early days. Seemingly from the outset, the new President would have a fraught relationship with the national press. A series of damaging stories would dominate the news in the first months of the new team's tenure, providing an image of ineptitude, disorganization, and failure in the White House. A frustrated Bill Clinton, knowing—in the words of his campaign consultant, James Carville—that it was "the economy, stupid," which should have been at the center of everyone's attention, instead found himself engulfed in other issues. His administration never had the usual "honeymoon" accorded an incoming President and not without reason was he angry at an unfriendly Washington press corps. But some of the wounds were clearly self-inflicted. Contrary to his own instincts, he let advisers persuade him to stay away from the press and the Washington establishment, thus making them more hostile than they would have been otherwise.

Even before inauguration day, the Attorney General appointment had become a distraction. It only got worse in succeeding weeks and it became the Washington punditry's first example of lack of discipline in the new White House. Zoe Baird's "nanny problem" immediately threatened her confirmation. When one of her supporters told Joe Biden, the Senate committee chair, that it was just the equivalent of a parking ticket, he replied, "No, this is like a wreck on a Los Angeles freeway." A mistake had been made in vetting her background. George Stephanopoulos noted that right-wing talk show celebrity Rush Limbaugh and powerful GOP Congressman Newt Gingrich were "bearing down on us from the right: hammering us as self-indulgent, overprivileged yuppies who thought it was permissible to break the law if you were wealthy and went to Yale." Now it was clear her support was collapsing on the Hill, and Clinton, just entering office, decided not to press the matter. He asked her to step down. She initially resisted but finally agreed to do so, insisting that the new President publicly shoulder the blame.

Her initial replacement was to be U.S. District Court Judge Kimba Wood. But even before she was formally asked, a staff member leaked her name and news immediately emerged that she, too, had "nanny problems." (Clinton later complained that his White House "leaked worse than a tar-paper shack with holes in the roof and gaps in the walls.") Wood insisted that her difficulties were different than Baird's, but a livid Clinton pulled the plug on her nomination. He then turned to Floridian Janet Reno, the prosecuting attorney in Dade County, who had been recommended by friends. Earlier, he had decided that one of the "big four" cabinet appointments (along with State, Defense, and Treasury) must be a woman; all slots now were filled but Attorney General. Still, he knew Reno was "a stranger to Washington's ways" and felt that there was "something about her approach to the job" he found troubling. But the appointment went forward, and he would discover that her aloofness weakened executive control, and as a team they would be a mismatched pair.[2]

More damaging even than this appointment debacle was the "gays in the military" issue. It was another reason why, as one Washington observer said, "They hit the ground barely standing."

During the campaign, Clinton had told gay leaders and fund-raisers (one of whom said that "he became the Abraham Lincoln of our movement") that one of his first acts in office would be ending the ban on gays serving in the military. Paul Begala said later, "It was not a big thing. . . . We clearly had no appreciation of the offense that would be taken at a presidential directive ending the ban." But during the transition, both Sam Nunn, the powerful Senate Armed Services Committee chair, and General Colin Powell, chairman of the Joint Chiefs of Staff, warned Clinton that this was a complicated and highly controversial measure, particularly within the military.

While Clinton had told an NBC correspondent, when asked whether he would fulfill his campaign pledge, "Yes, I want to," he said now that he must consult the chiefs of the armed services on the best way to go about this. With inauguration, Begala and pollster Stan Greenberg had advised Bill Clinton to put off the issue. There were more pressing items on his agenda. Moreover, his first executive orders had focused on reproductive rights; continuing to seek a female attorney general while fixating on the gays/military matter would make it seem he was simply bowing to liberal interest groups like the McGovernite Democrats of the past. He would not look like a New Democrat offering a new way forward.

Bill Clinton did not want to focus on this, he wanted to deal with the economy. He asked new Defense Secretary Les Aspin and Sandy Berger at the National Security staff to report back in six months on how to implement an executive order. But it was too late. The Republicans had seen an opening. During the campaign, the Bush reelection team had not attacked Clinton on his position, but now Bob Dole, the Senate minority leader (and presidential aspirant) introduced a Senate bill prohibiting gays in the military.

Dole promised to keep the incendiary matter alive. The White House had been blindsided. And now the issue broke into the press and became a major political and cultural controversy. The *New York Times* reported strong military opposition to relaxing sanctions against gays, and the Joint Chiefs of Staff urgently requested a meeting in the White House to discuss it.

It was a memorable gathering. All the chiefs were adamantly opposed, and the Commandant of the Marine Corps, who believed homosexuality was immoral, was particularly passionate. (One senior military official thought they came very close to insubordination.) Although Clinton, articulate as always, made a powerful case for ending the ban—pointing out that the concern for "unit cohesion" was the same argument used against integrating the armed services in the Truman years—there was no convincing them. Many in the Pentagon were deeply suspicious of the new President. One writer noted that some thought of him as a "draft-dodging naïf on military policy," and they were profoundly apprehensive of plans to cut the military budget. They considered his young staff arrogant and uninformed. One story circulating was that a young woman White House staffer, upon been greeted by a senior military official, said, "I don't talk to the military."

Two days later he met with members of the Armed Services Committee and heard venerable Senator Robert Byrd, who considered homosexuality a sin, lecture the assemblage on the how the Roman Empire fell because of the pervasive homosexual conduct in the Roman legions. Clinton responded that the Joint Chiefs seemed to "need hypocrisy and demanded inconsistency"; they "tolerated homosexual troops by the tens of thousands so long as these troops stayed closeted and vulnerable. It was a soldier saying he was gay that offended them more than the lies."[3]

But there was no winning this battle. The House passed a resolution opposing Clinton's position by more than three to one, and the Senate opposition was almost as strong. If he persisted with an executive order, Congress would overturn his position with an amendment to the defense appropriations bill, and there were the votes to override a veto in both houses. He had to accept Sam Nunn's suggestion of a compromise, worked out with Colin Powell: "Don't Ask, Don't Tell." If you don't say you are gay, you cannot be forced out of the service even if you have gay friends or support gay organizations. But it could not work. In practice, many anti-gay officers simply ignored the new policy and worked even harder to root out homosexuals. And in the gay community, there was profound disappointment with this new President. (It would take almost a generation—seventeen years—to change the law. It happened in a more enlightened age but, even in 2010, was achieved only by the narrowest of margins.)[4]

And so the first stories about the Clinton White House painted a picture of failure, confusion, and indiscipline. The President, it was reported, kept erratic hours, allowed his self-impressed young staff to walk into the Oval Office in informal dress, seemed unconcerned about the pizza boxes and soft drink bottles littering the West Wing after the late-night, seemingly endless meetings. White House reporters made fun of Clinton's notorious failure to keep on schedule; they coined the phrase "Clinton Standard Time." But Bill Clinton's managerial style had always been extraordinarily relaxed: his instinct was always to talk through issues. To Capitol veterans, however, it seemed like college bull sessions had been brought to the Executive Mansion.

The winning team had won a remarkable election victory; they had been feted in newsmagazines as extraordinarily smart, tough, and talented. Was hubris the problem? Did they enter office believing the puffery and thinking governing would be as easy as campaigning? Or was it simply a failure to learn enough about "the ways of Washington"? Stephanopoulos, writing of one early problem, said, "The political team just blew it. . . . Our antennae went down after the election and we lost our common touch."[5]

Bill Clinton was frustrated by the negative stories, for he knew his White House team was more disciplined than the media critics thought and that he had come to office better prepared than most of his predecessors, determined to implement a series of programs he had clearly described before and during the campaign. And "the old Washington media hands," as Paul Begala later observed, "were understandably shocked at President Clinton's level of involvement and his love of debate—even when it became rancorous. The accomplishments of Clinton's first two years speak for themselves. But it is also a fair point that as he (and his team) grew into the job, the Clinton White House became far more disciplined, efficient, and loyal."

At the time, the Clintons, one journalist wrote, "felt that they were surrounded by hostile strangers" and that the "face of this perceived hostility was the national news media. At the outset of his term, the President did not like Washington reporters." Whether or not this was an accurate portrayal, the Clintons gave the press corps ample reason to think so with two early actions that angered Washington journalists.[6]

The first concerned closing off the corridor connecting the press room to the rest of the West Wing, meaning that reporters would no longer have walk-in privileges to the press secretary's office; they would be confined to the basement. "They were pissed," Stephanopoulos noted, and senior members of the White House press corps furiously noted that this reversed thirty years of practice. But the President had not ordered the change—he had even asked his press aide, "Why are we closing the door?" It was Hillary Clinton, Stephanopoulos noted, who was behind the new policy.

Then there was the matter of the White House Travel Office. This office made all arrangements for the press when they traveled with the President, billing their employers for the costs. Bill and Hillary Clinton both had asked Mack McLarty to look into the operations of the Travel Office because they had heard it allowed no competitive bidding. An investigation turned up several irregularities, and the director and his staff of six were summarily fired. But the White House press corps liked director Billy Dale and liked the way they were cared for by his office, particularly on foreign trips. Several famous journalists would testify on Dale's behalf when he was indicted for embezzlement, leading to his acquittal. And now it was suggested by some press members that the real reason for the firings was that friends of the President could profit by taking over control of the office. Suddenly, a mini-scandal was in the news: It was "Travelgate." There was no substance to allegations of White House impropriety, but the linking of Nixonian wrongdoing during Watergate to this minor episode was an indication of the Clintons' initial difficulties with the press.[7]

The "haircut" affair was a further measure of the problem. The President had traveled to Los Angeles to promote investments in education and inner-city development, even playing an impromptu basketball game with neighborhood kids on an outdoor court in South Central, where riots had occurred a year earlier. Before returning to Washington, he decided to have his hair cut and asked Cristophe, the fashionable Beverly Hills hairstylist, a friend of the Thomasons who had done Hillary's hair, to come to Air Force One. The cut took ten minutes, but a story soon circulated that LAX, third busiest airport in America, was tied up for an hour, inconveniencing thousands so Bill Clinton could spend $200 on a fancy hairdresser. In fact, FAA records, released weeks later, showed that no planes were delayed; only the press corps on board was irritated. But the damage was done. The widely circulated image of an arrogant, self-indulgent young President infuriated Clinton and he was still seething weeks later. It added to his growing hostility to the press.[8]

This President was dealing with revolutionary changes that had helped transform media coverage of Washington. There was the growing influence of talk radio, increasingly dominated by conservative commentators, on air hour after hour assailing administration policies and amplifying any tidbit of negative gossip from the White House. Rush Limbaugh alone, with his daily audience of many millions, had become a major force in conservative circles. And there was the developing popularity of cable television news, with its insatiable appetite for scandalous tales. It was not only the mainstream media, with its White House press corps, that troubled Clinton.

But the press was not responsible for some of the administration's early problems.

For example, the Clinton team miscalculated the opposition to its relatively modest $16 billion stimulus bill. The President had laid out his economic plan in his State of the Union address in February, but the major budget bill at the heart of the program would not be acted on by Congress for months, and the stimulus was intended to give a quick boost to the economy. The White House, outmaneuvered, did not anticipate the hostile response by Republicans. It unwisely rejected amendments by moderate Democrats and then was shocked when GOP senators, voting in a bloc, killed the bill with a filibuster, requiring an unobtainable sixty-vote "supermajority" for passage. It was a tactic the opposition would rely on increasingly in the future.

And just as the stimulus bill, designed to create 500,000 jobs, was being defeated, Bill Clinton's reputation as leader was further damaged by his failure to rely on his instincts during the bizarre confrontation outside Waco, Texas, between two government law enforcement agencies and a religious cult, the Branch Davidians. A messianic cult leader, David Koresh, had assembled a large arsenal in his Waco compound, where he seemingly had hypnotic power over his large following, including numerous women and children. The Bureau of Alcohol, Tobacco and Firearms had called for Koresh to surrender illegal weapons. But after a firefight in which four ATF agents were killed and several cultists injured, a standoff had begun, continuing for almost two months. The FBI and Attorney General Reno now told the President they feared Koresh was sexually abusing the children and might be planning a mass suicide. They proposed a federal raid on the compound.

Clinton, as governor of Arkansas, had successfully counseled patience and cutting off food supplies in dealing with another standoff, that time at the Ozark compound of a right-wing extremist group known as The Covenant, the Sword and the Arm of the Lord. This time, he finally agreed to follow Reno's suggestion. It was a disastrous decision. The FBI had not consulted appropriate academic experts on the behavior of such cults and had rejected the policy of waiting out the unstable leader. The Davidians started a fire and eighty people died, including twenty-five children; only nine survived. The nation was fixated on the television pictures from Waco. Hesitating before speaking as the debacle came to a close, Clinton heard Janet Reno take full responsibility for the raid. The President was not only criticized for mismanaging the crisis but letting her take the fall.

Now Bill Clinton decided to make staff changes. He brought in David Gergen as counselor to the President and replaced Stephanopoulos as communications director, although keeping him on as a senior adviser helping to coordinate policy and strategy. Gergen was a political centrist, yet had served in three Republican White Houses, working for both Nixon and Reagan. But he was a newsmagazine editor and no ideologue. If Bill Moyers, another respected Washington journalist (and former press secretary to

Lyndon Johnson), as much a figure of the left as Gergen was of the center-right, was not available, this was a good choice.

The President felt a mature new presence was needed in his White House. The "kids" who had helped him win in November were showing their inexperience. And perhaps so too was Mack McLarty, the "Friend of Bill's" turned presidential chief of staff. The seasoned, well-connected Gergen could reach out to the major figures in the media. Too many members of the Washington elite, heavyweight journalists and other members of the Capitol establishment, seemed to view the Clintons from Arkansas, despite their Ivy League credentials, like the Clampetts of *The Beverly Hillbillies.* (At best, they were seen as hostile outsiders from a small southern state known for corrupt politics.) The problems with the press must be brought under control, because what was essential now was pushing through the economic agenda.[9]

The awkwardly named 1993 Omnibus Budget Reconciliation Act would be at the heart of all of Bill Clinton's plans to turn around the economy. Each house earlier had passed individual bills in agonizingly close votes; only now, in August, after final negotiations between House and Senate leaders and the White House, was the critical reconciliation act at last ready. But pushing it through Congress was an excruciating ordeal. It involved compromises among both the more liberal and moderate groups within the Clinton camp, as well as concessions to Democratic representatives and senators who had their own ideological commitments or their own fears about alienating key constituents in forthcoming elections. As the final vote approached in both houses, the President and his team were working the phones, imploring reluctant voters to come aboard, not sure of the outcome until the very end.

The final bill called for an increase in income taxes for the wealthiest Americans (the top 1.2 percent of wage earners), modest increases in the income tax rate for corporations, and the repeal of the cap on Medicare taxes (involving a small tax raise for the most affluent). There would be an increase in gasoline taxes. And there were changes in several taxation rules, which created even more federal revenue. In all, there would be $241 billion in tax increases. And there would be no "middle-class tax cut" that candidate Clinton had promised during the campaign, for the bill represented the "bond market/deficit reduction strategy" that the President-elect had decided on during the transition. Alan Greenspan at the Federal Reserve must be persuaded not to raise interest rates and the bond market traders must be appeased; these lords of finance, fixated on the deficit, must not act to choke off economic growth and expansion.

The bill also provided for a huge expansion of the Earned Income Tax Credit for the poorest Americans. Robert Reich noted that "5 million people working at the bottom will each get about $3,000 a year" in the form of this expanded EITC, and 10 million others, "just above them will also have lower taxes."

But the plans for major increases in public investment—in mass transit, child care, schools in poorer areas, employment for the jobless, and technology—had been pared to the minimum, gutted during congressional negotiations due to fears of raising the deficit. Speaking for the liberals in the administration, Reich complained, "It's now a tiny morsel of what we sought." The *New York Times* agreed, and in a damaging editorial titled "A Budget Worthy of Mr. Bush" complained that "Mr. Clinton promised voters more than a rehash. . . . [I]t won't be a budget that invests in the future and it won't be a victory for those who voted for an economic turnabout."[10]

In fact, there would be $255 billion in budget cuts, achieved through cutting spending on the entitlements of Medicaid and Medicare as well as significant cuts for defense, the realization of the post–Cold War "peace dividend." Together with the tax increases, this represented a half-trillion-dollar assault on the massive deficit the new President had inherited.

But all these efforts stimulated opposition in different circles. While liberal Democrats lamented the failure to expand social programs, conservatives in Clinton's own party wanted deeper program cuts and wanted to protect some defense expenditures, particularly in their own states or areas. And for those Democrats in marginal districts, some of them congressional newcomers and narrow winners in 1992 (but facing uncertain prospects in the midterm elections the next year), raising taxes was a poisonous subject. As the House was preparing to vote, Bill Clinton made a nationally televised address from the Oval Office, his last pitch for public support, promising that the bill would create 8 million jobs in the next four years and agreeing to sign an executive order establishing a deficit-reduction trust fund, to make sure that all taxes and spending cuts would be used for that purpose only.

Even with last-minute deals made to secure individual votes from reluctant Democrats (like promising to shift more government work to a plant in one member's district), Clinton and the congressional leadership feared they were one or two votes short in the House. And there would be no bipartisan support. Every single Republican representative was committed to voting no.

Particularly irritating was the refusal of the President's own Democratic congressman, Ray Thornton from Little Rock, to support the bill; he was in an absolutely safe seat but said he had never voted for a gas tax and he would not start now.

It was left to Marjorie Margolies-Mezvinsky of Pennsylvania, a freshman from perhaps the most Republican district in the country represented by a

Democrat (Philadelphia's Main Line), who had promised not to vote for any tax increases in her campaign but knew the bill, and perhaps the President's agenda, hung on her decision. "I won't let it fail," she finally had promised. "I will vote last but if you need me, you will have my vote." Democrats cheered as she voted yes; Republicans waved and sang, "Good-by Margie." She would lose in 1994, but it was a historic moment. The bill carried in the House 218 to 216 (a tie vote would have meant defeat). Bill Clinton said later, "I let out a whoop of joy, and relief."

Now it was the Senate's turn. If anything, securing a majority was even a harder task there. The first Senate bill had passed 50 to 49, with five conservative Democrats voting no. Now, two of the previous yes voters, Senators David Boren of Oklahoma and Bob Kerrey of Nebraska, both from heavily Republican states, were wavering on the reconciliation bill. With every Republican senator committed to voting no, losing either could mean disaster.

Boren, a fellow Rhodes Scholar from a neighboring state, a key member of the Finance Committee, a man who had called himself a "New Democrat" but was clearly more conservative than the rival elevated to the presidency, now insisted on more spending cuts, including eliminating much of the EITC. He wanted to reduce taxes on the wealthy and—from oil-rich Oklahoma—to virtually scrap energy taxes. Despite entreaties from Clinton and senior Democrats, he announced his implacable opposition on a national Sunday talk show. But when Senator Dennis DeConcini of Arizona, after an urgent personal appeal from the President, decided to switch in favor of the bill, it all came down to Bob Kerrey.

The Clinton–Kerrey relationship, one observer noted, was very complex, a potpourri of "rivalry, envy, and kinship almost of brothers. . . . It was like fighting the Vietnam War over again." Now Kerrey told Bill Clinton he would vote no because the plan didn't solve the entitlement problem and would not achieve long-term economic recovery. "My presidency's going to go down!" Clinton exclaimed in a passionate, expletive-filled telephone exchange. "I really resent the argument that somehow I'm responsible for your presidency surviving!" was the angry response. But in the early evening of the day of the vote, Bob Kerrey relented, calling Clinton and telling him he had his support. Before the vote, Kerrey delivered a powerful speech critical of Clinton, explaining he was voting yes only because "I don't trust what my colleagues will do on the other side of the aisle" and, speaking directly to the President, "I could not and should not cast a vote that brings down your presidency."

The vote was 50 to 50 and senatorial ties can be broken by the Vice President. Al Gore broke the tie. It was after 11 P.M., and at the White House, Bill Clinton said, "What we heard tonight at the other end of Pennsylvania Avenue was the sound of gridlock breaking."[11]

But it was not bipartisan gridlock breaking. The Republicans to a person had opposed the bill. Raising taxes had become anathema to the GOP. Shaped by the Reagan Revolution and their iconic figure's pledge to "get the government out of our pockets," mindful of George H. W. Bush's problems when, after promising to "read my lips," he had infuriated their base voters by supporting a tax increase, the Republican leadership now gathered on the steps of the Capitol after the vote. They predicted economic disaster resulting from the tax raises in the reconciliation act.

For months, GOP politicians had been repeating the same phrases. Representative Newt Gingrich (R-Georgia): "I believe that it will in fact kill the current recovery and put us back in a recession"; John Kaisch (R-Ohio): "This bill is going to kill jobs"; Christopher Cox (R-California): "It will kill jobs, kill businesses, and yes, kill even the higher tax revenues that these suicidal tax increasers hope to gain." The mantra of GOP politicians in succeeding years, into the second decade of the twenty-first century, that raising taxes on the wealthy was raising taxes on "job creators," with all the downside risks of that, was present in 1993. Representative Phil Crane of Illinois: "These higher taxes will only stifle job creation and economic growth"; Dick Armey of Texas: "The impact on job creation is going to be devastating"; and Joel Hefley of Colorado: "It will raise your taxes, increase the deficit, and kill over 1 million jobs."[12]

History would prove them all wrong. But the rigid opposition of the entire GOP congressional delegation to the budget bill, as well as the nerve-jangling difficulties in persuading barely enough conservative or moderate Democrats to support the bill, might have been a message to those liberals in Clinton's party complaining that he had not done enough to promote their programs. Whatever they thought of Clinton's New Democrat vision, the liberal elites in academia, the media, and the party might have noted that this certainly was not the political environment confronting FDR or LBJ.

In fact, in the coming election, Bill Clinton and his party would be assailed for the budget act that raised taxes on the rich. Angering—and energizing—the traditional, hard-right conservatives would be one factor in that midterm electoral setback. But another would be the disappointment of Clinton's own supporters because of his promotion of a second key part of his domestic agenda, removing barriers to international trade.

The North American Free Trade Agreement had been negotiated on the watch of Clinton's predecessor, but despite the efforts of President Bush to "fast track" the signing before the end of his term, he had run out of time. It remained for Bill Clinton to deal with this proposal to create the world's largest free trade area, which eventually would eliminate all duties and qualitative restrictions on trade between the United States, Canada, and Mexico.

Clinton, as he had during the campaign, endorsed the measure but with some reservations. He had long been for free trade. It would, he argued, create a "giant market of nearly 400 million people" and it would underscore U.S. leadership in pushing the hemisphere and the world toward a global, interdependent economic environment. Failure to support it would make the "loss of jobs to low-wage competition from Mexico [where tariffs were two-and-one-half times as high as those of the United States] more, not less likely."

But changes in the bill were needed. Now he moved to negotiate a side agreement on the environment with Canada and Mexico, to alleviate fears that NAFTA would lead to a "race to the bottom" in environmental regulation. And to secure the votes on the Hill, he had to promise separate deals with various agricultural constituencies and their congressional representatives. Florida members feared a surge in Mexican exports of citrus fruits and vegetables; Midwestern-state members were concerned about Canadian exports of durum wheat.

Still, little could be done to appease labor, whose leaders had become increasingly vocal in opposing the agreement. The industrial unions— the Auto Workers, Electrical Workers, Textile Workers, as well as the Teamsters—were furious, as was organized labor's umbrella organization, the AFL-CIO. They all seemed sure that, as Ross Perot had suggested in the campaign, NAFTA would result in a "giant sucking sound" of jobs lost to Mexico.

It would be a strange and difficult vote in Congress in November. The Clinton camp was helped by CNN, which sponsored a televised debate between Vice President Al Gore and Perot, in which Gore demolished the undisciplined former presidential aspirant, who lacked a critical grasp of facts and became increasingly blustering and angry. But in the House and Senate, this was a measure that would fracture Democratic support for the administration. Victory would come only with massive Republican help. In the House, where the bill passed 234 to 200, 132 Republicans and 102 Democrats were in the majority; in the Senate, where passage was 61 to 38, there were 34 Republicans and 27 Democrats for the bill.[13]

Bill Clinton's critical first year in the White House had been marked by major achievements for his ambitious economic agenda. By year's end, interest rates remained low, investment was up, and progress was already being seen in reviving the economy; more private-sector jobs had been produced than in the previous four years.

He was proud of other significant initiatives. There was the reversal of those repressive Reagan–Bush abortion policies and passage of both the family leave act and the motor voter bill. There was his program to sharply cut the cost of college loans, which would save students and taxpayers billions in succeeding years. There was the bill creating AmeriCorps, a national service program modeled on FDR's Civilian Conservation Corps and JFK's Peace Corps, which would attract nearly 200,000 young Americans in the next five years. And there was the crime bill he had promised during the campaign, now passed in both Houses with funding for 100,000 community police officers. Certainly, international crises had occupied much of his time and he had to endure constant attacks from well-funded enemies dedicated to demeaning him and paralyzing his administration. Yet for the most part, he successfully kept focus on pushing through his domestic program.

But one big part of this effort, the plan to reform health care delivery in America, could not be achieved the first year and would have to be decided in 1994.

Only days after the inauguration, Bill Clinton announced the creation of the Task Force on National Health Care Reform. It would include cabinet secretaries and other major figures, but the key player would be the chair, Hillary Rodham Clinton. The President had made health care an important part of his campaign. Now he proposed to do what FDR, Harry Truman, JFK, and even LBJ (with Medicare and Medicaid) had not accomplished: push through legislation that would ensure full medical coverage for all Americans.

Hillary's appointment surprised some, but it was already clear that she was no traditional first lady. Unlike any of her predecessors, she had an office in the West Wing of the White House and a strong, devoted, politically savvy staff. (Her group soon became known as "Hillaryland," and this band of loyalists, she later noted, unlike others in the Executive Mansion, never leaked.) Clearly, she was a key adviser to the President on a wide range of issues, even as she had been when he was governor of Arkansas. Now she was given a huge portfolio, although many might have agreed with Governor Mario Cuomo, who asked her: "What did you do to make your husband so mad at you? . . . He'd have to be awfully upset to put you in charge of such a thankless task."[14]

Working closely with her would be Ira Magaziner, an old friend, whose commencement address, when graduating from Brown, was featured, along with Hillary's from Wellesley, in national newsmagazines. Magaziner was also a Friend of Bill's, whom he had met as a Rhodes at Oxford. Now a successful business consultant who had written an important study on health care costs, he became second in command of the effort to shape the health care plan for congressional approval.

In one sense, this seemed like the perfect moment for the United States to end what one observer, a former president of Harvard, characterized as "the dubious distinction of having the highest health care costs in the world while being the only major democracy with a substantial fraction of the population still lacking basic medical insurance."

Rising health care costs now threatened to hurt American business in world markets, making corporate leaders responsive to any plan that might shift such costs to the government. Every major health care interest group suddenly seemed interested in reform, including those great opponents of compulsory health insurance, the American Medical Association and the Health Insurance Association of America (HIAA), which had helped to torpedo previous activist Presidents' plans to address the matter.

Even some influential Republicans, long opposed to federal health reforms, now stated that they favored universal coverage. In fact, twenty-three GOP senators cosponsored a bill introduced by Senator John Chafee seeking such coverage through a mandate on individuals to buy insurance. (Inspired by a paper from the Heritage Foundation designed to head off a single-payer system or an employer mandate, it contained no serous funding mechanism and so was not a true national health plan.)[15]

Nonetheless, rapid action seemed the only way to achieve the long-elusive goal. James Carville told the Clintons that "the more time we allow for the defenders of the status quo to organize, the more they will be able to marshal opposition to your plan and better their chances of killing it." House majority leader Dick Gephardt (D-Mo.) and Senate majority leader George Mitchell (D-Maine) both feared problems within their Democratic ranks, where there was overwhelming support for health care reform but strong disagreements about how to achieve it. And both believed that Republicans would vigorously oppose any Clinton plan. With the Democratic majority of 56 to 44 in the Senate, any GOP filibuster would require an unobtainable sixty votes and would kill it. So they strongly advised putting health care into the budget reconciliation bill, which required only a simple majority.

But the President and his economic team, confronting the daunting task of simply getting the budget through reconciliation, had reservations about adding this enormous measure to that fight for votes. And the matter became moot when Hillary discovered that Senator Robert Byrd of West Virginia, the Senate's "unofficial historian," that parliamentary master and the inventor, she noted, of the "procedural hurdle called the 'Byrd rule' to ensure the items placed in the Budget Reconciliation Act were germane to budget and tax law," said no to her request.[16]

The plan itself would take time in shaping—it was not ready until early summer—and when introduced ran 1,342 pages, eliciting scathing criticism for being overly complex. It was the product of what journalists and important figures on the Hill complained was a secret process, dominated by the Task Force's chair and her deputy.

In fact, there were numerous experts from academia and the health care world involved in its creation. And it was a carefully constructed measure, not as radical a departure from present practices as some had feared it might be (and others believed it should be). It was structured to have a chance at passage. This would not be "socialized medicine," the frightening phrase used to attack earlier efforts to provide universal medical coverage in the land of the individualist ethos.

Bill and Hillary Clinton rejected the "single payer" model, used widely in Europe and in Canada, where the federal government is sole financier, through tax payments, of most medical care. They also rejected the "Medicare for All" approach, in which the government ultimately covers all uninsured Americans, not only those age 65 or older. Instead, they offered a quasi-private system called "managed competition" that relied, as Hillary argued, "on private market forces to drive down costs through competition." The hope was, of course, that the gigantic private health care insurance industry, not fearing for its future, would not become implacably opposed and that most Americans need not fear disruptions in their existing coverage.

The federal government would play a role, but it was a smaller one, "setting standards for benefit packages and helping to organize purchasing cooperatives." Everyone would be covered, with businesses (where most Americans already received coverage), involved through an employer mandate, and groups of these businesses and individuals, through the cooperatives (alliances) using their leverage as large units, able to bargain with insurance companies for better prices and benefits. Self-employed individuals—with the least affluent provided subsidies—would be part of the cooperatives and thus be insulated from confiscatory prices or insurance refusals because of preexisting conditions.

All Americans could choose their own health plan and keep their own doctors, and none need fear insurance would be lost when there was an illness or job change. Moreover, hospitals and doctors no longer had to bear the expense of treating uncovered patients in emergency rooms. Everyone would be covered, through Medicare, Medicaid, the veterans or military health care plans, or, now, through one of the purchasing groups.

It was a measure designed to appeal, if possible, to conservative Democrats and moderate Republicans. But it was already facing political problems when Bill Clinton went before a joint session of Congress on September 22 to kick off the drive for its passage. It was a brilliant address, made more remarkable because the first part was done with the text of an earlier speech having been loaded onto the teleprompter, a challenge even for this legendary extemporaneous speaker.

"Millions of Americans are just a pink slip away from losing their health insurance, and one serious illness away from losing all their savings . . . and on any given day, over 37 million Americans, most of them working people and their little children, have no health insurance at all," the President exclaimed. "And in spite of all this, our medical bills are growing at over twice the rate of inflation, and the United States spends over a third more of its income on health care than any other nation on earth. . . . There is no excuse for this kind of system."[17]

The President now planned a major effort to sell the plan across the country. But the multifaceted challenges of the presidency intervened. There were foreign policy crises in Russia, continuing problems in Haiti, Bosnia, and—less than eleven days after the speech—Somalia, when the death of American servicemen in the "Black Hawk Down" incident would roil the political landscape for weeks to come.

Into the fall, as the Democratic congressional leaders had predicted, there was growing Republican opposition to any Clinton plan. Then William Kristol, major neo-conservative writer and editor, a key GOP strategist and chairman of the Project for the Republican Future, sent a famous memorandum to Republican congressional leaders warning them that health care reform was "a serious political threat to the Republican party"—remember what happened when Social Security was passed on FDR's watch—and the death of the plan would be "a monumental setback for the President." His instructions to his party: Don't negotiate on the bill, don't compromise; the only good strategy is to kill the bill outright.

Now other GOP luminaries were joining the effort, helping with a variety of targeted radio and television ads against health care reform. And the insurance industry, through HIAA, unappeased that this was "managed competition" and not "single payer," was already at work trying to destroy support for the plan. In an elaborate, $20 million advertising campaign featuring actors Harry Johnson and Louise Claire Clark, the "typical" middle-class American wife (Louise) complains: "This plan forces us to buy our insurance through these new mandatory government health alliances," which, adds the husband (Harry), are "run by tens of thousands of new bureaucrats." Having "choices we don't like is no choice at all. They choose, we lose."

Health care was in deep trouble in the first part of 1994 and for Bill Clinton, bad news was coming in waves. The President had to deal with the death of his mother in early January. Soon he would confront new editorial attacks in major national newspapers connected to stories about Whitewater; finally, he agreed to appoint a special prosecutor to investigate the matter. Now there was political blood in the water, and his enemies focused, among other things, on health care.

So effective had been the attacks, notably the Harry and Louise ads (although skewered by academic analysts as largely misleading), that one

White House memo warned, "Whatever you do, don't get caught up in the details of the policy." This fear that hostility to government and to new taxes would derail any support made it seem that the President was "proposing a virtually government-free national health security plan." Not surprisingly, voters became more rather than less confused during the course of the debate. When other health plans proliferated in Congress in 1994, pollsters found that the majority of respondents, when offered the details of different alternatives, did favor the Clinton proposal but had no idea it was the President's plan.

Now it was hopeless. Searching for a compromise, there was no way to accept the Republican alternatives. They all rejected the employer mandate, which major business leaders refused to support, and they all rejected broad-based taxes, meaning that these schemes lacked serious federal funding and amounted only to "individual mandates," involving sharp increases in costs for middle-class households. (Of course, twenty years later, attacking President Barack Obama's health care plan, Republicans suddenly claimed that such individual mandates, originally promoted by a conservative think tank, were unconstitutional.)

By late summer, when Senator Mitchell of Maine tried one last compromise, offering to make the alliances (cooperatives) voluntary and deferring the possibility of an employer mandate, it made no difference. Nothing would mollify opponents. By September, one year after the Clinton speech, health care reform was dead.

Who killed health care reform? While some liberals argued Clinton should have endorsed single payer or an expansion of Medicare, no serious observer believed Congress would have passed such a plan. Paul Wellstone, single payer's key advocate in the Senate, found only four cosponsors for his bill.

Others believe he should have been less ambitious, should have tried to make a deal with moderate Republicans like Senator Chafee or conservative Democrats like Representative Jim Cooper, both of whom submitted plans. In fact, Bill Clinton later regretted not reaching out to Bob Dole and Chafee in an effort to use the individual mandate concept in the Chafee bill to shape a bipartisan agreement. But a minimal program with thin and dubious financing would have failed to excite passionate supporters, would have stimulated vociferous resistance by liberals in the House, and probably would have faced the same kind of opposition by conservatives opposed to any plan.

In fact, Republicans were resolved not to accept a plan that carried the Clinton name. One supporter argued that Clinton, by "putting his personal signature on health care, gave the Republicans an incentive to defeat it and humiliate him," but this was not the critical problem. For even a concerted effort to present health care reform as a bipartisan achievement would not have met the Kristol test: With midterms coming up in November and a presidential campaign two years off, give him nothing.

Bill Clinton had discovered what his predecessors (and his successors) had experienced: This was a maddeningly daunting task. Key Democratic heavyweights, like Senators Daniel Patrick Moynihan, Bob Kerrey, and David Boren, irritated that Hillary and her team, not Congress, had created the plan, dragged their feet; Moynihan, in particular, was angry because he wanted welfare reform to come before health care. But even with unanimous and dedicated support in his party's caucus, the leaders of the opposition, brandishing the threat of filibuster, would have the final say. Certainly, they came to believe there was a vested interest in killing health care reform. The executive director of the Republican National Committee would recall: "Health care was the first time since the '92 election that Republicans all rose up together and said, 'We're going to defeat this thing.' And when it was defeated, Republicans felt alive again. They hadn't felt alive in years." (Certainly, this was more a measure of how threatened the GOP felt by Bill Clinton than any reality; Republicans had controlled the White House for twelve years before his victory.)[18]

Now Clinton faced the midterm elections, and even before the fall campaigning season, it was clear the Democrats were facing heavy weather. Bill Clinton's poll numbers were plunging—down to 40 percent approval— and many of his party's candidates now were afraid to embrace the White House, refusing to campaign on national issues.

For the President, it was an immensely frustrating time. His economic program seemed to be working: Unemployment fell to under 6 percent, the lowest since 1990, with over 4.5 million new jobs created. Economic growth for the third quarter of the year was 3.4 percent, with inflation at 1.6 percent. There had been the first back-to-back years of deficit reduction in two decades. The "reinventing government" initiative, led by Vice President Gore, was having its impact, with the federal payroll reduced by 272,000. Despite the cuts in social programs in the big budget bill, investments in education and other areas were increasing compared with years before.

Moreover, not only had the crime bill finally passed both houses, but the Brady bill was set to survive the threat of Senate filibuster in November. This pioneering gun control measure, seven years in gestation, had been bitterly opposed by the National Rifle Association. Named for Ronald Reagan's press aide, who was permanently injured by a pistol shot in a failed presidential assassination attempt in 1981, it required a waiting period for handgun purchases and introduced restrictions on assault weapons sales. It would keep half a million felons, fugitives, and domestic abusers from buying guns.

With all of these affirmatives, why was Clinton in trouble? Perhaps his problems with the Washington media had something to do with the image problem; he would later cite one national survey showing an unusually high amount of negative press coverage for a President in his first years. And, certainly, the continuing attacks on his character, linked to stories of "scandal," took their toll. But more important was how some of his successful initiatives were too easily misunderstood or even counterproductive in mobilizing support, and how the Republican opposition, now under new leadership, was able to shape a devastatingly effective assault on his administration.

The budget bill was a critical victory, but reviled by liberals for its shortcomings and by conservatives for increasing taxes, it elicited few passionate supporters. EITC was too hard for some to understand (could they not think of a more evocative name?) and angered others for giving money to the "undeserving" poor. NAFTA infuriated organized labor and the unions, key factors in mobilizing the Democratic base at election time, would punish Clinton by largely sitting out the midterms. The Brady bill mobilized the gun lobby to redouble its efforts to purge Democrats in Congress. And the failure of health care reform not only discouraged the liberal constituency, now more likely to stay home on election day, but energized right-wing opponents, whose hostility to "big government programs" and "faceless bureaucrats" would be manipulated by the GOP to bring out the vote and crush further efforts by this "European social democrat" in the White House.

One part of the Republican counterattack was mobilized by a shadowy new force, the revived Christian Coalition. Created by televangelist Pat Robertson and notably unsuccessful during Robertson's failed bid for the party presidential nomination in 1988, the Coalition now was under the leadership of Ralph Reed, a history PhD who had been a director of the College Republican National Committee and worked for Representative Newt Gingrich. He remarked he now had "an advanced degree in hardball politics" and shaped a campaign in which he would reach voters through church newsletters, leaflets, and "in pew" registration. He told a writer: "I want to be invisible. I do guerrilla warfare. I paint my face and travel at night. You don't know it is over until you are in a body bag. You don't know until election night."

On election night 1994, when the GOP reversed four decades of Democratic dominance in a momentous victory, one exit poll survey revealed that over 20 percent of voters identified themselves as evangelicals or born-again Christians and that three out of four of these voters supported Republican candidates. Over 60 percent of the 600 candidates endorsed by the religious right won. Infuriated by Clinton's support of gay rights, abortion rights, fetal research, and other threats to "traditional family values," the social conservatives made their voices heard. In Oklahoma, Senator Dave McCurdy said he was beaten in a race in which his opponent focused on "God, gays, guns, and Clinton."[19]

But it was the traditional political hard-right conservatives, led by Newt Gingrich, who led the way in the 1994 election.

Gingrich, another history PhD, had arrived in 1979 in Washington after a brief academic career, a freshman Republican intent on using alleged ethical wrongdoing as the wedge issue to attack the Democratic opposition. One of the objects of his early attacks, Representative Barney Frank of Massachusetts, characterized Gingrich as "the single most influential factor in replacing the politics in which you accepted the bona fides of your opposition and disagreed with them civilly with the politics of insisting that your opponents are bad people." In 1987, Gingrich, now a major force in his party, was characterizing his fight with Democrats as "a civil war," and stated that "one culture or the other would have to go."

By this time, he had become the leader of GOPAC, a political action committee dedicated to electing Republicans. He made it into a formidable fund-raising and training organization, producing cassette tapes instructing GOP candidates, as one of them later recalled, on "how to demonize the opposition, how to use invective and scary language . . . how to wage nasty partisan war against your opponent." In 1990, Gingrich, now the House Republican Whip, had GOPAC circulate a pamphlet titled *Language: A Key Mechanism of Control*: "As we mail tapes to candidates, we hear a plaintive plea, 'I wish I could speak like Newt.' That takes years of practice. But . . . we have created this list of words and phrases. . . . [A]pply these to the opponent, his record, proposals and party." Among the suggested words and phrases were "anti-child, anti-flag, lie, cheat, radical, steal, corrupt, coercion, destructive, bureaucracy, hypocrisy, betray, shame, decay, pathetic, traitors, disgrace, sick."[20]

Gingrich had used Frank Luntz, Republican strategist and author of a future best seller, *Words that Work: It's Not What You Say It's What People Hear*, to prepare the cassettes. (It was Luntz who invented the term "job creators" to be used instead of "rich," "wealthy," or "affluent" in heading off any effort at raising taxes on the richest Americans.) He now had Luntz's help in shaping the central campaign document for the midterm election: the GOP's "Contract With America."

The "Contract" was a potpourri of conservative proposals, many of them having kicked around for years, some the product of the right-wing Heritage Foundation. But it was Luntz and other spinmeisters who gave it its seductive appeal, designed as a "positive" program of change offered by Republicans, even as they used negative attacks to demonize Clinton and the opposition. Words were critical. For example, the proposal for a bal-anced budget amendment was called "The Fiscal Responsibility Act"; for more prison construction and death penalty sentences as well as repeal-ing prevention programs in the Clinton crime bill, "The Taking Back Our Streets Act"; for prohibiting welfare to minor mothers, "The Personal Responsibility Act"; for massive capital gains tax cuts and weakening regu-latory controls, "The Job Creation and Wage Enhancement Act"; for "loser pays" provisions that would discourage lawsuits concerning product liabil-ity, "The Common Sense Legal Reform Act."

Bill Clinton could agree with some of the particulars of the Contract—he was already pushing welfare reform and long had supported a line-item veto and ending unfunded mandates in congressional bills—but found the entire document "simplistic and hypocritical."

Polls later indicated that few Americans had even heard of the Contract by election time, and only a tiny number were influenced by it. But it ener-gized the Republican candidates and was used by the party to national-ize what are often midterm elections keyed to local issues. If Clinton was unpopular, the plan was to tie Democratic congressional candidates to him and his programs. It "gave a symbolic and substantive vehicle for the Republicans to make this a change versus status quo" race, one Democratic aide would recall. And when the results were in, it underscored the critical role played by Newt Gingrich. He had led his party to a historic victory, grasping majority control on both sides of Capitol Hill for the first time in decades. In the Senate, the GOP gained 9 seats, and would now have a 53 to 47 margin. In the House, there was a 54-seat gain, with Republicans assuming the majority, 230 to 204. With House GOP minority leader Bob Michael retiring, Newt Gingrich—the architect of victory—would become Speaker of the House.

It was a bitter moment for the President. He had been in Israel, Kuwait, and Saudi Arabia days before the vote, but now, he would remember, "I had to go home to face the election music." Even though on his watch far more Americans had received tax cuts than income tax increases and government had been reduced, smaller than it had been under Reagan and Bush, the GOP had won with "their same old promises of lower taxes and smaller government." They were, he said, "even rewarded for problems they had created," for they killed health care reform, campaign finance reform, and lobbying reform with Senate filibusters. But they had outma-neuvered the Clinton team and hijacked the campaign narrative. Even on New Year's night 1995, one aide found Bill Clinton still in a towering rage over the outcome. Now, it would be an even more challenging term ahead.[21]

Distressed at the setback, the President—with Hillary's support—had brought back Dick Morris as a consultant. Key liberal advisers lost influence. Stephanopoulos was pushed further into the background, Paul Begala would leave the White House, Stan Greenberg was displaced as pollster by Mark Penn. Dee Dee Myers resigned as press secretary. Mack McLarty already had left the chief of staff post, replaced by Leon Panetta.

Morris, of course, was a deeply divisive figure, and one Clinton aide called him "a man without a real center, he could advise Hitler or he could advise Mother Teresa—on the same night." Stephanopoulos despised him, and a fellow West Wing regular said of Morris: "He could not see anything except political consequences—there was no right and wrong, no best interest of the country." Indeed, he seemed worried that in working with the White House he would alienate his largely Republican political clientele. In succeeding years, he would move further to the right, becoming a poisonous critic of Bill Clinton. But now he once more had the President's ear.[22]

His major contribution was to push for more executive action, to encourage Bill Clinton to get out of Washington and be seen as doing things, to use the day's events to tell a story and not have the media portray him as bogged down in dealing with Gingrich. Morris commissioned several complex polls and Clinton met with him for hours to consider "strategy" in a new and unsettled political environment. One poll suggested that some people, responding to the drumbeat of scandal stories, considered the President immoral, and some others considered him weak. The consultant suggested that if Hillary took a lower profile, the President would appear stronger. She agreed to do so.

Later, critics would despair that all of this meant that the President, like that "Slick Willie" of past caricatures, had no real convictions, that he was "poll driven," now easily led by a toxic figure, a manipulator without principals. But in fact, Morris, whose more bizarre suggestions would be dismissed by the boss, was now only endorsing what Bill Clinton had long believed. He might call it "triangulation," a way of "bridging the divide between Republicans and Democrats and taking the best ideas of both," but Clinton had long proposed a "third way," the way to build a new consensus by becoming a "New Democrat." This is what he had advocated as governor, with the DLC, in the Covenant Speeches.

So when Morris encouraged the President to endorse some of the most popular premises of the new Republican majority, it was no problem: Clinton already believed in reducing the deficit (and was doing something about it), in shrinking the government workforce (and already had made progress there), in overhauling welfare to demand work from recipients.[23]

But Gingrich had shaped an attack on Bill Clinton and his party that went far beyond political or economic policy. He had shrewdly fixated on those negative stereotypes of liberal Democrats that had become a staple of right-wing rhetoric since the days of George Wallace in 1968. Now he alleged—without any proof—that 25 percent of White House aides were recent drug users, that Democratic "values" were the reason for the large number of out-of-wedlock births to teen mothers, even that "permissive" liberal ideas had created a moral climate leading to crime and sexual abuse across the land. He referred to the President and the first lady as "counter-culture McGovernicks." It would be no small task to deal with an adversary using such arguments.

In the early days of their new congressional majority, Republicans proposed draconian cuts in funds for education, drug-prevention, and school lunch and nutrition programs; they advocated eliminating the Department of Education. In the House, they would produce bills gutting consumer protection and environmental and worker safety regulations. They passed a Balanced Budget Amendment bill, although not with an extraordinary provision—supported by many newly elected GOP representatives—that a three-fifths majority was henceforth needed for any future tax increases. While some liberal legislators and pundits felt Clinton should have been more animated in attacking these efforts, which could never make it through the Senate or a presidential veto, Clinton was resolved to resist this assault from the right.

In fact, he had some marked successes in the first part of 1995. Congress passed, with large bipartisan majorities, the Global Agreement on Tariffs and Trade. GATT reduced tariffs worldwide by almost $750 billion, opened closed markets to American products and services, and helped poor countries sell to consumers beyond their borders. It led to the establishment of the World Trade Organization. It was another part of Clinton's plan to foster a global interdependent marketplace. Ross Perot and others opposed it, but organized labor was less vociferous than in its rejection of NAFTA.

Earlier, the President also succeeded in passage of the Retirement Protection Act, which required corporations with large underfunded plans (and there were many) to increase their contributions, stabilizing the national pension insurance system for 40 million Americans.

He supported Robert Rubin, newly elevated to Secretary of the Treasury when Lloyd Bentsen left after the first term, when Rubin and his deputy, Lawrence Summers, proposed a highly controversial $25 billion loan to Mexico. The neighboring state could not finance its short-term debt and the value of the peso was declining precipitously. Suddenly it had become a nation on the brink of collapse, in economic meltdown, facing default. Most Americans opposed a risky rescue package requiring American loan guarantees, and Leon Panetta warned that if Mexico didn't repay us, it could cost Clinton the election in 1996.

But the President felt it was the essential move. As Mexico slid closer to the brink (Rubin told Clinton, "Mexico has about forty-eight hours to live"), it was clear that the Republican leadership on the Hill could not produce a majority for bailout relief. And so the President acted unilaterally, announcing the aid package with money from the Exchange Stabilization Fund. There were, Clinton noted, "howls of protest in Congress," but it turned out to be strikingly successful. Mexico rapidly recovered and within months repaid its loan in full, with interest, three years ahead of schedule.

In April, Bill Clinton rose to the occasion after the nation was shocked when an enormous terrorist bomb shattered the Murrah Federal Building in Oklahoma City. It took 168 lives (including 19 children), injured almost 700 people, and destroyed structures and cars in a sixteen-block area. It was an American extremist fanatic, Timothy McVeigh, a militia-movement sympathizer consumed with hatred for the federal government, who was the perpetrator; he was caught and arrested within hours.

Clinton believed that those government employees working at the federal building "somehow had been morphed into heartless parasites of tax dollars and abusers of power, not only in the twisted minds of Timothy McVeigh and his sympathizers, but also by too many others who bashed them for power and profit."

The end of the Cold War and the disintegration of the Soviet Union made fear of Communists no longer plausible. Those who might have been inhibited in attacking the federal government in the past because a powerful Washington was needed to protect America from a formidable, nuclear-armed Moscow now found fewer constraints in assailing the federal government and its workforce. This included mainstream politicians and pundits as well as the leaders and followers of violent, fringe movements. The President used the terms "radical" and "extremist" to refer to the overheated rhetoric of all those who reviled government. One bumper sticker in Missouri in 1995 announced: I LOVE MY COUNTRY BUT I FEAR MY GOVERNMENT. Bill Clinton responded: "There is nothing patriotic . . . [in] pretending that you can love your country but despise your government."

At the memorial service four days after the bombing, he eloquently spoke for the nation: "This terrible sin took the lives of our American family . . ., citizens in the building and many there who served the rest of us and served us well. . . . To all the members of the families here present who have suffered loss, though we share your grief, your pain is unimaginable, and we know that. We cannot undo it. That is God's work. . . . You have lost too much, but you have not lost everything. And you have certainly not lost America, for we will stand with you for as many tomorrows as it takes. . . . To all my fellow Americans beyond this hall, I say, one thing we owe those who have sacrificed is the duty to purge ourselves of the dark forces which gave rise to this evil. They are forces that threaten our common peace, our freedom, our way of life. . . . Those who trouble their own house will inherit the wind."[24]

It was a moving moment. But partisan warfare in Washington continued, and the budget bill became the critical issue for the rest of the year. In
June, Newt Gingrich was on the cover of *Time* magazine; "King of the Hill"
was the caption. Now 50 years old, rotund, white-haired, self-infatuated,
comparing himself to major figures of history—and in one Orwellian
moment claiming that *he* was the revolutionary and the Clintonians were
the reactionaries—he was leading the charge in Congress to make major
cuts in federal programs endorsed by the White House. For a time he
seemed to dominate news coverage from the Capitol, and one journalist
even asked Bill Clinton if the President was "still relevant." The response
seemed strained: "The Constitution gives me relevance. The power of our
ideas gives me relevance."

In some ways, Gingrich was easier for Clinton to deal with than members of his team. The House majority leader was now Dick Armey of Texas,
a true right-wing ideologue who threatened Clinton that if he did not surrender on the budget, "your presidency would be over." The House GOP
whip was now Tom DeLay, who had run a pest extermination business
before entering politics. He was tough and politically ruthless, a central figure in that successful effort at the heart of the "Republican revolution" to
purge moderates from leadership positions and drive the party further to
the right. One such moderate told a reporter, "You can talk to Newt. He'll
listen. Talking to Armey and DeLay is like talking to a wall."[25]

In June, Clinton decided to embrace a key Republican demand. In a
nationally televised speech, he offered a plan to balance the budget in ten
years. Although he insisted that this would not involve cuts for education
or health services and that he still embraced a middle-class tax reduction,
there was an outcry from Democrats on the Hill. The Republicans were
playing with the President "like a kitten with a string," exclaimed one con-
gresswoman. But these protestors misunderstood the man in the White
House.

His was a political tactic. (And, of course, the budget-balancing promise was easily fulfilled in the next few years when the economy continued
to expand and there were significant budget surpluses during the Clinton
boom of the late Nineties.) He was much tougher than even some of his
supporters understood.

When Paul Begala told Bill Clinton in August that "Newt and those guys
think they can roll you," the President could not believe it. "We were jog-
ging at Ft. McNair in Washington," Begala recalled, "and he literally stopped
short. Sweat dripping off his nose, he squinted at me and said that couldn't
be. The smarter play would be to give him a proposal that was nuanced
enough that he might have to support, but would alienate him from his
Democratic base." If Newt "was going to be unreasonable and insist on

hammering Medicare," he simply could "play Gary Cooper" as in his favorite movie, *High Noon*, "stand my ground unflinchingly" and win.

He said, "I couldn't be that lucky. They wouldn't be that stupid. That is the easiest kind of leadership. I just say no and I win. They are misreading me."[26]

The late summer and fall were a crowded time in the White House. There were critical foreign policy matters in the Middle East, and the brutal ethnic conflict in Bosnia called for American action. Of course, there was an intensifying round of investigations by a new special prosecutor—appointed by Clinton's adversaries—to look into "Clinton scandals" from the past. But the budget battle was approaching a climax. The fiscal year ended on September 30 and there was still no budget. The Republicans proposed massive cuts in Medicare and Medicaid as well as food stamps, the student loan program, AmeriCorps, and environmental enforcement. They proposed reducing the Earned Income Tax Credit, thus raising taxes for lower-income working families, even while calling for tax cuts for the wealthiest Americans.

If the President did not accept their budget, Gingrich threatened to refuse to raise the debt limit. Raising this limit was a technical exercise, and no congressional majority had ever come close to putting the nation in default. In fact, it had only been in 1917, when the Wilson administration was funding U.S. involvement in World War I, that the debt ceiling matter had even been raised; and for years after, the votes on it had been pro forma, with a few members using the occasion to lament "runaway spending" while all knew that no majority would ever risk the dire consequences of such an act for both the American economy and for the world. In fact, from 1980 to 1995, there had had been no votes needed; the Democratic leader had persuaded Republicans (in power in the White House most of these years) that the whole thing was a no-brainer. And so while Newt Gingrich had suddenly brought back the issue to harass him, Clinton thought this was simply a GOP blackmail gesture; if Congress did not raise the debt limit, millions of Americans would have their mortgages rise, and a "Gingrich surcharge" on their monthly payments would be devastating for the Republicans.

Now Gingrich and his congressional allies provided a series of continuing resolutions (CRs) to keep the government going while they pressured Clinton to give in to their demands. If he did not, there would be no budget and no federal money and the government would be shut down. Although some of his aides and congressional allies feared he would capitulate, he held firm.

In early November, Gingrich offered one last CR. Without more White House concessions, this CR would increase Medicare premiums 25 percent and make draconian cuts in environmental and other key federal programs. Included was a provision to lower the debt limit again after thirty days, ensuring a default that would undermine the full faith and credit of the U.S. dollar across the globe. On November 13, Clinton and the Democratic leadership met with Gingrich, Armey, and Bob Dole, the Senate majority leader and frontrunner for the GOP presidential nomination in 1996.

Dole said he did not want the government to shut down. But Armey, a large, blustering figure wearing cowboy boots, angrily threatened the President, saying Dole "does not speak" for House Republicans. Clinton, who had noted the devastating impact on a wide range of social programs with a report on "82 reasons for vetoing the GOP budget," responded that he would never allow their budget to become law, "even if I drop to 5 percent in the polls. If you want your budget, you'll have to get someone else to sit in this chair." There was no deal.

The next day, the President vetoed the CR and debt ceiling bills; America was being "held hostage" to these extremist demands, he argued. Over 800,000 federal workers were sent home. Social Security, veterans' benefits, and business loans went unprocessed, national parks were closed, the lives of millions disrupted.

While the media focused on this unprecedented national crisis, Bill Clinton met with Gingrich, who at first remained adamant, admitting later, "We made a mistake, we thought you would cave." But Bill Clinton had taken the measure of his opponent. He had recovered quickly from the shock of the 1994 midterm defeat and understood how to use Gingrich's hubris and overreaching against him. Newt might have been a bright man, Begala later noted, but "he lacked Clinton's emotional intelligence and psychological and intuitive insights. . . . He never got the better of Clinton in any of their dealings."

Now the President offered a modest concession, saying he would work for a seven-year balanced budget agreement, knowing that his economics team felt that balancing the budget in seven years was eminently doable without harsh cuts. And polls were showing that the public overwhelmingly was blaming the GOP Congress for the shutdown.

Gingrich, full of himself during this season of media focus on his powerful role, made another signal blunder. In the midst of the budget standoff, Clinton had received the shattering news of the assassination of Israeli leader Yitzhak Rabin, with whom he had worked closely to achieve Arab-Israeli peace. He immediately flew to Jerusalem for the funeral, and important congressional leaders accompanied him, seated near the rear of Air Force One during the flights. Arriving home, Gingrich complained that the President had not called him to the front of the plane to talk about the budget. But he was particularly irritated that White House aides asked him to leave the plane by the back ramp instead of the front door with the President. He said he was snubbed: "It's petty but I think it's human"; it was "part of why you ended up with us sending down a tougher continuing resolution." To Americans, irritated by the continuing shutdown paralysis, this did not play well. The New York *Daily News* front-page headline was "Cry Baby," with a grotesque cartoon of a wailing, infant Newt and the caption: "Newt's Tantrum: He closed down the government because Clinton made him sit at back of plane."

By early January, Clinton had won. At first a few appropriations bills were passed and 200,000 federal employees went back to work. There had been another brief government shutdown in December, but the GOP was on the defensive. Bob Dole, looking to the presidential race, pushed for a resolution and soon all government workers were back on the job, without major concessions from the White House. The State of the Union address later that month was a triumphant moment for the President and his gleeful Democrats, cheering as he exclaimed, "Let's never, ever shut the federal government down again." The unhappy Republicans recognized that their "Contract for America" had been blocked, and now the year ahead would bring them a President riding the wave of new popular support.[27]

It was, of course, an election year. Bill Clinton, the consummate political analyst, understood the tide that had swept in the opposition in 1994. He recognized the need to recalibrate his agenda in view of GOP majorities on the Hill and the failure of the big health care initiative. He would now move carefully to ensure reelection in the fall. This meant giving both verbal and legislative nods to conservative sentiments in 1996. But it also meant shaping modest but significant progressive programs across the year that had a chance of congressional approval.

In his State of the Union address, he said: "We know that big government does not have all the answers. We know there is not a program for every problem." That was right out of his Covenant Speeches of the past. But now he added: "The era of big government is over." This gratuitous phrase, suggested in a speech revision by Dick Morris, would haunt him with liberal critics in years to come. Yet he had immediately added: "But we cannot go back to the time when citizens are left to fend for themselves. We must go forward as one America, one nation working together to meet the challenges we face together."

Responding perhaps to one of Morris's poll-driven suggestions in signing the landmark Telecommunications Act, which passed unanimously and included lower Internet rates for schools, libraries, and hospitals, he agreed to the requirement for the V-chip, allowing parents to control their children's access to television programs. That pleased the advocates of "traditional family values."

So too did the so-called Defense of Marriage Act, which held that states would not have to recognize same-sex marriage in other states. Clinton called the measure election-year "gay baiting" but signed it at one in the morning. Republicans in the House and Senate had introduced and passionately supported the bill; their party platform at the nominating convention later in the year would strongly endorse it. It had passed both houses overwhelmingly, 85 to 14 in the Senate, 342 to 67 in the House, and so a presidential veto might have been easily overridden. In later years, Clinton would support equal treatment of gay couples and call for repeal of DOMA, but in this election season, he would not.

In run-ups to an election, Bill Clinton would often soften the ideological edge before certain audiences, even if this meant seeming to undermine his own accomplishments and his party's appeal. In Houston, speaking to an affluent crowd in late 1995, he said, "Probably there are people in this room still mad at me because you think I raised your taxes too much. It might surprise you to know that I think I raised them too much, too." Democrats were furious. They had voted for that tax increase and many had lost seats in 1994. Daniel Patrick Moynihan exclaimed, "It just knocked us over when we saw that this morning. . . . He keeps conceding these things . . . What he should have said was: 'Is there a man in this room who's not richer than he was two years ago?'"

When Cuba shot down two aircraft flown by an anti-Castro group, Clinton agreed to put further restrictions on travel to and commerce with Cuba and to sign the Helms-Burton bill, denying presidential authority to lift the embargo against Cuba without congressional authority. This would make it impossible to work for positive changes within Cuba in a second term. But it was good election-year politics in Florida.

Still, there were occasions when he would act despite the terrible politics involved. Congress passed a late-term abortion bill (called by its proponents "partial-birth abortion"), which, Clinton believed, paid no heed to how badly damaged mothers' bodies would be if they carried their doomed babies to term. It was a transparent effort to erode *Roe v. Wade*, but it was popular. Despite the political consequences, he vetoed it. Similarly, he signed a bill expanding federal power over tobacco advertising, a blow to the cigarette industry that might cost him votes in tobacco-producing states like Kentucky and Tennessee (but in the end did not, since he carried both in 1996).

In a more constructive way, he was able to push through the Kennedy-Kassebaum bill, which helped millions of people by allowing them to take their health insurance from job to job and prohibiting insurance companies from denying coverage for preexisting health problems.

He signed the Food Quality Protection Act and the Safe Drinking Water Act. He won on a bill to increase the minimum wage and another providing tax credits for adopting a child, and even more for a child with special needs.

He moved to protect the beautiful red rock area of southern Utah, threatened when a proposal for a large coal mine was supported by state officials, by invoking the Antiquities Act to establish the 1.7 million acre Grand Staircase–Escalante National Monument. It was a major environmental initiative; he signed it standing next to Robert Redford. It was part of a remarkable environmental agenda under President Clinton that expanded the National Park System by 4 million acres (with thirteen new National Parks created and others significantly enlarged), seventeen new National Monuments designated, and tens of millions of acres of national forest protected from exploitation and development.

After the budget battle triumph, now it was possible to achieve all these successes.[28]

More controversial within the Democratic camp was welfare reform. For Bill Clinton, reforming welfare in America had been a critical issue for many years before he came to the White House. He had advocated humanely moving people form "welfare to work" as governor, issuing a report on "Why Welfare Reform? Why Now?" in 1988, and sponsoring a "Welfare Reform Conference" in Little Rock in 1990. The pledge to achieve this reform, to "end welfare as we know it," was a central part of his presidential campaign. He had long been convinced that too many had become trapped in a cycle of dependency and robbed of self-esteem, had become the "welfare-dependent poor."

Fundamental to his philosophy, his chief of staff (1998–20001) John Podesta would note, was "the importance of work to an individual's sense of self and well-being." Dignity comes from work; work organizes life; government should support structures so people could work. Welfare reform was "not a punitive act but a way of creating opportunity for those who had few options in their lives."

Some in the administration believed he had a made a strategic error in not making welfare a priority early in his term, before pushing for the big health care bill. Indeed, Clinton may have agreed that success with welfare reform—when the Democrats were in power on the Hill—rather than failure on health care, would have meant a better outcome in the 1994 midterms. But that was history. Now there was a Republican majority, and while that party long advocated changes in welfare—which polls indicated was politically popular across the land—their very different vision of welfare reform would make achieving his goal far more difficult. GOP Congressman Clay Shaw, a key player in their effort, told the U.S. Chamber of Commerce, the "welfare state has failed"; Congress "equated compassion with money" but now "we" are going "to make the tough decisions that must be made."

Twice, the Republicans passed welfare bills that Clinton found mean-spirited: cruelly cutting off people from aid without providing adequate help in returning to the job market and putting the most vulnerable at risk. He vetoed both measures. He then worked with the new GOP Senate majority leader, Trent Lott, to shape a more acceptable bill, and by summer there was a new version, supported by most Democrats in the House and Senate. It contained more financial support for moving people to work, offering much more money for child care (up 40 percent to $14 billion), tougher child-support enforcement, and restoring federal guarantees of food stamps and medical benefits.

But when Lott called on July 30 with the final terms of the bill emerging from conference committee and ready for his signature, Clinton was furious. It contained several provisions Republicans knew he found repellent. The most odious was the denial of food stamps and medical care to low-income immigrants. The GOP had larded the measure with poison pills, giving the President the alternative of vetoing a politically popular act (and just before the election) on an issue he was passionately concerned with or signing something that contained ugly provisions, thus infuriating his liberal base. An angry President finished the call and told an aide: "This is not about welfare. It is about screwing immigrants and screwing me."

Bill Clinton now called together his cabinet and closest advisers in the Roosevelt Room of the White House and asked for their judgment. The majority were in favor of vetoing the bill. Health and Human Services Secretary Donna Shalala, Labor Secretary Robert Reich, Housing Secretary Henry Cisneros, even Treasury Secretary Robert Rubin were opposed to the bill, as were Stephanopoulos, Leon Panetta, and Deputy Chief of Staff Harold Ickes. But after a lengthy discussion, Clinton came to a different conclusion. "This is a decent welfare bill wrapped in a sack of shit," he said. It was the last and best chance for welfare reform; pragmatism demanded that he sign it.

His closest adviser, Hillary Rodham Clinton, was not present at the meeting. Both Clintons knew that Marian Wright Edelman, Hillary's old boss at the Children's Defense Fund, and her husband, Peter Edelman, Assistant Secretary for Health and Human Services, were bitterly opposed to this bill. They warned it could have a calamitous impact on poor children because it ended the Aid for Dependent Children program and put a five-year limit on welfare support. (Later, Bill Clinton regretted not ensuring that this limit be lifted in periods of extensive recession if there were months of negative growth.) But Hillary did not share their longtime friends' negative view. She agreed to work hard to round up votes for the bill's passage. In the event, Edelman and two other high officials in his department resigned in protest.

The President signed the bill three weeks before the Democratic National Convention, which would nominate him once more for the nation's highest office. "The legislation is far from perfect," he stated. "There are parts of it that are wrong and I will work to redress them. But on balance, this is a real step forward for our country, our values and for people who are on welfare." In his statement, he vowed to fight to restore immigrant benefits. And two years later, there had been some progress; working with Congress, Social Security and food stamp benefits were reinstated for some legal immigrants, including children, the elderly, and the disabled.

In fact, by the end of Bill Clinton's second term, welfare reform—which he would say was "one of the most important decisions of my presidency"— seemed to be a smashing success. As he left office in 2001, welfare rolls had been reduced from 14.1 million to 5.8 million, a 60 percent decrease, and child poverty was down 25 percent, its lowest point since before the election of Ronald Reagan.[29]

Now it was time for the 1996 presidential election. The Republicans held their convention in San Diego in mid-August, nominating Bob Dole, who had resigned from the Senate to make the race. Dole, a heroic veteran, wounded in World War II, easily had overcome the challenges of two more right-wing figures, Congressman Phil Gramm of Texas and Steve Forbes, the heir to a business magazine fortune who advocated radically reducing taxes on the wealthy. The candidate made a good acceptance speech, Clinton thought. But in it, Dole derided the President as "part of the baby boomer elite who never grew up, never did anything real, never sacrificed, never suffered, never learned." And he promised to build a bridge back to a "better past of tranquility, faith, and confidence in the nation."

When the Democrats gathered in Chicago, Clinton was already well ahead in tracking polls. Later, he noted his acceptance speech was easy to give, because he focused on the record: lowest combined rate of unemployment and inflation in twenty-eight years, 10 million new jobs, 10 million people with minimum wage increases, 25 million who were benefiting from the Kennedy-Kassebaum Act, 15 million working Americans with tax cuts, 12 million taking advantage of the family leave law, 10 million students saving money through the Direct Student Loan program, 40 million workers with more pension security. He ended by saying, "We do not need to build a bridge to the past, we need to build a bridge to the future, let us resolve to build that bridge to the twenty-first century." It became the theme of his campaign and the rest of his presidency.

It would be a one-sided race. Ross Perot was back as a third-party candidate, as was Ralph Nader, but they made little impact. Clinton, as always, was a brilliant campaigner. He flew across America, speaking at rallies, working the rope lines. And his deficit-cutting budgets, his crime bill (for which he had won the endorsement of the Fraternal Order of Police), and trade acts, as well as welfare reform, had allowed him to grasp the political center.

The Democratic National Committee raised $180 million in an effort to match wealthy Republican fund-raisers. Near the end of the campaign, but more dramatically early the next year, stories emerged assailing the Clinton–Gore team for overly zealous efforts, accepting donations from some dubious individuals and demeaning the office by allowing donors to stay overnight in the White House. There was, of course, no illegality involved. (And compared with the massive election-year spending by corporations and billionaires the next decade, encouraged by the Supreme Court's "Citizens United" decision, the dollars were puny indeed.) But critics would call this the "Lincoln Bedroom Scandal."

Much of the money was used to fund television ad campaigns that skewered Newt Gingrich as a radical extremist—as opposed to Bill Clinton, the prudent protector of popular government programs like Medicare. And they pictured Bob Dole as Gingrich's partner, the narrator referring to them as "Gingrich-Dole." Paul Begala observed: "Gingrich was out of central casting in a way that Bob Dole could never be. Dole was essentially agreeable, pleasant, accommodating. . . . They could never have demonized him without Newt. Newt was like a Thomas Nast cartoon of a right-wing thug: overweight, bombastic, given to hysterical rants. . . . He says these crazy things. He was a gift."

Dole, a well-liked political figure but an uninspiring presidential candidate, never had a chance. The Republicans emphasized their "family values" agenda, and some of their spokespeople pushed the "character" issue, referring darkly to "Clinton scandals." But they found little leverage. With two weeks to go, polls had the President ahead by twenty points, which Clinton later felt took "some of the life out of our campaign." On election night, Bill Clinton won a striking victory in the electoral college, 379 to 159, and he had 49 percent of the vote to Dole's 41 percent (with Perot at 8.4.) He lost only three states he had carried in 1992—Montana, Colorado, and Georgia (where the Christian Coalition had been particularly effective)—but carried two new ones, Arizona and Florida.

Still, as he later observed: "My share of the vote was considerably lower than my job rating, my personal approval rating, the percentage of people who said they felt comfortable with my presidency." It was "a sober reminder of the power of cultural issues like guns, gays, and abortion, especially among white married couples in the south, the intermountain west, and the rural Midwest, and white men all across the country." All that was true, but it did not diminish the fact that Clinton was the first Democrat to be elected to a second term since Franklin D. Roosevelt sixty years before.[30]

After the election, there was the expected turnover in the cabinet, as key players, some exhausted after the intense years in power, submitted resignations. Warren Christopher left the State Department; Robert Reich, who disagreed with some of his old friend's budget and economic policies, left the Labor Department; and both Stephanopoulos and Leon Panetta would depart.

Clinton's second inauguration would be, like the November victory celebration, a more serene affair than that of 1993. In his inaugural address, he said that Americans had not "returned to office a President of one party and a Congress of another . . . to advance the politics of petty bickering and extreme partisanship they plainly deplore." A nice thought, but events would prove it a forlorn hope.

For this remained a Congress of a different party. Clinton's sweeping victory did not bring the Democrats back to majority. Some party professionals blamed the stories of improprieties in White House fund-raising just before the election for the failure to gain more ground; in the House they won only 9 more seats, and the new Senate would find the GOP even increasing its margin by two, now at 55 to 45. In his State of the Union address on February 4, the President quoted scripture, saying that if both sides worked together to get something done, "they shall be called the repairer of the breach . . . the restorer of paths to dwell in."

He focused on education, asking for it to be "our number one priority." In his ten-point educational plan, he proposed scholarship credit for the first two years of college and a $10,000 tuition deduction for all higher education after high school. Two days later, he sent his budget to Congress, calling for an increased investment in education by 20 percent, cutting some other programs, and offering middle-class tax relief and health insurance for uninsured children. And he promised a balanced budget after five years.[31]

The President's new chief of staff, Erskine Bowles, a successful North Carolina businessman, a strong supporter of the New Democrat approach long before Clinton came to the White House, but somewhat more conservative than other major figures in the administration, played a key role in budget negotiations. This time, the Republican leader, chastened by Bill Clinton's victory and still bruised by how he had outmaneuvered them in the government shutdown crisis, proved amenable to compromise.

Newt Gingrich knew he must be ready to deal. In June, he once again recognized how formidable was his opponent when Republicans tried to load a disaster relief bill with partisan riders, only to have Clinton veto it and force them to retreat. "Why are you sticking your head up and letting him beat you?" was the Speaker's response. This willingness to now work with Bill Clinton infuriated DeLay and Armey. DeLay, biographers noted, had called Gingrich a "think tank pontificator and fake." More important was the Texan Armey's intense hatred of Clinton, a "liberal" with "a brand of anti-Americanism," whose popularity and success infuriated him. And so the majority leader and the majority whip attempted a coup, trying to push Gingrich out of the leadership. But it was an abortive effort, as Speaker Gingrich mobilized support in the GOP caucus and held on to power. The budget discussion could go forward.

Clinton was dealing from strength. Economic growth in the first quarter of 1997 was at 5.6 percent, unemployment was under 5 percent, the estimated deficit down to $75 billion. At year's end, the growth rate would top 8 percent, and with tax revenue up, deficit reduction was even faster than Clinton's team predicted, the deficit now $22 billion, down more than 80 percent from the $290 billion problem he had inherited in 1993. In fact, the deficit was on target to be gone by the first week in 1998, something the *New York Times* characterized as "the fiscal equivalent of the fall of the Berlin Wall."

The GOP, as always, wanted massive tax cuts for the richest Americans and an agreement to balance the budget, now not a major issue in view of what was happening in the economy. Clinton agreed to two-thirds of the tax cuts they wanted, particularly the capital gains tax rate reduction, but felt he was getting much more in return. Working with Gingrich and Trent Lott, he got Republican agreement to 95 percent of the new investments he had recommended, as well as middle-class tax cuts.

The budget bill not only extended the life of Medicare for a decade, it provided new health coverage for 5 million more children. This was SCHIP, the State Children's Health Insurance Program. Administered by the Department of Health and Human Services, it provided matching funds to states for health insurance, covering uninsured children in families with modest incomes but too high to qualify for Medicaid. It constituted the largest expansion of taxpayer-funded health insurance since the passage of Medicaid in the 1960s. The act would have bipartisan sponsorship, introduced by Senators Edward Kennedy and Orrin Hatch, with Kennedy, Senator Jay Rockefeller, and Hillary Rodham Clinton playing the key roles in supporting it.

The new budget did much more. It provided for the HOPE (Helping Outstanding Pupils Educationally) Scholarship and Lifetime Learning Credits, which would open the doors of college to a new generation, with the largest investment in higher education since the G.I. Bill fifty years before. The HOPE Scholarship provided a $1,500 tax credit for students in the first two years of college; the Lifetime Learning program offered tax relief for college juniors, seniors, graduate students, and working Americans pursuing lifelong learning to upgrade their skills. This would be more than $38 billion in tax relief over five years. And there were additional provisions for education savings accounts and student loan interest deductions, as well as tax reductions for employer-provided education benefits.

Bill Clinton, dealing with Republican majorities on the Hill that offered an insuperable barrier to most activist legislation, had hit on a way to achieve liberal goals through conservative means. These education titles, like the Earned Income Tax Credit, used the tax code to expand opportunity to less affluent Americans.

The 1997 budget also contained significant new dollars for environmental efforts. It restored disability and health benefits to legal immigrants. It raised taxes on cigarettes, both to discourage smoking and to help pay for SCHIP.[32]

Some Democrats objected to the tax cuts and voted against the budget bill, but the vast majority of House and Senate Democrats and Republicans supported the budget. Clinton, signing the bill, invited Gingrich and Lott to share the moment.

Of course, years later, trying for his party's presidential nomination in 2011, Gingrich would take credit for the economic successes of the Nineties, saying that he'd played the essential role in the budget surpluses in the Clinton years. But while it was true that political realism did force him to be less rigid than more extremist figures in his party in 1997, this claim elicited only contemptuous scorn from members of the Clinton team. James Carville observed that "the idea that he had anything to do with balancing the budget is ludicrous"; Begala exclaimed, "He was involved in it—just on the losing side!" And another Clinton aide suggested that "Gingrich taking credit for the budget successes and economic boom of the '90s is like George Wallace taking credit for integration."

Into 1998, it appeared for a moment that Bill Clinton could build on his earlier achievements to pursue an expanded agenda in the last years of his presidency. A Gallup poll on New Year's day put Clinton atop the list of the public's "most admired men."

In his State of the Union address at the end of January, Clinton noted that the deficit would be eliminated that year and surpluses were on the way. Before spending this money on tax cuts, he argued, we should strengthen the Social Security reserves and improve education, through hiring 100,000 new teachers, cutting class sizes, building thousands of new schools, and providing after-school programs. He called for a renewed effort to address health care by opening Medicare to Americans between ages 55 and 65, expanding the Family and Medical Leave Act, and providing a Patients' Bill of Rights. He asked for massive increases for the National Institutes of Health and the National Science Foundation and new dollars for environmental protection and poverty programs.

The GOP majorities on the Hill made it unlikely that he could push through most of these ambitious items, but perhaps there was a real opening for Social Security reform. Gingrich now seemed flexible and Clinton met with him and Bill Archer, chair of the House Ways and Means Committee. The President was considering a modest increase in the retirement age but also a private-investment option, knowing it was the perennial Republican favorite "reform," always offered by the party that celebrated free enterprise and individual risk-taking.

Such an option would be fiercely opposed by liberal activists, particularly organized labor, appalled at any indication that Social Security would be "privatized" and turned over to Wall Street. But in fact it would be an option that did not replace Social Security, but only added to the existing program. And the government would match voluntary contributions dollar-for-dollar for poor and middle-class taxpayers. The Social Security system and its benefits would remain in place, the private accounts built on top of it. (Al Gore would propose something similar in the 2000 campaign.) Because of the economic expansion and the looming surplus billions, this was an achievable goal, without the expected pain that had throttled earlier schemes to "fix" Social Security.[33]

It would not happen. The sex scandal that almost ended the Clinton presidency would intervene.

Kenneth Starr, the special prosecutor zealously pursuing an alleged Whitewater "scandal," had failed to find incriminating evidence, despite his lengthy, expensive inquiry during the previous three years. Other supposed Clinton-era "scandals"—investigated by Starr and others—had also yielded no damaging results for the President. But in early January, even before the State of the Union address, the nation became fixated on word that he was accused of having an affair with a young White House intern. This was a different kind of scandal.

News of it had leaked out after Bill Clinton was forced to testify in a court case in Arkansas (early in January) about the allegations of an Arkansas woman, Paula Jones, who claimed he had made inappropriate sexual overtures to her years before, when he was governor. During his testimony, he had been asked about an affair with a White House intern, Monica Lewinsky. Surprised, he had denied any such wrongdoing.

Bill Clinton now repeated the denial in a nationally televised interview. It was a grotesque error. Barney Frank, a survivor of a sex scandal of his own years earlier, said, "The instinct is: Don't tell anybody anything other than what they already know for sure. Well, the problem with that is, if you are caught not being open and honest, you make the press into enemies. They have a vested interest . . . in almost destroying you." And Clinton was dealing with a press corps that had long imbibed the Slick Willie stories, with many reporters already prepared to doubt his word. He now compounded the problem with the media and, of course, created a huge problem with the public.

He wrote later: "Since 1991, I had been called a liar about everything under the sun, when in fact I had been honest in my public life and financial affairs, as all the investigations would show. Now I was misleading every-one about my personal failings. I was embarrassed and wanted to keep it from my wife and daughter. I didn't want to help Ken Starr criminalize my personal life, and I didn't want the American people to know I'd let them down." And in an oblique reference to secrets he always had kept about the violence in his childhood home with an alcoholic stepfather, he added: "I was back to my parallel lives with a vengeance."[34]

Of course, the story would become a media sensation. Newspapers, magazines, online websites, talk radio, cable TV, and network television news were dominated by the tale of the President and the intern. And other women had come forward accusing Clinton of sexual misconduct. Starr was on the case, calling White House staffers before a grand jury.

Bill Clinton tried to keep focus on the demands of the office. He had to deal with several critical foreign policy matters across the succeeding months and he traveled overseas often. But even before he testified to the grand jury on August 15—in which he finally admitted that "on certain occasions in 1996 and once in 1997" he had engaged in wrongful con-duct that included inappropriate intimate contact with the intern, Monica Lewinsky—any hope of pushing forward the heart of his domestic program for 1998 was long gone.

Clinton's sex scandal had destroyed any chance of furthering an activist agenda. The GOP blocked the Patients' Bill of Rights, killed tobacco legis-lation and an anti–teen-smoking measure, filibustered campaign finance reform, stopped another minimum wage increase, and refused to build or repair thousands of schools. Of course, there was no movement on entitle-ment reform.

Into the fall, House Republicans, Gingrich in the lead, now sensed the perfect opportunity to finally destroy the charming, charismatic man who had so often outmaneuvered them. They pushed for the impeachment of the President. A central issue: that Clinton had not truthfully answered questions about the Lewinsky affair while under oath in the Arkansas trial.

Of course, it also was a campaign season. With the 1998 midterms just ahead, Republicans, as one writer observed, thought that "they had at last struck political gold." After Clinton's grand jury testimony, followed imme-diately by his painful television statement apologizing to the nation, GOP leaders poured money into congressional races. They were certain they could increase their margin in the House by twenty or more seats. In the Senate, knowing that the Democrats were defending most of the vulner-able seats, they had hopes of winning a filibuster-proof sixty-seat major-ity. They would nationalize the campaign. As one southern Republican exclaimed about his congressional district: "Bill Clinton has re-energized our base. . . . We will gratuitously use Clinton's face on all our literature." But they could not have been more wrong.

When the votes were counted, the Democrats gained 5 seats, leaving the GOP with a narrow 223 to 211 majority. In the Senate, the parties broke even, each taking 3 seats from the other to keep the Republican margin at 55 to 45. In a midterm after losing the general election two years earlier, the opposition party expects gains on Capitol Hill. Now, even with impeachment in the air, they had suffered a humiliating setback. Furious members of his caucus turned on Newt Gingrich, and within a week of the election, he announced his resignation as Speaker and from the House of Representatives. *Time* magazine once more put him on the cover, this time his picture slipping off the bottom of the page. The title: "The Fall of Newt."

What had happened? The economic boom had happened. Americans were feeling better about their lives and more confident about their future, and the President was getting credit for it. The so-called misery index, a compilation of inflation and unemployment data, fell to its lowest level in more than forty years. Real incomes were up, 8 percent higher than in 1994. The stock market was bullish. Violent crime was down 28 percent during the Clinton presidency, and down 35 percent from its 1981 peak. The proportion of Americans on the welfare rolls was 46 percent lower than in 1994. And of course, the federal budget had moved from deficit to surplus on Clinton's watch. The President's standing in the final Gallup poll taken before the election showed 66 percent approving of his job performance, the highest for any president in any midterm pre-election poll since Gallup began asking the question fifty years earlier.[35]

Somehow, the Republicans still did not get the message. Polls indicated that most people believed that the media coverage had been "irresponsible," that it had been "All Monica all the time." There had been too much discussion of sex and not enough of the economy. Other polls suggested that the public was disenchanted with Starr and repelled by the time, effort, and money spent on his investigation. (Clinton believed that if more Democratic candidates for Congress had been brave enough to make anti-impeachment arguments, instead of being intimidated by the media blitz and running away from the President, the Democrats might even have regained a majority in the House.) But the right-wing leaders in the GOP House caucus, furious at the defeat and loathing the man in the White House, pushed on with their impeachment effort even after Gingrich departed. Bob Livingston of Louisiana was the designated Speaker, but the real power in the caucus was majority whip Tom DeLay, and he exerted enormous pressure on Republicans to vote against any compromise, such as a vote of censure. There must be impeachment.

On December 11, the Judiciary Committee voted along party lines to refer four articles of impeachment to the full House. The heated debate went on for days, but just before voting began, Livingston, after demanding the President's resignation, admitted that he too had "strayed" in his marriage and, amid angry shouts from the floor, announced his own resignation as Speaker. The vote went forward, along party lines, with only five Republicans voting no to the charge of "lying to a grand jury."

The President had been impeached and the Constitution called for a trial in the Senate, with a two-thirds vote needed for conviction. The Senate would take up the matter early the next month. But in the trial, stretching into February, there was never any question that the votes for conviction were lacking. All Democrats and five Republicans voted no to the central charge. Bill Clinton easily survived this effort to force him from the White House.

In the midst of this exhausting, media-dominated process of impeachment and trial came the publication of the massive "Starr Report"—which soon became a best-selling book. Its sordid, explicit descriptions of sexual activity, like the whole anticlimactic impeachment affair, did more damage to the President's enemies—including Kenneth Starr—than to Bill Clinton. But because the activity itself was pretty sordid, all of it would cast a shadow across the remaining months of his presidency.

Certainly, the last two years of the second and final term of any President hoping to promote an ambitious domestic agenda is a challenging time. The specter of being a lame duck and the growing interest in the upcoming presidential election has to limit the effectiveness of the person in the White House. And for Clinton, facing daunting foreign policy challenges, dealing with the emotional backwash of the Lewinsky scandal and the impeachment crisis, confronting a hostile House dominated by DeLay and his team, there now would be little chance of major legislative achievements.

In his 1999 State of the Union message, Clinton had called for new initiatives but found that even some members of his own party thought they would be better off without much legislative activity, believing they could then run against a GOP "do nothing" Congress. As for the Republicans, he noted long after leaving office, they "seemed to have reverted to the theme they had trumpeted since 1992: I was a person without character who could not be trusted."

He focused on actions that did not need strong congressional support. Hoping to build on the historic economic expansion, he negotiated more trade agreements and helped create 130 empowerment zones as well as community development banks. Selling more products and services overseas and opening new markets in America, where unemployment was high and investment too low, was now in order.

But he also used his veto pen to block Republican efforts at large cuts in education, health care, and environmental protection. And he stopped their plan for a tax cut that would cost $1 trillion over the next decade. They had justified this proposal by pointing to projected budget surpluses. Clinton wryly noted that he was "far more conservative" than GOP leaders on this issue; he did not want to push the nation back to deficit-prone policies of the Reagan years. (Of course, his Republican successor would successfully drive through a cut focused on those with the highest incomes, with predictable results.)[36]

His willingness to sign another piece of Republican legislation, the Gramm-Leach-Biley Act, would prove to be far more controversial. Senator Phil Gramm was the central force pushing the bill; his cosponsors in the House were two GOP representatives, Jim Leach of Iowa and Thomas Biley of Virginia. The bill represented the final repeal of the New Deal–era Glass-Steagall Act. That landmark legislation had separated commercial and investment banking, preventing commercial banks from engaging in the kind of dangerous, speculative, predatory practices that had helped bring on the Great Depression. It had been the goal of the banking industry throughout the Eighties and Nineties to tear down the firewall between the two kinds of banks; they wanted deregulation, and GLB would make this happen.

Almost a decade after he left office, Bill Clinton would be assailed by liberal critics for signing this bill. They linked his action to the financial crisis and resulting recession of 2008–2010. One prominent liberal economist, Simon Johnson, noted that the passage of GLB freed "commercial megabanks created by the ongoing merger wave to plunge headlong into the business of buying, securitizing, selling, and trading mortgages and mortgage-backed securities," using deposits insured by the FDIC. It was these risky, self-serving, immensely profitable gambles with taxpayer dollars that would enormously enrich a few bankers but play a key role on the road to the economic panic and downturn that had a devastating effect on the lives of so many average Americans. The act, some economists argued, was partially responsible for the creation of banks that were "too big to fail."

Other scholars would not view it that way. For many years, they argued, Glass-Steagall had been weakened by the rulings of the conservative, free-market–loving figure at the helm of the Federal Reserve as well as a series of deregulatory actions taken since the late 1970s. It had been outflanked by the emergence of new and different financial entities—hedge funds, private equity firms, and others—as well as new and complex financial products, including derivatives based on computer-generated data. Thus there was an emerging "shadow banking system" whose bad practices could not have been prevented even if Glass-Steagall was still on the books. That cat was already out of the bag.

For his part, Bill Clinton did not have regrets about signing GLB, arguing during the economic crisis of 2008 that "one of the things that helped stabilize the current situation" was the purchase of one failing large investment bank (Merrill Lynch) by a huge commercial bank (Bank of America).

Regulating derivatives themselves was a different matter. Collateralized debt obligations (CDOs), those vast collections of mortgage-backed securities, and credit default swaps (CDSs) grew enormously in size and significance in the years after the Clinton White House. Revisiting his economic legacy a decade after leaving office, the former President said he was "wrong to listen to the wrong advice about regulating derivatives."

The critical action was his signing—on December 21, less than a month before leaving office—the Commodity Futures Modernization Act of 2000. Phil Gramm, a free-market ideologue as an academic economist before coming to the Senate and soon to be a highly paid senior bank executive and banking lobbyist when he left Congress shortly after the passage of the bill, again was the driving force behind the CFMA. It essentially deregulated the entire derivatives market. Included here was energy, notably a special "Enron loophole" for the Houston-based company much admired by Gramm of Texas; this was later to be abused by Enron in the largest corporate fraud in American history. More damaging still, it deregulated CDSs. Among others, this allowed AIG, the world's largest insurance company, to issue such swaps (essentially insurance policies against possible losses) to investment banks, hedge funds, and other large units speculating recklessly in an unregulated and untransparent derivatives marketplace. The AIG bankers made millions from the sales, but the company did not have the trillions of dollars to back the policies when the market crumbled in 2008. This helped plunge the nation (and the world) into a financial abyss and necessitated a vast, taxpayer-financed federal bailout in 2008–9.

The deregulation effort had been a Republican priority for years and had been forcefully pushed by well-funded lobbyists for the financial industry and, of course, supported by Alan Greenspan at the Federal Reserve. But Robert Rubin, Clinton's Treasury Secretary, a famous investment banker before coming to the White House and a major figure at Citibank, the banking giant, after leaving the administration in 1999, strongly supported this effort. He was not alone. Not only did his predecessor at Treasury, Lloyd Bentsen, back the industry, but Lawrence Summers, the prominent Harvard economist who replaced him as Secretary, shared this view. With Greenspan, they helped to undermine the campaign of Brooksley Born, chair of the Commodity Futures Trading Commission (CFTC), when she presciently expressed concern that the buildup of large derivative positions invisible to regulatory oversight could create risks for the financial system as a whole.

Still, it was Gramm's shrewd move to insert CFMA into the budget act for fiscal 2001, just before the Christmas recess in 2000, that would have the most damaging effect. It foreclosed any possibility of regulation by the CFTC or the Securities and Exchange Commission of these derivatives. It was passed, as one writer put it, by a lame duck Congress and signed by a lame duck President and went far beyond the regulatory debates of earlier years by allowing the financial sector to "seal off" a central profit-making engine from any further government interference.

In expressing regret that he took advice from Rubin and Summers on this matter, Bill Clinton noted that "the argument on derivatives was that these things are expensive and sophisticated and only a handful of investors will buy them and they don't need any extra protection and any extra transparency." But the "flaw in that argument was that sometimes people with a lot of money make stupid decisions and make it without transparency . . . and that even if less than one percent of the total investment community is involved in derivative exchanges, so much money was involved that if they went bad they could affect . . . one hundred percent of citizens, not investors."

Nonetheless, the argument that Bill Clinton could have prevented deregulation, and thus was in part responsible for the economic disaster at the end of the next decade, seems strained. He would note that "if I had tried to regulate them," the Republicans, in the majority in Congress "would have stopped it. But I wish I should have been caught trying. That was a mistake I made." Indeed, if he had not signed Gramm's CFMA (which had huge bipartisan support in both houses of Congress) just before leaving office, a new Republican-dominated Congress, already elected, and a new, strongly right-wing Republican President would have had the opportunity to push it through in the months after he was gone.

In 2010, reflecting on the financial carnage of the previous few years, the former President would observe that if "Arthur Levitt had been on the job at the SEC, my last SEC commissioner, an enormous percentage of what we've been through in the last eight or nine years would not have happened."[37]

Of course, Levitt (who had not opposed the derivatives legislation at the time) would not be on the job, because a new President, George W. Bush, was in office. And he would act once more on Ronald Reagan's old anthem, "getting the government off our backs," by replacing all key figures in regulatory agencies with administrators opposed to "interfering" with the workings of the free market.

How Bush was elected would become one of the great debatable issues in American history. His ultimate hair-thin victory over Vice President Al Gore in the electoral college would follow his defeat by over one-half million in the popular vote count. It was the result of the bitter, disputed

Florida vote and the unprecedented action of the Supreme Court in stopping a recount.

Long before the polls opened in 2000, the presidential contest had dominated political life in America and had made the final months of Bill Clinton's administration less focused on an effort to expand his domestic agenda. Inside the White House, one important new development was Hillary Rodham Clinton's emergence as candidate for the Senate from New York. The retirement announcement of Senator Daniel Patrick Moynihan created the opportunity, and key New York political figures urged the first lady to run. The President was strongly supportive, and Hillary, who proved to be a strong, articulate, and powerful campaigner, won a striking victory on election night. It was a shining moment for the Clintons in the midst of the confused presidential outcome.

Yet, while Bill Clinton was energetically supporting his wife's effort, this legendary figure on the campaign trail was not as active across the nation working for Al Gore. The shadow of the Lewinsky scandal somehow made the Vice President—whose wife Tipper was particularly angry about Clinton's affair with the intern—reluctant to call upon the President to campaign in a number of critical states, particularly border, "battleground" states. "Why are you not out on the trail?" governors, mayors, and political leaders in these states would ask the man in the White House. "I would like to [be], but they won't let me," was the reply. It was, of course, a signal error by Gore the candidate.

The struggle over the Florida vote count dragged on for weeks, through the month of November. As the President focused on a last effort at what would have been a historic peace treaty in the Middle East, his two-term presidency was coming to a close. And his popularity, despite the sex scandal, was nearing its zenith. Many speculated that, despite it all, including the impeachment trial, if not for the constitutional provision limiting a President to two terms, Clinton would have been unbeatable in 2000.

The reason was the state of the economy and the public's satisfaction with the direction of the country under the leadership of President Bill Clinton.

By 2000, Clinton had presided over the longest economic expansion in United States history. The gross domestic product rose to over $11 trillion, up some $3 trillion from 1992 and the recession-wracked period before. Yearly productivity was growing at 3.9 percent, far eclipsing the figures for the Reagan and George H. W. Bush years, when the comparable figure had been a miserable 1.8 percent per year. In fact, output was up three-quarters of a trillion dollars more each year than in those "supply side" Reagan days of "unshackling American capitalism." That amounted to $7,000 per American household per year. These truly were the "boom years" of the Nineties. The "Clinton prosperity" was no illusion.

Employment was dramatically expanding, with over 22 million new jobs created since 1993, far more than in the entire three terms of the Reagan–Bush era. In fact, American employment skyrocketed from 108 million when Clinton entered office to 130 million as he prepared to leave. (Under Clinton, the economy was adding an average of 255,000 new jobs per month; there had been 52,000 under Bush and 167,000 under Reagan.) Of course, unemployment would decline; by 2000 it was down to 4 percent from the grim 7.5 percent in 1992. In fact, the unemployment rate had fallen for seven years in a row, remaining below 5 percent for the previous three years. By the end of Bill Clinton's presidency, it was the lowest in three decades.

And many of the jobs now widely available in America were "good jobs at good wages." The Clinton years marked the longest real wage growth in more than thirty years, with hourly earnings climbing far faster than the rise in prices. Since 1993, real wages (adjusted for inflation) were up 6.5 percent, after actually declining 3.3 percent during the Reagan and Bush years. This was true across the country, as those groups of Americans most likely to be victimized by discrimination in the past found their prospects sharply improved. African American unemployment was down by fully half from 1992 (to 7.2 percent), the lowest rate on record. Hispanic unemployment was down from 11.6 percent to 5.4 percent, also a record. Unemployment for women was at 4.0 percent, the lowest in forty years.

There was more. The poverty rate fell from 14.8 percent in 1992 to 11.3 percent, the lowest since before Ronald Reagan's election, the largest five-year drop in poverty since the Great Society. African American poverty declined to the lowest level ever recorded and, of course, there was also the largest drop in the child poverty rate—to under 19 percent—since the Sixties.

While all this was happening, the nation was moving from record deficits to record surplus. In 1992, the federal budget deficit was almost $300 billion, the largest dollar deficit in American history. In January 1993, as Bill Clinton was taking the presidential oath for the first time, the Congressional Budget Office projected that the deficit would grow to $455 billion by 2000. But in 2000, the Office of Management and Budget was projecting a surplus of over $200 billion for 2000, the third consecutive surplus and the largest ever, even after adjusting for inflation. The surplus was over 2 percent of gross domestic product, a spectacular change from the situation only eight years before, when the deficit had reached 5 percent of GDP.

On New Year's Eve 2000, as the year, the century, and the millennium were ending, Bill Clinton, preparing to leave the White House in less than three weeks, could look back with satisfaction on the pledge he had made to the American people. He had talked of promising to "build a bridge to a new millennium." In a prosperous land of full employment, an America now unburdened by crippling economic problems, a nation offering new opportunities for its citizens, his was a promise that had been fulfilled.[38]

Certainly, he had not done it by himself. It was the private sector that had produced the jobs. A critical element here was the rise of the "new economy," the computer, software, telecommunications, and Web search firms that were the driving force in the economic boom of the Nineties. Companies concerned with information technology and industrial machinery (including computers, semiconductors, and related equipment) created growth in output per hour worked an average of 15 percent per year between the mid-Nineties and 2000. This rapid growth was responsible for at least half of the national productivity upsurge.

Microsoft had become a huge company years before Clinton's inauguration, Bill Gates already among the world's richest people. But it prospered in the Nineties, even as other new giants of the telecommunications explosion emerged. Steve Jobs returned to Apple in 1996, to drive that company to new heights. The use of desktop PCs and laptop computers was becoming universal. Then Google was founded in 1998, soon to eclipse Yahoo (founded in 1994) and Altavista (founded in 1995) as the dominant Web search engine. For it was in the mid-Nineties that the World Wide Web truly became an "information superhighway," the Internet the transforming phenomenon of the age. The first mobile phone with Internet connectivity was launched in 1996, and cell phones, already proliferating across the world in this decade, would soon be transformed into "smart phones."

But even the hugely successful private companies in this era of new technology owed much to the government. The armed forces had pioneered the Internet and GPS positioning and provided early funding for Silicon Valley. (As one publication would note: federal dollars put the "smart" into Apple's smartphones.) Academic scientists in great private and publicly funded research universities and labs developed, with the critical help of federal grants, the touchscreen and HTML language. The research producing Google's search algorithm, the source of its wealth, was financed by money from the National Science Foundation. (Similarly, numerous pharmaceutical companies were beneficiaries of massive grants from the National Institutes of Health for the development of their revolutionary—and immensely profitable—new drugs.)

Many new companies, hoping to capitalize on the opportunity to find customers in a new world of easy, universal access, would prosper by selling toys or groceries, cartoons or legal advice, airline or hotel reservations on "the web." (Others, of course, organized by inept or unlucky dreamers, incompetents, or con men, proved disastrous failures; the bursting of a "dot com" bubble would bring a halt to the spectacular rise in the stock market, which had quadrupled the Dow Jones Industrial Average from the early Nineties to 2000.)

But the "new economy" was only part of the story of the booming Nineties. Companies from the "old economy" were also expanding. New hires in manufacturing, sales, and services in more traditional sectors of the economy were making the recession-ravaged years of the past a distant memory.

The domestic agenda of the Clinton administration had played a critical role in making all this possible. It was not just "good luck" that made the Clinton years a time of record-breaking prosperity while the Reagan–Bush era before had a been an age in which real wages declined, and the George Bush administration to follow would see economic stagnation followed by disastrous recession.

Certainly, the budget of 1993, that agonizingly close triumph of Bill Clinton over the monolithic opposition of all the Republicans on Capitol Hill, was a central event. Raising taxes, particularly on the richest Americans, while making key cuts in spending, tamed the deficit. It helped dissuade Alan Greenspan and the Fed from raising interest rates, which were kept at historically low levels through much of the Nineties. Low interest rates encouraged business investment (notably in the "new economy") and home building, so that between 1992 and 2000, investment rose by 4 percent of GDP. This, in turn, stimulated the upturn in productivity growth, and with it came lowered production costs and inflation, because increases in real (or inflation-adjusted) wages were a key factor in reducing the demand of workers for higher money wages and helped keep the inflation rate in check.

While conservative critics warned at the time that tax increases on the affluent would strangle the economy, the exact opposite was true. And even though they paid higher marginal rates, the richest Americans themselves would enormously profit by the boom of the Nineties, with the top 1 percent taking over 40 percent of total income gains. (But all Americans were doing well in the Clinton years, unlike the troubled next decade, when— after George W. Bush pushed through enormous tax cuts for the rich—the top 1 percent took between 63 and 93 percent of income gains.) It was only through acts of total historical amnesia that right-wing activists by 2010 could argue that higher taxes on the affluent were not only unfair to the rich but would mean recession for all. It was as if the Clinton years and the Clinton policies had never happened.

A key part of federal government spending cuts in the 1993 budget and after was in the defense sector. There was a bonus at the end of the Cold War; defense spending on Clinton's watch declined by 2.6 percent as a share of GDP. Adjusted for inflation, this was the equivalent of almost $300 billion. Despite protests from some parts of the military-industrial-political complex, these cuts not only made perfect sense in the years immediately after the collapse of the Soviet Union and its formidable armed forces, but made it far easier to pursue the domestic agenda of the administration, freeing dollars for more constructive purposes.[39]

And as Clinton and his team moved to address the economic challenges of the Nineties, he acted on his long-standing belief in encouraging a larger world market for American goods. This led to the passage of NAFTA and the creation of the World Trade Organization. There would be downside risks in a global, interdependent marketplace. But during the boom years of the Nineties, it often helped U.S. businesses in both the old economy and the new as they expanded, seeking customers and partners in distant lands.

If his campaign anthem, "It's the economy, stupid," was the most important reason why Bill Clinton was elected President of the United States in 1992, by the end of his second term, he had been strikingly successful in dealing with this central issue of his time. In his farewell address, he stated: "To those who say the progress of these last eight years was just some sort of accident, let me be clear. America's success was not a matter of chance; it was a matter of choice." President Clinton had presided over the revival of the American economy and the restoring of hope and prosperity for millions.

His conservative foes would not forgive him for his success. They would be relentless in efforts to humiliate him and damage his administration. (We will consider some elements of these attacks in Chapter Five.) Many of these enemies on the right had been certain that he had to fail; inheriting the huge deficits of the Reagan–Bush years, they believed, would so "starve the beast" that it would paralyze activist leadership. But he had read the message of the recent past and confounded these foes with his economic strategy.

Still, the fear of federal power, the belief in the dangers of "big government," had been so effectively inculcated by the makers of the Reagan Revolution, so shrewdly circulated for years by the masters of the conservative media machine, that even Bill Clinton's success in reviving the American economy never gave him a supportive environment in Washington.

He knew this going in, and the shaping of his New Democrat, Third Way vision was the response. Even as he implemented the economic policies that would help bring prosperity to the nation, he had to carefully maneuver a progressive agenda seeking to expand opportunity, address inequality, protect the environment, and help the most vulnerable. (Of course, he would not be helped by the damaging sex scandal his behavior allowed to darken the last two years of his presidency.)

Liberal critics would not be satisfied with his successes on this front: His were only "niche initiatives," he was "the fixer of tiny things," some insisted. EITC and SCHIP, HOPE Scholarships and AmeriCorps, Family and Medical Leave Act and Kennedy-Kassebaum, the Brady bill and the Direct Student Loan program, environment and conservation investments, strengthening reproductive rights and spending more on public schools, among others, were not enough for them. And they were not happy with welfare reform. Where was his "New Deal," his "Great Society"? they would ask. Why the failure on health care reform?

The answer, of course, was that he had to operate inside the historical setting he had inherited. He would leave it to history to determine whether he had fulfilled his promise to build a bridge to the new millennium.

NOTES

1. Clinton, *My Life* (New York: Alfred A. Knopf, 2004), pp. 481–482, 490.
2. Ibid., pp. 481, 490–491; *New York Times,* January 14, 1993; Taylor Branch, *The Clinton Tapes: Conversations with a President, 1993–2001* (New York: Simon and Schuster, 2009), pp. 11–12; Elizabeth Drew, *On the Edge: The Clinton Presidency* (New York: Simon and Schuster, 1994), pp. 37–41, 54–56; George Stephanopoulos, *All Too Human* (New York: Little Brown, 1999), pp. 118–120.
3. Branch, *Clinton Tapes,* pp. 5–8; interview with Sandy Berger, July 25, 2012; Drew, *On the Edge,* pp. 42–48; Clinton, *My Life,* pp. 483–486.
4. Ibid., p. 485.
5. Stephanopoulos, p. 119; John Harris, *The Survivor* (New York: Random House, 2005), pp. 54–58.
6. Ibid., p. 35; interview with Paul Begala, October 3, 2012.
7. Stephanopoulos, pp. 111–112; Clinton, *My Life,* pp. 519–520.
8. Drew, *On the Edge,* pp. 174–183; Clinton, *My Life,* pp. 518–519.
9. Ibid., pp. 520–522; Harris, pp. 65–66; Drew, *On the Edge,* pp. 185–188; Stephanopoulos, pp. 142–152; Bob Woodward, *The Agenda: Inside the Clinton White House* (New York: Simon and Schuster, 1994), pp. 212–225; interview with John Podesta, July 24, 2012.
10. Robert B. Reich, *Locked in the Cabinet* (New York: Vintage Books, 1998), pp. 121–122; Woodward, *The Agenda,* pp. 277–279.
11. Clinton, *My Life,* pp. 531–538; "Conference Agreement on President Clinton's Deficit Reduction Plan," OMB—1993 Budget Deal, Box 45, Clinton Presidential Library; Drew, *On the Edge,* pp. 260–272; Woodward, *The Agenda,* pp. 282–309; Harris, pp. 90–93.
12. *New York Times,* August 5–6, 1993; *Congressional Record, 1993,* pp. H1344, H2649, H1454. H5745.
13. Drew, *On the Edge,* pp. 338–355; Harris, p. 95; Clinton, *My Life,* pp. 546–547.
14. Ibid., p. 536; Hillary Rodham Clinton, *Living History* (New York: Scribner, 2003), pp. 116, 133, 143–149.
15. Paul Starr, "What Happened to Health Care Reform?" *The American Prospect* 20 (Winter 1995): 20–31; Derek Bok, "The Great Health Care Debate 1993-94." http://www.upenn.edu/pnc/ptbok.html
16. Hillary Rodham Clinton, pp. 151–152.
17. Ibid.; *New York Times,* September 23, 1993, pp. 150–152.
18. Starr, "What Happened to Heath Care?" pp. 22–28; Bok, "The Great Health Care Debate"; Hillary Rodham Clinton, pp. 238–233; Harris, pp. 112–119; Michael Takiff, *A Complicated Man: The Life of Bill Clinton as Told by Those Who Know Him* (New Haven: Yale University Press, 2010), pp. 191–195; Clinton, *My Life,* pp. 554–555, 564–571, 620–621; Ezra Klein, "Unpopular Mandate," *The New Yorker,* June 25, 2012, pp. 30–31.

19. David H. Bennett, *The Party of Fear: The American Far Right from Nativism to the Militia Movement* (New York: Vintage Books, Random House, 1995), pp. 416–420; Takiff, pp. 238–239.
20. *New York Times*, January 27, 2012; Newt Gingrich, "Language: A Key Mechanism of Control." http://www.informationclearinghouse.info/article4443.htm.
21. Jeffrey B. Gayner, "The Contract with America: Implementing New Ideas in the United States," http://www.heritage.org/research/lecture/the-contract-with-america-implementing-new-ideas-in-the-us; Walter Dean Burnham, "A Transforming Election: 1994 in Context," http://www.nathannewman.org/EDIN/.election/.1994/.1994anal/.WDB.html; Steven M. Gillon, *The Pact: Bill Clinton, Newt Gingrich and the Rivalry that Defined a Generation* (New York: Oxford University Press, 2008), pp. 121–126; Clinton, *My Life*, pp. 621–622, 628–632; Branch, p. 218.
22. Takiff, pp. 253–254; Stephanopoulos, pp. 328–341; Harris, pp. 154–155.
23. Ibid., pp. 169–172; Clinton, *My Life*, p. 660; interview with John Podesta, July 24, 2012.
24. Clinton, *My Life*, pp. 636–645, 651–654; Bennett, pp. xi, 409–410; "Remarks by the President During 'A Time of Healing Prayer Service,'" April 23, 1996, Oklahoma City. http://clinton4.nara.gov/WH/EOP/OP/html/okla.html
25. Elizabeth Drew, *Showdown: the Struggle Between the Gingrich Congress and the Clinton White House* (New York: Simon and Schuster, 1996), pp. 55–58; Takiff, pp. 246–247.
26. Ibid., p. 256; Harris, pp. 214–215; interview with Paul Begala, October 3, 2012.
27. Harris, pp. 216–217; Clinton, *My Life*, pp. 680–684, 694–696; Drew, *Showdown*, pp. 324–372; "President Clinton's Reasons for Vetoing the Republican Budget," December 6, 1995, File 1497454, NEC Government Shutdown, Box 40 (1), Clinton Library; "Cry Baby," (New York) *Daily News*, November 16, 1995; interview with Paul Begala, October 3, 2012.
28. Harris, pp. 244–245; Branch, p. 551; Clinton, *My Life*, pp. 700–701, 707, 719; Steve Kornacki, "Bill Clinton Praises Bain," *Salon*, June 1, 2012, http://www.salon.com/2012/06/01/bill_clinton_being_bill_clinton; "President William Jefferson Clinton: State of the Union Address, U.S. Capitol, January 23, 1996," http://clinton2.nara.gov/WH/New/other/sotu.html; Michael Waldman, *Potus Speaks: Finding the Words that Defined the Clinton Presidency* (New York: Simon and Schuster, 2000), p. 106.
29. Clinton, *My Life*, pp. 694, 720–721; Hillary Rodham Clinton, pp. 365–370; Harris, pp. 230–239; John Podesta, *The Power of Progress* (New York: Crown, 2008), pp. 120–124; Gillon, pp. 178–179; Takiff, pp. 285–287; "Remarks by E. Clay Shaw to U.S. Chamber of Commerce," February 9, 1995, "Memorandum for the President on Welfare Reform Conference Strategy" from Bruce Reed and Rahm Emanuel, September 22, 1995, "Statement by President Clinton on Welfare Reform Legislation," July 31, 1996, Domestic Policy Council, Welfare Reform, NGA OA/ID 8505, Boxes 132, 139, Clinton Library; Bob Woodward, *The Choice: How Bill Clinton Won* (New York: Simon and Schuster, 1996), pp. 352–353.
30. Ibid., pp. 235–237, 446–440; Takiff, p. 294; Clinton, *My Life*, pp. 730–734.
31. Ibid., pp. 735–745; Harris, pp. 266–273; Reich, pp. 344–346.
32. Clinton, *My Life*, pp. 754–755, 761; Gillon, pp. 197–203; "SCHIP History," http://www.news-medical.net/health/SCHIP-History.aspx; U.S. Department of Education, "The HOPE Scholarship and Lifetime Leaning Credits," http://www.2ed.gov/offices/OPE/PPI/HOPE/index.html; "President Clinton's Hope and Opportunity for Post-Secondary Education (HOPE) Act," March 20, 1997, NEC "HOPE Scholarships," Box 42 (2) Clinton Library.
33. Gillon, pp. 205–221, 264–266; Harris, pp. 354–355; Klein, pp. 197–198; Maggie Haberman, "Newt, Clinton Battle over 90s Legacy," *Politico*, December 26, 2011.
34. Jonathan Van Meter, "The Post-Scandal Playbook," *New York Times Magazine*, April 14, 2013, p. 28; Clinton, *My Life*, p. 775.
35. Ibid., pp. 800, 813–825; Harris, pp. 354–355; Gary C. Jacobson, "Impeachment Politics in 1998 Congressional Elections," *Political Science Quarterly* 114 (Spring 1999): 31–38.
36. Ibid., 45–47; Clinton, *My Life*, pp. 843, 861, 866–867, 871–880.

37. Simon Johnson and James Kwak, *13 Bankers: The Wall Street Takeover* (New York: Random House, 2010), pp. 133–137; Dana Goldstein, "Bill Clinton Revisits His Economic Legacy," *The American Prospect* (September 23, 2008); Evan Harris, "Clinton: I Was Wrong to Listen to Wrong Advice Against Regulating Derivatives," April 17, 2010, http://abcnews.go.com/blogs/politics/2010/04/clinton-rubin-and-summers-gave-me-wrong-advice-on-derivatives-and-i-was-wrong-to-take-it; Eric Lipton and Stephen Labaton, "Phil Gramm Looks Back, Unswayed," *New York Times*, November 16, 2008; Bill Clinton, *Back to Work: Why We Need Smart Government for a Strong Economy* (New York: Random House, 2011), pp. 48–52.

38. The White House, "The Clinton-Gore Administration: A Record of Progress," http://clinton4.nara.gov/WH/Accomplishments/additional.html

39. William D. Nordhaus, "The Story of a Bubble," *New York Review of Books* (January 15, 2004); "The Entrepreneurial State," *The Economist*, August 31, 2013, 59; Alan S. Blinder and Janet L. Yellen, *The Fabulous Decade: Macroeconomic Lessons from the 1990's* (New York: Century Foundation Press, 2004); Joseph Stiglitz, "The Roaring Nineties," *Atlantic Monthly* (October 2002); Steven Rattner, "The Rich Get Even Richer," *New York Times*, March 26, 2012.

CHAPTER 4

FOREIGN CHALLENGES IN A
POST–COLD WAR ENVIRONMENT

As Bill Clinton prepared for Inauguration Day, he understood his first, critical challenge in foreign affairs. For over four decades, the central pivot of American foreign policy had been the Cold War. The United States, emerging from World War II as the giant of the West, had faced the threat of a continent-sized Soviet Union and its empire of satellite states for almost forty-five years. The American policy, in this bipolar world, was containment, blocking the feared expansion of Soviet dominance short of a shooting war between the thermonuclear superpowers, a catastrophic conflict that would destroy them both and reduce the world to ashes. But now the Cold War was ending, and managing the transition from that long twilight struggle to a new and less threatening environment was the essential first task of the incoming President.

So the fate of Boris Yeltsin became priority number one. As the new leader of Russia, Yeltsin rejected the autocratic practices of the Soviet past and pursued cooperation with the West. Strobe Talbott, Clinton's old friend and noted expert on Russia, citing the famous Isaiah Berlin, whose lectures Clinton and Talbott attended together at Oxford so many years before, said that actors in history can be divided into two categories, the hedgehog and the fox. "The fox knows many things, but the hedgehog knows one big thing." And Bill Clinton knew one big thing: On "the twin issues that had constituted the casus belli of the cold war—democracy versus dictatorship at home and cooperation versus competition abroad—he and Boris Yeltsin were now, in principle, on the same side."[1]

But Yeltsin needed help. He had come to power just as Clinton was announcing his candidacy for the presidency. But he was menaced by angry members of the old Communist hierarchy, infuriated by the direction he was moving the nation.

The final stage in the collapse of the USSR had occurred in the mid-Eighties, when first Leonid Brezhnev, then Yuri Andropov, and finally Konstantin Chernenko had died within a two-year period and the way had been cleared for the elevation of the 54-year-old Mikhail Gorbachev to the leadership of the Soviet Union. Gorbachev, of course, had become a transformational figure. His advocacy of glasnost (openness) and perestroika (restructuring) led not only to the removal of the Iron Curtain and the liberation of nations in Eastern Europe, but ultimately to the disintegration of the USSR itself. And as he turned away from totalitarian controls and promoted a more pluralistic society at home, he was confronted, in August 1991, with revolution: a cabal involving almost all of his Communist comrades staging a coup d'état and placing him under house arrest.

At that moment, Boris Yeltsin, who had cut his ties to the Communist Party after being pushed out as head of the Moscow party organization, establishing himself as leader of the Russian Soviet Federative Republic, intervened to block the coup. He famously stood atop a tank in front of the Russian legislature, known as the White House, and the putsch ended in the arrest of the conspirators. But Gorbachev, fatally weakened, resigned as head of the Party, and the Communist regime and the Soviet Union both collapsed. On December 24, the USSR gave up its seat in the United Nations to a different entity, a country now called the Russian Federation. Its leader, Boris Yeltsin, moved from the White House to the Kremlin.

As Yeltsin attempted to reshape political power in favor of reform, he confronted daunting problems. Resentment over the loss of important parts of the old Soviet Union—with the independence of Ukraine and other states—was a festering sore. More significant, perhaps, would be the privatizing of state property, which helped create a new class of robber barons (later called the Oligarchs) and criminal bosses in a land long plagued by crime and corruption. Leaders of the old regime went into opposition in the Russian parliament, hoping to paralyze and then displace Yeltsin, who desperately needed financial help from America. Candidate Clinton responded, attacking the Bush administration for being "overly cautious on the issue of aid to Russia."

Now President George Bush announced new efforts to support Russia. Yeltsin then visited the White House, but candidate Clinton managed to have a brief meeting with him as well, at Blair House, the official visitor's residence.

During the campaign, when Bush tried to take credit for having won the Cold War, Bill Clinton, in a speech in Los Angeles, said that reminded him of "the rooster who took credit for the dawn." It was not the Republicans who had triumphed in the Cold War, he said, it was the bipartisan chain of presidents, starting with Harry Truman, who shaped policies that ultimately resulted in victory. (In fact, if those three old men had not died in a row in the Eighties—and Andropov, the tough ex-KGB leader, had not contracted a deadly liver ailment—the Cold War might not have ended on the Reagan–Bush watch.)

While no Russian leader would appreciate triumphalist comments of Americans concerning the end of the Cold War, Yeltsin had appreciated Bush's efforts to help. But he now recognized there would be a new American chief executive. Even before he entered the White House, Clinton had a call from Yeltsin, pleading with him to come to Moscow "as soon as possible." He then sent a letter that "reads like a cry of pain," Clinton told Talbott. "I really want to help him, he is up to his ass in alligators. He needs friends abroad because he's got so many enemies at home." His main concern in foreign affairs, Bill Clinton said, was whether "Russia is going to blow up in our face."

After inauguration, Clinton moved to help his new friend. He agreed to meet with Yeltsin, although it would be in Vancouver, Canada, not in the White House. (Yeltsin had proposed meeting the new President "halfway," not wanting to seem summoned to Washington or seen in Russia as a puppet of the West.) And while key members of his foreign policy team— Secretary of State Warren Christopher, Vice President Gore, Ambassador to the United Nations Madeleine Albright, Tony Lake, Sandy Berger—all worried that Clinton might stand by Yeltsin "no matter what," the President said: "What is going on over there is about people, some people versus other people. This is a zero-sum thing. That's why we've got to take sides." Despite the reservations of Larry Summers and some others, the President now arranged a package of $1.6 billion in American assistance.

The Clinton–Yeltsin relationship strengthened. It became "Bill" and "Boris." They would meet eighteen times across the years of Clinton's presidency, almost as many meetings as Bill Clinton's nine predecessors had had with Soviet leaders over a forty-six–year period. The meetings were often intense. Yeltsin, a big, bear-like man, mercurial, heavy drinking, prone to fits of depression but a proud spokesman for Russian interests, was a difficult partner in the search for peaceful solutions. But the Cold War was not replaced by a new conflict between the world's only two military superpowers.[2]

Two issues involving Yeltsin had special significance early in Clinton's first term. One had to do with nuclear proliferation, a matter that haunted thoughtful people across the planet; the other with Bosnia, a foreign policy crisis inherited from the outgoing administration.

The disintegration of the Soviet Union had left a huge arsenal of nuclear weapons in the newly independent states of Ukraine, Belarus, and Kazakhstan. Ukraine would pose the most difficult problem, and there were 130

SS-19 intercontinental ballistic missiles with their thermonuclear warheads, almost 50 intermediate-range missiles, and dozens of strategic bombers equipped with long-range cruise missiles stationed there. The United States and the USSR had been working on efforts to reduce the numbers of such systems in the years before the collapse of the USSR. Now, in spring 1993, it was essential to ensure that the Ukraine-based weapons be returned to Russia.

Not only was this an important step in blocking nuclear proliferation, it would remove doomsday weapons from an unstable new state, for a polarized Ukraine, containing two dominant groups—Ukrainians and ethnic Russians—struggling for power, might well descend into chaos.

But it was a difficult task. President Clinton, with Vice President Gore, Secretary of State Christopher, and Strobe Talbott playing important roles, achieved the goal: Ukraine's agreement to transfer all the weapons to Russia for disposal, with the United States financing the return and supplying economic and technical assistance to dismantle them. There would be guarantees to respect Ukraine's sovereignty, and in turn it would formally agree to become a non-nuclear state.

Deep suspicions and mutual contempt between the leaders of Ukraine and Russia had to be managed. President Leonid Kravchuk's efforts to secure billions of dollars in compensation from the United States and guarantees that the United States would treat an attack on Ukraine as an attack on America had to be blocked. Clinton used blunt language to force a final agreement. When it seemed at the last moment that Kravchuk was trying to back out on the arrangement, the President coldly warned how this would impact his future relations with the United States. The deal was done.[3]

But Bosnia proved a far more difficult problem. Yeltsin's government opposed American efforts to address the murderous ethnic cleansing conducted by Serb warlords against Bosnian Muslims.

With the fall of the Soviet empire, many of the newly freed states behind the old Iron Curtain—Poland, Hungary, Czechoslovakia, and the three small Baltic countries—had moved in the direction of democracy. But in the Balkans in southeastern Europe, Yugoslavia was a different story. The Serbs had long dominated this tottering, multiethnic regime, despite the restive presence of different ethnic and religious groups. And Slobodan Milošević, a Communist strongman now reinventing himself as a Serbian nationalist, was willing to use any coercive force available to keep dissident populations under his control.

The dissolution of Yugoslavia had begun in the summer of 1991. First Slovenia, then Croatia, and finally Bosnia declared independence. In the northwestern corner of Yugoslavia, the Slovenes, physically separated by Croatia from territory inhabited by Serbs, escaped after only a brief conflict and created their own state. The well-armed Croatians, under their own autocratic nationalist leader, Franjo Tudjman, also needed a brief but violent military campaign against Milošević's forces to gain full sovereignty.

Bosnia, the truly multiethnic, multireligious province, would not be so fortunate. In its 1991 census, 44 percent of the population considered themselves Bosnian Muslims; just over 32 percent were Serbs, predominantly Orthodox; and 17 percent were Croats, a largely Catholic population. But with Slovenia and Croatia now recognized by the international community, the leading Muslim politician, Alija Izetbegović, knew that the only way Bosnia could escape Serb domination was to follow suit. The subsequent referendum endorsed independence but was boycotted by the Serb minority.

What followed was brutal warfare. Croats as well as Serbs fought to carve out territory from Bosnia. But it was the Bosnian Serbs, under Radovan Karadžić, supplied with overwhelming firepower from Milošević's military (so well stocked with Soviet weapon systems), who made this the bloodiest struggle in Europe since the end of World War II.

In 1992, the outgoing Bush administration had urged the United Nations to impose economic sanctions on the Serbs, but it was largely a gesture. Secretary of State James A. Baker had made it clear that the Balkans were unimportant to Washington. In Baker's words, "We have no dog in that fight."

During the presidential campaign, after the European Community had recognized Bosnia as an independent state, with American television and print media describing the terrible consequences of Serbian "ethnic cleansing" and the inhuman conditions in Serb-run detention camps, Bill Clinton spoke out in favor of NATO air strikes with U.S. involvement. The Serbs were targeting local leaders for extermination and this had become a nightmare struggle. Karadžić promised: "There will be five hundred thousand dead in a month and Muslims will be annihilated in Bosnia."

The UN had imposed an arms embargo in the area, but it merely proved helpful to the aggressors; only the Bosnian Muslims in Sarajevo seemed defenseless. Clinton called for lifting the embargo, but the British and French, fearing deeper involvement in a Balkan swamp, insisted this would only prolong the war. They argued that it might endanger the lightly armed UN peacekeeping forces (which included a few of their own troops but no Americans) already on the ground.

After inauguration, Bill Clinton found his foreign policy team divided on the matter. Vice President Gore, Ambassador Albright, National Security aides Tony Lake, Sandy Berger, and Leo Fuerth—particularly Lake—called for "lift and strike": The United States would end the embargo on arms shipments to Sarajevo while threatening the use of American airpower against the Bosnian Serbs unless they refrained from further aggression.

General Colin Powell, chairman of the Joint Chiefs of Staff, was skeptical. While insisting he had no opinion on what the President should do in Bosnia, he emphasized how ineffective air strikes might be in a mountainous and wooded environment. He warned of the dangers involved in sending American ground troops, noting how large would be the commitment and uncertain the outcome of fighting in difficult terrain, marked by tunnels dating from World War II. Like others in the U.S. armed forces, he was haunted by the specter of Vietnam, concerned about the consequences of intervention in civil wars with no clear exit strategy. Each time he was asked if something could not be done about the Serbian artillery bombarding civilian populations, he would insist that any American action inevitably would lead to at least 100,000 U.S. ground troops. There were repeated references to the "Pottery Barn" metaphor: If you break it, you own it; America could be facing a quagmire without end.

After hearing this again and again, an exasperated Madeleine Albright exclaimed: "What are you saving this superb military for, Colin, if we can't use it?" But Bill Clinton had a lot of respect for Powell, and later, when Warren Christopher was preparing to leave the State Department, would even ask his friend Vernon Jordan to sound out the general on replacing him.

Secretary of Defense Les Aspin also was unenthusiastic about an expanded U.S. role in Bosnia, feeling it was "a loser from the start." Secretary of State Christopher was a reluctant supporter. "Our conscience revolts at the idea of passively accepting such brutality," he had said. But when he flew to Europe and again encountered strenuous British and French resistance, he did not come as the representative of the world's most powerful nation to insist on action, but to "consult." He was easily rebuffed.

The Italian Prime Minister had said, "This would be like throwing a log on a burning fire." The French would agree to air strikes only if the United States sent in ground troops. The Europeans from the start thought of Bosnia only as a humanitarian mission; they were resistant to a strong military response. Christopher not only was ineffectual with them but was outmaneuvered when he felt he had won a commitment from Karadžić on a cease-fire, only to have the Serb legislature contemptuously vote down this agreement even as Serb attacks intensified.

Meantime, Boris Yeltsin was providing a clear obstacle to a peaceful solution, refusing to accede to effective international action to block the Serb offensive. His aides talked of the dangers of Muslim extremists and terrorists in Europe and some used the language of pan-Slavic nationalism, a reminder that Russia in the past had claimed to be the protective "big brother" of the Orthodox "little Slavs" of the Balkans. Most significant, there was concern that Yeltsin's own position was fragile; Russian nationalists were waiting for his misstep, and he must not be pressed on this issue.

At home, Stan Greenberg's poll indicated public endorsement for action in Bosnia in conjunction with the UN but no enthusiasm for a unilateral move. On Capitol Hill, there was very limited congressional support for aggressive American involvement.

Bill Clinton now was reading a recent best seller by Robert Kaplan, *Balkan Ghosts*, which described the long history of conflict in the area, a morass of ethnic and religious mistrust and hatred across the centuries. Maybe nothing could change this. He was concerned, according to one report, about getting drawn in deeper and deeper. He asked, "Couldn't the use of force embolden the Serbs?"

He pushed for action to provide humanitarian help to embattled Muslims, authorizing the airdrop of food supplies. Of course, lift and strike would require much more. Only if the United States was prepared to act unilaterally might its allies come along. But it was clear that Clinton was ambivalent about committing the U.S. military to what he feared might be a quagmire. Like Colin Powell, he was thinking of Vietnam.

It was May 1993. He wanted to concentrate on his domestic agenda. With the Pentagon resisting and negative feelings on the Hill, with the Secretaries of State and Defense offering no strong support, with his White House foreign policy team—only months on the job—not fully up to speed yet, with opposition across Europe and concern for dividing the NATO alliance if he acted alone, and not wanting to send American troops in harm's way, he declined to push forward.

So "lift and strike" was not implemented in 1993. The war continued and, if anything, became much worse. But Bosnia would not go away.[4]

And soon Clinton and his team would confront another painful foreign policy dilemma, also inherited from the previous administration. Like Bosnia, it was an international crisis rooted in a struggle within a nation, rather than between nations.

In late September, the President was working to gain approval for a new aid package for Russia, facing yet another round of instability. According to radio reports from Moscow, hardliners were maneuvering to replace Yeltsin. Armed men linked to these opposition delegates raided a military compound and killed several militiamen. Thousands of rioters stormed the streets near the Kremlin carrying hammer-and-sickle flags and portraits of Stalin. Václav Havel, president of the Czech Republic, said: "What is happening in Moscow is not a power struggle but a fight between democracy and totalitarianism." And in a concerned White House, as Yeltsin worked to put down another coup attempt, Clinton told his Russian adviser, "I guess we've just got to pull up our socks and back ole Boris again." But when Strobe Talbott spoke to the President hours later, a weary Bill Clinton said, "Bad as that Moscow deal is, believe me, it is worse in Mogadishu." The Somalia crisis had erupted.

As the Clinton team dealt with events in Somalia, National Security adviser Anthony Lake would exclaim, "Boy, do I ever miss the Cold War." (Bill Clinton would not agree; failure in the Cold War carried with it the threat of nuclear annihilation.) Still, while helping to head off disaster in Russia might be essential, dealing with the difficulties of internecine warfare in small, failed states was far more complicated. Like Bosnia, Somalia proved a foreign policy nightmare. The death of eighteen American servicemen would impact Clinton's actions in years to come.

In October, Task Force Ranger, an assault force comprising members of elite special units from the U.S. Army, Air Force, and Navy, had conducted a raid into the center of the Somalian capital of Mogadishu and something went terribly wrong. Their mission had been to capture Mohammed Farah Aidid, the clan warlord whose heavily armed followers not only controlled much of the city, but had killed twenty-four Pakistani peacekeeping troops, part of the United Nations mission to Somalia.

The UN was in this impoverished land on the horn of Africa because it had become a collapsed state, a place of mass starvation and despair. In January 1991, Somalia's President was overthrown by a coalition of opposing clans. The warlords of these groups began a series of bitter battles to dominate the nation, which was now without a functioning government. The ruthless struggle led to famine and disease. Efforts to provide relief from outside failed, as local clan leaders, indifferent to human suffering, hijacked 80 percent of the food to purchase weapons. By the end of 1992, 350,000 had died in this chaotic civil war.

When an effort to negotiate a cease-fire between opposing clans failed, the United Nations sent military observers to watch distribution of food. President Bush had provided planes and troops for Operation Provide Relief in August 1992, but when that failed to stop the slaughter—with over a million displaced persons and thousands more dead—the United States launched Operation Restore Hope. It was December, and the United States was assuming command of the military effort to bring order out of the chaos. Now Marines and elements of the U.S. Army's 10th Mountain Division arrived in country, 25,000 in all. Brent Scowcroft, National Security chief in the outgoing administration, told Sandy Berger, the President-elect's National Security aide, that they would be home before Clinton's inauguration.

It was not to be. Over the next several months, as the United Nations sent in 20,000 troops and the United States reduced its force to 4,000, there were signs of progress: Starvation ended, refugees were returning, some schools and hospitals were reopening. There was hope of reconciliation and stability; fifteen Somali parties, representing many of the clashing clans, agreed to restore peace and democracy. But by May, it was clear that Mohammed Aidid's faction would not cooperate, for he was planning on taking power across the land. The warlord now controlled Radio Mogadishu and used it for anti-UN propaganda. He thought he was being marginalized and he declared war on the United Nations peacekeepers.

In early June, his forces killed the Pakistanis. Reacting immediately, UN leaders, notably the Secretary General, felt that there was no alternative but to arrest and punish Aidid and asked the United States to help. In the White House, there was no meeting of the Principals Committee, composed of the State and Defense Secretaries, the CIA director, Joint Chiefs chair Colin Powell, and other key foreign policy advisers. The resolution agreeing to the request was drafted at the State Department, and there was no dissent. It was felt that action was needed or peacekeepers all over the globe would be in jeopardy. In retrospect, one writer noted, this seemed a casually made decision. Bill Clinton clearly was hoping to extricate American troops and was concerned that forces might be needed for the unresolved Bosnia matter. In a press conference, he had promised that U.S. operations in Somalia would be over. No one could remember whether the President was consulted.

Late that month, a U.S.-led operation on a safe house where Aidid supposedly was hiding led to a violent confrontation involving helicopter gunships. Aidid was not present, but dozens of Somalis were killed and angry mobs stormed the streets, leading to the death of four journalists. Aidid's militia, seemingly with increased public support after that firefight, now killed four American soldiers with remote-controlled bombs. Admiral Jonathan Howe, the frustrated U.S. representative to the UN who was leading the fruitless search for Aidid, had been calling for elite units, including the Army's Delta Force. General Powell and Tony Lake now agreed. Thus was created Task Force Ranger.

By fall, key administration figures became uneasy about the direction of events. They had decided to try to get the UN to change the mission, but that was taking time. In fact, the Pentagon did not "own" Somalia; neither the military chiefs nor the White House were making decisions about it at a strategic level.

Now some members of Congress were drafting a resolution setting a firm date for withdrawal. Bill Clinton wanted to aggressively pursue a political solution and bring American troops home. (He had other pressing matters; he was soon to deliver his speech on health care to the Joint Session and begin the effort to sell this critical measure.) But his message on Somalia was never clearly delivered. A day after the raid, he erupted, "This is stupid! . . . How could they be going after Aidid when we're working the political end?" Yet Secretary of Defense Aspin would say, "The Pentagon's understanding of the policy was to move to more diplomatic efforts but snatch Aidid on the side, if you can."

In his memoirs, Clinton notes that "just a few days before he retired as chairman of the Joint Chiefs [on September 30], Colin Powell came to me with a recommendation to approve an American effort to capture Aidid, though he thought we had only a 50 percent chance of getting him." The President had agreed. But neither the White House nor the Pentagon would be consulted about the mission to follow. General Powell, about to retire, placed no parameters on the commander on the ground. There was no requirement for even CentCom (the armed forces command for the region) to approve a raid.

And so, acting on a tip about the presence of Aidid's top aides at a particular site, on October 3, Major General Garrison, Ranger commander, ordered the 160 members of the Ranger force to fly into Mogadishu on Black Hawk helicopters in daylight. A ground extraction convoy of Humvees and trucks followed on to take the captive targets back to base but encountered intense fire on the way in.

After capturing some of Aidid's aides, the raid became a debacle. Enemy militiamen, firing rocket-propelled grenades, shot down two of the Black Hawks. One pilot was caught in the wreckage, other troops killed or injured. As Rangers gathered to protect the trapped and wounded, a firefight ensued with hundreds of Somalis. Two of the brave defenders, both killed in action, would be awarded Medals of Honor. But before a relief column, involving American and allied UN forces (including their obsolescent M48 tanks), was able to fight its way in to rescue the besieged Rangers, there would be eighteen Americans killed, seventy-three wounded, and one captured, along with several Malaysian and Pakistani casualties.

The exact toll of Somali militia and civilian casualties is unknown. There was a torrent of bullets and grenades fired during the encounter, and while Aidid insisted that there were fewer than 400 Somali dead, some U.S. observers estimated over 1,500 killed and wounded.

As first reports of the mission gone awry came in, Bill Clinton was shocked. He had not envisioned a daytime assault in a crowded urban environment, assuming "we would try to get him when he was on the move, away from large numbers of civilians and the cover they could give his armed supporters." Now, his face reddening, according to Stephanopoulos, he exclaimed: "I can't believe we're being pushed around by these two-bit pricks!"

But within hours the President could see the full dimensions of this disaster. Television was showing footage of a dead American—a helicopter crew chief—being dragged through the streets and every network was showing videotape of the captured pilot. Soon they would be on the cover of the newsmagazines, and "Black Hawk Down" would become the infamous title—in books and a film—for the "battle of Mogadishu," the largest firefight Americans had been involved in since Vietnam. While General Garrison said he took "full responsibility," it was clear that the commander-in-chief could not, as the general put it, "be taken off the blame line."

Across the country, there was outrage. Pundits asked if the United States was now doing the UN's bidding. They suggested that this humiliating public setback for the American military superpower could encourage insurgent enemies everywhere. Senator John McCain said, "Clinton's got to bring them home." Members of Congress flocked to the White House, demanding immediate withdrawal. The President, appalled at the American casualties, would have liked to have gotten Aidid, but he feared that even if successful, this would have meant "we would own Somalia," not the UN, and there was no way of knowing if the United States could "put it together again." (Of course, even after Aidid died of natural causes in 1996, Somalia continued to be a chaotic and divided land. It would be a classic failed state, soon to be the base of pirates.)

Bill Clinton refused to "cut and run," that ugly term for retreat after failure. He negotiated a six-month transition period with Congress. He ordered American forces in Somalia strengthened for this interim period, with heavy weapons—M-1 tanks and Bradley armored personnel carriers—sent in to face down the lightly armed militiamen who had seen success against the fragile helicopters.

But who would pay the price for the failure? It was Les Aspin, who had resisted sending modern tanks to Mogadishu earlier in the year. Already dealing with problems in the military over Aspin's "relaxed leadership," Clinton ordered the change. Tony Lake, an old friend, told him in mid-December, "Les, I've got some bad news to tell you." Concerned, Aspin responded, "What, you're not leaving?" "No, Les, you are." The new Secretary of Defense would be William J. Perry, Aspin's deputy, a man respected as a logical, precise, and authoritative figure.[5]

The Somalia affair would haunt the President. Clearly, it damaged the health care initiative because it would dominate media and public discourse for weeks. It further undermined his support in certain circles of the armed forces. It was cited by political enemies as evidence of weakness and ineptitude in foreign and military matters. Most important, precious lives now had been lost on his watch. Would it mean a more cautious approach in the future?

Events that fall in another impoverished third world country—one much closer to home—reinforced the Clinton critics' belief that he was reluctant to use American power. It was in Haiti, the poorest state in the western hemisphere, where yet another crisis carrying over from the previous administration led at first to another humiliating setback.

The scene of numerous interventions by American forces earlier in the century, Haiti had suffered for years under repressive dictatorships until

1990, when Jean-Bertrand Aristide was overwhelmingly elected President. But one year later, he was overthrown in a coup led by General Raul Cedras and a group of military men, supported by the nation's elites, who feared Aristide was a radical planning to redistribute wealth. This junta brutalized opponents, stimulating an exodus of "boat people" fleeing toward the nearby United States. Candidate Bill Clinton had criticized the Bush administration's policy of blocking these desperate migrants. But after inauguration, intelligence agencies warned the President that 200,000 more might be on the Caribbean in makeshift, overcrowded boats. To prevent a humanitarian disaster at sea and an immigration crisis at home, Clinton decided to continue the Bush restrictions while moving to negotiate a peaceful return of Aristide.

At a meeting on Governors Island in New York, it appeared that Cedras's regime had agreed to the return. But this brokered agreement proved but a cynical play for time by the junta. In October, pursuant to the agreement, the Pentagon sent 200 army engineers and trainers to Haiti. Instead of a friendly welcome, Cedras sent a mass of gun-bearing thugs to prevent the docking of their landing ship, the *Harlan County*. This vessel was not equipped for an invasion, the troops aboard were not heavily armed. They heard the shouts of the angry mob ashore: "We are going to turn this into another Somalia."

For two days, the ship waited listlessly offshore while Washington debated what to do. The decision was to order the vessel to turn around and come home. The President, in a public statement, exclaimed, "I want the Haitians to know I am dead serious about seeing them honor the agreement they have made." But it was obvious, as Warren Christopher later admitted, that the *Harlan County* should have been accompanied by fighting ships and well-armed personnel. There was no masking the fact that this was another ignominious setback, undermining the credibility of the nation and its chief executive.[6]

Certainly, this would not be the end of the story. As in Bosnia, the Clinton administration, months later, would use military muscle in Haiti and achieve its objectives. But before that happened, in 1994, there would be yet another instance of a failure to use force to stop terror in a country caught up in a civil conflict.

In Rwanda during April, May, and June, there was the mass murder of an estimated 800,000 people. Tension and violence between two ethnic groups, the Tutsis and the Hutus, had marked the history of this East African nation. But the speed of this slaughter was astonishing and the scale appalling.

Most of the dead were Tutsis, the minority group (with 15 percent of the population) favored by Belgian colonists with better jobs and opportunities in the nineteenth and early twentieth century. They had been victims of repressive, revengeful rage when the majority Hutus gained power at the end of the colonial era. Tutsi refugees, living in Uganda and supported by some moderate Hutus, long had plans to overthrow the Rwanda government to secure their right of return. Their rebel army, the Rwandan Patriotic Front (RPF), finally had invaded, leading to negotiations for a power-sharing arrangement. But unrest continued and militant Hutus, who for years had been stockpiling weapons, planned a different outcome. Then, on April 6, 1994, a plane carrying the Rwanda President was shot down. With the militants in control, the presidential guard immediately initiated wide-scale killing. The murderous assault had begun.

Military officials, politicians, and many others joined the slaughter. Radio propaganda—characterizing all Tutsis as "cockroaches"—encouraged the formation of an unofficial militia group, called the Interahamwe, which grew to mobs numbering 30,000. With soldiers and police pressing ordinary citizens to take part, with incentives of food or money or property offered if more Tutsis were killed (and any Hutu who tried to protect them), there was mass murder with machetes, knives, and guns. Neighbor attacked neighbor. And there was mass rape. This genocidal rampage would become one of the great crimes of recent history. It went on for weeks before the RPF launched an offensive and finally took the capital, Kigali, in early July.

Where was the United States during all this? There was no lesson from Somalia, Madeleine Albright would argue: "Somalia was something close to anarchy. Rwanda was planned mass murder. Somalia counseled caution; Rwanda demanded action."

Why was there no action? In mid-May, the UN had proposed sending 55,000 troops to Rwanda but the United States lobbied to cut the number. When ten Belgian peacekeepers had been killed and their bodies mutilated by Hutu militiamen, it was clear that only a formidable military power could stop the slaughter. But the United States government did not bomb or jam extremist radio stations inciting the killing (despite pleas from the African Bureau at the State Department), would not authorize officials to use the term "genocide" for weeks after the mass murder had begun, seemed dead to information from the International Red Cross reporting the killings, and would send no troops. It was not ignorance of developments in Rwanda that was the reason for the inaction.

The process simply broke down. Said National Security director Anthony Lake, an Africanist who was the most knowledgeable White House figure about these developments: "We never had a serious meeting about whether to intervene. . . . Why didn't we have that meeting? I've asked myself that question about five hundred times. I think it was essentially a failure of imagination. Not just after Somalia, but in general, there was 'a consensus' that 'we were not going to intervene in the middle of Africa.' I deeply, deeply regret that."

For President Bill Clinton, "the failure to stop Rwanda's tragedies became one the greatest regrets of my presidency." Looking back, he wrote that it was clear "with a few thousand troops and help from our allies, even making allowances for the time it would have taken to deploy them, we could have saved lives." But the reason he did not act? "We were so preoccupied with Bosnia, with the memory of Somalia just six months old, and with opposition in Congress to military deployments in faraway places not vital to our national interests that neither I nor anyone on my foreign policy team adequately focused on sending troops to stop the slaughter." And six years after leaving office, thirteen years after the genocide, Clinton was still obsessed with it; discussing entirely unrelated subjects with Strobe Talbott, "out of the blue, Clinton would suddenly say, 'Explain to me again why we blew it in Rwanda.'"

Was it, as some later argued, the "fog of war," which affected policymakers in Washington fixated on other issues, unable to grasp the scope or rapidity of the slaughter? Or was there also a lack of confidence about going in and making a difference without a substantial commitment of troops? Certainly a few hundred Rangers would not do it after the Belgian peacekeepers had been butchered; two divisions at least would be required, and large-scale intervention in civil wars evoked those memories of Somalia and Bosnia, if not Vietnam.

After the RPF intervened, and the killing stopped, the Clinton administration poured in aid to Rwandan refugee camps. The United States established a base in Uganda to support around-the-clock shipments of relief supplies: 1,300 tons of food and medicine and 100,000 gallons of safe water a day. In all, the United States sent 4,000 troops and spent $500 million. It was too late to stop the genocide. But some lives were saved.[7]

Rwanda was a tragic failure. But the President now would become more assertive about deploying America's military power in the service of essential foreign policy goals, including humanitarian missions. Lessons were being learned. Haiti and Bosnia would be revisited and this time force would be used.

By September 1994, Clinton had reports from Haiti of how Cedras and his gang were intensifying their brutal regime. There were stories of young girls raped, priests killed, victims slashed with machetes while their children watched, mutilated bodies left in the open to terrify the population. It had been over a year since the general had signed an agreement to surrender power, only to have the *Harlan County* humiliation. Finally, Bill Clinton said he was "fed up." Former President Bush along with his Secretary of State, James Baker, had argued that the national interest did not justify the use of force in Haiti, and Republicans in Congress remained solidly opposed to military intervention to restore democracy. But the President now was resolved to drive out Cedras, even if it took an overwhelming display of American power.

Speaking from the Oval Office, the President told a national television audience: "The nations of the world have tried every possible way to restore Haiti's democratic government peacefully. The message of the United States to the Haitian dictators is clear. Your time is up. Leave now or we will force you from power."

To provide international support for action, the Clinton administration had taken the issue to the Organization of American States to forge a hemispheric agreement endorsing the use of force against Cedras. Ambassador Albright then introduced the Security Council resolution authorizing "all necessary means" to depose the autocratic regime. It would be the first time the UN had acted expressly for the purpose of defending democracy.

Now the President gave the petty tyrant one last chance to get out peacefully. He sent to Haiti a remarkable three-person delegation: former president Jimmy Carter, Colin Powell, and Sam Nunn. Carter and Nunn did not trust Aristide; both were skeptical about his commitment to democracy, and Powell felt that the police and Haitian army would not work with him. None of them shared Clinton's resolve to use force. But they were there to persuade Cedras to peacefully accept Aristide's return.

The President established a deadline and reviewed invasion plans with General John Shalikashvili, the new chairman of the Joint Chiefs. The result was a multiservice task force involving two aircraft carriers, landing vessels, special operations units, 82nd Airborne Division paratroopers, Navy SEALs, Air Force fighter bombers, and more.

With Cedras stalling for time and President Carter asking for another delay in the assault, Bill Clinton finally insisted that the delegation leave Port-au-Prince. They would be personally at risk because the paratroops were en route and would be over the capital within the hour. Only then did Cedras agree to leave power and cooperate with the American commander of the invasion force. The issue was resolved without guns being fired.

Haiti would continue to be plagued by economic and political problems. Aristide would prove no angel, and future developments in that troubled land—as with other countries—would continue to depend on domestic factors, with all the severe limits to what the United States (or any outsiders) could do to affect them. But at least the thugs who had overthrown Aristide were pushed out and there was a new message about the use of American power.[8]

In Bosnia, which Warren Christopher called "the problem from hell," it would take a year longer for forceful action. After the United States had failed to use military muscle against the Serbs in 1993, the United Nations Protective Force had deployed a few more lightly armed troops to shield the embattled Bosnian Muslims. Six UN "safe areas" were announced, but there was little safety for outgunned Muslims.

In February 1994, the Serbs fired a mortar shell into the central market of Sarajevo, killing 68 people, wounding almost 200. NATO, its forces under UN command, issued its first real ultimatum: The Serbs had to pull back artillery from around the capital. But the cease-fire around Sarajevo was spotty, and the siege of the capital remained in place. In April, Serb paramilitary forces overran the Muslim town of Gorazde (one of the "safe areas"), with devastating results for the civilian population. Two F-16 jets now attacked an artillery command bunker, the first time in NATO's forty-five–year history that alliance forces had fired in anger. But the strike was merely a pinprick. In fact, this puny response—although stimulating angry protests from the Serbs' would-be protectors in Moscow—merely encouraged subsequent Serb aggression. NATO, without America taking the lead, was incapable of assertive action.

At this time, Bill Clinton was still opposed even to a unilateral lifting of the arms embargo to help the embattled Muslims. The President welcomed the UN "green light" for limited air attacks but he did not want "others to use a unilateral abandonment of the Bosnia embargo as an excuse to disregard the embargoes we supported in Haiti, Libya, and Iraq." What the administration could do was to help negotiate an agreement between the Bosnian Muslims and the Croatians. This would finally stop the fighting between them. The Presidents of Bosnia and Croatia signed the pact in the White House.

But the Serb attacks continued. Certain that the feckless response by the Western powers was no barrier to their grasping more territory, engaging in hideous war crimes against combatants and civilians as they imposed their will on weaker foes, in 1995 the Bosnian Serbs finally went too far.

In March, they tightened the blockade around Sarajevo, and as CNN and other Western media aimed their cameras, Serb snipers in the surrounding hills fired down on innocent men, women, and children in the city. In May, after NATO air forces, still under UN control, made limited strikes on the Serb stronghold of Pale, Serbian forces retaliated by seizing UN peacekeepers and chaining them to ammunition dumps as hostages against further air attacks.

In early July, Bosnian Serb troops, under the command of the ruthless General Ratko Mladić (who would be indicted—along with Radovan Karadžić—by the Hague International War Crimes Tribunal for genocide) overran two UN safe areas, Zepa and Srebrenica. The towns were filled with Muslim refugees from surrounding areas. In Srebrenica, civilians sought protection in the UN compound. But the few hundred Dutch UN troops, uniformed in their blue peacekeeper helmets, outnumbered and vastly outgunned by 2,000 Serb soldiers equipped with tanks and armored personnel carriers, proved helpless.

After two Dutch F-16 jets dropped a few bombs and the Serbs threatened to kill Dutch troops and French hostages unless they stopped, the "peacekeepers" meekly cooperated as Muslim men and boys were separated from their families. Many women were sent on buses to Muslim areas but other young women and girls had been forced into camps, where they were tortured, raped, and sexually abused, sometimes as their mothers watched. The men and boys were taken to killing grounds where they were executed over open pits. More than 7,000 died in the Srebrenica massacre. "You must kill everyone!" the Bosnian Serb commander exclaimed in a radio transmission intercepted by the West. "We don't need anyone alive." It seemed incomprehensible that this could be happening in Europe only four decades after the end of the Holocaust.

Cleary, the cowed European troops could not defend themselves, much less the Muslims. Now there was even momentum for withdrawal of UN forces from Bosnia, a pathetic response to the humiliations they had suffered. It was obvious that something had to be done. The United States loosened the arms embargo on the Bosnians and Croatians. Foreign and defense ministers from Europe and North America were called to a meeting in London where the ludicrous "dual key" system, in which the United Nations and its overly cautious Secretary General Boutros-Ghali had foiled effective use of airpower, was changed. (It would not be long before the United States played the key role in replacing Boutros-Ghali with new Secretary General Kofi Annan.) A "line in the sand" was drawn around the enclave of Gorazde, the first time that NATO had indicated that there was a place where it would make a stand. And the Russian representative promised cooperation, if Russia would have a "dignified and meaningful" role in the peacekeeping operation once NATO had forced the Serbs into negotiations.

Bill Clinton was ambivalent about the use of American power no longer. The President had resolved that the United States would act alone if the British, French, and Germans did not want to act with it. His National Security team supported the move. Speaker of the House Newt Gingrich, at the height of his power that summer, did not. After observing that Srebrenica was the worst humiliation for the Western democracies since the 1930s, Gingrich insisted that "there are twenty ways to solve this problem without involving a single American directly in this thing."

Clinton told Tony Lake, "I am risking my presidency." But the United States was taking ownership of the outcome in Bosnia. The President said to his advisers, "If we let this moment slip away, we're history."

In early August, the Croatians launched a major offensive to retake Krajina, and the Croatian Serbs were abandoned by Milošević, who did not send heavy units of the national army from Belgrade to help defend this Serb enclave in Croat territory. This was the first defeat in four years for any Serb forces. Was the balance of power shifting in these Balkan lands? Clinton decided to make one last effort at negotiations to end the conflict between the Bosnians and Milošević before using American airpower. He sent a team headed by Richard Holbrooke to Zagreb, Belgrade, and Sarajevo to sound out the leaders of all the combatant states.

Holbrooke was a veteran statesman who had served in Vietnam. He was in private life when Clinton made him Ambassador to Germany and, while unhappy that he had not been offered a more senior post, agreed to return to Washington as Undersecretary of State for European Affairs. A forceful, articulate presence, he long had favored lifting the arms embargo and had criticized what he felt was America's weak and ineffectual policy in Bosnia. Now, after visiting the Croatian and Serbian capitals and being told that General Mladić would not guarantee safe arrival at the Sarajevo airport, Holbrooke had to lead his diplomatic team—in two vehicles—over Mount Igman, on the most dangerous road in Europe. General Wesley Clark suggested Holbrooke ride with him in a Humvee, to see how it was "better than the jeeps you were used to in Vietnam." Three senior figures from the Pentagon, the National Security Council, and the State Department rode with aides and troops in a French armored personnel carrier. This was the vehicle that slipped off the mountain road and down a ravine, killing several, including the three American diplomats.

Days later in Washington, immediately following an emotional memorial service in which the President said the three men "made reason their weapon, freedom their cause, and peace their goal," Clinton and his foreign/military policy team discussed the final outlines of a resolution to the crisis. Newspaper headlines now announced: "U.S. Officials Say Bosnian Serbs Face NATO Attack if Talks Fail." When the Serb response was a mortar shell into the heart of Sarajevo that killed thirty-eight people and wounded eighty-five, Strobe Talbott called Holbrooke, saying he believed a military response to this latest outrage was essential. The head of the negotiating team agreed that "this was the most important test of American leadership since the end of the Cold War."

It was August 30. Bill Clinton authorized Operation Deliberate Force. From the aircraft carrier *Theodore Roosevelt* in the Adriatic and from U.S. Air Force bases in Italy, sixty American aircraft pounded Serb positions around Sarajevo. When French and British artillery from the Rapid Reaction force joined in, targeting Serb barracks near the capital, NATO, led by the United States, had finally intervened to punish the barbarous aggressors and bring an end to the war.

The bombing worked. Holbrooke was right. While he had opposed the air campaign against North Vietnam back in the Seventies, he argued that not only were American objectives different this time, but the Bosnian Serbs were not the Vietcong or the NVA and Belgrade was not Hanoi. The Bosnian Serbs were poorly trained bullies and criminals and would not stand up to NATO air strikes.

Milošević now was anxious to meet Holbrooke, who flew to Belgrade and found the Serbian leader ready for peace talks. For sixteen months, he had not cooperated in getting Bosnian Serbs to participate in negotiations, claiming he could not speak for Karadžić or Mladić. Now Milošević offered to lead the Serbian effort himself. Holbrooke made it clear that those Bosnian Serbs, indicted war criminals, not only could have no part in the upcoming talks, but would be arrested if they set foot on American soil.

In rapid order, the siege of Sarajevo was lifted, there was a brief Western offensive to retake territory lost to the Serbs, and a peace conference was arranged. It would be held in the United States, at the Wright Patterson Air Force Base in Dayton, Ohio, in November.

It took the tough, knowledgeable, and relentless leader of the American negotiating group, Richard Holbrooke, to bully Milošević and the others into agreeing to the Dayton Accords. But Holbrooke would credit Bill Clinton with stepping in at the decisive moments to achieve success. The document contained a general framework for peace in the contested region, mandated a continuing cease-fire, ensured recognition of Bosnia, established borders, and provided for free elections, a constitution, and a banking system. It contained provisions for refugees and displaced persons, called for an investigation of human rights violations, and established an international police task force, including American troops.

Implementation would not be easy and there would be setbacks along the way. But when President Clinton, his family, members of Congress, and his defeated rival in the late presidential election, Bob Dole, arrived in Bosnia in late 1997, it was clear that Dayton had been a success. Peace had come to a former war zone and the United States was committed to not walking away from the state it had played the critical role in rescuing.

Bill Clinton had come to the White House focusing on his domestic agenda and the imperative need to revive the American economy. The end of the Cold War had seemed to offer a respite from major foreign policy crises, allowing him to concentrate on his efforts to build the bridge to the next century. But beginning with Somalia in the first months of office, he had been forced to deal with a new era of bitter ethnic and religious conflicts in small states.

He faced political opponents at home who vociferously opposed American involvement in these matters and blamed him for the deaths at Black Hawk Down. Public opinion did not support foreign interventions. He was acutely aware of recent history, how the abyss of Vietnam—when the

United States last became militarily involved in a civil war—had devoured the domestic agenda of Lyndon Johnson. He knew not only that committing ground forces in these new conflicts would create a political firestorm but that key players in the Pentagon felt that using airpower alone would be ineffectual, merely serving as a precursor to "boots on the ground." So, he had been reluctant to use American forces in Haiti, Bosnia, and Rwanda.

The result was scathing criticism for his failure to act to protect the vulnerable, an image of weakness and indecision as a foreign policy strategist and military leader. That began to change in Haiti in 1994. It would be finally put to rest in Bosnia in 1995. There would be need to use force again in his White House years ahead, but Bill Clinton now demonstrated new mastery in his role as commander-in-chief.

And in foreign affairs, he and his administration could refocus energy on other matters. In September, Hillary Clinton led the American delegation to Beijing for the United Nations Fourth World Conference on Women. There had been growing tensions with China over the sale of missiles to Pakistan, Chinese military exercises in the Taiwan Strait, and ongoing human rights abuses. But in a powerful speech that had resonance across the world, she exclaimed that "on the eve of a new millennium, it is time to break our silence . . . to say here in Beijing that it is no longer acceptable to discuss women's rights as separate from human rights." Meanwhile, the President would turn to new diplomatic efforts to resolve ancient conflicts and address the menace of weapons of mass destruction.[9]

Dealing with one of these conflicts became more difficult even as the peace arrangements for Bosnia were being shaped at Dayton. On the third day of that meeting, Clinton received word of Yitzhak Rabin's assassination. The President had been deeply involved in efforts to end the Israeli-Palestinian conflict and create a "two state solution" to the crisis. He had become very close to the Israeli leader. When Tony Lake gave him the news, "it was as if somebody had punched him in the stomach." He was "openly weeping," said a press secretary. A few hours later, in a television statement from the Rose Garden, he said, "Yitzhak Rabin was my partner and my friend. I admired him and I loved him very much." And with his death, the extraordinarily complicated effort to bring peace to this enduring conflict in the Middle East, the flashpoint for anger and violence throughout the region, entered a new and uncertain phase.

Rabin, the legendary Israeli military figure, had taken great risks in reaching out to Yasir Arafat, the leader of the Palestinian Liberation Organization (PLO). In January 1993, at Oslo, Norway, the two had met in secret and shaped the Oslo Accords, a landmark agreement in which Israel would withdraw from parts of the Gaza Strip and the West Bank and be replaced by a Palestinian national authority. There would be a five-year interim period during which further transfers of land to the Palestinian Authority would occur and mutual trust built for negotiating a final status agreement. This would involve the most difficult issues: Jerusalem, claims of Palestinian refugees, the fate of Israeli settlements in the West Bank, Israel's security needs, water rights, and final borders.

Clinton had not been involved in the Oslo meeting. But he had already bonded with Rabin, whom he met for the first time as a Democratic candidate, when the newly elected Israeli Prime Minister visited Washington in August 1992. Martin Indyk, Clinton's Middle Eastern affairs adviser during the campaign (and named, in 1995, Ambassador to Israel), had told him that if elected, he had a good chance of helping to shape several peace agreements in the troubled region. "I want to do that," Bill Clinton had replied. Later, Indyk would recall: "He made a commitment to be the peacemaker in the Middle East . . . and right up to the last day in office he was pursuing those agreements. He made it a priority."

When Rabin called to tell him of the peace agreement in Oslo, Clinton pledged financial support and worked to gain the commitment of other countries, including Saudi Arabia, to the peace process ahead. More important, he persuaded the Israeli leader and the PLO chief to come to the White House for an extraordinary signing ceremony. It was more than a symbolic occasion, for it was, as Clinton put it, "a gamble for both of them." That Rabin would stand next to Arafat, whom he held personally responsible for the deaths of many of his countrymen, was a signal achievement.

Clinton gave a remarkable speech: "A peace of the brave is within our reach. Throughout the Middle East there is a great yearning for the quiet miracle of normal life." Then, standing between them, he watched the historic handshake. Rabin had resisted doing this, but Clinton told him, "The whole world will be watching and the handshake is what they will be looking for." At last, Rabin, sighing, said, "I suppose one does not make peace with one's friends." And after the handshake, he spoke eloquently: "We are destined to live together, on the same soil in the same land. We, the soldiers who have returned from battles stained with blood . . ., say to you today, in a loud and clear voice: Enough of blood and tears. Enough."

After the ceremony, at a private lunch, Clinton asked Rabin why he had decided to support the Oslo Agreement after spending much of his life in uniform. His response: He had come to realize that the territory Israel had occupied since 1967 was no longer necessary to its security but, in fact, was a source of insecurity. If Israel were to hold on to the West Bank permanently, it would have to let Arabs there vote in Israeli elections. If the Palestinians got the right to vote, within decades, Israel would no longer be a Jewish state. If they were denied the right to vote, Israel would no longer be a democracy but an apartheid state.

In 1993, this analysis of the meaning of the West Bank to Israel, Clinton said, was "novel, insightful, and courageous." He had admired Rabin even before meeting him, but that day, "listening to his argument for peace, I had seen greatness. . . . I had never met anyone quite like him and I was determined to help him achieve his dream of peace."

Bill Clinton's efforts to shape an agreement between Israel and Syria did not bear fruit, despite his trips to Damascus—where no American President had been in twenty years—to talk to Syrian strongman Hafez al-Assad. But earlier, in July 1994, King Hussein and Prime Minister Rabin were in Washington for the formal ending of the state of belligerency between Jordan and Israel, committed to negotiating a full peace agreement.

Still, the critical peace issue involved the Palestinians. And there had been movement during the first part of that five-year interim period following the handshake. But in November 1995, after addressing 100,000 people gathered in Tel Aviv to show their support for the Oslo peace process, the 73-year-old Rabin was shot and killed by a 25-year-old Jewish law student, an anti-Oslo zealot, who said the Prime Minister wanted "to give our country to the Arabs." In March 1993, Clinton had told his friend, "You take risks for peace and we'll act to minimize these risks." Now the President was profoundly shaken, and not only by the loss of someone he so admired. One aide noted that "he saw that everything was built around Rabin. . . . How were we going to deal without him?"

Shimon Peres, the foreign minister, became Prime Minister. But he would be defeated (by less than 1 percent of the vote) in an upcoming election. The victor was the right-wing Likud Party leader, Benjamin Netanyahu, who promised to be tough on terrorism and to slow the peace process. American neo-conservatives had been advisers to Likud, and Netanyahu used television ads created by Republican media consultants from New York.

At first, President Clinton was optimistic that the new Prime Minister wanted to maneuver against the "crazies" within his own coalition. But within a year, it seemed clear that "Bibi" Netanyahu, despite his promises, was blocking meaningful progress. There could be no real two-state solution to the Israeli-Palestinian conflict without movement on the West Bank settlements, the status of East Jerusalem, and other critical issues needing resolution before a final status agreement. There was a brief period when Netanyahu appeared more flexible. When Bill Clinton organized a meeting involving him, Arafat, and the King of Jordan at the Wye Conference Center in Maryland in 1998, there was some progress on prisoner exchanges and plans for a link between Gaza and the West Bank. But on the hardest issues, the Israeli did not seem to want a deal. In the end, Bill Clinton recognized that the realization of Yitzhak Rabin's dream, and the creation of peace in the Middle East, would be possible only with another leader of

Israel at the helm. And that would not happen until the last year of Clinton's presidency.[10]

But if the peaceful resolution in one land ravaged by ancient animosities had to be on hold, Bill Clinton found another place to use his skills as peacemaker.

He had been interested in the conflict in Northern Ireland between Catholics and Protestants since "the Troubles" had erupted in 1968, when he was a student at Oxford. During the primary struggle in 1992, after he had addressed a gathering of the Irish American Forum in New York, a law school classmate (a former congressman, Bruce Morrison of Connecticut) organized Irish Americans for Clinton. Clinton would later recall that "I first got involved in the Irish issue because of the politics of New York, but it became one of the great passions of my presidency."

During the campaign, he had promised, if elected, to issue a visa to Gerry Adams, president of Sinn Fein, the political arm of the leading Catholic paramilitary group in Northern Ireland, the Irish Republican Army. This was a controversial proposal. Some in his circle opposed it, insisting that allowing Adams to come to the United States would "reward" him for the IRA's terrorist crimes against British soldiers and Protestants in Northern Ireland.

In office, he decided to issue the visa, despite Warren Christopher's impassioned plea not to do it. The British, believing that Adams was a "deceiver who had no intention of giving up violence," which had included an attempt to assassinate Margaret Thatcher, were furious. But Bill Clinton was willing to reach out to the extremes on both sides to help shape an agreement. It was early 1994, and he would recall long afterward that it was Yitzhak Rabin's remark about not making peace with your friends that played a significant role in his decision. The FBI, one observer noted, "went nuts," and tried to stop it at the State Department. But Clinton was insistent.

Adams made a brief visit and would return again a few months later after Clinton issued a second visa, contingent on Sinn Fein's agreement to discuss the IRA's laying down of arms and acceptance of a truce with the British government. This time, he invited Adams to the White House reception on St. Patrick's Day. Also invited: John Hume, the moderate leader in Northern Ireland, a champion of peaceful change, along with members of other main parties (Protestant and Catholic) in the troubled land, both Unionist and Republican.

A few months later, he selected George Mitchell, recently retired after serving as majority leader in the Senate, as his special representative for the Irish issue. It was an inspired choice. An Irish American supporter would say: "Bill Clinton changed American policy 180 degrees. He went from a policy of hands off to putting America's weight in favor of a peace process."

In November 1995 he flew to Europe and visited London, Dublin, and Belfast. On the eve of this journey, the Prime Ministers of Great Britain and Ireland announced a breakthrough in the Irish peace process, calling for separate talks on arms decommissioning and the resolution of political issues, with all parties, including Sinn Fein, invited to participate. George Mitchell would chair the international panel overseeing the process, which finally would lead to the historic Good Friday Agreement in 1998.

In Britain, Prime Minister John Major said that Clinton's trip helped to "concentrate the mind" on the peace efforts under way. In Northern Ireland, where he was the first American President ever to visit, tens of thousands filled Belfast's Donegall Square, shouting "We want Bill!" He met with leaders of both sides but his message was the same everywhere. In Derry, he asked the crowd: "Are you going to be someone who defines yourself in terms of what you are against or what you are for?"

Even when his work for peace suffered a setback, as in February 1996, when the IRA broke its seventeen-month truce, setting off a bomb in London's Dockland district, he was not discouraged. It would be another seventeen months until the IRA reinstated the cease-fire. But as an Irish supporter observed, "He never took the reverses personally, it was always future oriented, continuing to work on the project."

The effort of all parties—from Great Britain, the Republic of Ireland, and both sides of the bitter divide in Northern Ireland—would be realized in the agreement signed on April 10, 1998. This provided for a Northern Ireland assembly with a power-sharing executive and new cross-border institutions involving the Irish Republic. It was a multiparty agreement binding all participants to "exclusively democratic and peaceful means of resolving differences on political issues" and to oppose "any use or threat of force by others for any purpose."

The Good Friday Agreement was subject to a referendum in both Ireland and Northern Ireland. The day before the vote, Bill Clinton delivered a radio address to the people of Northern Ireland, pledging America's support if they voted for a "lasting peace for yourselves and your children." The next day, with 56 percent voting in Ireland, 94 percent said yes. In Northern Ireland, with a massive turnout of 81 percent, the yes vote for peace was 71 percent.

In September, in the midst of the Lewinsky scandal, just as Kenneth Starr was sending his 445-page report to Congress alleging impeachable offenses, Bill and Hillary Clinton once again visited Northern Ireland. There had been violence by militants opposing the agreement, and Clinton, again demonstrating his ability to focus on the responsibilities of his office in the midst of an extraordinary personal and public crisis, eloquently addressed a large "Gathering for Peace" in Armagh. There would be trouble ahead across the months in implementing the accords, but Clinton—along with Mitchell—would play a role in dealing with the anger and misunderstandings.

Shortly after Thanksgiving 1999, there would be news that a new Northern Ireland government was formed, with parties from both sides in key cabinet roles. It was, as President Clinton put it, "unthinkable not long before."

Certainly Bill Clinton did not work miracles to bring peace to Northern Ireland. But he played a critical role in having the United States, with its enormous political and financial power, involved. His efforts, one historian wrote, "fundamentally altered the equation and provided a catalyst" for the historic agreement.[11]

Still, peacemaking in smaller nations confronting old religious and ethnic tensions would be only part of the foreign policy issues confronting the leader of the great power. Dealing with the threat of weapons of mass destruction was a continuing concern throughout his administration.

There was some progress here. Belarus and Kazakhstan joined Ukraine in 1994 in destroying or transferring to Russia the nuclear weapons they had inherited from the USSR. Along with the successor states from the breakups of Yugoslavia and Czechoslovakia, they would now sign the Treaty on the Non-Proliferation of Nuclear Weapons (NPT), which had been implemented since 1970 but was extended indefinitely in May 1995. Many other nations joined in the late Nineties, including Argentina, Chile, and Brazil.

But keeping this nuclear genie inside the bottle would not be easy. Pakistan, angered by yet another nuclear test in bitter rival India—which had detonated its first device in 1974—announced possession of a nuclear weapon in 1998. And earlier, in the first year of the Clinton White House, North Korea had become the first country to announce plans to withdraw from NPT (to which it had become a signatory in 1985) and from the nuclear safeguards regime instituted by the International Atomic Energy Agency. They refused IAEA inspectors access to the nuclear complex at Yongbyon, and there was evidence that they were building an even larger reactor, capable of producing plutonium for ten to twelve nuclear bombs a year.

This was unacceptable. The Clinton team, although first endorsing economic sanctions, was willing to use military strikes at the reactors to keep the insulated, brutal, duplicitous, and dangerous regime of dictator Kim Il Sung—who had pushed his country into a shooting war with the United States four decades earlier—from getting the bomb.

There was an opening for a diplomatic solution in June 1994 when an intimidated North Korea invited former President Jimmy Carter to visit. Kim now said he would not expel the inspectors, and Clinton replied that if North Korea was prepared to freeze its nuclear program, we would return to talks. Just as negotiations began in Geneva, with Ambassador Robert Galucci leading the U.S. delegation, Kim Il Sung died. The "Great Leader's" death was but a minor setback. The "Agreed Framework" would stipulate that North Korea would adhere to the NPT and permit IAEA inspections, outlining specific steps for it to freeze and later dismantle its nuclear program. In turn, the United States and its allies agreed to help North Korea cope with immediate fuel shortages and pay for construction of civilian nuclear plants.

The crisis was resolved. Only after Clinton left office would it be revealed that in 1998, North Korea began to violate the spirit of the agreement made four years before by procuring highly enriched uranium in a laboratory. It was perhaps enough for one or two bombs. But the plutonium program ended in 1994 was much larger than this later effort. If it had proceeded, and it did not, weapons-grade material for dozens of weapons would have been produced by 2000.[12]

There would be other challenges. Aiding Russian efforts to secure the vast numbers of obsolescent tactical nuclear weapons (and amounts of fissionable material) created in the old Soviet Union was a priority. But so too was reducing the number of thermonuclear bombs and warheads in the modern arsenals of the two great powers themselves. This was harder to achieve.

The final enactment of the second Strategic Arms Reduction Treaty (START II), negotiated at the end of the previous administration, would not happen on Bill Clinton's watch. This treaty put a ceiling of 3,500 strategic warheads for each side. It called for "de-MIRVing" land-based intercontinental ballistic missiles, which meant no multiple, independently targeted re-entry vehicles (MIRVs) atop the ICBMs, a development that had enormously increased the number and lethality of deployed weapons. But the Russian parliament, with powerful anti-Yeltsin forces making their influence felt, would not vote for ratification. The President had wanted to move on to START III, with even further cuts to the vast nuclear arsenals of the superpowers. "What's going on here?" he asked in a meeting of defense aides in fall 1994. "The Cold War's supposed to be over. What do we need this much overkill for?" But his efforts to have the United States push forward on its own faced Defense Department objections to cutbacks in the number of U.S. strategic weapons. And Congress now refused to allow unilateral reduction below the levels in START I in the absence of START II ratification in Russia.

Powerful Republican opposition in Congress also damaged the President's efforts to preserve a critical element in early arms control efforts, the ABM treaty, which essentially eliminated antiballistic missiles (ABMs). Agreed to in the early Seventies, the ABM treaty was a key element in ensuring that thermonuclear war would result in mutual assured destruction. It did so by eliminating the possibility that ABMs, which no expert believed provided a secure umbrella of defense against the arsenals of the superpowers, might allow one of them to miscalculate and actually use its fearsome offensive weapons, in the belief it could survive and "win" a thermonuclear war.

President Ronald Reagan's Strategic Defense Initiative in the Eighties, a scheme for space-based antimissile laser weapons, termed "Star Wars" by critics—who recognized it as a wildly expensive but technologically infeasible effort—had threatened the treaty. But it had mesmerized Republicans. They believed it played the critical role, despite its demonstrable failure as a functioning ABM system, in defeating the USSR.

Bill Clinton was committed to reducing ABM spending, calling only for a theater missile defense (TMD) against shorter-range rockets, such as might be deployed by "rogue states" like Libya, Iran, Iraq, and North Korea. However, even this TMD alarmed the Russians, and Clinton responded by promising to adhere to the ABM treaty, insisting that these new defensive weapons posed no threat to Soviet-era ICBMs. But in mid-1998, when North Korea attempted (and failed) to launch a multistage rocket which in theory could reach American shores, the Senate and House passed bills calling for the United States to deploy an antimissile system capable of "defending the territory of the United States." Now the TMD would become the NMD (National Missile Defense). In the last years of his administration, Bill Clinton and his advisers would try to persuade the Russians to accept it (still focused on rogue states) and maintain the ABM treaty. However, with Boris Yeltsin out of office and Vladimir Putin in during Bill Clinton's final White House year, no such agreement could be negotiated. And in the subsequent administration of George W. Bush, the United States would end its adherence to the ABM treaty.[13]

It was with some of these rogue states that the Clinton team would have to shape other responses to their aggressive actions. At the start of the administration, there was a policy of "dual containment" of two dangerous dictatorial regimes, Iran and Iraq. Both were considered, as Madeleine Albright asserted, "repeat violators of international law," undemocratic and hostile to U.S. interests. "Our policy was to isolate them . . . deny them the capacity to develop advanced arms."

There was a special effort to pressure Russia to not help Iran develop nuclear arms and ballistic missile technology. In the first year of the administration, the issue was Moscow's contract to build a reactor, which, if completed, would contribute to a covert nuclear weapons program. Vice President Gore, Strobe Talbott, and Sandy Berger worked to block this. Yeltsin and Prime Minister Victor Chernomyrdin—who had a close working relationship with Al Gore—seemed responsive.

But in the next two years it became clear that the Russian minister for atomic energy was bypassing his own government's export controls and preventing newer ones. He was cutting deals with Iran to accelerate its nuclear program by offering the Iranians gas centrifuges and four nuclear reactors. A Yeltsin aide insisted that the minister was "out of control" and his boss was unaware of his action. Yeltsin now promised to publicly announce that Russia would give Iran no militarily useful technology.

Yet problems still remained. The Clinton team discovered that Russian commercial firms, spun off from the old Soviet military-industrial complex, were providing Iranians with materials useful in making ballistic missiles. Finally, after more negotiations, the Russians "put in place new controls," Talbott noted, "tightened existing ones, and cracked down on the offenders."

Even while acting to restrict its military power, Bill Clinton worked to improve ties with Iran. He had inherited almost fifteen years of troubled relations with a state with which the United States had no diplomatic contact since Islamic revolutionaries had come to power amidst the U.S. embassy takeover and the hostage crisis that marked the end of the Carter years.

The President was aware of Iran's role in terrorist acts in the Middle East. In 1995, he issued an executive order banning most trade between U.S. businesses and the Iranian government and had declared Iran a "state sponsor of terrorism." In 1996, when a truck bomb exploded at the U.S. Air Force facility in Khobar, Saudi Arabia, killing 19 Americans and wounding over 350, intelligence indicated that it was the work of a Saudi Shiite group with links to Iran's Revolutionary Guards. The White House responded by hardening U.S. installations in the Gulf, deploying U.S. warplanes to remote air bases in the Saudi desert, and taking targeted actions through the CIA against Revolutionary Guards and Iranian intelligence personnel around the world.

But this did not prevent Clinton from reaching out to Mohammad Khatami, after this moderate's surprise victory in Iran's 1997 presidential elections. Khatami had said, on CNN, that he was open to a new relationship, wanting to bring down the "wall of mistrust" with America. Over the next three years, Clinton's national security aides sent a series of public messages affirming interest in improving relations. There were discussions in multilateral forums and contests between U.S. and Iranian wrestling and soccer teams. But Khatami, restricted by the powerful presence of Ayatollah Khamenei and the other religious leaders who controlled ultimate power in his land, could go no further. Still, by the end of the second Clinton term, the United States and Iran had moved, in the words of Bruce Riedel, Clinton team member tasked with reaching out to the Iranians, "from the precipice of armed conflict to an indirect dialogue." While the climate had improved, policy differences remained wide, but a new effort to defuse tensions between Washington and Teheran had begun.[14]

Relations with Iraq would be a different matter. Less than three months in office, Bill Clinton was told that authorities in Kuwait had thwarted an assassination attempt against former President Bush during his visit to commemorate the second anniversary of the Gulf War. The FBI concluded that Iraqi intelligence agents were responsible and the White House ordered an attack—with sixteen cruise missiles fired from naval units—on the Iraqi Intelligence Service's headquarters in Baghdad.

Saddam Hussein ran a bandit regime. After its invasion of Kuwait had resulted in a crushing defeat at the hands of the American-led alliance, Iraq continued to thwart efforts to assure compliance with its agreement to eliminate all nuclear, chemical, and biological weapons programs. This stonewalling of UN weapons inspectors (and the terrorizing of domestic rivals) led to severe economic sanctions.

In 1994, frustrated by the sanctions, Iraq mobilized over 60,000 troops on the Kuwait border, but when the United States deployed overwhelming firepower in Operation Vigilant Warrior, Saddam Hussein backed down. In fall 1996, when he attempted a military offensive against Kurds, the United States launched a massive attack with fighter bombers and missiles from a carrier battle group as well as Air Force B-52s.

The Iraq tyrant would prove an intractable problem throughout Clinton's White House years. Saddam tried to appeal to international public opinion, arguing that half a million children had died as a result of the sanctions. But of course, the United States was not embargoing medicine or food; in fact, it was allowing Baghdad to sell limited amounts of oil in order to buy these commodities. But the dictator would not spend money on humanitarian goods. He built lavish palaces for himself, his murderous sons, and trusted aides.

In late 1997, the Iraq leader again blocked UN weapons experts and demanded American inspectors be fired. But Clinton was firm; the UN inspectors must be allowed to resume work with unfettered access. Once again, there was a military buildup, with more ships gathering in the Gulf. Secretary Albright visited capitals throughout the region and worked with Russian Foreign Minister Primakov, who had ties with Saddam, to relieve this crisis. But months later, there would be another. This time, the UN Secretary General, Kofi Annan, stepped in to assure continued inspection. Not for long. Unsuccessful in dividing the UN Security Council, in November 1998 Saddam abruptly shut down all international inspection and monitoring activities.

The result was Operation Desert Fox. Lasting seventy hours, 650 bomber air sorties and 400 cruise missiles hit a wide variety of security-related targets. Significant damage was inflicted on Iraq's command and control infrastructure.

Now, with UN and IAEA inspectors no longer in Iraq, U.S. policy shifted from containment with inspections to "containment plus." In practice, this meant "keeping Saddam in his box," as Secretary of State Albright put it, by stricter enforcement of existing no-fly zones over northern and southern Iraq, frequent attacks on anti-aircraft and radar facilities, and smarter and tougher sanctions to cause "Saddam more harm and his people less." This limited Saddam's options and extended his isolation while encouraging his internal opponents. And the President signed the Iraq Liberation Act, which advocated a policy of "regime change" in Iraq, but it specifically did not argue for an invasion with American military forces.[15]

While some congressional Republicans assailed Bill Clinton for the Desert Fox air campaign, with Trent Lott and Dick Armey complaining he had ordered the attacks in order to delay the House vote on impeachment, other right-wing critics of the President were insisting he did not go far enough. These were the people who would lead the United States into the Iraq war three years after Clinton left office.

In 1997, the Project for the New American Century, a neo-conservative think tank, was created in Washington to promote a militantly hawkish foreign policy. It was based on the belief—as one friendly pundit would put it—that this was a special "moment in history" for an America that ran a "uniquely benign imperium." After the collapse of the Soviet Union and before the rise of China, the United States was the dominant power in the world, with no global rival. There were rich possibilities for shaping policy in this environment, but the PNAC members, assailing "the incoherent policies" of the Clinton administration, warned that "we are in danger of squandering the opportunity."

William Kristol was a central figure in creating PNAC, but joining him, Robert Kagan, and other neo-con intellectuals were important figures from earlier and future GOP administrations. Paul Wolfowitz and Richard Perle, key players in the Defense Department under both George H. W. Bush and his son, were involved, along with Donald Rumsfeld, Dick Cheney, John Bolton, Douglas Feith, and I. Lewis Libby, among others. Many of them signed a widely circulated letter to President Clinton in January 1998, calling for the removal of Saddam Hussein and his regime, which "now needs to become the aim of American foreign policy." They authored books and articles calling for war against "the terror master." They wrote of lurking dangers even in an age of American military dominance, and were alarmed at a "steadily eroding policy of containment" of Saddam and the threat of weapons of mass destruction in his hands.

Of course, Clinton's policy of "containment plus" was working, as would become clear when no WMDs were found after the second Iraq war. (Some might argue that the brief but very powerful Desert Fox attack played a key role in persuading Saddam to abandon any new efforts to produce such weapons.) And an American invasion of Iraq, which Bill Clinton rejected, would have found no support at home or abroad in the late Nineties. But the hawks of the PNAC wanted to strike Saddam, as part of their larger agenda for change in the region. They found an excuse after 9/11. The costs and consequences of that invasion, which led to the long, deadly struggle with insurgents, remain a matter of controversy.[16]

Even as the White House was being attacked by the Republican right, it was dealing with objections from Russia about the Iraq bombing campaign. The Duma, by a vote of 394 to 1, passed a resolution denouncing the United States as an "international terrorist." Boris Yeltsin said America was "crudely violating" the UN charter; Talbott called his overheated rhetoric a "replay of what we'd experienced over Bosnia."

Managing relations with Yeltsin's Russia continued to be a challenge for Bill Clinton and his team. One major problem was NATO expansion. In April 1993, the Presidents of Poland, the Czech Republic, and Hungary made the case for their countries' admission to NATO directly to Clinton in Washington, when they visited for the opening of the Holocaust Museum. Yeltsin strongly opposed enlargement, seeing it as a strategy for moving the line of Western influence in Europe to the east and leaving Russia, a weakened and potentially unstable country following the collapse of the Soviet Union, isolated. He would resist expansion for years. He was not alone. In the United States, George Kennan, the famous diplomatic icon who had shaped the containment policy decades before, called enlargement the "greatest mistake in Western policy in the entire post–Cold War era." Liberal columnists also termed it "reckless."

But in 1994, President Clinton announced U.S. backing for a gradual process of enlarging NATO; in 1997 invitations were to be issued at the Alliance summit. Now, as Albright put it, "we had to walk a tightrope to keep faith with Europe's new democracies while not recreating an old enemy." Key members of Clinton's national security team, including Berger, Deputy National Security Council director James Steinberg, and Tom Donlon were playing critical roles pushing the project, and Bill Clinton used his personal ties with Yeltsin to advance the process.

He could deal with the Russian leader's rants even when Yeltsin was inebriated. (Save for one meeting when the two leaders were at FDR's home in Hyde Park, the Russian was never drunk during face-to-face sessions, but sometimes—with the time difference between Washington and the Kremlin—he was during international phone calls.) Clinton never became angry or self-righteous, he did not formalize opposition. Talbott observed that this was his "overall approach to diplomacy." His reply to almost any proposition would be, "I agree with that," even when he did not. "This default to agreeableness was not just a reflection of his desire to be liked, it was also a means, both calculated and intuitive, of disarming those he was trying to persuade, of pretending to begin a conversation on common ground in order to get there before it was over."

On NATO expansion, he got there. The President and his team dealt with a myriad of Russian objections, and Strobe Talbott would compare their negotiating strategy to a dental root canal: Moscow wanted the ordeal so painful that there would be no further rounds of enlargement. Madeleine Albright told Yeltsin, "Mr. President, if as you say, there is a new Russia, there is also a new NATO, not one of we versus you or you versus us, but one where we are on the same side." But she said that "Yeltsin believed anything was possible" if only he could talk one-on-one with his friend, the man whose name he pronounced "Beel." (And this friend never made the Russian believe he was doing the United States a favor, but persuaded him he was acting in his own interest in reaching agreements. Indeed it was Clinton who had encouraged Yeltsin to reduce internal tensions in Russia by giving housing to displaced former Soviet officers, pulled out of the Balkans after the collapse of the USSR.)

While Clinton would not give Russia the veto over NATO actions that Yeltsin requested, he offered to give Moscow a voice, a NATO–Russia Charter. And when Yeltsin asked for private assurance of no further NATO expansion involving former captive Soviet republics, Clinton said, "I'm not going to veto any country's eligibility, much less let you or anyone else do so." After a heated exchange with his aides, finally Yeltsin shrugged, "Okay, Beel, but I tried." In 1999, the Czech Republic, Hungary, and Poland were formally admitted to NATO.[17]

Relations between the former antagonists in the Cold War would be sorely tried once more in the last years of Clinton's presidency. Even the friendly "Boris" and "Beel" niceties would not work for this one. The issue was Kosovo and yet another challenge to peace presented by Slobodan Milošević, still seething from the humiliation in Dayton.

Kosovo was a southern province of the former Yugoslavia. Although ethnic Albanian Kosovars made up 90 percent of its population, Milošević insisted on Serbian control. In 1989 he had taken away the substantial measure of autonomy that Marshal Tito had given the Connecticut-sized region in 1974 and sent in his military to impose Serb rule. During the wars of independence involving the Slovenes, Croats, and Bosnian Muslims—and throughout the crisis in Bosnia ending with the American-led NATO air campaign in 1995—the Kosovo issue had simmered.

But in early 1998, in response to attacks by an Albanian resistance group calling itself the Kosovo Liberation Army (KLA), there was a wave of repression by ruthless Serbian paramilitary forces. In one small town,

Prekaz, women, children, and the elderly were victims, whole families were burnt alive in their houses and thousands were forced to flee. When the KLA launched a "summer offensive" in July, the guerrillas were soon overwhelmed by the powerful armored units of Milošević's Serb-dominated Yugoslavian army—which seized control of large areas of the province. In a campaign of intimidation, the Serbians killed at least 1,000 and drove 350,000 civilians into the mountains and woods. Their plight immediately created a new humanitarian dilemma.

This new Balkan crisis was a complicated matter. Kosovo had special historical meaning for Serbians, dating back to the Ottoman victory in the fourteenth century that had led to loss of Serb sovereignty for almost five centuries. And the KLA—with a widening appeal, particularly among jobless youths—had itself used murderous violence in its campaign against Serbs. But Milošević now seemed determined to crush Albanian opponents and use ethnic cleansing tactics, vividly remembered from the tragic scenes in Bosnia. Economic sanctions alone could not stop him. The President decided to push for a NATO Alliance decision on Kosovo.

Acting through the UN Security Council would not work. The Russians said they would veto any resolution on authorizing military action. The very idea of NATO authorizing use of force led Yeltsin to be "nearly unhinged on the subject of Kosovo." Over the phone, Strobe Talbott recalled, Yeltsin "raged for twelve minutes, pausing neither for interpretation into English nor for Clinton's reply." Repeatedly he used the Russian word for "inadmissible" and finally just hung up on the President. "Well," said Bill Clinton, "he hasn't done that before. I guess we've got a real problem here."

Bombing Serbians presented menacing dangers for Yeltsin and his team. His foreign minister told Secretary Albright, "Madeleine, don't you understand we have many Kosovos in Russia." He was referring to Chechnya, another Muslim-majority province with its own insurrectionary forces threatening to secede from a nation with a Slavic Orthodox majority.

The anti-American nationalists in Moscow who continued to seek Yeltsin's overthrow would be immensely strengthened. The Russian leader exclaimed that after all he had done to "turn my people toward the West," it would be "practically impossible" to keep them headed in that direction. (In fact, during one moment in the Balkan crises, Yeltsin, fearing his top brass had gone rogue, called Bill Clinton and said that the "the world is in peril" and proposed meeting secretly on a submarine.)

Nonetheless, in October, under American urging, NATO formally authorized the use of force. At first, Milošević seemed to be cowed and told Richard Holbrooke that he was ready to reduce troops and police in Kosovo and allow refugees and displaced persons to return to their homes. But he could not be trusted. In mid-December, Serb forces killed dozens of Albanians and the conflict heated up again. With Madeleine Albright now playing a critical role, there was a January meeting with key figures in the U.S. National Security establishment. Some of the principals expressed doubts about a peacekeeping force with U.S. troops on the ground in Kosovo; they did not want to support a second major mission in the Balkans and feared getting caught in the middle of a civil war. But Albright persevered. It was not for nothing that *Time* magazine would later call Kosovo "Madeleine's War."

She called a meeting in Rambouillet, France, with foreign ministers from the major European powers and factional leaders of the Albanian Kosovars. After difficult negotiations, Clinton's team got most of what it wanted; Milošević had to agree to the provisions or face a full-scale aerial assault. The terms: the restoration of Kosovo's autonomy for an interim period until its final status was determined by a referendum; all Serbian troops and police out of the province; and the settlement to be ensured by a NATO peacekeeping force of at least 30,000, with full participation of the U.S. military. In Washington, after strenuous efforts, Congress supported the President's plan to send troops to implement the agreement and use bombing if necessary. But most Republicans voted no as the measure passed the House 219 to 191 and Senate 58 to 41.

Milošević would not agree. His response: "We will have nothing to do with an outside military force. We will deal with the terrorist threat in our own way. And it will not take long."

Knowing his military was vastly inferior to NATO, he believed he could withstand the bombing longer than the West could keep it going. He thought the Russians would be supportive, and perhaps he hoped for a "reverse CNN" effect on world public opinion: television pictures of bombing victims in Belgrade underscoring his argument that there was "blood on the hands" of the United States and NATO. (It is not clear whether he thought that Clinton's domestic troubles—and the political firestorm in Washington—would help him as well.)

He was right about Russia's response once bombing began. For Boris Yeltsin, this was a bigger problem even than Bosnia. If events got out of hand, there was the specter of a ground war in Europe. The hardliners in the Kremlin were seething at the image of NATO strutting about the world. In another impassioned call, Yeltsin practically shouted in the phone to Bill Clinton: "Don't push Russia into this war! You know what Russia is! You know what it has at its disposal!" This was a warning of the danger of nuclear confrontation between the superpowers. But in a calm voice and with a sensitive, reasoned argument suggesting how the United States and Russia could work together, Clinton soothed Yeltsin, who finally concluded, "I think our discussion was candid, constructive, and balanced."

The bombing assault began. In charge was Wesley Clark, now a four-star general and the senior American and NATO commander in Europe. He knew that Milošević was amassing troops to solve the Kosovo problem his own way, through a combination of mass killing and mass eviction. Clark was a shrewd, tough leader. He argued that airpower would be no magic bullet. "It we start this thing, it'll be a long haul."

It was. The Serb plan was called Operation Horseshoe, and 40,000 troops and paramilitaries, with 300 tanks and 1,500 artillery pieces, poured into Kosovo for a ruthless campaign to empty the province of "Albanians" and create new facts "on the ground" before NATO could make its impact. Tens of thousands of Albanian Kosovars were driven over the border into Albania and Macedonia, threatening stability in these fragile lands and creating an even more gigantic refugee crisis. By April the United Nations reported that 850,000 people, mostly Albanians, had left Kosovo and that another 230,000 were internally displaced persons forced out of their homes. The Red Cross would later report the deaths of over 3,000 civilians, including 2,500 Albanians; other estimates ranged upward to 10,000 killed by Serbian forces.

On the ground, the Serbs now were facing growing opposition from a revived Kosovo Liberation Army, but the KLA was outnumbered and desperately needed NATO air cover.

The NATO response started slowly, with 350 aircraft, but became an extraordinary show of force. The European powers joined in, with aircraft carriers from Britain, France, and Italy taking part along with the Spanish air force and the German Luftwaffe, in its first combat participation since World War II.

But at first, there were problems in target selection. Jacques Chirac, the French leader, wanted to restrict the attack to Serbian "command and control" centers. "We don't want to hurt the people," he argued, and resisted bombing critical infrastructure targets in Belgrade and elsewhere. It took ten days to get everyone on the same page, with Tony Blair, the British Prime Minister, traveling to NATO headquarters to support U.S. insistence on striking targets that could bring Serbian capitulation.

At the height of the campaign, 700 air missions were flown a day, including 300 strike sorties. Of course, American firepower was the critical element. Sixty percent of all sorties, 53 percent of all strike missions, 95 percent of all cruise missile attacks—fired from ships and submarines—were U.S. contributions. There were over 1,000 aircraft involved, and the Americans used planes from all parts of the vast inventory of the Air Force and Navy, including every type of modern fighter plane—quickly smashing the MIG-29s of the Serbian air force—as well as fighter-bombers, huge B-52 strategic bombers, and even the B-2 stealth bomber, in its first combat role. (It was an errant bomb from a B-2 that created a diplomatic furor when it hit the Chinese embassy in Belgrade.) Efforts were made to limit civilian deaths in the air strikes on military and state targets, but Human Rights Watch would report over 500 civilians killed. At least 5,000 Serbian troops perished in the war that lasted from March 24 to June 11, 1999.

Milošević's forces proved much tougher and more resilient than some (including Madeleine Albright) had expected, recalling the rapid collapse of the Bosnian Serbs. As the weeks stretched into months, there were strains in the alliance and continued protests from Russia. Moscow called for a cessation of bombing and the continued presence of Serb military in Kosovo after the fighting stopped. But Clinton and his diplomatic/national security team remained resolute. The Serbs had to get out. At first Clinton had not supported using "boots on the ground," and he knew that 70 percent of Americans were telling pollsters they were opposed to this. But if it took a ground force to crush Milošević's army and push it out, then so be it.

General Wes Clark led the preparations for a NATO ground assault if air strikes were not enough, knowing it would take time to mobilize such a force. At first he estimated a sixty-day buildup but then called National Security director Sandy Berger, saying it would take ninety days to gear up for the long, difficult ground campaign; he wanted a green light from the White House the next day. Berger composed a memo at 2 in the morning to the President: Despite all the perils, the army must go in because "we cannot lose in Kosovo." It was a close call, but it did not come to that. Strobe Talbott called Berger that morning; the Soviet ambassador was confirming that Milošević was putting up the white flag.

The threat of a massive, U.S.-led ground campaign and the increasing costs of the concentrated air attacks played a central role in forcing Milošević to give up. With the Serbian power grid destroyed, computers running air defenses, the water system, and the country's banks were disabled. Not only was Belgrade's infrastructure ravaged, but factories, oil refineries, and electrical generating plants were smashed. With 100,000 Serbs out of work and many fleeing the country, U.S. broadcasts asked Serbs, "How long will you suffer for Milošević? Don't let him hold you hostage to his atrocities."

Another key factor was the grudging agreement of the Russians that all Yugoslav security forces had to withdraw and Russian troops would be part of the peacekeeping force under NATO leadership. (It was another success for the Clinton–Yeltsin relationship; in fact, all through the several Balkan crises, Russia never did break with the United States.) Milošević had already been charged by the International Criminal Tribunal with crimes against humanity. Now, with no hope of avoiding disastrous defeat, he capitulated, ordering his troops out of Kosovo in early June. The peacekeepers, numbering 48,000, prepared to deploy.

Even after victory, there were tense moments ahead. Yeltsin, along with his defense and foreign ministry aides, feared the image of a Russian leader as a puppet of NATO. They were dealing with angry hawks in the Russian military, and there was fear that Russian troops were on the move and might enter Kosovo ahead of NATO forces. General Clark ordered runways at Pristina airfield blocked in order to keep Russian Il-76 transports from landing such forces. It took hard diplomatic bargaining to head off conflict and smooth out the occupation arrangements.

The end of fighting in Kosovo brought Bill Clinton, in his words, "an enormous sense of relief and satisfaction." Slobodan Milošević's "bloody ten-year campaign to exploit ethnic and religious differences" was over. Clinton and his team had achieved a striking success.

The triumphant use of U.S. military strength in Kosovo also put the final exclamation point on Bill Clinton's transformed relationship with the American armed services. Even before the end of his first term, the rocky early period of dealing with the leaders of the fighting forces was ending. The President had been respectful of the military, made numerous trips to the Pentagon, met with the commanders of all the services, invited them to the White House, and took hard decisions that gained the respect of many. He visited military bases across the nation and the world. Moreover, he had shown a willingness to listen to Pentagon arguments even when supporting them angered his political base; certainly he took heat from the arms control community in the case of his opposition to the Land Mine Convention, because the Army insisted it needed mines—for at least a few more years—to protect forces in Korea.

As for the triumph in the Balkans, Václav Havel said that if any war could be called ethical, Kosovo could, for "this war placed human rights above the rights of the state." But it would cast its own shadow across the future. Historian John Keegan believed it proved "a war can be won by air power alone." In a book published in 2000, Michael Ignatieff said it demonstrated that war could be waged with scarcely any loss of life, at least for "our side." But he wondered that if Western nations could employ violence with seeming impunity, "Will they be tempted to use it more often?" Ahead lay the fateful decision to invade Iraq in 2003.[18]

Those who made that decision, in the administration of President George W. Bush, linked it to the threat of terrorism. Many critics would scoff at such a connection. But terrorism did not emerge as a major issue only after the attacks of 9/11. Terrorism became a central concern of Bill Clinton and his White House, particularly in his second term. And his efforts to combat terrorists are often misunderstood.

Yet, as the President focused on this new national security issue, particularly in the last two years of his administration, he had to deal with

a daunting series of other critical matters. There was, of course, unprecedented political turmoil at home, with the Lewinsky scandal and the looming impeachment crisis intersecting the final resolution of the Kosovo war.
And he had other foreign policy goals to pursue.

Early in the year, he and Hillary made a lengthy and memorable journey
to Africa, the continent too often ignored by American leaders. Bill Clinton
began the trip in Ghana, speaking to a crowd of more than 500,000 in Independence Square in the capital, Accra. He went to Uganda, visiting small
villages, discussing growing efforts to combat the AIDS epidemic, and
highlighting the importance of education and American-financed micro-
credit loans. He flew to Rwanda and met not only with national leaders but
with survivors of the genocide. And he made the first visit of any American
President to South Africa, speaking to parliament, building a real friend-
ship—which endured through succeeding years—with Nelson Mandela,
who took him to Robben Island, where the famed leader of the anti-apart-
heid movement had been imprisoned.

The Africa journey was one of many trips. Clinton became the most traveled President in history, visiting seventy-four nations on six continents in
eight years. Of course, Air Force One has long been a prized perquisite of
the President of the United States, and as Bill Clinton used it to fly across the
country and the world, he spent the hours aloft on business. Key administration members often were on the plane for meetings. The elaborate communications equipment onboard allowed him to talk to figures all across
the globe. But he also needed a break from the grinding pressure. He was an
inveterate card player, and hearts was his favorite game. As usual, he played
late into the night, almost always animated and competitive. This led to some
bizarre moments. After getting the right combination and about to win, he
slammed down his card at a critical juncture in one game, shouting the
slang term, "Sit down, Alice!" just as budget director Alice Rivlin entered the
compartment. This distinguished, senior figure immediately sat down in the
first seat available. Clinton, who had his back to her, was told, "Uh, Mr. President, the director is here." Bill Clinton, turning around, laughing, had to
stay, "Oh, I didn't mean you, Alice." On another occasion, playing an intense
game while chewing on an unlit cigar, he got a call from Boris Yeltsin at
a critical, losing moment for his hand and he let out a stream of colorful
expletives. The alarmed interpreter had to be told: "Don't translate that."

Yet there was unending pressure. Across 1998, along with the terrorist
threat, there was also the eruption of a very different but deeply threatening international matter: the explosive economic downturn in the financial
markets of Asia, which menaced the economies of Russia and other lands.

The problem began in July 1997 in Thailand, when the value of the Thai
currency, the baht, tumbled by 50 percent. Across succeeding months, the

"Asian flu" would infect other rapidly developing lands, the so-called Asian Tigers. It spread to Indonesia, Malaysia, the Philippines, and South Korea. Currencies were devalued and key banks faced collapse. High investment rates had powered the spectacular growth of these "Tigers" for a while, but they also fostered financial fragility. This was exposed when exports slowed, investment faltered, and foreign capital fled. Flawed banking systems, bad loans, and crony capitalism were problems throughout the region, and the situation was aggravated, Clinton knew, by the lack of economic growth in Japan (the region's largest economy) for the past half-decade.

By August 1998, the disease had spread to Brazil and, even more alarmingly, to Moscow. Russia was at risk because of dependence on energy exports, now battered by the fall in oil prices during a global downturn. The government devalued the ruble and defaulted on foreign debt. In the United States, this Russian collapse panicked Wall Street. The Dow Jones Index plunged 300 points on August 3; four weeks later, there was a 512-point decline, the second worst in the Dow's history.

But Clinton's economic team had been at work for months to deal with the crisis. The formula for recovery was the extension of sizable loans from the International Monetary Fund and from wealthy countries. Recipients were expected to make necessary reforms, politically difficult in each nation because they often required fiscal austerity along with threats to entrenched interests. The United States supported IMF efforts in Thailand, Indonesia, and South Korea and made additional contributions in the last two cases. (Clinton later regretted a failure to give more help to the Thais.)

Russia was a particular problem, because it failed to cut spending or increase or even collect taxes, and millions of rubles were being taken out of the country. Clinton, in yet another visit to Yeltsin, who was dealing with Communists and ultra-nationalists in the Duma blocking his reform measures, had to explain that more IMF money would be released only when these measures were taken.

Bob Rubin and Larry Summers were the key Clinton team members helping to address the worldwide economic emergency. The efforts were successful. By early 1999, the sense of crisis had ebbed; Asia was pulling out of its slump. With Russia's oil revenues on the rise, the ruble was stabilized and the IMF endorsed the growth of the Russian economy. Financial markets recovered. In late March, the Dow closed above 10,000 for the first time in its history; it would top 11,000 six weeks later.

Time magazine now put Rubin and Summers, along with Alan Greenspan, on its cover. These "Three Marketeers," the editors announced, were "the Committee to Save the World." No one would make such a statement about their views on deregulating financial derivatives when another economic crisis emerged in 2009. But in 1998 and 1999, dealing with what Clinton called the "biggest financial challenge facing the world in a half-century," the President's team had been effective. (Rubin told colleagues how fortunate it was that he was working for a President who actually understood currency flows and had appreciated the large stakes at risk. If a Republican had been in the White House for this crisis, the Treasury Secretary said, "they would be building a monument to him on the National Mall.")[19]

But few were cheering Bill Clinton for the rapid resolution of the crisis. And during this enormously stressful time, facing enemies trying to push him out of the White House and a daily, humiliating media feeding frenzy fixated on sexual rumors and transgressions, he concentrated on doing his job.

As both John Podesta, his chief of staff, and Sandy Berger, the National Security director, would later observe, this President had a remarkable ability to focus, to compartmentalize the issues before him, and to deal with the pressing matters of national import in domestic and foreign policy even while the drumbeat of scandal was occupying Washington and much of the country. Unlike some of his predecessors—who had become paralyzed prisoners in the White House during personal crises—he not only had enormous confidence in his governing skills, but as these aides noted, he was honored by the privilege of serving as President, refusing to allow anything to keep him from doing his job. The sex scandal might be making it harder for him and his foreign policy/national security team, but he stayed focused. And the job now involved confronting terrorist fanatics who had sworn to attack Americans and American interests.[20]

In early August 1998, two U.S. embassies in East Africa—at Nairobi, Kenya, and Dar es Salaam, Tanzania—were shattered by huge explosions detonated simultaneously by terrorists, leaving 258 dead (including 12 Americans) and more than 5,000 injured. These enormous truck bombs—with 2,000 pounds of TNT in the Nairobi device—brought a rapid and lethal response from the White House. Efforts to track down and punish those responsible for such acts would continue throughout Clinton's presidency.

The embassy bombings were not the first terrorist acts during the Clinton years. Even before the Oklahoma City attack—the work of two right-wing domestic fanatics—and the Khobar, Saudi Arabia, truck-bombing, there had been the effort to destroy the World Trade Center in New York City in February 1993, a month after the inauguration. A giant truck bomb was detonated below the North Tower of the Center, intended to knock it into the twin South Tower, killing thousands when the two huge buildings were flattened. The plot was a failure, but six were killed and more than one thousand injured.

The subsequent investigation led to the arrest and conviction of a group of Middle Eastern conspirators, six of whom received long prison sentences.

These plotters—and their leader, Ramzi Yousef—had plans to bomb UN Headquarters as well as the Lincoln and Holland Tunnels. Richard Clarke, President Clinton's national director for counterterrorism, said there was no answer when the FBI and CIA were asked: "Who are these guys?" Intelligence agencies had not yet heard of al-Qaeda. And they never heard of its founder, Osama bin Laden, the scion of an enormously wealthy Saudi family, who had fought against the Soviets in Afghanistan in the Eighties and later committed himself to a jihadist struggle against the satanic West, forming al-Qaeda three years before the New York bombing.

The Clinton national security team had come into office in 1993 with little thought of terrorism, but by 1996, Clarke noted, "they were preoccupied with it." By 1997 and 1998, Berger would say, "we were obsessed with it."

But at first they were not thinking of al-Qaeda. Iraqi intelligence was responsible for the attempt on the life of President Bush, Iranian intelligence responsible for the Khobar bombing, and a band of murderers led by a blind Egyptian Islamic cleric had tried to blow up the Trade Center. But Clarke, Tony Lake, and Sandy Berger had persisted in asking questions about bin Laden, the man whose name kept appearing in the CIA's raw reporting as a "terrorist financier." (Later, it would be clear that he was behind the New York plots.) Now al-Qaeda would become one of the major terrorist threats tracked by the key players in National Security. Bill Clinton issued a secret "finding" authorizing covert action, what he characterized as a "snatch operation against bin Laden," perhaps using Afghan local tribes contracted to do the job.

In the aftermath of the East African tragedies, both the FBI and the CIA provided detailed evidence that the operation had been carried out by al-Qaeda. National Security director Berger called together the "Small Group," composed of the Secretaries of Defense and State, the chairman of the Joint Chiefs, and the heads of CIA and counterterrorism. They planned a major American military strike against the terrorists' leadership cadre. But Clinton also asked for an overall plan to deal with al-Qaeda: "Retaliating for these attacks is all well and good, but we gotta get rid of these guys once and for all."

The retaliatory strikes involved seventy-five Tomahawk cruise missiles fired from surface warships and submarines in the northern Arabian Sea and Red Sea. The targets: terrorist training camps in Khost, Afghanistan, along with a pharmaceutical factory in Sudan, which the CIA believed bin Laden was using to produce deadly VX nerve gas. Later, many would insist the Sudan intelligence was faulty and that chemical weapons were not being made at the plant.

As for the Afghan strikes, bin Laden was not in the camp the CIA thought he would be in when the missiles hit; some reports said he had left less than an hour earlier. (But other terrorists were killed, along with members of Pakistan's Inter-Service Intelligence Directorate [ISI], who had worked with al-Qaeda and seemed to share bin Laden's anti-Western ideology.) And only at the last moment—in fact just two minutes before the cruise missiles crossed over into Pakistan territory en route to Afghanistan—did the United States inform the Pakistani ambassador about the raid.

At home, some congressional Republicans were in an uproar and there was scathing contempt from media heavyweights. Bill Clinton's admission that he'd had relations with Monica Lewinsky, after months of denial, was dominating the news. His critics now shouted that the attack was a fraud, he is just "wagging the dog." The reference was to *Wag the Dog*, a movie released earlier in the year in which fictional presidential advisers invent an artificial crisis with Albania to attack it and divert attention from domestic problems. But, of course, that was not the case. As Clarke noted, "Clinton made it clear we were to give him our best national security advice. . . . If we thought this was the best time to hit the Afghan camps, he would order it and take the heat for the 'Wag the Dog' criticism we all knew would happen."

President Clinton, of course, was acting the way he had throughout his years in office. Early, he told Sandy Berger: "Let me handle the politics. Just tell me about policy." When the Mexican bailout and the Kosovo ground troop proposals were eliciting media and political opposition, Clinton wanted Berger and the National Security team to keep the White House political people out of any consideration of policy alternatives, as they did. And on the missile attack decision, apparently the American public was not unhappy; a new poll had 73 percent supporting the strikes.

These attacks were only the beginning. Clinton amended his earlier "finding" by signing three highly classified memoranda of notification (MONs). They authorized the CIA to use lethal force to apprehend or, if necessary, kill bin Laden, added several of bin Laden's senior lieutenants to the deadly list, and, finally, approved the shooting down of private civilian aircraft on which they flew.

In fact, bin Laden had already targeted Bill Clinton for death. Later, it was revealed that only the prompt action by Secret Service agents thwarted a successful assassination attempt when members of the elite Presidential Protection Division, acting on last-minute intelligence, changed the route of the President's motorcade during Clinton's visit to the Philippines in November 1996. Late to a meeting, the President was not happy with the rerouting, but it avoided crossing a bridge under which al-Qaeda operatives had placed a bomb powerful enough to kill him and others in his entourage.

Clinton now ordered the Navy to place two Los Angeles–class submarines on permanent station in the nearest available waters so that Tomahawk cruise missiles could be on target within eight hours of receiving the order to fire. (Arab sensitivities precluded use of U.S. air bases in the Persian Gulf.) Three times after August 20, 1998, the CIA came close enough to pinpointing bin Laden that the President authorized final preparations to launch. Yet in every case, doubts about intelligence aborted the mission.

One of the potential targets turned out to be a Gulf sheik's falconing party, another was a tent in a desert encampment, the third was a stone compound full of al-Qaeda operatives. Clinton refused to authorize the use of "area weapons," a warhead of cluster bombs that would have killed women and children around bin Laden. So it had to be the Tomahawk's standard warhead—which allowed a person 100 yards away to survive the strike. But the CIA was having trouble providing actionable intelligence, definitive proof of the exact location of bin Laden; after the near miss in August, he was redoubling efforts to mask his whereabouts.

Director George Tenant said, "I can tell you where he's been, I can tell you where he's going, the problem is, can I tell you where he'll be for the next six to ten hours." Yet the slow-flying cruise missiles needed that long. On the third of the occasions, in autumn 2000, Tenant called to say, "We have one source here," only to call back and say, "We just don't have it." And so the Tomahawks' launch would be canceled once more.

Frustrated by the difficulties in using air strikes to decapitate al-Qaeda, other avenues—involving allied forces—were explored. None of them worked. One involved lavish funding of a militia element hostile to both al-Qaeda and its Taliban protectors in Afghanistan. Another concerned using Uzbekistan commandos. A third came at Pakistan's initiative, when its Prime Minister offered a small special force (to be trained by the CIA) that would cross the Afghan border to kill or capture bin Laden. Berger, Albright, and Steinberg were skeptical, believing that this Pakistani proposal would come to nothing. (After a military coup that led to a new government, it collapsed, and the National Security Agency later reported the plan had been compromised by the ISI, long penetrated by al-Qaeda.)

The Clinton administration worked to choke off al-Qaeda's financial network, threatening states and banking institutions with sanctions if they failed to cut off assistance to those who did business with the terrorist group or the Taliban. And it endorsed use of a new intelligence device in the search for bin Laden, a small, unmanned aircraft to be sent into Afghanistan. The tiny Predator drone brought back startling videos, and Richard Clarke now strenuously argued to have it carry a missile to eliminate the terror master. But it was early in drone development; some Air Force and CIA leaders scoffed at having a 950-pound aircraft carry a 100-pound warhead. It would only be after Clinton left the White House that such new weapons would be utilized.

The only certain way to kill or capture Osama bin Laden might be the use of American troops. While U.S. diplomats told the leaders of the Taliban, who controlled most of Afghanistan and were allied with al-Qaeda, "If bin Laden or any of the organizations affiliated with him attack the United States, we will hold you personally accountable," this was long before 9/11 and no one was proposing a large-scale invasion of a neutral nation. But Berger and Albright, in the Small Group, repeatedly called for a limited use of "boots on the ground," a small, elite Special Forces mission into Afghanistan to get bin Laden. Bill Clinton strongly pushed the idea with General Hugh Shelton, now chairman of the Joint Chiefs. The general looked pained, but said he would "look into it."

The Pentagon would not support such an effort. Fixated on the memory of Vietnam as well as the example of the first Iraq war, fearful of a debacle such as the burning helicopters at Desert One during the Iranian hostage rescue mission in Carter's time—which had so embarrassed their predecessors—the generals could think only in terms of using "overwhelming force." Perhaps even more important, they still were dealing with the lingering trauma over the "Blackhawk Down" tragedy in Somalia. Shelton refused to even give the President a plan to execute a raid. He was reported to have privately referred to the proposal as "going Hollywood." Of course, the military would change its view of dealing with non-state enemies in subsequent years. New Pentagon leaders had a more affirmative view when the Obama administration endorsed the Special Forces attack into Pakistan that killed bin Laden in 2010.

Al-Qaeda remained a threat. In mid-October 2000, just before the presidential election for Bill Clinton's successor—and just days after the last of the canceled Tomahawk strikes—there was a terrorist attack on an American destroyer, the USS Cole, at anchor in Yemen, killing seventeen American sailors, injuring thirty-nine. Now the administration considered a military operation to overthrow the Taliban and find bin Laden, but the CIA and FBI could not certify that bin Laden was responsible for the attack until after Clinton left office and the military could not secure basing rights in Uzbekistan.

Just after 9/11, Bill Clinton was subjected to attacks by right-wing pundits and politicians. Rush Limbaugh exclaimed, "Mr. Clinton can be held culpable for not doing enough when he was commander-in-chief to combat the terrorists." Newt Gingrich chimed in, calling Clinton "pathetically weak." Clarke—who continued to serve as counterterrorism leader for George W. Bush—would contemptuously dismiss such broadsides. He described how "the incoming leadership thought that Clinton and his administration were overly obsessed with al-Qaeda," they believed the "recommendation that eliminating al-Qaeda be one of their highest priorities was rather odd," for at the beginning, the new Bush National Security group was much more concerned about missiles coming from rogue states. Their whole experience was with dealing with powerful, well-armed nations; they could not believe that people living in a cave could offer a new peril.

As Clarke wrote, "Clinton left office with bin Laden alive, but having authorized actions to eliminate him and step up the attacks on al-Qaeda." He "had seen earlier than anyone that terrorism was the major new threat facing America" and "greatly increased funding for counterterrorism and initiated homeland protection programs." To the end of his White House days, Bill Clinton never lost his focus on the menace of terrorism. He called it "the threat of our generation."[21]

But as his final days in office approached, the President was also deeply involved in another foreign policy challenge, the quest to fulfill Rabin's dream and bring a peaceful resolution to the Israeli-Palestinian crisis. Benjamin Netanyahu had been defeated and there was a new leader in Jerusalem. In July, Bill Clinton announced his invitation to Prime Minister Ehud Barak and Palestinian Authority chairman Yasir Arafat to come to Camp David to continue negotiating a Middle East peace settlement. It would be a historic if failed effort to find a solution to the most intractable diplomatic issue of the post–Cold War era.

Barak, a famous former military leader, came to office hoping to replace incremental efforts at the final status settlement (called for at Oslo) with a series of dramatic diplomatic breakthroughs not only with the Palestinians but also with Syria and Lebanon.

At this point, Bill Clinton made his last effort to end hostilities between Israel and Syria. He called Assad, now a frail and sickly figure, and arranged for meetings among the Syrian foreign minister, Ehud Barak, and U.S. representatives. At a conference center in Shepherdstown, West Virginia, in January 2000, a deal was almost achieved. Barak was committed to doing what Rabin had agreed to years earlier: returning to Syria all of the strategic Golan Heights (conquered by the Israelis decades before) in return for peace and security agreements. But disputes over a tiny strip of land on the border and the date of Israel's final withdrawal proved obstacles. And Barak, feeling political pressure at home, now decided, as a disappointed Clinton noted, to "slow-walk" the process, finally suggesting he wanted to first deal with the Lebanese matter. So the moment was lost. Within months, in June, Assad would be dead. There would be no peace with Syria, which might have made it easier in turn to achieve the critical Palestinian settlement.

But on Clinton's urging, Arafat and the Palestinian delegation joined Barak and his Israeli team at the presidential retreat, Camp David, in the Catoctin Mountains outside Washington. For two weeks, the discussions went on, with the President using all his charm and skill to bring the sides together. He was, Albright wrote, eloquent and inspiring in the opening sessions. Later, he spent many hours meeting separately with each leader, sometimes into the wee hours of the morning, trying to bridge the enormous gulf that decades of violence, hostility, and mistrust had created between them.

Clinton knew that there was not a high probability of success for this summit but he had called the meeting because "the collapse of the peace process would be a near certainty if I didn't."

Arafat was a problem. He had not wanted to come. He wanted more time to prepare, was irritated that the Israeli had turned first to the "the Syrian track," and angry that Barak had not kept previous commitments to turn over more of the West Bank. While he feared that some kind of trap was being set for him at Camp David, he was even more rigid than usual because he believed Barak's unilateral withdrawal from occupied land in southern Lebanon and the offer to give back the Golan to Syria had weakened the Israeli. Moreover, he feared the personal consequences of success. Anwar Sadat and Yitzhak Rabin had been assassinated for their efforts to bring peace; at one point he told Madeleine Albright, "The next time you see me is when you are walking behind my coffin."

Ehud Barak, a brilliant but remote and sometimes prickly figure, was incapable of personally reaching out to Arafat, and thus there was no chemistry between the two. But he was ready to deal. Bill Clinton grasped the opportunity. He helped shape the terms of a settlement, understanding that taboos at last were being broken and the essential needs of each side addressed.

Barak would agree to the establishment of a Palestinian capital in East Jerusalem, an enormous concession, with Palestinian sovereignty over both the Moslem and Christian quarters of the Old City as well as most of the outer suburbs. There was an offer to return 91 percent of the West Bank, withdraw from some of the settlements there, and accept the principle of a swap of some land for the continued existence of the major population centers in the area, where 180,000 Israelis had homes. Of course, there could be no "right of return" for all Palestinians (and their descendants) made homeless by the 1948 and 1967 wars, a core objective of the PLO throughout its history, for this population now numbered 4 million, and if they all came back Israel would no longer be a predominantly Jewish state. But a limited number might be allowed to return and others would be compensated.

These were path-breaking proposals presenting an extraordinary opportunity. But Arafat did not grasp it. The Palestinian, as a key member of the U.S. delegation observed, almost revered Clinton; he was a symbol of American power and thus of Arafat's "acceptance on the world stage." Clinton was masterful at making him feel comfortable, treating him as a leader. Yet Yasir Arafat would not move. His group offered no real alternatives. Finally, Bill Clinton blew up: "I've been here for two weeks and the only thing you've said is no. You haven't offered one damn thing!"

In the end, Arafat refused to budge on demands for the "right of return" or the issue of sovereignty over the site of both the Western Wall, sacred to Jews, and the Dome of the Rock and al-Aqsa mosque, sacred to Muslims. This tiny piece of land in the center of ancient Jerusalem, known as the Temple Mount/Haram al-Sharif, for which Barak had made substantial concessions, became the final unbridgeable obstacle. Arafat inexplicably told Clinton that the Western Wall, part of the Jewish Second Temple complex, destroyed by the Romans in AD 70, actually had been located in Nablus, not Jerusalem.

Arafat's final word at Camp David was to be no. Abba Eban, the legendary Israeli diplomat, long before had observed that "the Palestinians never miss an opportunity to miss an opportunity." But there had never been an opportunity like this.

Yet Clinton was not ready to give up. But as he planned a final effort to bring a settlement before he left office, there were new complications. Ariel Sharon, the tough, militant former Israeli general, now a right-wing political leader soon to defeat Barak and become the next Prime Minister, led a thousand armed police and soldiers, along with a group of Likud politicians, to the Temple Mount, the plaza containing the al-Aqsa mosque and the Dome of the Rock. The reaction was a massive Palestinian demonstration, and in responding to the stone-throwing crowd, Israeli police killed 4 and wounded 200. The "Second Intifada" was to begin, this time featuring suicide bombers sent into Israeli cities. Sharon's act was deliberately provocative, but Arafat, while it is unclear whether he called for the violence, did not restrain it.

Still, Clinton persevered. The Palestinian and Israeli negotiators were called back to Washington, and on December 23, less than a month before leaving office, Clinton brought them to the White House and in the Cabinet Room read them his parameters for proceeding. On territory: 94 to 96 percent of the West Bank for the Palestinians with a land swap from Israel of 1 to 3 percent (and 80 percent of the settlers in the West Bank blocs would be included in land kept by Israel). On security: Israeli forces to withdraw from what would be the new and demilitarized Palestinian state over a three-year period, with an international force introduced. Israel would be able to maintain security early-warning stations with Palestinian liaison presence. The resolution of the Jerusalem and refugee matters would be similar in most respects to the Camp David proposals.

Clinton said that the parameters were nonnegotiable. Barak's cabinet endorsed them; there would be a Palestinian state with roughly 97 percent of the West Bank and all of Gaza. Arafat, after trying to wiggle out of the right of return issue, agreed to further meetings. The parties continued their talks in Taba, Egypt, in January and got close but could not make the deal. Arafat never said no, Clinton would write, he just could not bring himself to say yes.

There continues to be debate over why: whether he feared for his life, could not tolerate a peace settlement in which his role as world-famous insurgent leader ended, lacked strong support for an agreement from Egyptian leader Hosni Mubarak and from the Saudis, or simply felt he couldn't sell the terms to his followers. But in his last conversation with Bill Clinton, he said that the President was a great man. Clinton's response: "Mr. Chairman, I am not a great man. I am a failure, and you have made me one." (He then warned Arafat that he was single-handedly electing Sharon and that he would "reap the whirlwind.")[22]

Of course, Bill Clinton was not a failure. He had helped shape the terms of what most consider the only feasible two-state solution to the Arab-Israeli crisis. And he was not a failure in the far larger task of shaping America's response to the foreign challenges of the post–Cold War era.

Throughout his eight years in office, he patiently, shrewdly, and successfully managed relations with Russia and its volatile leader. He worked to prevent the spread of weapons of mass destruction, responded to dangers presented by the emerging rogue states of Iraq, Iran, and North Korea, calmly dealt with perilous international economic crises, and served as peacemaker in Northern Ireland as well as the Middle East. After initial reluctance to use American military power, which had such tragic consequences in Rwanda and Bosnia, he became both an authoritative and effective commander-in-chief in Haiti, Bosnia, Kosovo, and elsewhere. And he recognized the new threat of international terrorism, responding appropriately.

Initially, he was less concerned about international issues, as he addressed the big home-front economic, social, and political questions that had preoccupied him while running for office. But he would shape a progressive and pragmatic foreign policy for a highly complex post–Cold War world. It proved as successful as his domestic achievements.

All through these years of meeting challenges at home and abroad, he had to deal as well with implacable political enemies seeking to humiliate him and destabilize his administration. While these adversaries continuously insisted that his White House was wracked by wrongdoing, most of their allegations and investigations merely amounted to illusory but destructive politics of scandal. Yet there was one scandal that was not illusory. And it almost cost Bill Clinton the presidency.

Notes

1. Strobe Talbott, *The Russia Hand: A Memoir of Presidential Diplomacy* (New York: Random House, 2003), p. 10; interview with Strobe Talbott, November 2, 2012.
2. Ibid.; Talbott, *Russia Hand*, pp. 8, 23–71.
3. Ibid., pp. 79–84, 107–109, 112–114.
4. Interview with Strobe Talbott, November 2, 2012; interview with James Steinberg, December 13, 2012; Talbott, *Russia Hand*, pp. 72–78, 89–90; Madeleine Albright, *Madam Secretary* (New York: Hyperion, 2003), pp. 228–231; Clinton, *My Life* (New York: Alfred A. Knopf, 2004), pp. 509–513; John Harris, *The Survivor* (New York: Random House, 2005), pp. 42–52; Elizabeth Drew, *On the Edge: The Clinton Presidency* (New York: Simon and Schuster, 1994), pp. 139–163; Warren Christopher, *In the Stream of History* (Stanford: Stanford University Press, 1998), pp. 343–347; interview with Sandy Berger, July 25, 2012; Jane Perlez, "Showdown in Yugoslavia: The Diplomacy," *New York Times*, October 8, 2000.
5. Clinton, *My Life*, pp. 550–554; Harris, pp. 121–123; Drew, *On the Edge*, pp. 313–332; Stephanopoulos, pp. 214–216; interview with Sandy Berger, July 25, 2012; Albright, pp. 178–184; *New York Times*, October 1, 1995.
6. Christopher, pp. 175–177; Harris, p. 123; Albright, pp. 195–197.
7. Ibid., pp. 185–194; Michael Takiff, *A Complicated Man: The Life of Bill Clinton as Told by Those Who Know Him* (New Haven: Yale University Press, 2010), pp. 204–206; Clinton, *My Life*, pp. 592–593, 609; interview with Strobe Talbott, November 2, 2012; interview with James Steinberg, December 13, 2012; Strobe Talbott, *The Great Experiment* (New York: Simon and Schuster, 2008), pp. 294–298.
8. Clinton, *My Life*, pp. 616–619; Takiff, pp. 214–215; Christopher, pp. 180–188; Albright, pp. 195–203; interview with Strobe Talbott, November 2, 2012.
9. Talbott, *Russia Hand*, pp. 122–123, 170–183; Clinton, *My Life*, pp. 581–583, 590–591, 655–656, 665–669; Harris, pp. 192–202; Mark Danner, "Bosnia: The Great Betrayal," *New York Review of Books*, March 26, 1998; Peter Maas, "Paying for the Powell Doctrine" in Nicolaus Mills and Kira Brunner, eds., *The New Killing Fields: Massacre and the Politics of Intervention* (New York: Basic Books, 2002), pp. 71–87; Richard Holbrooke, *To End a War* (New York: Random House, 1998), pp. 3–141, 156–161, 199–312; Richard Holbrooke in Takiff, pp. 271–276; U.S. Department of State, "Summary of the Dayton Peace Agreement on Bosnia-Herzegovina," http://www.pbs.org/newshour/bb/bosnia/dayton_peace.html. Hillary Rodham Clinton, *Living History* (New York: Scribner, 2003), pp. 298–308.
10. Clinton, *My Life*, pp. 541–546, 609–610, 626–627, 678–680, 714, 747, 831–833; Takiff, pp. 216–221, 263–267; Branch, pp. 488–490; Albright, pp. 380–405.
11. Takiff, pp. 276–284, 341–343; Clinton, *My Life*, pp. 401, 686–693, 700, 787, 900; Branch, 126–127, 328–330; "Wistful Bill Clinton Remembers Good Friday," *New York Observer*, October 4, 2008; William Hazleton, "Clinton's Role in the Good Friday Agreement," *Irish Studies in International Affairs* 11 (2000), pp. 103–119.
12. Albright, pp. 578–582; Christopher, pp. 213–216; Clinton, *My Life*, pp. 62–63, 624–625.
13. Ibid., pp. 751–752; Talbott, *Russia Hand*, pp. 269–270, 376–378, 393–395.
14. Ibid., pp. 65, 143, 158–161, 254–256, 265–273; Albright, pp. 406–414; Clinton, *My Life*, pp. 654–655; Bruce O. Riedel, "The Iran Primer: The Clinton Administration," United States Institute for Peace, http://iranprimer.usip.org/resource/clinton-administration
15. Albright, pp. 346–365; Clinton, *My Life*, pp. 833–834; Talbott, *Russia Hand*, pp. 293–294.
16. Project for the New American Century, "Statement of Principles," June 3, 1997, http://www.newamericancentury.org/statementofprinciples.htm; Project for the New American Century, Letter to President Clinton on Iraq, January 26, 1998, http://www.newamericancentury.org/iraqclintonletter.htm
17. Talbott, *Russia Hand*, pp. 93–101, 110–111, 184–185, 382; Albright, pp. 318–332; Vladimir Baranovsky, "NATO Enlargement: Russia's Attitudes," European Security Forum, Brussels,

2001, http://www.eusec.org/baranovsky.htm; interview with Strobe Talbott, November 12, 2012; interview with James Steinberg, December 13, 2012.

18. Albright, pp. 481–543; Talbott, *Russia Hand*, pp. 298–331; Clinton, *My Life*, pp. 848–860; Richard Sale, *Clinton's Secret Wars* (New York: St. Martin's Press, 2009), pp. 344–381; Paul Wilson, "The Dilemma of Madeleine Albright," *New York Review of Books*, June 7, 2012, pp. 35–36; interview with Sandy Berger, July 25, 2012; interview with James Steinberg, December 13, 2012; interview with Strobe Talbott, November 2, 2012; Wesley K. Clark, *Waging Modern War* (New York: Public Affairs, 2001), pp. 68–69, 138–139, 171–182, 308–321, 381–403; Ivo H. Daalder and Michael E. O'Hanlon, *Winning Ugly: NATO's War to Save Kosovo* (Washington: Brookings Institute Press, 2000), pp. 143–175.

19. Clinton, *My Life*, pp. 780–784, 806–807; Talbott, *Russia Hand*, pp. 275–291; Harris, pp. 328–329; "The Three Marketeers," *Time*, February 15, 1999.

20. Interview with John Podesta, July 24, 2012; interview with Sandy Berger, July 25, 2012.

21. Richard A. Clarke, *Against All Enemies: Inside America's War on Terror* (New York: Free Press, 2004), pp. 73–80, 101–107, 114–121, 184–196, 225–226; Lawrence Wright, *The Looming Tower: Al-Qaeda and the Road to 9/11* (New York: Random House, 2006), pp. 200–212, 230–253, 297–324; Ken Gormley, *The Death of American Virtue: Clinton vs. Starr* (New York: Crown, 2010), pp. 491–492; Harris, pp. 405–415; Albright, pp. 459–480; Takiff, pp. 362–367; Barton Gellman, "Broad Effort Launched after '98 Attacks," *Washington Post*, December 19, 2001; *New York Times*, August 21, 1998, December 30, 2001; Bill Press, "Don't Blame It on Bill Clinton," CNN.com, October 18, 2001, http://archives.cnn.com/2001/ALLPOLITICS/10/18/column.billpress; interview with Sandy Berger, July 25, 2012; interview with James Steinberg, December 13, 2012; interview with Strobe Talbott, November 2, 2012; Clinton, *My Life*, pp. 789, 803–805.

22. Ibid., pp. 883–887, 911–916, 943–944; Albright, pp. 601–633; Takiff, pp. 385–392; Robert Malley and Hussein Agha, "Camp David: the Tragedy of Errors," *New York Review of Books*, August 9, 2001; Dennis Ross and Gidi Grinstein, reply by Hussein Agha and Robert Malley, "Camp David: An Exchange," *New York Review of Books*, September 20, 2001; Ehud Barak and Benny Morris, "Camp David and After," *New York Review of Books*, June 27, 2002; interview with James Steinberg, December 13, 2012.

CHAPTER 5

THE POLITICS OF SCANDAL
AND THE IMPEACHMENT CRISIS

In the White House, Bill Clinton had to focus on two multifaceted challenges. The first was reviving a sagging U.S. economy: implementing policies that would leave America stronger and Americans more secure, more prosperous, more hopeful. The second was dealing with a post–Cold War world in upheaval: new crises in failed states or rogue states, emerging threats from terrorists, opportunities to both strengthen relations with old rival Russia and help bring peace to troubled lands long marked by ethnic-religious hostilities.

But during his years in office and even after he left the White House, some journalists and pundits, independent scholars, and academic specialists too often paid scant attention to Clinton's domestic and international policies. They fixated instead on "scandals." It was as if the dramatic and often momentous history of this period was being offered with the sensibility of a late night TV comic.

Of course, dealing with bruising politics at the pinnacle of national power is another obligation of presidential office, and it is expected that any figure in the White House will be under an unremitting media spotlight. But the torrent of scandal stories that often dominated newspaper and TV coverage throughout the Clinton years, which led to a vast literature excoriating (or defending) the President, was extraordinary.

It was the result of a number of interrelated developments. First, there were the relentless efforts by political enemies who feared and hated Bill Clinton; they created foundations, institutes, and publications dedicated to assailing him and questioning his legitimate claim to the office, working in public and sometimes in secret to destroy his presidency, hoping to undo the elections of 1992 and 1996. Second, there were revolutionary changes

under way in the media, reshaping political coverage for print and electronic journalists in the so-called mainstream media—where many already
were deeply suspicious of the man they considered "Slick Willie"—and giving rise to Internet gossips, talk show ideologues, and cable TV performers
all eager for explosive revelations of real or imagined wrongdoing. Third,
there was the legal system at a peculiar moment in American history, when
the "independent counsel" law, championed by Democrats in the past, now
would be reauthorized and used by Clinton's adversaries to pursue a wide
variety of allegations against him and his appointees.

Finally, there was the action of the President himself, which provided the
one issue—after all the largely empty scandal stories that preceded it—that
could be used to humiliate him. But Bill Clinton's affair with Monica Lewinsky, the White House intern less than half his age with whom he had oral
sex right in the Oval Office, was behavior so tawdry that it exposed him to
the scandal his enemies would use to try to force him from office.

The sex scandal came relatively late in the Clinton presidency. It was
preceded by numerous other efforts to tie this President to illegal or unethical conduct. And to put all this in context, it is important to consider the
meaning of scandal in American political history.

The typical American political scandal had to do with the corruption of
money, how officeholders or their appointees used their temporary positions of power to line their own pockets.

In the post–Civil War period, when vast government land grants were
funding the building of transcontinental railroads and huge bribes were
offered for favored treatment, the self-dealing machinations of congressmen
and members of the White House administration made the Ulysses S. Grant
era (although not President Grant himself) synonymous with corruption.

In the post–World War I period, a complex series of activities wrecked
the reputation of President Warren Harding, who also did not personally
profit: "I have no trouble with my enemies. I can take care of them. It is
my friends, my friends that are giving me my trouble," he complained to
writer William Allen White. There were the notorious schemes of Harding's home-state cronies, "the Ohio Gang," led by the Attorney General, as
well as his friends who were the grafters bilking the Veterans Bureau and
the Alien Property Custodian office. Finally there was the central scandal
of the time, the one that gave its name to all the others, which involved
massive bribes to the inept Harding's corrupt Secretary of the Interior,
allowing two immensely wealthy and powerful oil men to take control of
federal naval oil reserves, including one located in Wyoming known as
Teapot Dome.[1]

Greed, graft, and ill-gotten gain have been the classic American political
scandals. Many governors, mayors, and legislators at all levels of government

have been involved, some convicted and sent to prison. In Richard Nixon's administration, the Vice President of the United States, Spiro Agnew, had to resign and plead no contest to avoid jail, guilty of taking kickbacks from contractors during his years as Maryland's governor.

But it was in the Nixon years that a new kind of White House scandal eclipsed the old. This was the corruption of power. The presidency had changed since Harding's time, and so had presidential scandal. The concentration of enormous power in the White House during FDR's New Deal and the crisis years of World War II and the Cold War created a different kind of presidential government. And while rumors of unethical behavior and minor scandals of the old type—involving allegations of graft by the President's aides—emerged from time to time, notably in the Truman and Eisenhower years, the next great scandal would be different. Richard Nixon was no presidential lightweight like Grant or Harding. But he had fatal flaws of character that had been revealed years before in his campaigns for the Senate and Vice Presidency. Supporters claimed in the Sixties that there was a "new Nixon," but there was not. As President, he would do almost anything to thwart real or imagined adversaries, and—not surprisingly—always was certain they were plotting against him.

This was the reason for the series of shadowy, unethical, and illegal schemes that preceded the Watergate break-in at the Democratic campaign headquarters that brought down this President. There was the crew of political "dirty tricksters" created to disrupt and discredit Democratic presidential candidates and the bumbling band of "plumbers" tasked with "plugging leaks" in the administration by any means necessary. There was secret surveillance of the opposition and bizarre plots for unleashing mugging squads and kidnapping teams, characterized as the "White House horrors" by Nixon's former Attorney General, John Mitchell. Of course, Watergate and the cover-up that followed it became the central scandal of the Nixon years. Like the others, it was linked to a feeling by the chief executive and his key aides that they were justified in whatever they were doing in order to fulfill the lofty goals of the administration.

Fifty years earlier, the confused Warren Harding had led a government by cronyism, and some of those closest to him used their positions for private plunder of the nation's resources. Richard Nixon had organized a modern presidential government, and those closest to him talked with pride of their dedication to the great job they confronted; they thought of themselves as figures of rectitude and there were allusions to the "greatest presidency of the twentieth century." Asked about the cover-up, Mitchell said, "The most important thing for this country was the reelection of Richard Nixon. And I was not about to countenance anything that would stand in the way of that." In any case, they were not making money, so how could this be scandal? "What scandal?" Mitchell exclaimed. "I never made a cent from Watergate."[2]

The fall of Richard Nixon weakened the presidency and undermined public faith in government. It also would lead to a new institutional arrangement to check executive power—the Independent Counsel Act—and an intensification of the adversarial attitude by the national media toward the White House. These developments, of course, would play a central role in the politics of the Nineties. But curiously, they had little impact during the next great scandal, one that also involved the corruption of power.

It was true that on Ronald Reagan's watch, the old-style corruption was at work in smaller scandals. At the Environmental Protection Agency, the Nuclear Regulatory Commission, and the Department of Housing and Urban Development, graft rewarded the ideologues put in charge, people who did not believe in government regulation or development grants, yet found an opportunity to personally profit by their misallocation of federal resources. And, of course, in the enormous $1.5 trillion defense buildup, kickbacks were part of the price of doing business for some contractors.

Yet the great scandal of the time concerned how the President and his aides persevered with policies that were clearly illegal, simply because they believed they were right and their opponents, who inconveniently controlled the majority in the legislative branch, were wrong. This was another classic case of the corruption of power. It was Iran-Contra. It involved two foreign policy fixations of the Reagan team: one concerning fear of "communist" penetration in "our" hemisphere; the other involving fear of appearing weak, of being "like Jimmy Carter," of not protecting Americans from hostage takers in the Middle East. The man who had promised to make the United States "stand tall" once more in the world could not afford to fail on these issues.

And so the Reagan White House, having created the secretly financed Contra War against the left-leaning Sandinistas in Nicaragua in Central America, would be willing to violate explicit congressional directives (the Boland amendments) against funding this effort. While one key administrative figure warned that it could be an "impeachable offense" to fund an activity that Congress had expressly prohibited, what followed were secret solicitations from foreign nationals and vulnerable governments, essentially diplomatic shakedowns.

Meanwhile, in Lebanon, the small land torn by civil strife and abandoned by the Reagan administration after suicide bombers destroyed a Marine barracks, a few American hostages were being held by militias seemingly under the influence of the Iranian mullahs. How to free the hostages? The infamous scheme to secretly trade arms to Iran (locked in its bitter war with Iraq) was born. And while this involved selling weapons to a country whose leader had humiliated the United States in 1979 and daily excoriated "the American Satan," a nation characterized as a "terrorist state" by Ronald Reagan, it did not seem to matter as long as the outcome would be freedom for the hostages and a special bonus: more money for the Contras.

The Iran-Contra plans were hatched by an administration indifferent to legal restraints, contemptuous of its opponents, and unconcerned about violating the law, certain that the press, the public, and Congress need not know what was being done in the name of America. In the end, the whole sordid matter was exposed, not because of American investigative journalists but only because a plane was shot down in Nicaragua and stories emerged from Middle Eastern publications.

In the Iran-Contra affair, an independent counsel played a role, but it was not to be a central one. A presidential commission (which would embrace a "rogue staff" theory, holding White House aides, not the President, responsible) was organized to investigate, along with congressional committees. Still, everyone seeking answers would be inhibited in their work by destroyed, delayed, or denied documents; in this scandal, the cover-up worked. In the congressional committees, while there was considerable partisan skirmishing, Democrats made it clear, as the Senate majority leader put it, that "the last thing we need[ed] was an impeachment outcry, a frontal assault on the President's integrity." The country, it was argued, "did not need another Watergate."

Thus Ronald Reagan emerged from the scandal to the warm support of the public in his last year in office. "We took a hit," the White House counsel noted, "but we survived." Yet the passions unleashed during Iran-Contra would not disappear so easily. For conservative activists of the Nineties, the politics of scandal could cut both ways.

In these years, the organized Clinton haters would accuse the President both of corruption by money and corruption of power. (Some parts of the media would share in making this case.) Yet only a third kind of scandal, a sex scandal, would have the truly damaging impact.

Certainly, Clinton's enemies were well organized and richly funded. A key figure was a reclusive right-wing billionaire, Richard Mellon Scaife of Pittsburgh. An heir to the Mellon banking fortune, Scaife long had lavishly supported conservative causes. Now he would financially back an ultraconservative magazine named the *American Spectator* that focused on printing anti-Clinton stories. And in 1993 he would be behind the creation of the secretive "Arkansas Project," a four-year, $2.4 million effort to gather intelligence that could lead to the ruin of President Bill Clinton.

Scaife, his magazine, and his Arkansas Project were not alone. Other right-wing organizations and individuals, notably the Rutherford Institute, Floyd Brown and his Citizens United, Reed Irvine's Accuracy in the Media, and televangelists Pat Robertson and Jerry Falwell, would be actively involved in the campaign to demonize Clinton.

Some of the early efforts to damage him were almost comically preposterous. The President was accused, as Arkansas governor, of supporting illegal cocaine importation, gun-running, and murder at a small airport in Mena, in western Arkansas. There had been stories of CIA involvement in nefarious activities in Mena during the Iran-Contra years. But just after Clinton entered the White House, right-wing propagandists hit on the bizarre idea of naming him—not the makers of the great scandal of the Eighties—as the perpetrator of the "crimes of Mena." Larry Nichols, the man Clinton had fired back in 1990 for misusing his office to support Iran-Contra, played a key role.

He also was involved in making *The Clinton Chronicles*, a scurrilous 1994 film marketed by Falwell on his television show and introduced by old Clinton enemy Justice Jim Johnson, which concluded with a plea for Bill Clinton's impeachment. More than 150,000 copies of this video were sold. Along with an anti-Clinton book called *The Secret Life of Bill Clinton*, it linked the President to evil activity in Mena and other wrongdoing. There was the alleged murder of an Arkansas private investigator, the murder of the wife of a state trooper, the appointment of corrupt judges, and the killing of witnesses.[3]

Scaife, interviewed by John F. Kennedy Jr. for a magazine piece, said, "Listen, Clinton can order people done away with at his will. He's got the entire federal government behind him. . . . God, there must be 60 people associated with him who have died mysteriously." The implication that this President was a murderous criminal took on a particularly lurid tone after the suicide of Bill and Hillary Clinton's close friend, Vince Foster.

It was July 20, 1993, six months into the Clinton presidency, when Foster, deputy counsel in the White House, shot himself with an old revolver in Ft. Marcy Park across the Potomac. Bill Clinton was devastated by the death of his boyhood friend: "How could this have happened? I should have stopped it somehow." Hillary, in tears, stayed up all night, crying and talking to friends, wondering if it could have been prevented. But the Clinton haters, and some in the mainstream media, had a different response.

Foster had been assailed by the *Wall Street Journal* and other papers for involvement in the Travel Office affair, characterized as "Travelgate" in the press. In his briefcase, found at the scene of his death, was a note: "The public will never believe the innocence of the Clintons and their loyal staff. The WSJ editors lie without consequence. I was not meant for the job or the spotlight of public life in Washington. Here ruining people is considered sport."

Foster, overworked and under stress, was suffering from untreated clinical depression. There was no evidence of any other reason for his action.

But the grieving Clintons could not bury their friend before the conspiracy stories began to be circulated.

"Suicide or murder?" Pat Robertson asked on this network broadcast; was Foster killed to cover up wrongdoings about Whitewater or other crimes? Rush Limbaugh claimed that Foster died in a Clinton "safe house" and that the corpse was deposited at the site where it was found to make the death appear a suicide. On another occasion, after cautioning his vast audience of millions that he was passing on a rumor, Limbaugh suggested that Vince Foster was murdered in an apartment owned by Hillary Clinton. Right-wing writer Christopher Ruddy, with support from the Arkansas Project, published *The Strange Death of Vincent Foster*. Another Clinton-despising author, Ambrose Evans-Pritchard, speculated that the death was really an "extra-judicial execution," a sign of incipient fascism, for "a government that winks at murder will wink at anything."

Even if it was not murder, "Was dread of further scandal a triggering cause of this apparent suicide?" asked famous *New York Times* columnist William Safire. "What terrible secret drove Vincent Foster?"[4]

Perhaps it was not surprising that a prominent figure at a major newspaper would sound like that band of Clinton haters circulating conspiracy tales to damage the object of their animus. Even before his election, the "mainstream media" was deeply involved in major efforts at uncovering evidence that Bill Clinton was guilty of corruption by money and/or corruption of power.

On March 8, 1992, the *New York Times* ran the first of what became a long series of front-page stories by reporter Jeff Gerth on Whitewater. It was just before Super Tuesday, in the midst of the presidential primary season. Gerth was a well-known journalist who would win the Pulitzer Prize, but not for his coverage of Clinton or the Whitewater matter. The article, headlined "Clintons Joined S&L Operator in an Ozark Real Estate Venture," implied that Bill and Hillary Clinton "stood to lose little" if Whitewater failed but might have "cashed in" if it had done well. There were several charges of possible wrongdoing by the Clintons and a clear indication that Governor Bill Clinton was in a position to help his business partner, Jim McDougal, owner of a failing savings and loan association that was subject to state regulation.

After the inauguration, the *Times* returned again and again to Whitewater. Gerth, examining documents and interviewing a number of people, was getting some information from Sheffield Nelson, perhaps the most bitter of Clinton's political enemies in Arkansas, and Floyd Brown of Citizens United. (Brown, a right-wing political operative, was creator of the infamous Willie Horton ad during the Dukakis campaign in 1988 and the author, in 1992, of *Slick Willie: Why America Cannot Trust Bill Clinton*, an angry campaign piece.)

Gerth's work would be severely challenged, and not only by Clinton supporters. Arkansas journalist Gene Lyons argued that an arrogant but credulous eastern writer, "parachuting" into Little Rock for a few months, had been manipulated by Clinton haters. Lyons's *Harper's Magazine* article was titled "Fools for Scandal: How The New York Times Got Whitewater Wrong." (Even that first headline in March 1992 was incorrect, Lyons noted; when Bill and Hillary Clinton made their misbegotten investment in 1978, McDougal was not even involved in the banking or savings and loan business.)

Why did America's most important newspaper seem fixated on an obscure Arkansas land deal? Bill Clinton and some others believed one reason was the transparent animosity of Howell Raines, the editorial page editor, a prize-winning writer and, like Clinton, a southerner. Both had been shaped by the civil rights movement, but Clinton's friend Taylor Branch, author of the famous book trilogy *America in the King Years*, felt that Raines, responding to the unflattering stories about this newcomer to Washington, might have viewed Clinton as a sleazy character, "some hillbilly Bubba" from Arkansas. Yet the *New York Times* would not have Whitewater to itself. The *Los Angeles Times* and the *Wall Street Journal* were both on the case. And from November 1993 to February 1994, the New York City "paper of record's" most important rival for national journalistic prominence, the *Washington Post*, published sixty-two articles on Whitewater, sixteen on the front page. Editor Leonard Downie, knowing that the *Times* had beaten the *Post* to the initial story, wanted to expose what he believed might be an elaborate cover-up. One of his colleagues said, "Len thinks this is his Watergate." Others speculated that Downie felt that Clinton had lied during the campaign about the draft and marijuana use and, perhaps like Raines, was offended by the stories of sexual improprieties.

Whatever the reasons, the fact that the two most influential newspapers in America were relentlessly flogging this story would have an important impact on subsequent events. Their articles influenced prominent Democrats, including Senators Daniel Patrick Moynihan and Bill Bradley. Already under pressure from fiercely partisan Republicans on the Hill to name an outsider to investigate the increasingly complicated reports coming from Arkansas, assailed in the editorial pages of the *Times*, the *Post*, and the *Journal* to bypass his Attorney General, who reported to the President, and appoint a Special Prosecutor, Clinton finally gave in.

White House counsel Bernard Nussbaum warned that this would be a disastrous error. Whoever was appointed would keep widening the investigation until something was found; it could become an endless hunting expedition against a sitting President, a "magnet for allegations." Here is "an institution I understand," Nussbaum, a man who had been involved in the Watergate prosecutions, told Clinton. "They have one case. They have unlimited resources. They have no time limit. Their entire reputation hinges on making that one case."

They will "broaden the investigation," he predicted, "to areas we haven't even contemplated. . . . They will chase you, your family, and friends throughout the presidency and beyond." Finally, Nussbaum even asked Hillary, who had been on his staff back in the Watergate investigation, "Why are you going to put your head in that noose?"

But Bill Clinton, saying he was not worried about an investigation because he had done nothing wrong, at last agreed to the appointment. He would recall: "Though I had said I could live with it, I almost didn't live through it." It was, he would write, "the worst presidential decision I ever made, wrong on the facts, wrong on the law, wrong on the politics, wrong for the presidency and the Constitution. Perhaps I did it because I was completely exhausted and grieving over Mother; it took all the concentration I could muster just to do the job I had left her funeral to do. What I should have done is release the records, resist the prosecutor, give an extensive briefing to all the Democrats who wanted it, and ask for their support."[5]

Instead, Clinton now asked Attorney General Janet Reno to appoint a special prosecutor. Reno was reluctant; a member of the President's cabinet appointing an investigator of the President smacked of inside dealing and would be attacked by anti-Clinton activists, GOP adversaries, and national editors. But there was no alternative, for the paradox was that Republicans, seething at what they viewed as the unfair treatment of Ronald Reagan (and, earlier, Richard Nixon) by such special prosecutors, had opposed the continuation of the Independent Counsel Act, which had expired in 1992. Prominent GOP figures had considered it, in the words of one writer, "not as post-Watergate reform but as an unconstitutional monstrosity, clearly designed by partisan Democrats to harass Republican administrations." Some notable (and conservative) legal experts had agreed. Supreme Court Justice Antonin Scalia, the court's preeminent conservative, writing the single dissenting opinion when the court deemed the independent counsel law constitutional in 1988, reviled the existence of "an unaccountable prosecutor," arguing that the "context of this statute is acrid with the smell of threatened impeachment."

Reno asked three deputies to nominate an experienced attorney who would be viewed as an impartial investigator. The choice was Robert B. Fiske Jr., careful, taciturn 63-year-old senior partner at a major New York law firm, a former U.S. Attorney for the Southern District of New York and so an individual with wide experience as both a prosecutor and a defense attorney. He was a notable figure in the American Bar Association, and a moderate Republican who had voted for George H. W. Bush.

After insisting on the authority to essentially investigate anyone for any-thing, a broader jurisdiction granted than for other special counsels, Fiske accepted the appointment. He would respond to the press and political clamor about the Foster suicide by adding it to the Whitewater allegations, which included charges of illegal interference by Treasury Department officials. Newspaper stories—some from Gerth's reporting—about Hill-ary Rodham Clinton's profits from her success in speculating in the com-modities market back in the Arkansas days made that an issue. Fiske's team questioned White House aides, and the special prosecutor interviewed the President and the first lady. (As the wide-ranging inquiry proceeded, Web-ster Hubbell, the Clintons' old friend who had become a member of the Justice Department, suddenly resigned when there were revelations of his questionable billing practices back at the Rose law firm.)

The special prosecutor was opposed to congressional hearings until he was able to complete much of his work; he was aware of how such hearings had weakened the cases prepared by the prosecutor in Iran-Contra. But angry Republicans were anxious to hold such hearings and pressed ahead with them. Roger Ailes, president of CNBC and soon to be head of Fox News, accused the administration of a "cover-up with regard to Whitewater that includes . . . land fraud, illegal contributions, abuse of power . . ., suicide cover up, [and] possible murder."

At this point, some columnists and editorial writers at the *Times* and the *Wall Street Journal* began to accuse Fiske himself of complicity in a White House cover-up, and key conservative political figures joined in, convinced now that Fiske was an apostate Republican. But he ignored his critics and pushed forward with his investigation, and five months after his appoint-ment, in late June, released two preliminary reports. One simply confirmed the suicide of Foster: "There is no evidence to the contrary" or "links from it to Whitewater." The other stated that no crimes had been committed in the White House–Treasury contacts.

Only hours after these reports were made public, Bill Clinton signed the bill reauthorizing the Independent Counsel Act. Both Houses of Congress had voted for this law, which seemed only reasonable because the President himself had, months before, appointed a special prosecutor. "Do I have to?" Clinton asked his chief of staff before signing, yet he knew there was no choice.

When the Attorney General made application for a Whitewater inde-pendent counsel under the new law, and formally requested Fiske be the one selected "so that he may continue his ongoing investigation," the request was denied. The act, as in the past, called for a three-judge panel—appointed by the Chief Justice of the Supreme Court—that would name the special prosecutor. And this three-judge panel rejected Fiske and appointed

Kenneth Starr. It was a shock to Fiske and many in the White House, but it was applauded by GOP opponents.[6]

"Wait a minute! Just wait a goddamn minute!" shouted James Carville in a call to the President. He recounted a chance encounter with Starr at National Airport, in which Starr had openly criticized Clinton to Carville. He argued that it was obvious that Starr was a partisan pawn. But other White House figures persuaded Bill Clinton that there was no point in fighting the appointment or attacking this new appointee. Carville's response was a letter calling it a "historic and unconscionable violation of fairness and justice," relinquishing his White House pass so he would not be constrained from speaking out against the decision to make Starr the special prosecutor.

Still, for many in Washington, in the words of one Clinton supporter, Starr was considered "an eminently respectable choice." He was partner in a famous law firm, earning perhaps $1 million a year, a seemingly mild-mannered, 48-year-old bespectacled Washington insider who cultivated a reputation for reasonableness. He had served as clerk for Chief Justice Warren Burger, had sat on the U.S. Court of Appeals for the District of Columbia from 1983 to 1987 (he liked to be called "Judge" Starr long after leaving the court), and had earned the deference of the *Washington Post* when he had handed down a landmark First Amendment decision in a libel suit brought against the paper. He was in the Justice Department in the Reagan years and was Solicitor General in the administration of George H. W. Bush.

But critics had a different view. They saw an intense partisan who had told *Time* magazine he looked forward to a new Republican administration, perhaps headed by his good friend, former Vice President Dan Quayle. They viewed Starr as a passionate social conservative, indoctrinated in biblical inerrancy by his father, a Church of Christ minister renowned for deeply fundamentalist interpretations of the scripture. The biggest clients of Kenneth Starr's law firm were tobacco and auto companies—which opposed government regulation and had repeatedly clashed with the Clinton administration—as well as the Republican National Committee and a number of wealthy right-wing foundations. His close friends belonged, as did Starr, to the Federalist Society, "a partisan fellowship," one legal writer noted, "that provided the intellectual energy behind the Reagan revolution in the courts." He had been hired by the Bradley Foundation, which had financed, among other things, the *American Spectator*. He had joined the advisory board of the Washington Legal Foundation, which had spearheaded a campaign to attack Robert Fiske. He already had spoken out against the President's position in the Paula Jones case, in which Bill Clinton was accused of sexual misconduct, and was about to submit a brief on her behalf for another conservative organization, an antifeminist group called Independent Woman's Forum, funded by Richard Mellon Scaife.

Why was Starr the choice? Critics pointed to the composition of the three-judge panel, known as the Special Division, which had been appointed by Chief Justice William Rehnquist, who had been nominated to the court by Richard Nixon. On it were two strong conservatives: Joseph Sneed of Texas and David Santelle of North Carolina, one of the federal judiciary's most extreme right-wing figures. In 1991, Santelle, another member of the Federalist Society like Justices Rehnquist and Scalia, had published a law review article in which he accused "leftist heretics" of trying to turn the United States into a "collectivist, egalitarian, materialistic, race-conscious, hyper-secular and socially permissive state." Before the appointment, Santelle had met for lunch with the two Republican senators from North Carolina, Lauch Faircloth—who would soon hire Santelle's wife for work in his office—and Jesse Helms, who had been Santelle's close political ally and champion. Both senators were on the right wing of their own party and were virulent critics of the Clinton White House and of Robert Fiske. Santelle later admitted that the subject of the independent counsel "might have come up."

When word of this lunch appeared in the press, there was an uproar. The *New York Times* editorial was headlined "Mr. Starr's Duty to Resign," arguing that there must be "the appearance as well as the reality of impartial justice." (Five former presidents of the American Bar Association had already called on Starr to refuse to serve.) But Starr did not resign. And one scholar would argue that it was Sneed, not Santelle, who might have been Starr's strongest advocate, a fellow Texan who had Kenneth Starr as an outstanding student when he taught at Duke Law School.[7]

Now appointed, Starr assembled Fiske's staff, but most of them resigned, angered at their boss's dismissal. His new Office of Independent Counsel (OIC) staff would include Hickman Ewing Jr. and Jackie Bennett. Ewing, a tough former federal prosecutor from Memphis, was a political conservative and born-again Christian who had been praised by several Christian-right organizations for his work. Bennett, a tall, aggressive attorney from Indiana with prosecutorial experience, later told an interviewer: "A lot of people would like to make the case that Ken Starr staffed his office with a bunch of right-wingers who were determined to take Clinton down. And I'm probably not a good argument in rebuttal." But, he added, "no personal views I had" affected his ability to remain neutral.

As the new team began its work in late summer 1994, the House and Senate Banking committees began hearings on Whitewater. Twenty-nine Clinton administration officials were subpoenaed or testified. All would be cleared of any wrongdoing. At the beginning of January, the Democratic majority on the Senate Banking Committee released a report finding that no laws were broken in the Whitewater matter. But, of course, the GOP had won majorities in both houses of Congress in the November election, and when the new bodies were sworn in, the tone of the inquiries would change.

In July, the Senate special Whitewater Committee, chaired by Republican Alfonse D'Amato of New York, who would serve as chairman of Bob Dole's presidential campaign, began hearings on Whitewater and the Foster suicide. The hearings would last eleven months. Forty-nine subpoenas were issued to federal agencies and others involved in the affair, and there was continuous media attention. Over at the House, the Whitewater inquiry would resume, not to be concluded until mid-June 1996, with a final report in which Republicans accused the Clinton White House of stonewalling and Democrats, in a minority response, claimed that the President and first lady were victimized by a modern-day witch hunt. The politics of scandal were on display.

Meanwhile, Starr was pushing forward with work begun under Fiske, pursuing Jim McDougal, who back in 1978 had invited the Clintons to invest in Whitewater. Four years later, McDougal had bought a small savings and loan, naming it Madison Guaranty. In 1984, federal regulators had begun to question the financial stability of Madison Guaranty and the owner's numerous speculative land deals. McDougal, who had asked the Rose law firm to do legal work, later borrowed $300,000 from a company owned by David Hale, a former Little Rock municipal judge, and Hale's company subsequently received federal funds from the Small Business Administration (SBA).

In 1989, Morgan Guaranty finally collapsed after a series of bad loans, and the federal government shut it down, spending millions bailing it out. It was one of many such institutions—and a relatively small one, a twentieth the size of another failed S&L in Arkansas alone—that foundered during the "savings and loan scandal" in the Reagan years, when lax federal regulation had necessitated a massive, half-trillion-dollar federal rescue mission. McDougal would be acquitted after indictment on federal fraud charges, but the federal Resolution Trust Company (RTC), created to manage the bail-out, was investigating the causes of the Morgan collapse.

In August, McDougal, his former wife Susan, and Arkansas governor Jim Guy Tucker were charged with bank fraud relating to the questionable SBA loans. All three targets of this action were being pressed by Starr's team to link both Clintons to illegal activities.

A key figure in the case was David Hale, the pudgy wheeler-dealer who was known, as one writer put it, for "skating along the edge of the law." An Arkansas journalist had characterized him as a "paranoid liar and embezzler"; he was called "just a crook, plain and simple" by the attorney who once had prosecuted him for bilking money from poor and elderly African American families. Facing the federal grand jury indictment charging him with massively defrauding the SBA, he began telling national news-paper correspondents (and Little Rock now was filled with them) that Jim McDougal and then-Governor Bill Clinton had pressured him into giving the $300,000 loan to Susan McDougal's advertising company.

Fearing a long jail sentence, the frightened Hale had gone to an old friend, "Justice Jim" Johnson, Clinton's enemy of long standing, the aging racist politician who referred to the President as that "queer-mongering, whore-happening adulterer, a baby-killing, draft-dodging, dope-tolerating, lying, two-faced treasonist activist." After asking Hale what he was indicted for and hearing the response, "conspiring to defraud," Johnson—who sub-sequently had more than forty phone conversations with Hale—said: "Then you've got to have some conspirators." At this point, Hale exclaimed: "Clin-ton and his gang were part of it."

The SBA reported that it had lost more than $3 million due to Hale's self-dealing transactions. But after he pleaded guilty to defrauding the government, David Hale's sentencing was postponed until just before the McDougal trial. He became a critical player in the effort to tie Bill Clinton to a criminal act. He was kept out of jail and paid a tax-free annual sti-pend by the OIC after agreeing to testify. Meanwhile, he was also paid by the Arkansas Project. And he was receiving legal counsel from Ted Olson, a famous eastern attorney, the powerful and well-connected old friend of Ken Starr who also served as a lawyer for both the Arkansas Project and the *American Spectator*, where his published essays, under the pseudonym "Nasty, Brutish and Short," accused Clinton of wrongdoing.

At the McDougal/Tucker trial, which at first seemed headed for the acquittal of the accused, James McDougal, who earlier vociferously had denied stories about joining Bill Clinton in pressuring Hale to make loans, now suddenly became "a cooperating witness" for the Starr team. His former wife continued to deny any such involvement. She insisted that McDougal's erratic behavior appalled her; she believed he was acting this way because it might help him with the sentencing. He shouted at her: "F— the Clintons! What'd they ever do for us?" He had a history of mental illness and had been under psychiatric care. At the trial, Jim McDougal was a sick man with a clogged carotid artery who twice during the course of proceedings required hospitalization. But his testimony, while damaging him, his wife, and Tucker, did not damage President Bill Clinton, who testified on vid-eotape. After the verdict, the jury forewoman would tell ABC News, "The President's credibility was never an issue."

McDougal was found guilty on eighteen counts of conspiracy and fraud. (Starr asked for a reduced sentence for his cooperating witness, and McDou-gal, given three years, would die in prison.) An angry Governor Tucker, who believed he was simply an incidental victim of an OIC witch hunt aimed at the President, was acquitted on the major charges but convicted of one count of conspiracy and one count of mail fraud and had to resign his office. His replacement was Lieutenant Governor Mike Huckabee, a Baptist minister who would become the third Republican to occupy the Arkansas chief executive's office since the Civil War.

In August 1996, Susan McDougal was sentenced to serve two years in jail for making false statements and for misuse of some of the SBA funds for personal purposes. But Starr wanted her to implicate Clinton. In the months to come, he pursued her relentlessly, convinced that she was lying and privately speculating that she was protecting the President because she had had an affair with him earlier. Certain that Starr and his colleagues would use her denials of any Clinton wrongdoing as a way of bringing perjury charges, she refused to testify before Starr's grand jury; he responded by convicting her of contempt, with more prison time. She was incarcerated with drug dealers and murderers, put in a Plexiglas bubble in the middle of a jail pod, and then forced to spend twenty-three hours a day in a windowless cell usually reserved for convicted killers. She was refused contact with other prisoners and photographed chained in orange jail garb during transfer again and again from one prison to another. This "Hannibal Lecter–like confinement," Bill Clinton would write, came to an end only after the American Civil Liberties Union filed a suit alleging that she was held in "barbaric" conditions at Starr's request.

Nothing was working for the OIC with Ms. McDougal or with Starr's entire Whitewater hunt for evidence of Clinton criminality. Hale's allegations had gone nowhere. Starr's ever-widening probe had rocked Arkansas political circles, involving businessmen and lawyers who had not even a vague connection to the Whitewater Development Corporation, but it had not touched Clinton. A second "Whitewater trial" brought little satisfaction to the OIC. This time it was two rural county bankers who were accused of illegally funneling cash from their small bank into Bill Clinton's campaigns in 1990 and 1992. But the jury returned innocent verdicts on felony counts and no one disputed that the money had belonged to the campaign or was spent legally. The frustrated Hick Ewing promised there would be a new trial, but Starr refused to proceed.

All the leads pointing to Clinton illegal activity were going nowhere. At the RTC, that temporary federal agency created during the Bush administration to bail out S&L depositors and liquidate assets of institutions seized by the government, L. Jean Lewis, an RTC investigator, had alleged that the Clintons might be involved in criminal behavior connected to the collapse of Madison Guaranty. A self-described conservative Republican who once referred to Clinton as a "lying bastard," Lewis, who was neither a lawyer nor a CPA, had become a star witness on Capitol Hill. First she appeared before the House Banking Committee hearings on Whitewater. (These sessions were presided over by committee chair Jim Leach of Iowa, who compared Bill Clinton's Arkansas to Huey Long's Louisiana.) Months later, Lewis was back in D.C. at the Senate investigation.

Her charges attracted attention in the national newspapers. "Senate Hearing Touches on Clinton's Integrity" was the *New York Times* headline. But her appearance was a failure for Senator D'Amato, and she crumbled under questioning. Even worse, her intemperate behavior at work had led to an internal inquiry at the RTC's Kansas City, Missouri, office. She was accused of improper handling and disclosure of confidential documents and of secretly tape-recording her colleagues. Although Starr's office had intervened to defend Lewis and turn the investigation against her supervisors, it was a failed effort, for the RTC had hired a prominent San Francisco law firm, Pillsbury, Madison & Sutro, to investigate the issue of the Clintons and Whitewater. George Stephanopoulos at first complained about the partisan bias of the firm because a senior partner, Jay Stephens, the former Reagan and Bush U.S. Attorney for the District of Columbia, had been fired by Clinton in 1993. But the Pillsbury Report, a massive document issued in December 1995 after a lengthy $3.6 million investigation, concluded that the President and the first lady had told the truth about their Whitewater investment.

It found no evidence that Whitewater's losses had been subsidized by taxpayers in the savings and loan bailout: "There is no basis to assert that the Clintons knew anything of substance about the McDougals' advances to Whitewater, the source of funds used ... [or] the source of the funds used to make payment on bank debt. . . . [T]here is no basis to charge the Clintons with any kind of primary liability or fraud or misconduct. This investigation has revealed no evidence to support any such claims."[8]

The Pillsbury Report did not impress the Washington press corps; their papers, which had featured Jean Lewis's charges in her initial testimony, buried the stories about it.

Weeks later, there would be a new scandal story to pursue. The White House announced that a number of documents, including some papers detailing legal work Hillary Clinton had done at the Rose law firm in the mid-Eighties for Madison Guaranty, had been discovered misfiled in the Executive Mansion. It was true that Hillary Clinton, believing any cooperation with Starr would only lead to further harassing requests, had resisted sending documents from her Little Rock time to the special prosecutor. (Washington insiders would argue that the best way for the Clintons to have handled the whole Whitewater matter was to immediately have released all materials having anything to do with these Little Rock years, and the first lady's resistance was a problem.) But in this case, a friend and aide of

Hillary's, who had worked with her back in Little Rock before coming to Washington, had mistaken the sheaf of folded papers for old records and mistakenly put it in a box with other files. They were finally sent to the OIC, which had subpoenaed billing records many months before.

Senator D'Amato's committee immediately looked for evidence, never found, of obstruction of justice and perjury. William Safire, in a commentary titled "Blizzard of Lies," called Hillary Clinton a "congenital liar" in his widely read *Times* column. White House press secretary Michael McCurry said that that if Bill Clinton were not President, he would have "delivered a more forceful response to that column on the bridge of Mr. Safire's nose."

But Kenneth Starr now summoned the first lady to testify before his grand jury, insisting that she not be questioned privately under oath as before or even on videotape but to present herself at the courthouse like anyone accused of a felony. It was clear that photographers and TV crews would be stationed outside. Bill Clinton was furious at Starr's conduct. Fresh from his victory in outmaneuvering Gingrich and the GOP in the government shutdown affair, the President of the United States was powerless to protect his wife from this humiliation. Of course, these tactics by the OIC were now standard operating procedure in dealing with the Clinton White House, where so many on the staff had been forced to hire lawyers. One of Bill Clinton's top advisers whispered to Hillary, "Until you've testified at least five times before the grand jury like I have, you're just small potatoes."

In a few months, the RTC would file a supplemental report confirming that the billing records supported Hillary Clinton's account of her legal activities. But Starr and his pugnacious aides would not be satisfied. Even two years later, Ewing was still trying to persuade the OIC team to indict Hillary Rodham Clinton as part of a criminal conspiracy involving the bank records, Rose law firm work, Whitewater, and Madison Guaranty. "As far as I'm concerned, she did it," exclaimed the prosecutor. But his colleagues, as one of them put it, felt that if they attempted a trial of Mrs. Clinton, "we were going to get our asses kicked." Kenneth Starr would not take that risk and finally Ewing agreed. Death had sealed the troubled Jim McDougal's lips, he conceded, and neither Susan McDougal nor Webb Hubbell seemed interested in cooperating: "We shouldn't go."[9]

There had been a concerted effort to dig into Whitewater. Starr and his prosecutors were the major players but they were not alone. There were the staffs of the congressional committees and those several prominent eastern journalists. There was James Stewart, the well-known investigative reporter whose book, *Blood Sport*, would gain national attention, with the author featured on numerous network television programs alleging questionable behavior by both Clintons, although not offering any specific documentation. And there was that wide variety of Arkansas Project figures, some working with old Clinton adversaries from his home state. All had been digging for evidence that Bill Clinton and his wife were guilty of criminal behavior or, at least, unethical conduct. But Whitewater had proven a dry hole.

Starr and his OIC team explored other alleged scandals that might reveal Clinton culpability. One example was the issue of FBI background files, some involving Reagan and Bush officials, kept in the Clinton White House by error rather than returned to the FBI when Clinton took office. Two midlevel employees, both later forced to resign, were assembling a list of those who had legitimate security pass clearance for the Clinton White House and had not recognized the mistake when documents involving GOP administration figures were sent to the archives. Of course, this would be called "Filegate" and lead to dark tales of Bill Clinton trying to politicize the FBI and having a cavalier approach to sensitive security matters.

Starr took over the "Filegate" matter. Already, he had joined Republican congressional efforts to continue a seemingly endless inquiry into Vincent Foster's death, not satisfied with the Fiske report. He also elected to delve once more into the mysteries of the White House Travel Office firings, "Travelgate." For years he would hint that all these matters were still under investigation. But only in fall 1998, near the end of his tenure at OIC, would he admit that he had no additional evidence relating to them or to Whitewater. Furious Democrats asked why he had not come forward to exonerate the President and first lady long before. He had no plausible answer. Even one of his Republican champions, Congressman Henry Hyde, confessed his shock: "We were really surprised at his testimony, that he did not have more material on any of these matters."

In fact, these all were pseudo scandals and there was no real substance to them (although not to the sex scandal to come). A culture of conspiracy had arisen concerning the Clinton White House and the special prosecutor law had allowed for seemingly endless fishing expeditions into alleged crimes. It affected not only the President, his wife, and administrative staff but his cabinet. Five Clinton Cabinet members would find themselves under investigation by separate special prosecutors: Secretary of the Interior Bruce Babbitt, Secretary of Agriculture Mike Espy, Secretary of Housing Henry Cisneros, Secretary of Commerce Ronald Brown, and Secretary of Labor Alexis Herman.

These inquiries stretched out for months and years at enormous cost. There was nothing of importance found in any of them, which focused on alleged misuse of campaign funds or influence-peddling charges. All were ultimately dismissed, many with scornful comments about the prosecutors. (After Special Prosecutor Donald Smalz spent almost $20 million and four years on the critical issue of whether Mike Espy was guilty of illicitly receiving gifts and gratuities, namely some sports tickets and airline trips, one juror, after hearing seventy witnesses in the trial that found Espy not guilty, told reporters: "This is the most bogus thing I ever saw. I can't believe they even brought this to trial.") There was, of course, one conviction. Henry Cisneros, after a fifty-two–month investigation costing almost $15 million, pled guilty to failing to report the total amount of payments he had made to a former mistress. He was fined $10,000.[10]

As the Whitewater matter (which itself cost over $50 million) and all the other investigations dragged on across the last years of Clinton's first term and into the second, they had to take a toll on the President and everyone in his administration caught up in them. But Bill Clinton, often seething with anger at the actions of Starr and his fellow prosecutors and feeling helpless to stop the continuous stream of scandal stories dominating the headlines, persevered in addressing the big domestic and foreign policy challenges of his moment in history.

And the efforts to link him to the traditional scandals found in American political history had failed. There was no real evidence of corruption by money or the corruption of power in the Clinton White House or in the life and work of Bill Clinton. There was no Teapot Dome scandal in the Nineties, no Watergate, no Iran-Contra.

All this had seemed obvious by early 1996. Kenneth Starr's ethics adviser, Professor Samuel Dash of Georgetown Law School, the well-known former majority counsel on the House Judiciary Committee during the Watergate investigation, told him, "You have nothing." Dash reportedly said: "Zero plus zero plus zero equals zero"; the job was over, it was time to "close up shop."

The special prosecutor refused. Was it because Starr and his OIC team now bore deep animosity toward the President, believing that Clinton was a bad person, a sinful person, who "ought to be punished for it," as Dash would recall? It distorted their judgment: "Ken allowed his personal concepts of morality to interfere with the role of a prosecutor." And one writer would speculate that "the reason for the smoke and mirrors" across 1996 was that "even if they could not pin anything on Clinton, the appearance of scandal might be enough to stop him from being reelected."

In February 1997, with Clinton safely inaugurated for a second term, Kenneth Starr announced he would leave the investigation and that he was accepting the position of dean at Pepperdine University in Malibu, California. But angry figures on the right now assailed him. William Safire's column was titled, "The Big Flinch," and he called Starr a "wimp." Richard Mellon Scaife, who had helped fund the Pepperdine position, expressed his contempt. Was Starr leaving because he had completed his work? Or was it now obvious that there was "no 'there' there," as one judge would put it, in the failed efforts to prosecute alleged Clinton criminality?[11]

Under pressure, Starr took back his resignation. Perhaps it was easier to continue because his staff soon discovered new leads in the pursuit of the President. Of course, this time, it would not be corruption by money or of power. It would be all about sex.

Certainly, sexual scandal had been a staple of rumor as well as news reports throughout the Clinton years. It long had been on the radar of the OIC, and Kenneth Starr, of course, had been involved in the Paula Jones matter before becoming the special prosecutor.

It must have been immensely frustrating for Bill Clinton to be the object of this intense scrutiny when he knew that so many predecessors had been given an almost free pass by both the press and their political adversaries in the matter of personal sexual activity. Powerful, popular, and successful Presidents in recent history not only had extramarital affairs, but even engaged in reckless womanizing without prominent Washington journalists, who knew them well and were aware of much of the activity, publishing a word.

John F. Kennedy, Clinton's old hero, reportedly had more affairs while in the office, even in his brief thousand days. Two of the many women allegedly involved were linked to a prostitution ring in Great Britain, another to liaisons with a notorious mafia leader, yet another to rumors of espionage for East Germany. There was even a White House intern on the list. And JFK certainly was not alone among recent Presidents in having the press allow his private life to be kept private. The belief was that their sexual activity had nothing to do with how they performed the duties of their office. But after his former mentor Gary Hart had seen his presidential aspirations destroyed by stories about an affair in 1988, Bill Clinton must have known that this was a different time.

The saga of the Jones legal case had begun with a call Ms. Jones placed to a local Little Rock lawyer in January 1994, complaining that her first name had appeared in a lurid story that month in the *American Spectator*, purporting to chronicle Bill Clinton's extramarital sexual activity while governor of Arkansas.

The article was written by David Brock, at the time a fervently conservative young writer. Brock had gained celebrity in 1992 with his poisonous attack on the woman who had accused Supreme Court nominee Clarence Thomas of sexual misbehavior. "The Real Anita Hill" was a devastating assault on Professor Hill and helped salvage the Thomas nomination and place him on the court. Later Brock would regret the "sloppy, skewed, slanderous material that poured off my keyboard," including his reference to Hill as being "a little nutty and a little slutty." But at the time it made the author an emerging star in right-wing circles and inside the Arkansas Project. It helped to double the readership of the *Spectator*, where Brock now had a full-time position, and the paper would gain many new readers after publishing the piece on Clinton.

Titled "His Cheatin' Heart," the article was the product of an effort by old Clinton enemy Cliff Jackson, who had been at the center of the draft-dodging charges during the campaign, to market a story being told by four state troopers who had worked at the Governor's Mansion in Little Rock. They described Bill Clinton, Brock later wrote, as a "sexually vora-cious, sociopathic cipher," and Hillary Clinton as a "foulmouthed, castrat-ing, power-mad harpy." It was an ugly tale, filled with explicit, gross, and degrading images. Brock later cast doubt on its veracity in his book *Blinded by the Right*. But after publication, while editors at the *New York Times* and other major national papers dismissed it as sleazy trash (although the *Los Angeles Times* was working on a similar article), CNN featured the trooper piece as its lead story. It would become known, of course, as "Troopergate."

Brock had not meant to name the various women the troopers claimed Clinton had been with in these pornographic tales. "Paula" somehow had appeared in the printed version and Jones now wanted to press charges. But suing a magazine, protected by freedom of the press, would be chancier than suing the President. Jackson persuaded Jones and her husband, Steve (who long had disparaged President Clinton), that bringing the subject "to the attention of the American people" would promote the case. It might force the President into a deeply damaging public apology for the alleged incident, during a brief encounter in the Excelsior Hotel in Little Rock in 1991. He brought Jones and the troopers to Washington for a press inter-view at the Conservative Political Action Conference (CPAC) meeting, where surrounded by bumper stickers asking WHO KILLED VINCE FOSTER? and doctored photographs of a naked Hillary Clinton, Jackson was greeted as a celebrity.[12]

Attending the CPAC session at the Omni Shoreham Hotel was a *Wash-ington Post* reporter, Michael Isikoff. The press conference did not go well for Jackson and his group. The White House dismissed Jones's claims, and the national press was unimpressed by the troopers and Paula Jones, casting doubt on any hopes for lucrative book and movie deals. (Ms. Jones sub-sequently would be paid a small fee for telling her tale of sexual abuse on the notorious *Clinton Chronicles* videotape.) Still, Isikoff saw a major story there. He would fly down to Little Rock for more interviews. Already, he had helped invent, in the words of one writer, a "new field in American journalism, sexual investigative reporting," for his articles exposing the illicit affair of religious right televangelist Jim Bakker. Now, as in the title of the book he would publish, he would attempt to "uncover Clinton."

As Isikoff pursued the sex story, trying to find women who might talk about Bill Clinton's extramarital sexual activity, the proposed Jones legal action against Clinton would move haltingly forward. Two new lawyers were recruited to handle the case against the President. Bill Clinton, who strongly denied sexually harassing Ms. Jones, had to hire a prominent (and expensive) Washington attorney, Robert Bennett. The two sides came close to an agreement in 1994. But it fell apart at the last moment, because, in the words of author Jeffrey Toobin, "Steve wanted an apology—and money."

Throughout 1995 and into election year 1996, the case faced a series of delays as the White House tried to settle or push any legal action into the future, so it would not be an issue in the campaign. It was stalled in the appellate courts for more than a year. After the election, Bill Clinton offered to settle. "I didn't want to, because it would take about half of everything Hillary and I had saved over twenty years and I knew that we would win the case if it ever went to trial. But I didn't want to waste any days of the three years I had left on it." The offer was $700,000, the full amount her legal team had demanded, but there would be no apology.

Jones refused the settlement, and her lawyers were astonished: "Our opponents may portray your refusal as a money-grubbing attempt to further develop this story for profitable book rights and portray you as . . . under the influence of right-wing Clinton haters." But Jones, now living in southern California with her husband, an airline ticket agent at LAX, in fact had come under the influence of an anti-abortion activist and religious-right radio personality named Susan Carpenter-McMillan. This new adviser, working to secure Jones a deal for a book (never published), was an accomplished self-advertiser. She soon was appearing on national television shows, characterizing Bill Clinton as a "liar" and "philanderer."

Jones's lawyers ultimately would leave her case, and the Rutherford Institute, a Christian right public-interest law firm in Virginia, contacting McMillan, offered a new a set of attorneys from Dallas. They would be less interested in a settlement than creating an expanding critique of Clinton's sexual activities.

But prior to the change in legal representation in September 1997, there had been important developments in the case. In her Arkansas court, Judge Susan Webber Wright had granted Clinton's motion for summary judgment, ruling that Jones could not show she had suffered any damages. The Eighth District Court of Appeals, in a two to one verdict, had overruled Wright. Clinton's counsel then brought the case to the Supreme Court, arguing that a sitting President should not be tried for an incident occurring prior to his time in office. They asked that any trial be delayed until after he left office.

Before this critical case reached the Supreme Court, a new, shadow team of lawyers emerged to help shape a favorable verdict for Jones. Three well-connected attorneys from major firms, graduates of prominent law schools, passionately conservative members of the Federalist Society who reviled Bill Clinton, secretly organized a virtual mock trial. Famous conservative Judge Robert Bork (close poker-playing friend of Justices Scalia and Rehnquist) served as adviser; the goal: to game-plan a strategy to persuade the Supreme Court to allow the trial to go forward. Along with Ted Olson, the notable appellate attorney and Arkansas Project figure who had wide experience appearing before the court, the shadow team would provide the arguments used by the Jones lawyers.

Because they worked behind the scenes and did not want their names used, they were called the "elves," a term apparently coined by their friend Ann Coulter: "There are a lot of us busy elves working away in Santa's workshop." (Coulter was a right-wing lawyer and media figure, deeply involved in the anti-Clinton effort, soon to gain notoriety as author of a series of shrill books with incendiary titles aimed at ideological true believers, accusing liberals and Democrats of being "treasonous," "godless," and "demonic.")[13]

The elves were successful. On May 27, 1997, the court ordered the case to trial and depositions would begin in October.

The man who faced trial was a lawyer and a former law professor. And throughout his presidency, Clinton had demonstrated the importance of his legal training. He had held extensive meetings on candidates for lower court judicial appointments, carefully reviewing their backgrounds and legal positions. In considering Supreme Court justices, he had delved into the work of his nominees, choosing centrists, not ideologues. Several members of the White House Counsel's Office would note that Clinton's background in constitutional law—as well as his agile mind—allowed him to immediately grasp the legal implications of numerous policy questions. He spent hours with White House lawyers on the Securities Law Reform Act, the Brady bill, the Oklahoma City bombing. On the matter of the Religious Freedom Restoration Act, one counsel recalled that "after discussing the case for thirty minutes or so, the President walked in and engaged in an invigorating and free-ranging debate—the kind law professors die for—about tithing, the meaning of the Religious Clauses, and the application of the law to the case."

But this was not a constitutional law matter. It was about personal behavior and it was about sex. Before Bill Clinton would give his deposition, among those who had already given their statements in October were Gennifer Flowers and Kathleen Willey. And on December 19, Monica Lewinsky, the former White House employee, was served a subpoena ordering her to provide information in the suit. On January 16, 1998, a panel of federal judges authorized Kenneth Starr, the independent counsel, to expand his investigation to include allegations that the President encouraged Ms. Lewinsky to lie under oath. The next day, January 17, Bill Clinton was to give his deposition.

The elves had wanted the case to come to trial to embarrass and humiliate the President in a public setting. But in the months after the Supreme Court allowed the case to go forward, new developments provided a new opportunity: If the OIC could be brought into the case and if Bill Clinton could be trapped into lying about the Lewinsky affair under oath, this might be the issue that would lead to impeachment and destroy his presidency.

It started with the intrepid sex reporter, Michael Isikoff, and with Ms. Willey. Hearing from one of the Jones lawyers that an anonymous caller claimed she had been sexually harassed by the President in the Oval Office, Isikoff tracked down Willey, a White House volunteer and Democratic activist. She directed him to two sources who might confirm her tale of being "groped" by Bill Clinton. One was a friend who ultimately would deny that the troubled Willey, reeling from the suicide of her bankrupt husband, had ever told her this story. But the other was Linda Tripp, a former West Wing employee who had been transferred to the Pentagon. While Tripp would not give credence to a harassment narrative—"[Willey] was disheveled . . . but smiled from ear to ear"—she told Isikoff that she had a bigger story, because "you're barking up the wrong tree." The reporter pressed her for details and she agreed to tell him about the 23-year-old Monica Lewinsky, who was having an affair with the President.

Lewinsky, a Californian and a graduate of Lewis and Clark University, arrived at the White House in 1995 as an unpaid intern, later becoming a staff member in the legislative affairs office. She began a flirtatious and then sexual relationship with President Bill Clinton, starting in November 1995. There were perhaps twelve or fourteen very brief sexual encounters over the next eighteen months. But they happened right in the Oval Office, where she performed fellatio on him. Reporters knew nothing about it, nor did most members of the White House staff. But a few had suspicions. Deputy chief of staff Evelyn Lieberman, one of "the meanies" who kept Lewinsky away from the man she referred to as "Handsome," had seen Monica around the President and his quarters too often. Lieberman told Lewinsky's boss, "I want her out of here," and citing the former intern's "overfamiliarity," had her transferred to the Pentagon press office in 1996. It was there that Monica Lewinsky had been befriended by Tripp.

Linda Tripp, 47, had worked in the West Wing Counsel's Office in the George H. W. Bush years, staying on when Clinton won. An admirer of Bush, she disliked Clinton and his team. There were growing concerns about her leaking hostile stories to the press and finally she was pushed out, moving to the Pentagon in 1994. Now Tripp would characterize former West Wing colleagues as incompetent or inebriated (or worse) in testimony during the Senate investigation of Vince Foster. She began serving as a source for Tony Snow, the conservative columnist and Fox News talk show host. Her name appeared in Isikoff's *Newsweek* stories (he was no longer at the *Washington Post*) chronicling Willey's allegations. When she told Snow about her interest in a book deal for a White House exposé, he put her in touch with Lucianne Goldberg, a writer, literary agent, and right-wing political activist.

Would there be a market for such a book? Gary Aldrich, the Clinton-hating former FBI man, had made a splash with his alleged tell-all book, *Unlimited Access: An FBI Agent Inside the Clinton White House*, which had been subsidized by Scaife through the Southeastern Legal Federation. Among other tales, Aldrich repeated the rumors of Clinton's supposed late-night trysts at a Washington hotel. Perhaps Tripp's book idea might sell, but Goldberg had a larger agenda. Like some others, she wanted to destroy the Clinton presidency. She had been in touch with reporters, the Jones lawyers, and the young, conservative Internet gossip Matt Drudge. It was Goldberg who persuaded Linda Tripp to begin to tape her telephone conversations with Monica Lewinsky, who, on Tripp's urging, was relating intimate details of her affair with the President. It was Goldberg who contacted attorney (and prominent elf) Richard Porter with the tale of the intern and the President. And so when Paul Rosenzweig, one of Starr's OIC lawyers, visited his University of Chicago law school classmates, Porter and Jerome Marcus, two of the three elves, he was told about the affair. Kenneth Starr now would know about Lewinsky.

But how could OIC link her to the Jones case? It soon became clear that Ms. Lewinsky, both distressed because Clinton was no longer sexually involved with her (she told a biographer that May 24, 1997, had been "dump day") and wanting out of the Pentagon, had asked the President for help with new employment. Bill Clinton had referred her to his friend Vernon Jordan, who might aid the job search for a post outside of government. (She would be hired in public relations at Revlon, yet at a modest salary, less than her Pentagon position.) Starr went to Judge David Santelle. Arguing his OIC was already investigating Jordan for helping arrange employment for Webster Hubbell, Starr asked that he be allowed to add the Clinton–Lewinsky matter to his charge. Santelle agreed.[14]

Three days before Clinton gave his fateful deposition, the Starr team, now working closely with Linda Tripp as well as the Jones lawyers (which would raise serious questions of legal ethics), set up a sting operation aimed at Monica Lewinsky. The young woman had confided in Tripp but had no knowledge of this alleged friend's anti-Clinton plotting; she accepted an invitation for a lunch at the Pentagon City Mall on January 16, 1998. Three days before, the OIC had equipped Tripp with a wire for the late lunch meeting; the goal was to have Lewinsky say on tape that Clinton had encouraged her to deny their sexual relationship. Earlier, Lewinsky had been formally deposed for the Jones trial and had stated that she had not had a sexual affair with the President. So this could be the hard, incriminating evidence that Bill Clinton had suborned perjury, an impeachable offense.

Two FBI agents approached a shocked Lewinsky, took her from the Mall to a room in the adjacent Ritz Carlton Hotel, and during eleven hours of interrogation by Jackie Bennett and other OIC prosecutors, she was told that she could face up to twenty-seven years in prison for lying under oath. After her family provided legal counsel, the frightened young woman ultimately would agree to cooperate with the OIC, but not until she was offered immunity. And she would never say that Bill Clinton had asked her to lie.

At the Jones case deposition hearing, Clinton was prepared for many of the questions about his sexual conduct. He denied allegations of harassment concerning Paula Jones, Kathleen Willey, and several other women, "Jane Does," on the list prepared by new Jones attorneys. (He would later settle his case with Jones, paying $850,000 to her but offering no apology or admission of guilt.) Before the hearing, his lawyer had asked about Monica Lewinsky, whose name had been added to that list; Clinton had said there was nothing to worry about. Now, under oath, he stated: "I have never had sexual relations with Monica Lewinsky." The perjury trap had been sprung.

Within 36 hours, the story exploded in the national news. Isikoff long had been involved with Tripp, Goldberg, and the Jones lawyers. He knew what had been transpiring prior to the Lewinsky sting at the Mall and had told the OIC he would keep from publishing his scoop before the Clinton deposition (a story that would almost certainly have changed the President's testimony and subsequent history) only if given a copy of Tripp's tapes. But his editors hesitated before printing his exposé the day after Clinton's deposition and Drudge broke the story with a "world exclusive" on the *Drudge Report* at 1 A.M. on January 18. Now the detailed Isikoff article would be published, along with huge headline stories in the *Washington Post* and other major newspapers, on ABC news and other TV networks. By the end of January, 305 stories, or more than one-third of all network news airtime, concerned the "Lewinsky scandal."

Bill Clinton's sexual activities became the media's central fixation. Gary Aldrich's stories, "Troopergate" tales from the Arkansas years, and the saga of Paula Jones had been featured in many publications, not only supermarket scandal sheets, for months. But now Kathleen Willey would be a television heroine after a lengthy, sympathetic interview on *60 Minutes* in March. And "Monica" became the name known to all.

Clinton tried to head off the media storm on January 26 at a press conference, where, standing with his wife, he exclaimed, while wagging his finger: "I want you to listen to me. I'm going to say this again: I did not have sexual relations with that woman, Ms. Lewinsky. I never told anybody to lie, not a single time. Never. These allegations are false." The next day, on

NBC's *Today* show, Hillary Clinton defended Bill, saying, "The great story here for anybody willing to find it and write about it . . . is this vast right-wing conspiracy that has been conspiring against my husband since the day he announced for President." Clinton had not told his wife about the affair and he had made matters far worse by doubling down on his false denial. Certainly some kind of a concerted right-wing effort to damage him had long been at work against her husband, but Hillary could not know that this was not the moment to use such a phrase.

"Monicagate" consumed Washington and much of the nation's news outlets into the summer. But critics argued that Starr's OIC team was feeding the media firestorm, as they had throughout earlier years, with selective and damaging leaks about Bill Clinton to favored reporters. Was the President lying about sex with the former intern? Had he obstructed justice?

Finally, in late July, Ms. Lewinsky and her lawyers accepted an immunity deal. She also gave up the critical piece of evidence in the matter. It was a blue dress, purchased at the Gap, which she had saved on the suggestion of Linda Tripp, who then had told the prosecutors about it. It contained a stain, left after the last of Monica Lewinsky's oral sex encounters with Bill Clinton. (The date was February 28, 1997; they had not been alone together for nearly eleven months and, as Ms. Lewinsky testified to OIC investigators insisting on every detail involving sex, it was the only time there had been ejaculation.) Immediately sent by the OIC to the FBI lab, it confirmed through unimpeachable DNA evidence a sexual relationship.

Clinton was trapped in a falsehood. And within days, on August 18, he had to appear before Starr's grand jury. Kenneth Starr insisted that the testimony be videotaped; he clearly wanted the focus on the most humiliating and graphic discussions of sexual acts. Bill Clinton had to admit an "improper physical relationship" with Lewinsky. But he insisted he had not given false testimony at the Jones trial, because oral sex did not fall within his understanding of the definition of sexual relations—vaginal intercourse—used in the deposition. (This was the origin of his unfortunate statement that "it all depends on what the meaning of the word 'is' is," which would be the subject of such scorn in succeeding months.) In conclusion, he exclaimed: "This has been going on too long, cost too much, and hurt too many people. Now this is a matter between me, my wife and our daughter, and our God. . . . It's nobody's business but ours. Even Presidents have private lives. It is time to stop the pursuit of personal destruction."

That night, on all three national television networks, he admitted a relationship with Monica Lewinsky "that was not appropriate." His advisers counseled an apologetic speech, one marked by self-blame, repentance, and accountability. Instead, consumed by his anger at Kenneth Starr, whom he despised as an unethical partisan zealot, he assailed the independent

counsel. It was a damaging error. And now he would face the full consequences of his failure to be honest about the affair: with his family, his
friends, and his political future.[15]

Shortly before his grand jury confession, Clinton had to tell his wife the
truth. "She looked at me as if I had punched her in the gut, almost as angry
at me for lying to her in January as for what I had done. All I could do was
tell her that I was sorry and that I had felt I couldn't tell anyone, even her,
what had happened. . . . I didn't want to be run out of office on the flood tide
that followed my deposition in January. I still didn't fully understand why I
had done something so wrong and stupid." Hillary Clinton would recall: "I
was dumbfounded, heartbroken, and outraged. . . . This was the most devastating, shocking, and hurtful experience of my life." And they both now
had to tell Chelsea.

The next day, the three left for Martha's Vineyard for their long-sched-
uled annual vacation. It was a strained, painful journey. It would take much
time and reflection for the healing to begin for them. But even in the midst
of this family crisis, Bill Clinton could not ignore the enormous burden of
office; at 3 A.M.—he was sleeping downstairs on the couch—he would be
on the phone giving Sandy Berger the final order for the missile strike at
al-Qaeda targets in Afghanistan.

But why had he done it? The untruth he told about the Lewinsky affair
at the deposition might be explained as the consequence of his fear of what
his family (and the larger world) would think of him as well as his belief that
he was being unfairly pursued and pilloried for only a consensual sexual
dalliance. Less understandable was his panicky failure to recognize that
what seemed just another repetitive denial of extramarital sexual activity
was coming under oath, in a very different setting, and with potentially
devastating consequences.

But why was it that he'd had the affair? Many would wonder how this
brilliant man, the most gifted political figure of his time, could be so recklessly stupid, beginning a relationship with a naive young woman willing to
divulge all to someone like Linda Tripp. It did not matter what affairs JFK
may have had while in the White House. It did not matter what LBJ or FDR
or Dwight Eisenhower or any other leaders did with women who were not
their wives before or during their White House years. He knew full well
that the press (and Isikoff was not alone) would no longer allow a zone of
privacy in these matters to the President. And more than anyone else, he
knew that hostile reporters and political enemies were out there, seeking
damaging stories about him all the time. How could he have done it?

But that was the political question. More important was the personal
question. Some might say it was the arrogance of power; the President
thinks he can do anything he wants. Hadn't JFK, similarly devoted to his

family, also acted on his erotic impulses and not restrained his "out-of-control libido" before or during his White House years? Yet others would say, no, this was a self-destructive act. Bill Clinton intentionally was courting disaster; it is one thing to be a risk taker but far different to take suicidal chances as he did with this reckless choice. Moreover, there were deep moral implications in that choice, for while it be true that Monica Lewinsky certainly was not the victim of harassment and was the flirtatious aggressor at the beginning of the affair (as she has stated), he was the President of the United States and she was a young White House intern.

Was it that he was under particular pressure, following the death of his mother, grappling with the enormous demands of office during the government shutdown crisis, dealing all the time with the incessant attacks of enemies, and recently concerned about his own mortality? Was he unconsciously acting out against Hillary? Or was he just acting like his birth father, stepfather, and grandfather had in years gone by? Why could he not restrain himself, and keep from doing something that, if exposed, would seem to everyone, friend and foe alike, as dirty, hurtful, and squalid?

There is no answer to the oft-asked questions. The speculative responses are many, varied, and all unsatisfactory.

But Bill Clinton now had to face not only his family but the country, its media, and his pursuers. Friends and staff—many well aware of stories of past sexual activities—were shocked by what they learned about this behavior. Former aides Dee Dee Myers and George Stephanopoulos expressed deep disappointment, Ms. Myers telling CNBC that his action was "so reckless as to seem pathological." The newsmagazine quote from Stephanopoulos: "If I knew everything then that I know now, I wouldn't have worked for him." (Other Clinton staff, distressed at their much-admired boss's action, yet putting it not only in the context of the President's achievements in office but what they viewed as relentless and destructive efforts of unscrupulous enemies, soon referred to Stephanopoulos, who had become a television commentator, as the "commentraitor.")[16]

Of course, Clinton's ideological foes had rich new material for their attacks. William J. Bennett, Secretary of Education in the Reagan years and conservative savant, the noted moral scold who had written *The Book of Virtues*, issued what became a number one best seller titled *The Death of Outrage: Bill Clinton and the Assault on American Ideals*.

Media heavyweights offered their scornful comments. This had become an age of celebrity journalism, James Fallows noted in *Breaking the News*, of a star system with huge salaries for TV network anchors and a proliferation of well-paid "talking heads," some of them print journalists with new and lucrative electronic forums. In the rush to condemn the President's actions, many joined the posse calling for Bill Clinton to resign because "he had lied to the American people." "If he did it, he has to go," one exclaimed. "Just Go" shouted the cover of *The Economist*. And on all too many occasions, as Marvin Kalb would note, for prominent journalists, "gossip masqueraded as news."

Late-night television comedians had a gift that would keep on giving for years. Jay Leno had taken over the *Tonight Show* in 1992, a final replacement for the legendary Johnny Carson, on whose show Bill Clinton had rescued his presidential aspirations after the Dukakis nomination fiasco in 1988. Leno's rival, David Letterman, started his famous show, also at 11:30 each night, in August 1993. Their writing teams competed for Clinton sex jokes; a decade later, hundreds would fill pages on Internet sites. (After the President left office, Leno remarked: "Bill Clinton's spokesperson confirmed that he has had talks with NBC about doing his own daytime talk show. He'd have to do daytime, because you can't do late-night without doing Clinton jokes.")

Millions laughed at the scatological humor of late night and heard the sneering comments of some famous media figures. But the majority of Americans certainly were not convinced that this was a constitutional crisis. They seemed more impressed by the striking good news from Bill Clinton's Washington: the booming economy, the successes overseas, the legislative achievements of the Clinton domestic agenda. And many apparently agreed at least with the book title by prolific legal analyst Alan Dershowitz, who called his scathing 1998 takedown of Starr *Sexual McCarthyism*. National polls indicating support for the President, if distaste for his behavior in the Lewinsky matter, were one reason William Bennett despaired about the "death of outrage."[17]

But in Congress, Newt Gingrich thought he saw an opening in the midterm election year, and preparations for an impeachment effort were under way after Clinton's grand jury testimony. The GOP leadership rejected the House Democrats' proposal for a vote of censure and pressed ahead. But first there would be the issuance of the massive Starr Report, totaling 452 pages, with 1,660 footnotes and eighteen boxes of supporting material, including FBI interviews and grand jury testimony.

It was mostly about sex and how the President of the United States had lied about sex. Starr would tell an interviewer that though it personally repulsed him, he agreed to include the steamy sexual material: "There was no joy in it," there was an "enormous amount of discomfort." Perhaps. But it made this government report virtually X-rated. Larry Flynt, the publisher of *Hustler*, wrote that Starr did "something I've been trying to do for twenty-five years and had never been able to do: This man has expanded pornography to where no one thought it would go." And while Kenneth Starr said he did not want it made public, the GOP House majority voted immediately to put his report on the congressional website. Within a day or two, on September 11, less than two months before the midterm election, major newspapers across America printed large parts of it, often in fat special sections.

The House leadership grasped the opportunity to humiliate their enemy. Perhaps the shock effect of all this ugly, sexually explicit detail might create a tidal wave of public revulsion leading to an overwhelming call for the President's resignation. At least it would serve as a proper prelude for the impeachment effort.

In fact, in that first weekend following the publication of the report, there were fears in the White House that too many Democrats might join the GOP and a media chorus calling for Clinton to step down. House minority leader Richard Gephardt searched for a counterattack strategy; in part it would be to rally the troops by accusing partisan Republican leaders of treating Democrats—a "fractious, opinionated bunch," as one writer put it—unfairly. But there was no stopping the House Judiciary Committee majority, in a vote in early October on strict party lines, from recommending an impeachment inquiry.

Among the witnesses would be Kenneth Starr. He had an unpleasant experience. It was on this occasion that Starr was forced to admit he had found no actionable wrongdoing on the Clintons' part in any of the pre-Lewinsky scandal inquiries and that he had reached that conclusion "some months ago." Furthermore, he had to confess that he had talked to the press in violation of grand jury secrecy rules and that he had never disclosed to Attorney General Janet Reno, as he should have, that he had been involved in previously providing legal advice to the Jones attorneys. When pressed about his OIC's involvement in the Monica Lewinsky sting operation, the *Washington Post* would report that "Starr's denials . . . were shattered by his own FBI reports."

Henry Hyde, chair of the House Judiciary Committee, insisted that Starr had survived the testimony and the cross-examination, but others did not agree. Starr himself would be shaken by the word that his ethics adviser, Sam Dash, had resigned in protest, arguing that the special prosecutor had made himself an advocate of impeachment. Dash would say, "I thought the Constitution prevented him from doing it."[18]

Still, even after the Republican setbacks in the midterm election in early November were followed by Gingrich's humiliating resignation, the first presidential impeachment process since Watergate got under way, with Representative Hyde in the chair. It would be happening during the post-election lame duck session for the outgoing Congress. The Judiciary Committee's hearings included over twenty hours of taped conversations between Lewinsky and Tripp and the President's answers to eighty-one questions posed to him by committee members. On December 12, the Judiciary Committee majority approved four articles of impeachment, including perjury in a civil deposition and abuse of power. One week later, December 19, the full House voted to impeach President Bill Clinton, but on only the two other articles: perjury to a grand jury (by a 228–206 vote) and obstruction of justice (by a 221–212 vote). It was, unlike Watergate, largely a one-party show; only five Democrats supported any of the articles of impeachment and only four Republicans opposed any of them.

Both the debates leading to the impeachment in the House and the impeachment trial in the Senate to follow would be anticlimactic. It seemed clear that such a partisan effort in both houses never had any chance of conviction and removing Bill Clinton from office.

Instead, the process was marked by incessant moralizing about sex, infidelity, lying about sex, and lying under oath about sex. And here, pornographer Larry Flynt would once more play a role. In early October, he took out a full-page ad in the *Washington Post,* offering to pay $1 million to any women willing to go public about their affairs with government officials. There were 2,000 calls to his 800 number, but his private investigators looked closely at a restricted list. Some of the stories involved the man whom Tom DeLay and Dick Armey had chosen to replace Gingrich as Speaker of the House: Bob Livingston, recently pictured in a national newsmagazine pumping his fist in the air, a major cheerleader for impeachment.

Flynt would recall: "He said 'I may have strayed from my marriage, but it was never with anybody who worked for me or a lobbyist or anyone else in government.' . . . We had him, because one source was a federal judge in Louisiana, another was an intern in his office, and a third was a lobbyist on Capitol Hill." Now, when this new Speaker addressed the House and called for Bill Clinton to resign, furious Democrats shouted: "You resign!"

Livingston was forced to resign, another humiliating setback for his fellow Republicans. When he did, the *New York Times* called Flynt a "bottom feeder," and the publisher responded, "Yeah, but look what I found there." For it did not end with Livingston. The adultery of Bob Barr, the passionately pro-impeachment congressman from Georgia, soon was exposed, and even 74-year-old Henry Hyde would be involved, when an online magazine reported that he had engaged in an extramarital affair decades before. (Later, it would be revealed that several other congressional defenders of marital fidelity—and angry critics of the "faithless Clinton"—had engaged in their own extramarital affairs, including Gingrich himself and New Mexico's Pete Domenici, with his 100 percent rating from the Christian Coalition for his support of "family values.") Flynt had said: "We're not the morality police, we're the hypocrisy police."[19]

Tom DeLay, the House majority whip, who would later be forced out of office in an unconnected scandal, insisted that sex and sexual infidelity were not the issues: It was "all about honor, decency, integrity, and the truth." But most Americans did not agree. A CBS News poll showed that only 38 percent wanted their representatives to vote for impeachment, 58 percent wanted a no vote. If fact, many seemed more persuaded by the House minority whip, Representative David E. Bonior of Michigan, who exclaimed, after the impeachment votes, that the Republicans were trying to "hijack an election and hound the President out of office."

The Senate impeachment trial opened on January 7, with statements by five of the thirteen House GOP "managers for the prosecution." It continued on for over a month, before and after Bill Clinton's State of the Union Address on the 20th, until the vote on February 12. The managers produced but three witnesses, including Monica Lewinsky, deposed on videotape. The Constitution called for a two-thirds vote—sixty-seven senators—and with only fifty-five Republicans in the chamber, there was never any real chance of conviction.

The turning point, if one was needed, came with the speech by Arkansas's Dale Bumpers, who had just retired after twenty-four years in the Senate. "We are here because of a five-year, relentless, unending investigation of the President, $50 million, hundreds of FBI agents fanning across the nation, examining in detail the microscopic lives of people. . . . Here is a man who was unfaithful to his wife. That is not a high crime against the United States because if it was, you'd be guilty, you'd be guilty, you'd be guilty, you'd be guilty [pointing around the chamber], and would not that be a ridiculous outcome? . . . H. L. Mencken one time said: When you hear somebody say: 'This is not about money.' It's about money. And when you hear somebody say: 'This is not about sex.' It's about sex."

There was no drama. The vote for acquittal of the President was a foregone conclusion: 45 to 55 for conviction on the perjury count, 50 to 50 on the obstruction of justice matter.

Later, Henry Hyde would recall that shortly after the losing vote, he had attended an event at a posh Washington Hotel in which Justice Antonin Scalia put his arm around him and said, "You guys covered yourselves with glory." Most observers would not agree. Not only had the managers hardly distinguished themselves, but their task was hopeless from the start, the entire impeachment effort the misguided result of the partisan venom of Tom DeLay and Dick Armey. More important, while Scalia, the man who earlier claimed to hate the independent counsel law because it was "acrid with the smell of threatened impeachment," might have been impressed, noted legal writer Anthony Lewis would speak for many others in concluding, not only about the impeachment process but about the politics of scandal across the Clinton years: "People on the political right set out to unseat a President and they almost succeeded. In his folly, Clinton played into their hands. But that does not alter the facts that this country came close to a coup d'état."

Of course, Hyde also said that "I take consolation that George W. Bush would not have been elected if we had not impeached President Clinton." This was another dubious conclusion by the leader of a failed effort.

A few observers might speculate that Al Gore could have won if only Clinton had resigned and given the Vice President a year or so in office before the election. Yet not only was this impossible, for Bill Clinton would never have given his enemies such a victory, but even if such an unthinkable scenario had happened, Gore much more likely would have shared the fate of Gerald Ford, defeated after serving briefly in the Seventies after Nixon was forced from office.

A slightly more plausible view was that Al Gore lost the 2000 election because of moral revulsion with the behavior of the sitting President. But the far more persuasive argument is that Gore's failure to sufficiently use Bill Clinton was his problem in the campaign to come, particularly in the border, battleground states. Because it was not the personal behavior of Clinton in the Lewinsky affair that concerned most Americans casting their ballot for the next President. It was what Bill Clinton had done in office that really mattered. And Gore failed to capitalize on how voters recognized the striking improvement in the nation's strength, health, and prosperity on the Clinton watch.[20]

In the end, the politics of scandal and the impeachment crisis could not touch Bill Clinton's accomplishments in domestic and foreign affairs or his remarkable political successes, including the striking reelection victory.

After the acquittal vote in the Senate, the economic boom of the Clinton years continued into 2000. Any lame duck President, particularly one without a working majority in Congress—even a President who had not been the continuous target of scandal seekers—would have had difficulty significantly adding to his legislative accomplishments. So the impeachment affair, after all the intense media and political noise died away, had a limited impact on Bill Clinton's final record in office.

And as Bill Clinton faced life after the White House, he knew he was leaving the United States a richer, more prosperous, and more equitable country, crossing the bridge to a new millennium. But what was not clear during his last months in office was how remarkable would be his post-presidency career.

NOTES

1. William Allen White, *The Autobiography of William Allen White* (New York: Simon Publications, 1946), p. 623.
2. Staff of the New York Times (eds.), *The Watergate Hearings: Proceedings of the Senate Select Committee on Presidential Campaign Activities* (New York: Bantam, 1973), p. 390.
3. Joe Conason and Gene Lyons, *The Hunting of the President* (New York: St. Martin's Press, 2000), pp. 167–179; *New York Times*, February 23, 1997; Ambrose Evans-Pritchard, *The Secret*

   Life of Bill Clinton (Washington: Regnery, 2001), pp. 263, 309–311, 337–339, 350; Sidney Blumenthal, *The Clinton Wars* (New York: Plume, 2003), p. 86.

4. John D. Gartner, *In Search of Bill Clinton* (New York: St. Martin's Press, 2008), pp. 281–283;
   Hillary Rodham Clinton, *Living History* (New York: Scribner, 2003), pp. 175–178; Conason
   and Lyons, pp. 83–84; Blumenthal, pp. 65–71; *New York Times*, August 2, 12, 1993; *Wall Street
   Journal*, August 6, 1993; Evans-Pritchard, pp. 210–222.

5. *New York Times*, March 8, 1992, November 2, 1993, December 15, 1993; Gene Lyons and the
   Editors of Harper's Magazine, *Fools for Scandal: How the Media Invented Whitewater* (New
   York: Franklin Square Press, 1996), pp. 5–7, 30–56; Marvin Kalb, *One Scandalous Story* (New
   York: Free Press, 2001), pp. 17–21; Taylor Branch, *The Clinton Tapes: Conversations with a
   President, 1993-2001* (New York: Simon and Schuster, 2009), pp. 410–445; Bob Woodward,
   Shadow: Five Presidents and the Legacy of Watergate (New York: Touchstone, 1999), pp. 227–
   235; Jeffrey Toobin, *A Vast Conspiracy* (New York: Touchstone, 1999), pp. 66–68; Clinton, *My
   Life* (New York: Alfred A. Knopf, 2004), pp. 573–574.

6. Conason and Lyons, pp. 118–121, 127–130; Woodward, *Shadow*, pp. 241–243, 260–266; Hillary Rodham Clinton, pp. 220–227.

7. Toobin, pp. 73–78; Woodward, *Shadow*, pp. 266–269; Blumenthal, pp. 103–107; Conason and
   Lyons, pp. 131–135, 246–248; Ken Gormley, *The Death of American Virtue: Clinton vs. Starr*
   (New York: Crown, 2010), pp. 143–149; James B. Stewart, *Blood Sport: The President and His
   Adversaries* (New York: Simon and Schuster, 1996), pp. 423–425; Gartner, p. 286.

8. Gormley, pp. 99–104, 156–159; Toobin, pp. 190–193; Hillary Rodham Clinton, pp. 349–350;
   David Brock, *Blinded by the Right* (New York: Crown Publishers, 202), pp. 195–196; Conason
   and Lyons, pp. 31–45, 175–178, 198–205, 223–255, 271–274; Clinton, *My Life*, pp. 761–763;
   Wall Street Journal, June 26, 1995, December 18, 1995; *New York Times*, December 6, 1995;
   Washington Post, August 28, 1995, April 22, 28, May 26, 28, June 17–19, July 7, 15–18, August
   1, 19–20, September 23, 1996, July 30, 1997, May 5, 1998.

9. Hillary Rodham Clinton, pp. 328–337; *New York Times*, January 6, 7, 1996; *Washington Post*,
   January 4, 8, 15, 22, 26, 1996; Gormley, pp. 470–474.

10. Stewart, pp. 183–209, 312–376, 430–432; Lyons, pp. 94–95, 147–153; Blumenthal, p. 175;
    Conason and Lyons, pp. 208–210, 264–265; Gormley, pp. 596–597. *Washington Post*, June
    24, 27, 1996, October 1, 1996, November 20, 1998; *Chicago Tribune*, April 8, 2000; Hillary Rodham
    Clinton, pp. 172–173; Toobin, pp. 92–93, 348–349.

11. Toobin, pp. 92–93; Blumenthal, pp. 328–332, 382–383; Gormley, pp. 242–247; Gartner, pp.
    290–291; Joe Conason, "Filegate Judge: There's No There There—And Never Was," *Salon*,
    March 10, 2010, http://www.salon.com/2010/03/10/filegate; Brock, *Blinded*, pp. 134–165;
    Toobin, pp. 2–5, 19–41; David Brock, "His Cheatin' Heart," *American Spectator*, January 1994,
    http://spectator.org/archives/2012/09/07/his-cheatin-heart; Conason and Lyons, pp. 99–115.

12. Brock, *Blinded*, pp. 134–165; Toobin, pp. 2–5, 19–41; Brock, "His Cheatin' Heart"; Conason
    and Lyons, pp. 99–115.

13. Michael Isikoff, *Uncovering Clinton* (New York: Three Rivers Press, 2000), pp. 3–25; Toobin,
    pp. 28–37, 43; Conason and Lyons, pp. 120–127, 260–261; Clinton, *My Life*, pp. 768–769;
    Brock, *Blinded*, pp. 180–186; Gormley, pp. 255–261; Ann Coulter, *High Crimes and Misde-
    meanors: The Case Against Bill Clinton* (Washington: Regnery, 1998) pp. 39–76, 105–194.

14. David H. Bennett, "William Jefferson Clinton: Political Lawyer," in Norman Gross, ed., *Amer-
    ica's Lawyer-Presidents* (Evanston: Northwestern University Press, 2004), pp. 193–197; Cona-
    son and Lyons, pp. 277–290; Toobin, pp. 97–114; Isikoff, pp. 101–163, 230–232; Gormley, pp.
    143, 223–225, 281–288; Andrew Morton, *Monica's Story* (New York: St. Martin's Press, 1999),
    pp. 17, 72, 113–114, 120, 129; Kalb, pp. 24–35; Gary Aldrich, *Unlimited Access: An FBI Agent
    Inside the Clinton White House* (Washington: Regnery, 1998), pp. 27–168.

15. Gormley, pp. 348–362; Kalb, pp. 35–97, 156–159; "Jones v. Clinton," *Washington Post* Special
    Report, March 13, 1998; Dan Fromkin, "Case Closed," *Washington Post*, December 3, 1998;
    Isikoff, pp. 290–349; Morton, pp. 102–114, 175–193; Steven Brill, "Pressgate," *Brill's Content*,

135; Woodward, *Shadow*, pp. 403–407, 441–445. Hillary Rodham Clinton, p. 445; Toobin, pp. 312–315.

16. Hillary Rodham Clinton, pp. 467–470; Clinton, *My Life*, pp. 800–803; Gartner, pp. 315–316; Gail Sheehy, *Hillary's Choice* (New York: Random House, 1999), pp. 312–313; William H. Chafe, *Bill and Hillary: The Politics of the Personal* (New York: Farrar, Straus and Giroux, 2012), pp. 336–337.

17. William J. Bennett, *The Death of Outrage: Bill Clinton and the Assault on American Ideals* (New York: Touchstone, 1999) pp. 1–30, 40–51, 58–91, 128–134, 146–148; James Fallows, *Breaking the News: How the Media Undermine American Democracy* (New York: Pantheon, 1996), pp. 23–40, 74–116; "Bill Clinton Jokes," http://politicalhumor.about.com/od/billclinton/Bill_Clinton_Jokes.htm; Kalb, pp. 184, 242–245; Alan M. Dershowitz, *Sexual McCarthyism: Clinton, Starr and the Emerging Constitutional Crisis* (New York: Basic Books, 1998), pp. 1–48, 123–163.

18. Gormley, p. 363, 565–576, 582–586; 590–599; Toobin, pp. 326–337, 364–367; Clinton, *My Life*, pp. 828–829; Larry Flynt in Takiff, p. 345.

19. Ibid., pp. 368–371.

20. *New York Times*, December 20, 1998; Takiff, pp. 376–377; Gormley, p. 678; Anthony Lewis, "Nearly a Coup," *New York Review of Books*, April 13, 2000, pp. 22–29.

CHAPTER **6**

AFTER THE WHITE HOUSE

Leaving the presidency is difficult for anyone. But for Bill Clinton, only 54 and still at the height of his powers, a life of sitting on corporate boards and recreation was out of the question. As one former aide observed, he needed to be part of something larger than himself and to serve. He would shape one the most impressive post-presidency careers in American history.

First, there would be trying moments in the transition.

He would have to deal with a brief wave of nasty, bogus publicity coming from those in the new Bush administration. These were the phony stories, amplified by "reports" on Fox News and other networks, that he and Hillary had trashed the White House on the way out: desk drawers emptied on floors, pornographic pictures left in computer printers, cabinets glued shut, phone lines cut. One right-wing talk show host even said that the Clintons damaged Air Force One, the plane looking "as if it had been stripped by a skilled band of thieves, or perhaps wrecked by a trailer park twister." Apparently, some of the most deeply partisan Republicans, moving into the West Wing after the troubled 2000 election finally was settled by the highly controversial Supreme Court decision, still sought to discredit Bill Clinton and his staff, fabricating these tales even as they took over. There were precedents for pranks; when Clinton's team arrived in January 1993, they discovered posted signs reading "Draft Dodger" and headsets stuck to telephones. But these scurrilous stories were not just about pranks. They were, of course, false, as a subsequent General Services Administration report would make clear.

More troublesome was one of the 176 presidential pardons and commutations Clinton signed just before noon on January 20, even as he prepared to head to the Capitol for George W. Bush's inauguration. The pardon was for Marc Rich, a billionaire commodity trader who had run afoul of the law in 1983. He had been indicted for tax evasion, fraud, and other charges; rather than face trial and jail, he had fled to Switzerland. Rich's wife was a generous contributor to Democratic efforts (including the Clinton campaigns) and had pledged money to the Clinton presidential library. Perhaps more important, a large number of Israelis and American supporters of Israel, where Marc Rich had directed much of his philanthropy, had been in contact on the fugitive's behalf. Clinton's recent Camp David ally Ehud Barak had three phone conversations with him on the matter.

Bill Clinton, referring to the political contributions, insisted that there was "absolutely no quid pro quo." Still, the pardon, as many of his friends and supporters would argue, was an error; Rich had renounced his citizenship, as his wife would in later years, seemingly only for tax purposes. Clinton did not lose sleep over the Rich decision, taken at the last moment and with a small transition team. He has said he does regret not pardoning Webster Hubbell.

But now the former President of the United States would have to build a life after the White House. Senator Hillary Clinton, victorious in 2000, represented New York State and so the Clintons would be living in New York. They purchased a home in Chappaqua, in New York City's far suburbs. It would be the first place they had owned since Governor Clinton had returned to the Executive Mansion in 1982. But unlike that small house in Little Rock and the preceding one in Fayetteville, Arkansas, this would be an impressive, five-bedroom Dutch colonial. The sprawling white wood and stone house, over 5,200 square feet, is on a beautiful landscaped lot in one of the most sought after neighborhoods in affluent Westchester County. Later, they bought a second home in Washington, D.C.

The Chappaqua and Washington houses were expensive, in two of the costliest real estate markets in America. Yet Bill Clinton could afford it. For decades, he had been a public servant, and compared with many of his new neighbors, even the salaries of governors or a President are very modest. Moreover, he and his wife left the White House with millions of dollars in legal fees to pay. But there soon would be an influx of cash.

"You know, I never had any money until I got out of the White House, but I've done reasonably well since," he remarked at a forum in Cape Town, South Africa, in 2010.

The most famous man in America (if not the world), the leader of the United States through eight dramatic years, the most gifted public speaker of his time, Clinton would be in demand as a writer and a lecturer.

Reports were that he received a $12 million advance from Random House for his autobiography. *My Life*, the massive 950-page work published in 2004, set a worldwide record for single-day nonfiction book sales. Hillary

Rodham Clinton also received a multimillion-dollar advance for her memoir; *Living History*, like her husband's book, became an international best seller. According to records released in 2008, when Senator Clinton was campaigning for the Democratic presidential nomination, in the first seven years after leaving the White House, Clinton earned $29 million from his writing, and his wife more that $10 million for her two books.

Meantime, Bill Clinton became a phenomenon on the lecture circuit, in demand all across the planet. In 2001, in fifty-nine appearances in more than a dozen countries, he was paid more than $9.2 million. It was only the beginning. By 2011 he was delivering 54 paid speeches—there were 52 in 2010—and earned $13.4 million, his most lucrative year on the speaking circuit to date. At that point, he had delivered 471 compensated speeches in eleven years. He had spoken in twenty-seven states and fifty-two countries. In six overseas appearances in 2011, in Hong Kong, Shanghai, the United Arab Emirates, Austria, Holland, and Lagos, Nigeria (to a newspaper publishing company), he received at least $500,000 for each address. In fact, his popularity on the international circuit has earned him well over $50 million.

It is not unusual for former Presidents to command large speaking fees after leaving office. George W. Bush reportedly delivered 140 paid speeches for at least $15 million in his first two and a half years out of the White House. Yet because his wife has been a high-ranking federal official, first as a senator and then Secretary of State, Bill Clinton is the only one subjected to strict disclosure requirements. But the huge sums he has earned are a testament to far more than his stature as a former President of the United States. It is his enormous popularity across the land and around the globe, his worldwide philanthropic work, and his lifelong ability to shape talks touching each particular audience that have made him the incomparable star speaker of his age. "He is really gifted," exclaimed the organizer of a conference Clinton addressed in Vancouver, British Columbia. "He speaks in a language that everyone can understand."

For the first time in his life, Clinton became a wealthy man in the years since leaving the highest office. But clearly, this was not his driving ambition. "I've enjoyed the fact that I can pay all my debts," he told an interviewer. "I enjoy the protection of being financially self-sufficient . . . having some security for my family, but also the freedom to speak out against policies that concentrate wealth and power, which I passionately disagree with. Now I have more credibility 'cause I've got money."

Paul Begala has said, "I don't think I ever knew anyone less interested in money than Bill Clinton." Money made life easier for the former President, but he had much more important goals in mind for his post–White House years.[1]

The Clinton Presidential Center and the William J. Clinton Foundation (it was no longer just "Bill Clinton") would be at the heart of his plans for these years. The Center houses the Clinton library and museum and the offices of the foundation, as well as a new Clinton School of Public Service, a graduate division of the University of Arkansas, offering a master's in public service.

Set on seventeen acres alongside the Arkansas River and near Interstate 30 just east of downtown Little Rock, the Center is housed in a striking, five-story steel and glass bridgelike building that cantilevers almost to the edge of the river. (The Clinton School is in a nearby rebuilt former railroad station.) The structure evokes the physical image of Bill Clinton's campaign pledge to "build a bridge" to the next century and next millennium.

It is the largest presidential library, almost 70,000 square feet. The research wing, managed by the National Archives, houses 80 million pages of documents, millions of photographs and e-mail messages, as well as thousands of artifacts of the Clinton presidency. The museum section features a lengthy timeline of each of Bill Clinton's years in the presidency and a number of alcoves focusing on critical events during his time in office. There are theaters and a full-size replica of the Oval Office as it was in the Clinton years.

Planning for the library had begun in 1997, and Bill Clinton selected the architects, James Polshek and Richard Olcott. The project cost $165 million, with Clinton's friend and supporter Terry McAuliffe leading the intense, private fund-raising effort that would include over 110,000 donations. Much of the money came from various American organizations and wealthy individuals, but a significant part came from affluent foreigners and from foreign governments. The city of Little Rock donated land valued at over $11 million.

Over 30,000 people, including numerous celebrities, attended the dedication ceremony in November 2004. The Center immediately became a major tourist attraction, with a half million visitors the first twelve months and almost 2 million across the next years. It inspired a remarkable urban renewal development in the adjacent River Market district to the west, with many hotels, restaurants, apartment houses, and retail establishments costing over $1 billion transforming the area. And next to the Clinton presidential park, which formerly was a grim, dilapidated warehouse neighborhood, other nongovernmental organizations have built impressive headquarters. Clinton's library has been an enormous stimulant to his adopted city of Little Rock, the capital of his home state.[2]

Bill Clinton had a two-bedroom, 2,000 square foot apartment built on the top floor of the main library-museum building. For his Center serves as one of the two offices of the Clinton Foundation. The other is in New York

City, where Clinton established his personal office in Harlem. The choice of venue was more than symbolic. In 1998, prizewinning novelist Toni Morrison had called him America's "first black president," and while this was a tongue-in-cheek descriptor, as one writer put it, "hers was a serious theme" that referred to "Bill Clinton's humanity, his inherent empathy with those different from him."[3]

That spirit of humanity and empathy would be the driving force in the work of the William J. Clinton Foundation. Its agenda was multifaceted; from the start it included combating HIV/AIDS, promoting economic empowerment of poor people, and fostering ethnic and racial reconciliation. Its concerns would cross national frontiers, its motto: "To strengthen the capacity of people throughout the world to meet the challenges of global interdependence." It would work through partnerships with organizations, governments, prominent individuals, and corporations, seeking to shape new policies and practices. In 2005, the Clinton Global Initiative (CGI) was founded, expanding the work of the foundation in its areas of main concern, recruiting global leaders to help implement solutions to these pressing problems and to other challenges as well, including the specter of climate change.

Before CGI was founded, Bill Clinton had a major health scare. After suffering an angina episode in September 2004, he underwent quadruple coronary artery bypass surgery at the Columbia Presbyterian Medical Center in New York. He had not had a heart attack, but surgeons said that a massive attack might have occurred within months without the procedure. Complications, involving a partially collapsed lung, would bring him back to the hospital the following March for further surgery. He had a strong recovery, although he complained that he did not quite have the strength of the past: "If I'm really, really tired, it's more difficult for me than it was when I was back in politics before the heart problem." He told a visitor, "I didn't have any depression in my recovery, and I think it's because I haven't had any real time off in thirty-five years, since I've been in politics. So I loved being home all day and being more or less incapacitated. I had a long rest. I got to watch movies, which I hadn't done in a long time, and I got to read books. In my house in New York, I've got nearly five thousand books." And he exercised daily, in a gym in the converted barn behind the Chappaqua home, losing almost forty pounds.

Nonetheless, in February 2010, after experiencing chest pains, he had two coronary stents implanted in the arteries near his heart. Now, the man of legendary energy, who always could live on five hours' sleep, play cards, and keep talking with sleepy friends late into the night, the man who could consume large quantities of Big Macs, fully changed his regimen. He adopted a plant-based, whole-foods vegan diet. "I live on beans, legumes, vegetables, and fruits," he told CNN. "I drink a protein supplement every morning. No dairy. . . . I changed my whole metabolism and lost twenty-four pounds. I got back to basically what I weighed in high school." His ancestral family had not been long-lived, and Bill Clinton, thinner than ever before in his professional life, was taking steps to protect his health.

Even as he recovered from the first surgery, he was involved once more in presidential politics. In October 2004, only days before the election, he campaigned for John Kerry, then trailing in a close race against incumbent George W. Bush. Saying he promised his wife, his doctors, and himself that he wouldn't overdo it, Clinton had a crowd of almost 100,000 filling a Philadelphia park, cheering wildly. "If this isn't good for my heart, I don't know what is," said the famous stump speaker. He praised Kerry's programs and said that the "other side is trying to scare the undecided voters" and that "one of Clinton's laws of politics is this: If one candidate's appealing to your fears and the other one's appealing to your hopes, you better vote for the person who wants you to think and hope."

While he was willing to lend a hand for his party's candidate late in the 2004 campaign, Bill Clinton had taken a low profile in politics after leaving the White House. Like former Presidents before him, he thought it unwise and unseemly to use his position to criticize his successor. "We only have one President at a time" has been the motto, and George H. W. Bush had followed that axiom during Clinton's years in office. When possible, Clinton tried to be supportive. After 9/11, of course, he was present at the events in Washington when George W. Bush spoke for the nation.

But it must have been a strain not to speak out. For the Bush administration's policies were very much at odds with his own. In foreign and military affairs, there was the aggressive, isolationist vision of the neo-conservatives George W. Bush placed in the Pentagon, with their rejection of multilateral efforts to stem nuclear proliferation and the growth of antiballistic missiles, their contempt for international courts and organizations, and their insistence on America's right to launch a preventative war. In domestic affairs, the Bush team embraced huge tax cuts for the wealthy, placed administrators who did not believe in regulation in key regulatory positions, and called for cutbacks in many social and economic programs Clinton had embraced.

When the Bush White House was beating the drums for a "preemptive" military strike against Iraq in 2002, Bill Clinton did talk of unpleasant consequences of such action. Addressing the Progressive Governance Conference in London in 2003, he provided a blistering analysis of the domestic and foreign policies of the Bush administration. And in 2005, speaking at the United Nations Climate Change Conference in Montreal, he strongly criticized the Bush team for its handling of emissions controls. But he was out of power, and he would not play a major role in these or most other debates.

In fact, as the years passed, Bill Clinton was able to build warmer relations with both his predecessor and successor. In the words of journalist Peter Baker, "He has a remarkable capacity for reconciliation."

In the aftermath of the devastating 2004 tsunami in Asia, the UN Secretary General appointed Clinton to head relief efforts, and he worked with George H. W. Bush to establish the Bush-Clinton Tsunami Fund. After catastrophic Hurricane Katrina ravaged New Orleans and the adjacent region in 2005, they worked together again on the Bush-Clinton Katrina Fund. By 2009, the elder Bush had told a reporter that he considered Clinton a "real friend." Clinton had said, "We get along fine. . . . I understand him better than I did. We have good personal rapport and we can be very candid."

Earlier, when Bill Clinton had been unhappy at the whispering campaign trashing him after he left the White House, he called George W. Bush and ended by saying, "I'll make you a deal. If you ever need me to do something for you and I can do it consistent with my conscience, I'll do it." The cooperative work with Bush's father was one result. Then, after the huge earthquake in Haiti in 2010, Clinton, already having been named the United Nations special envoy to Haiti, teamed with the now-former President George W. Bush to create the Clinton-Bush Haiti Fund. "We just developed a relationship," Bill Clinton said. "He would call every now and then. I just made it a project. I wanted to figure him out and get to know him."

"He is likelier to find peace with people who hate him the most," Baker observed of Clinton, "than with friends who betray him." Even Christopher Ruddy, the conservative writer and author of the book proposing cover-up theories about Vincent Foster's death, now said, "I do consider Bill Clinton a friend [it was 2009] . . . and to think of all the wars we went through, it seems almost surreal." One reason for the new attitude: the Clinton Foundation. The work of the foundation not only impressed Ruddy, but even inspired Richard Mellon Scaife to be a contributor (as would Rupert Murdoch, whose Fox News regularly attacked President Clinton).

"You know," said Bill Clinton, "I'm a Baptist. We don't give up on anybody. We believe in deathbed conversions."

But how about Kenneth Starr? "Well," he said, "that's another kettle of fish."[4]

It was the foundation and the CGI that would remain at the center of his attention. A cover story in *Esquire* in late 2005 was called "The Third Term: the Dawning of a Different Sort of Post-presidency."

Former President Jimmy Carter's extraordinary career after he left the White House had impressed Bill Clinton, and near the end of his second term, he invited Carter up to Camp David to talk. Clinton would say of

Carter: "He eradicated river blindness in Africa, he worked on the green revolution to help people become more agriculturally self-sufficient, advanced human rights, and monitored elections." Now Bill Clinton blazed his own post-presidency path, raising billions on a variety of fronts to improve the lives of people in the United States and in many other lands.

In 2002, Nelson Mandela, at an international conference in Barcelona, urged Clinton to lead an effort to fight HIV/AIDS, to do what Western governments had not done, providing effective treatment for millions of the infected poor in Africa, Asia, and Latin America who lacked money (some $1,600 per person) for the diagnostic tests and drugs to save them. The Clinton HIV/AIDS Initiative became one of the first focal points of the William J. Clinton Foundation. In one sense, it was unfinished business; as President, Bill Clinton had addressed the AIDS crisis in the United States but had not done as much with global AIDS. Now, as rock star and activist Bono would remark, Clinton moved "into the fast lane in fighting this epidemic."

The former President brought in Ira Magaziner, the old friend who had worked on Hillary's ill-fated health care effort, and as they shaped a plan to reduce costs of treatment, Clinton lobbied government leaders in Europe and Canada to fund the program. Promising that they would prevent kickbacks or black-market sales, they took advantage of already reduced prices by manufacturers of generic antiretroviral drug combinations to broker drug distribution agreements. In October 2003, Clinton announced that his foundation would license countries to purchase drugs at an annual cost of $140. The foundation and its partners—several NGOs (including the major nonprofits fighting AIDS, such as the Gates Foundation and the Global Fund) and the governments of Ireland, Norway, Sweden, France, Canada, and the UK, along with the UN and the World Bank—would help put hundreds of thousands of people in treatment in the next few years.

Bill Clinton now made repeated journeys to Africa and Latin America, conferring with heads of government (many treating him like he was still the world's most powerful figure) and encouraging leaders in still other countries to sign agreements. He cultivated these relationships, a writer observed, "with the same care he once devoted to governors and mayors in America." But he also visited villages and hospitals. On one trip to Kenya, Lesotho, Mozambique, Rwanda, and Tanzania early in this effort, after delivering an upbeat message to local media, he said, "I am thrilled to be in Zanzibar. . . . Just now, I shook hands with an eleven-year-old orphan child who knows that he is HIV positive. His circumstances have changed. He doesn't have to be stigmatized and to resign himself to an early death."

In 2010, the Clinton HIV/AIDS effort became a separate part of the Clinton Health Access Initiative (CHAI), a global organization dedicated to strengthening health systems and expanding care and treatment of malaria, tuberculosis, and other diseases, as well as HIV/AIDS.

CHAI is but one element of the larger Clinton Global Initiative. CGI had its inaugural meeting in a Manhattan ballroom in 2005. Bill Clinton was soon joined on stage by Prime Minister Tony Blair of the UK, Secretary of State Condoleezza Rice, and the King of Jordan. In the reserved seats in front were current and former heads of state, rock legends, and movie stars. By the time the CGI gathering had concluded, after two days of panels, workshops, and reports, Clinton announced that the participants had signed agreements to sponsor and finance more than two hundred separate projects valued at nearly $2 billion. These participants were a remarkable group: the presidents of South Africa, Ukraine, Nigeria, and the Dominican Republic, the Prime Minister of Turkey, the CEOs of Sony, Time-Warner, General Electric, Goldman Sachs, and Starbucks, the president of the World Bank, numerous Nobel Prize winners, and the leaders of many of the world's largest nonprofit organizations. Their pledges involved investment of hundreds of millions of dollars for clean water in Africa, youth employment in the Balkans, renewable energy projects, credit for small business in developing nations, environmental protection in South America, and much more.

Only Bill Clinton could have brought such an extraordinary assemblage to a meeting, and inspired glittering show business celebrities—Angelina Jolie, Brad Pitt, Mick Jagger, Barbra Streisand, Tony Bennett, Leonardo DiCaprio—to attend in secondary roles.

Critics might complain that this gathering, mounted with special lighting, theme music, and an elaborate set, was just another opportunity for the man now out of office to shine the spotlight once more on himself. But Bill Clinton did not need the publicity, and if he wanted to hang out with the powerful and famous, he had plenty of other opportunities. The Clinton Global Initiative, this added dimension of the Clinton Foundation, was enlisting these notables in new efforts to address a variety of major challenges across the globe.

Each CGI member would be asked to develop a "Commitment to Action," specific plans to help make the world a better place. The CGI offered numerous tracks, including, among others, the Built Environment, Education and Workforce Development, Energy and Environmental Stewardship, and Global Health. Seven years after CGI's first gathering, members had made more than 2,300 commitments. As one journalist noted, "financed by Saudi princes, Indian tycoons, Hollywood moguls, and governments like Australia and Norway," Clinton had created a movement with 1,400 paid employees and volunteers working in forty countries to fight disease, poverty, and climate change. Money was raised to deal with these problems, but there was also a concerted effort to find market-based solutions bringing government, business, and the nonprofit sector together.

Following its first meeting, almost each year would bring new developments. During the second CGI annual meeting, 50,000 people worldwide viewed the affair by webcast; thousands of viewers made personal commitments online and the meeting brought an increase in the yearly value of commitments to $7.3 billion.

In 2007, newly inaugurated CGI University had its first gathering at Tulane, with succeeding sessions held at the University of Texas at Austin, the University of Miami, and the University of California–San Diego. Madeleine Albright, Jon Stewart, Bill and Chelsea Clinton, and Stephen Colbert were among those helping to stimulate interest by appearing at these meetings. CGI U students, representing all fifty states and more than fifty countries, have made 3,000 Commitments to Action in energy, climate change, global health, human rights, and poverty alleviation.

There was more. The Clinton Climate Initiative (CCI) was launched in 2006. Its first project: helping some large cities cut greenhouse gas emissions through retrofitting older buildings; five large banks committed $1 billion each for the effort. In late 2008, Bill Clinton convened the first CGI International meeting in Hong Kong; and there were 3,000 accredited delegates, including prominent business leaders from across Asia.

The Clinton Development Initiative (to improve food security, clean water, and sanitation) was founded in 2006. The Clinton Global Initiative America was created five years later to foster economic growth in the United States. More than 700 leaders of business, government, and nonprofits attended with major commitments to action; when fully funded and implemented, they could provide 140,000 people with job training and create 1,000 information technology jobs in rural areas.

Also put in place have been the Clinton Economic Opportunity Initiative, the Clinton Health Matters Initiative, with its focus on reducing preventable diseases across America, and the Sustainable Growth Initiative, with an initial focus on how business in Latin America might spur sustainable social and economic development.

When some in his party complained that he was not aggressive enough in leading opposition to Bush administration programs after Kerry's 2004 defeat, Clinton had responded: "I have to chart my own course. I have to do things that I think are important. I'm not the leader of the opposition anymore. I will always be loyal to my party, but if I spend time being leader of the opposition, I won't be able to help save lives doing what I'm doing. I have a different life now, and I've got to lead it."[5]

But this new life and career, focused on the foundation and CGI, would be interrupted by politics once again in 2007 and 2008. Hillary Rodham

Clinton, who made a major impact in the Senate and won an overwhelming reelection victory in 2006, had decided, clearly with her husband's encouragement, to run for President.

After announcing her candidacy in January, Senator Clinton quickly became the front-runner. April 2007 polls showed her at 41 percent against second-place John Edwards, Kerry's vice-presidential running mate (at 19 percent), and Barack Obama, the freshman senator from Illinois, whose keynote address had electrified the Democratic Convention in 2004, at 17 percent. But the race rapidly tightened across the summer and into the fall. No longer was Hillary the obvious, inevitable choice. Obama's brilliant campaign organization and the early debate results played a role as the Democratic Party now seemed ready to nominate either the first woman or the first African American as its presidential candidate.

Bill Clinton took his first campaign trip in July, serving, he said, "as an opening act" for his wife on a three-day tour. By December, with the Iowa Caucus and the New Hampshire and South Carolina primaries only weeks away, it was a horse race and there were indications that Obama might be ahead in Iowa. Now one national newsman, Al Hunt, reported that there was "trouble in Hillaryland," suggesting that the staffs of the candidate and her husband were at odds.

After Obama's victory in Iowa and Hillary Clinton's comeback win in New Hampshire, Bill Clinton's efforts in South Carolina became an issue. He called Barack Obama's claim to be a strong opponent of the Iraq war from the start "the biggest fairy tale I've ever seen," a comment considered by many both inaccurate and condescending. (Of course, Clinton saw it as an answer to Obama's criticism of Senator Clinton's early positions on the war.) More damaging was his statement, after Obama's primary victory, that "Jesse Jackson won South Carolina twice, in '84 and '88. And he ran a good campaign. Senator Obama ran a good campaign here." Some pundits, bloggers, and journalists interpreted this as implying that Barack Obama was just another black candidate. But so, too, did some key black politicians. Hillary would later apologize for the remark at a meeting of South Carolina African Americans.

James Clyburn, the powerful South Carolina representative, and a leader of the Congressional Black Caucus, complained that an angry Bill Clinton berated him on the phone for Clyburn's pointed criticism of the former President's campaign rhetoric. Another major African American political leader, and a Hillary Clinton endorser, Congressman Charles Rangel, was reported as suggesting that Clinton "pull back" and allow "the focus on Hillary."

For Bill Clinton, so long a hugely popular figure in the African American community, even the muted accusation of his using racist imagery was, in Paul Begala's words, "the unkindest cut of all." It was "the worst thing you could ever say about him, it was like a punch in the stomach." Clinton insisted that "I don't have to defend myself on civil rights," noting that famous civil rights leaders Andrew Young and John Lewis supported the Clintons. But the angry former President told one radio interviewer, "I think that they played the race card on me." The next year, long after the controversy was over, he observed, "None of them ever really took seriously the race rap. . . . They knew it was politics."

Still, had his campaigning helped or hurt his wife's presidential effort? There was little he could do about stories now circulating that Hillary's staff was trying to control him, that he had devoted days to speaking in South Carolina against the wishes of her strategists, that he often was ill-tempered on the trail, and never felt truly a part of Hillary's campaign.

Whatever the truth of this overheated political gossip, the fact was that there were reasons why Bill Clinton might take the race personally. It was not only that he was defending his wife and her work, or that he couldn't understand how a young upstart, a state senator four years earlier, somehow could overtake her in this critical primary race. It was also that he could not ignore the demeaning references that Barack Obama had made about his own years in the White House.

"For too long, through both Democratic and Republican administrations, the system has been rigged against everyday Americans by the lobbyists that Wall Street uses to get its way," Obama told one labor audience. "Jobs fell through the Clinton administration and the Bush administration." Clinton was more than offended and at a Pennsylvania campaign stop he exclaimed: "Hillary's opponent, in his entire campaign, has said that there really wasn't much difference in how America did when I was President and how America has done under Bush. If you believe that, you should probably vote for him, but you get a very bad grade in history."

On several occasions, Barack Obama seemingly had belittled Clinton's accomplishments, referring to the "transforming" presidencies of earlier chief executives but pointedly leaving out Bill Clinton. "I think Ronald Reagan changed the trajectory of America in a way Richard Nixon did not and in a way that Bill Clinton did not," he said in Reno in January. He implied that Clinton was yesterday's figure, a product of the old struggles over the Vietnam War and the upheavals of the Sixties and that he himself was of a new generation and perspective, that he would produce a new, "post-partisan" presidency, breaking the ideological gridlock of the past. Every observer, years later, could make a judgment about such claims, but at the time, they did not amuse Bill Clinton.

As the primary struggle carried through the winter and into the late spring, it became clear that while this was a close race, Obama was prevailing. At one point he won ten primaries in a row before a Hillary Clinton victory. And while Senator Clinton had some striking successes later in the campaign season, notably in Ohio and Pennsylvania, Obama's superior campaign organization and his eloquence in speaking to crowds large and small gave him an insurmountable lead.

Bill Clinton had continued to play an energetic role in the campaign, saying, "I literally went to 300 towns in March, April, and May alone, and I did way over 300 events in those three months." So when he responded angrily at a campaign stop in the spring to a nasty piece just published in *Vanity Fair*, Clinton said, "You might be a little testy too if you didn't get more sleep than I did." Titled "The Comeback Id," the article's author, a former *New York Times* correspondent, implied that Clinton had "never been the same" after his heart surgeries and attacked him for traveling about the world on the private planes of wealthy friends, "a motley crew constituting the post-presidential rat pack."

Still, it was the old Clinton on the campaign trail, even as the race wound down. In small towns in South Dakota at the very beginning of June, he was still working the rope lines, speaking without notes, astonishing his audiences with a torrent of policy details, but including the usual amount of folksy storytelling. "I thought I was out of politics until Hillary decided to run," he told one group, "but it has been one of the greatest honors in my life to be able to campaign for her for President." And while some mainstream media outlets continued to recycle their early narrative, with its unflattering portrait of Bill Clinton's efforts in this race, those watching him work knew he had not lost his edge. "Ninety-nine percent of the time, he has been the happy warrior on the campaign trial," one friend said. Yet, "The important stuff doesn't make news."[6]

But it was all in vain. On June 7, Hillary Clinton officially announced she was suspending her campaign and fully endorsing Barack Obama. At the Democratic Convention held in Denver in late August, both Clintons would be given major speaking roles. In eloquent addresses, they offered strong praise for presidential candidate Obama.

Bill Clinton was greeted by a huge standing ovation; he had to encourage the crowd to "please stop, sit down, we have important work to do tonight." He said, "What a year we Democrats have had. And it came down to two remarkable Americans locked in a hard-fought contest right to the very end. The campaign generated so much heat, it increased global warming." When the laughter stopped, he praised his wife for the campaign she ran and for the "magnificent speech" she had given in support of Barack Obama.

About candidate Obama, Clinton exclaimed, "he has a remarkable ability to inspire people, to raise our hopes and rally us to high purpose. He has the intelligence and curiosity every successful President needs. . . . His family heritage and his life experiences have given him a unique capacity to lead our increasingly diverse nation in an ever more interdependent world."

Near the end of his speech, he compared the outgoing George W. Bush administration with his own years in the White House: "They took us from record surpluses to an exploding debt, from over 22 million new jobs to just 5 million, from increasing working families' incomes to nearly $7,500 a year to a decline of more than $2,000 a year, from almost 8 million Americans lifted out of poverty to more than 5.5 million driven into poverty, and millions more losing their health insurance. . . . [Yet] in spite of all this evidence, their candidate is actually promising more of the same."

Sixteen years ago, he said, "you gave me the profound honor to lead our party to victory and to lead our nation to a new era of peace and broadly shared prosperity. . . . Republicans said I was too young and too inexperienced to be commander-in-chief. Sound familiar? It didn't work in 1992, because we were on the right side of history. And it will not work in 2008 because Barack Obama is on the right side of history. . . . So if like me you believe America must always be a place called hope, then join Hillary and Chelsea and me in making Barack Obama the next President of the United States."[7]

Bill Clinton played only a small role in the victorious Obama campaign in the fall. The Iraq debacle, George Bush's inept response to the Katrina disaster, and the stuttering economy all had weakened public support for the GOP long before the financial crisis of 2008, the stock market collapse, and the looming recession placed the Republican presidential ticket in deeper trouble. Barack Obama's superb campaign organization, strengthened now by a unified Democratic effort, along with the candidate's own skillful performance, produced a remarkable victory.

In the following weeks, as Bill Clinton resumed full-time commitment to his foundation, his wife would be asked to leave the Senate and assume the post of Secretary of State, the most prestigious of all cabinet positions. Clinton certainly approved of her taking the job, but he knew that his own work would be affected by it, as the Obama team carefully scrutinized the activities of the CGI.

And so this most extraordinary American couple would embark on four more event-filled years. Hillary Clinton—traveling to nations across the globe, dealing with a variety of foreign policy crises, speaking out for human rights, conferring with world leaders (many of whom she already knew), managing the immense State Department establishment—quickly established an enviable reputation as one of the most popular and effective Secretaries in recent history.

Meanwhile, Obama's aides had presented a set of conditions affecting the work of the first former President to serve as first spouse. For the Clinton

Foundation, they insisted on the disclosure of the previously secret list of donors. It was no surprise that foreign governments, including Saudi Arabia, Australia, Norway, Oman, Taiwan, and others, had contributed millions each. The names of many wealthy and well-connected individuals who had opened their wallets to CGI also were made known, including Scaife and Murdoch.

Among the other conditions for an organization run by the husband of the Secretary of State: no annual meetings of the CGI outside of the United States and no new contributions to the CGI from foreign governments. Also required: approval by the State Department ethics officials or the office of the White House counsel for each business activity and paid speech by the former President. Friends said that Bill Clinton was impressed with how clear and candid the Obama team was with him. He told them, of his hosting CGI events overseas, "I think they're good for the country, but if that's what you want, fine."[8]

Clinton returned to work. Three years later, he told a CNN reporter that he had been in Haiti twenty times between 2009 and 2012, helping to raise billions of dollars for that devastated land. He said that his foundation's mentoring programs for fighting childhood obesity had been established in 13,000 American schools. When the interviewer noted that everywhere we went, he was "greeted like a rock star," the former President agreed that he could "go places and do things," and that might be one reason that 400 million people in 180 countries had been impacted by the programs of his foundation. He was able to travel to 150 countries and involve a bewildering variety of celebrities, from Bill Gates to Matt Damon to twenty Nobel laureates, in these efforts.

Was there a downside to all of this? Writer George Packer has raised questions about a "jet-setting, Davos-attending crowd constituting its own superclass, who hang out at the same TED talks, big-idea conferences, and fund-raising galas, appear on the same talk shows, invest in one another's projects, champion one another's causes." For Packer, these "new aristocrats" had emerged in a time of a sluggish economy and chronic malaise, even as "the American dream quietly dies, a victim of the calcification of a class system that is nearly hereditary."

But Bill Clinton was different. The former President was not just another figure on the celebrity circuit—he was a unique, charismatic individual. And he alone had the ability to mobilize large numbers of the rich, powerful, and famous to address problems facing the United States and the world. It has been no small feat to secure 2,100 commitments from such people that amount to over $69 billion for these causes.[9]

Of course, private foundation efforts, even Clinton's, remarkable as they may be, can have only limited impact on the larger issues confronting the

United States in the second decade of the twenty-first century. What is required, Bill Clinton wrote in 2011 in a book titled *Back to Work*, is enlistment of "smart government" to help build "a strong economy." Government action is essential to fully address the problems of the growing number of Americans left behind and left out by developments since the turn of the millennium. And the man who led the nation for eight critical years in the Nineties, helping to shape a new prosperity and, by 2000, a more egalitarian moment in recent history, was the person to make that case.

In his book, Clinton assessed "our thirty-year anti-government obsession." He dismantled the arguments of the Tea Party activists, who had emerged in 2010 as the antigovernment ideologues helping to frustrate the work of the Obama administration. Restating the themes of his own time in power, he asked: "What kind of future do we want? Do we want a country where we work together to restore the American Dream and rebuild the middle class . . . with a strong economy and strong government working together? Or a weak government and powerful interest groups who scorn shared prosperity in favor of winner take all . . . for that's really where antigovernment, 'you're on your own' policies will lead us."[10]

Bill Clinton had been committed to his new career and to his foundation's agenda. But by election year 2012, he was ready once more to help progressive forces in the struggle against what he saw as antigovernment reactionaries, the new far right extremists who resisted any role for Washington and who were willing to paralyze the nation if their demands were not met, and who rejected even the concept of compromise. He would do what he could to help Barack Obama win reelection and help bring more Democrats to Congress.

The Obama administration from the start had a familiar look to students of the Clinton years. Barack Obama's chief of staff, national economics adviser, White House counsel, Treasury Secretary, Attorney General, UN Ambassador, climate czar, and Homeland Security Secretary all had served Clinton. In Obama's first year, over 40 percent of his appointees to Senate-confirmed posts were veterans of the Clinton administration. And, of course, there was the Secretary of State.

Some of these returnees now in the Obama White House initially praised the new boss at the expense of the old. They told one reporter that they admired "Obama's cool" as opposed to Clinton's "purple rages at his staff behind closed doors"; they marveled at Obama's discipline and "rolled their eyes" at memories of Clinton's "agonizing before making decisions." But as time passed, and congressional gridlock stalled many Obama initiatives, there would be growing concern about the new president's logical and unemotional persona, about how "no-drama Obama" lacked communication skills within his own party as well as with Republicans. There would be fond memories of Clinton's warmth, his adroit way of connecting with people, his political genius, and shrewd ability to outmaneuver his opponents.

As the election campaign heated up in 2012, the perceived differences in style and effectiveness of the two Presidents long had faded from view. Now what was important for Democrats was keeping the White House. With Mitt Romney, the most plausible of the GOP contenders, finally having won the Republican nomination, with polls indicating a very tight race, the Democratic Party Convention in Charlotte in early September would be a critical test in the run-up to voting day. And Bill Clinton was asked to give the speech nominating Barack Obama.

It proved to be a bravura performance, energizing Democrats everywhere, and a major reason why the party and its presidential candidate would leap ahead in the race. White haired, thinner than ever before, but commanding the stage as always, he spoke for fifty minutes. He was greeted, as usual, with rapturous applause and interrupted again and again with cheers, laughter, and boos as he shaped a brilliant defense of the Democratic record and a scathing if good-humored demolition of Republican policies. ("I often disagree with Republicans but I actually never learned to hate them the way the far right that now controls their party seems to hate our President and a lot of other Democrats.")

"The Republican argument against the President's reelection went something like this," he said. "We left him a total mess. He hasn't cleaned it up fast enough. So fire him and put us back in." As always, he effortlessly cited the critical statistical data and historical evidence supporting his argument, but did so without pedantry, without boring or losing the big crowd, which sat spellbound in front of him. In fact, the crowd—and from subsequent reports, apparently much of the huge television audience beyond—was often so involved with each of his arguments, wanting to cheer yet again, that he had to remind them that there was more: "No, wait, you got to listen to this, this is important." He was like a famous symphony conductor, and he was orchestrating a special moment in political history. On the Obama economic record (and the Bush and Clinton economic results in earlier years), on the debt, taxes, the stimulus plan, health matters, and the success of "Obamacare," on student loans, and so much more, he built his case for reelecting Barack Obama and rejecting Romney. "We simply cannot afford to give the reins of government to someone who will double down on trickle down."

Democrats, of course, were exultant. But Republicans were shaken. Said Steve Schmidt, John McCain's 2008 presidential campaign manager, now an MSNBC analyst: "I wish to God as a Republican we had someone on our side who had the ability to do that." At Fox News, Brit Hume exclaimed: "I've always said if I were ever in trouble . . . I would want Bill Clinton there to defend me. Nobody does it better." GOP strategist and CNN pundit

Alex Castellanos said the speech had tilted the scale: "Tonight when everybody leaves, lock the door. You don't have to come back tomorrow [when President Obama would speak]. This convention is done. This will be the moment that probably reelected Barack Obama."

Journalists and pundits tried to explain the magic. He had "shrunk the room," one wrote, putting himself on intimate terms with his audience. He knew the facts, he criticized without getting nasty, he drew sharp distinctions but kept it light and simple, he respected his listeners. Many were searching for the right term to describe this achievement, and soon there seemed to be a consensus. The *Washington Post* headlined: "The Big Dog Shows How It's Done." *Forbes* magazine would say: "Bill Clinton: the Big Dog Owns the Big Stage." And the *Miami Herald* would explain "Why They Call Bill Clinton 'Big Dog.'"

Bill Clinton was the "big dog" once more, America's most brilliant and effective political spokesman. Barack Obama now said that Clinton should be appointed "in charge of explaining stuff."

He worked hard during the fall campaign, serving as an active behind-the-scenes consultant, regularly in touch with Obama strategists Jim Messina and David Axelrod. Clinton went on the road numerous times after telling the Obama team: "I'm yours in the final weeks." Bill Clinton would even act as the President's surrogate speaker when Barack Obama had to leave the campaign trail and address the destruction in New Jersey, New York, and the eastern seaboard caused by Superstorm Sandy.

At one point, just days before the vote, after a whirlwind seventy-two–hour marathon of nine speeches in New Hampshire, Minnesota, North Carolina, and Virginia, a reporter said that Bill Clinton sounded awful, as if he had been "gargling with Liquid-Plumr." Wheezing while introducing Barack Obama at the final late-night event, he said, "As you can see, I have given my voice in service of my President."

On election day, the GOP went down to smashing defeat, with only 47 percent of the vote. Now, the former President could retreat again from the political spotlight. Hillary Clinton, having served four years, announced she was leaving the State Department, amidst blossoming rumors that she would be the presumptive candidate for the party in 2016 if she so desired. But for Bill Clinton, it was back to work with the foundation and the CGI.

He was happy at the prospect. "I love this work," he said, as once more he toured Africa, this time with daughter Chelsea, who now had taken a more active role in the charitable effort, at his side. He was 66, no longer the Boy Governor and youthful President of earlier years, but still full of intellectual energy and looking to the future. "Anybody who has had the life I have had, anybody who has been given the gift that I was given by the American people, would be crazy not to do it."[11]

NOTES

1. Michael Takiff, *A Complicated Man: The Life of Bill Clinton as Told by Those Who Know Him* (New Haven: Yale University Press, 2010), pp. 399–403, 411–413; *New York Times*, February 9–10, May 19, August 21, 2001; "The White House Scandal that Wasn't," *Salon*, May 23, 2001, www.salon.com/news/politics/feature/05/23/vandals; Robert Yoon, "Bill Clinton Has Most Lucrative Year on Speech Circuit," CNN Politics, July 3, 2012, http://www.cnn.com/2012/07/03/politics/clinton-speaking-fees; Joe Conason, "The Third Term: The Dawning of a Different Sort of Post-Presidency," *Esquire*, December 1, 2005, http://www.esquire.com/features/ESQ1205-1205CLINTON_190

2. William J. Clinton Presidential Center, "Building the Center," http://www.clintonpresidentialcenter.org/about-the-center/building-the-center

3. Jaris F. Kearney, *Conversations: William Jefferson Clinton from Hope to Harlem* (Chicago: Writing Our World Press, 2006), pp. xi, 362–363.

4. "Bill Clinton's Vegan Weight Loss Secret and His 4 Heart Disease Reversal Gurus," http://calorielab.com/news/2010/09/25/bill-clintons-vegan-weight-loss-secret-and-his-4-heart-disease-reversal-gurus; "Clinton Pumps Base from the Stump," CNN Politics, October 26, 2004, http://www.cnn.com/2004/ALLPOLITICS/10/25/clinton.monday; Bill Clinton, "Address to the Progressive Governance Conference, London, England, 07/11/2003," *A Decade of Difference: President Clinton, Select Remarks, 2001–2011* (Little Rock: William J. Clinton Foundation, 2011), pp. 29–41; Paul Begala in Takiff, p. 413; Peter Baker, "The Mellowing of William Jefferson Clinton," *New York Times Magazine*, May 26, 2009, http://www.nytimes.com/2009/05/31/magazine/31clinton-t.html?pagewanted=all&_r=0; Conason, "The Third Term."

5. Ibid.; Takiff, pp. 405–410; Address to Nelson Mandela's 90th Birthday Dinner, London, June 25, 2008; Clinton, *A Decade of Difference*, pp. 80–81; Clinton Foundation, "Clinton Global Initiative," http://www.clintonglobalinitiative.org; Clinton Foundation, "A Decade of Difference: Celebrating 10 Years of the Clinton Foundation: Clinton Global Initiative Milestones," http://www.clintonfoundation.org/main/about/our-10-years/10-clinton-global-initiative-milestones.html

6. Al Hunt, *Bloomberg News*, "Tensions in Hillaryland Grows as Plan Goes Awry," http://www.bloomberg.com/apps/news?pid=newsarchive&sid=anRcoLyfN0VM; *New York Times*, February 22, June 3, 8, 2008; Baker, "Mellowing"; "Bill Clinton Says Race, Gender to Decide S.C. Vote," *USA Today*, January 24, 2008; Mark Mooney, "Obama Played Race Card On Me," ABC News, www.abcnews.go.com/blogs/politics/2008/04/bill-clinton-ob-2; Ryan Lizza, Campaign Journal, "Bill vs. Barack," *The New Yorker*, May 5, 2008, http://www.newyorker.com/talk/2008/05/05/080505ta_talk_lizza; Todd S. Purdom, "The Comeback Id," *Vanity Fair*, July 2008, http://www.vanityfair.com/politics/features/2008/07/clinton200807; Takiff, pp. 414–420.

7. "Bill Clinton's Convention Speech," *New York Times*, August 27, 2008.

8. Takiff, pp. 424–425; *New York Times*, November 29, December 18, 2008.

9. "Bill Clinton: Life after the Presidency," CNN, January 29, 2012, http://www.youtube.com/watch?v=Mdrf0cVUe38; George Packer, "Celebrating Inequality," *New York Times*, May 20, 2013.

10. Bill Clinton, *Back to Work: Why We Need Smart Government for a Strong Economy* (New York: Random House, 2011), pp. 3–69, 234–240.

11. Baker, "Mellowing"; Clinton, *A Decade of Difference*, pp. 6–7; "Life after the Presidency," CNN, January 29, 2012; Transcript of Bill Clinton's Speech to the Democratic National Convention, *New York Times*, September 5, 2012; "The Big Dog Shows How It's Done," *Washington Post*, September 6, 2012; "Bill Clinton Media Reactions: Pundits Praise Former President's DNC Speech, Some Criticize Length," *Huffington Post*, September 5, 2012; http://www.huffingtonpost.com/2012/09/05/bill-clinton-media-reactions-dnc-speech_n_1859892.html; "Why They Call Bill Clinton 'Big Dog,'" *Miami Herald*, September 8, 2012; *Washington Post*, October 12, 2012; *The New York Times*, September 4, November 4, 2012, March 26, May 29, 2013.

Epilogue

On the Question of Presidential Greatness

At the end of his lengthy autobiography, Bill Clinton noted that he has had an "an improbable life and a wonderful one." Still, for all his remarkable achievements before and after the White House, this life and career surely reached its pinnacle when he was President of the United States.

But was Clinton a "great President"? For many years, historians and other "presidential scholars" have been called on to rank the American Presidents. Opinion surveys have repeatedly polled the general public on its "approval" of the present chief executive. Such surveys also have asked the public's view of the comparative ratings of all those who have been "POTUS," the most powerful and influential figure in the world, at least across most of the last century.

Clinton, of course, has done very well in the approval surveys. His end-of-presidency approval rating in the Gallup poll was 66 percent, substantially higher than Kennedy's or Reagan's, strikingly higher than all other Presidents since the surveys began at the end of World War II. (It is a measure of the futility of those enemies plotting to destroy him that his high point in such approval surveys was 73 percent in December 20, 1998, in the midst of the impeachment effort.)

The rankings of the scholarly "experts" have been less kind, with Bill Clinton almost never placed in the pantheon of the greatest Presidents. FDR and Abraham Lincoln, George Washington and Theodore Roosevelt, Jefferson, Madison, Wilson are usually ranked above Clinton. Even Harry S Truman, who had such lamentable public approval ratings upon leaving office, as well as Dwight Eisenhower and JFK in the post–World War II years, often rank above the "Man from Hope."

These ratings do change from year to year, and decade to decade, with Bill Clinton having moved up in the view of "presidential scholars" in recent times.[1]

Of course, there is a built-in arbitrariness to all such rankings. The relative rank often depends on the ideology of the rater. It depends on the moment in history: what crises presented a sitting President with opportunities to lead and to shape successful responses. It depends on the political environment confronting the POTUS; skill, charm, toughness, negotiating acumen, and willingness to compromise count far less in times of deep polarization and entrenched congressional opposition, when a President has no "working majority" on Capitol Hill.

For Bill Clinton, it is unlikely he will ever receive high marks from free market libertarians or passionate social conservatives, people who would view his domestic agenda as destructive of their vision for America. But he will not fare well with most committed liberals either, for the "third way"/New Democrat approach that he shaped is anathema to those who wanted a successful neo–New Deal run of victories in the Nineties and could not understand why he failed to deliver it. Scholars on both the political right and the political left are unhappy with the bridge Clinton was building to the future in his White House years. He will not be at the top of most of their presidential pyramids.

As for the "moment in history" he inherited, Bill Clinton in office did not have to deal with the calamities at home or abroad confronting some of his predecessors, which offered them a setting for "greatness." There was no new nation to shepherd through a post-revolutionary period. There was no Civil War to fight and win. There was no World War I ravaging Europe, no Great Depression to overcome, no world-menacing threat of Nazi or Japanese aggression to deal with. There was no emerging Cold War in a nuclear age, requiring a new response from traditionally isolationist Washington.

Moreover, Bill Clinton did not come to power at a favorable time for activist political leadership. Theodore Roosevelt first brought rising reform passions to the White House, but they were already coursing across the land at the turn of the twentieth century. Then Woodrow Wilson inherited a wave of Progressive support in Congress for his "New Freedom" agenda. FDR faced a dispirited conservative opposition, shattered by the economic disasters of the early Thirties, and brilliantly moved forward with his New Deal programs. LBJ grasped the opportunities presented by the booming prosperity of the Sixties, the perceived martyrdom of JFK, and the dominant liberal ethos in the country to push through his momentous Great Society effort, done before his fateful Vietnam decision. These modern Presidents, for all their legendary political skills, did not face the kind of implacable opposition in Congress that Bill Clinton had to deal with from day one. And none of them faced the intense, media-fueled politics of personal destruction that was the hallmark of the Clinton presidency.

President Bill Clinton would not have the challenge—and the opportunity—of dealing with a "big war," with its existential threat to the future of the nation. He even was eight months out of office on 9/11, that terrible day. His eloquence at the time of the Oklahoma City bombing, his growing confidence in managing measured military responses in regional conflicts and in facing the emerging terrorist menace give some sense of how he would have met this challenge.

But in foreign affairs, he did have to face a series of new, complex, and maddeningly difficult problems emerging from the end of the Cold War. And with his diplomatic and national security team, he devised ways of dealing with them. Under Clinton, America avoided new conflicts with old adversary Russia, dealt with the threats posed by hostile rogue states, grasped the opportunity to serve as peacemaker in ancient quarrels, confronted terrorism, and eventually used force to end aggression in some lands torn by ethnic strife. Yet in one sense, Bill Clinton was concerned with an even larger agenda: shaping American leadership in an age of globalization.

He was frustrated, Strobe Talbott would observe, that he and his team could find no single phrase that defined his foreign policy. He was searching for the critical word, like the famous "containment" after World War II. He couldn't seem to escape the "post–Cold War era," but that, he once observed, is "where we are in terms of where we've been rather than where we're going. I'm tomorrow's boy and I don't like being seen as doing yesterday's business." But in fact he was doing tomorrow's business. "Communications and commerce are global," he said, in his first inaugural address. Investment is mobile, "technology almost magical, ambition for a better life now universal. We earn our livelihood in peaceful competition with people all across the earth. Profound and powerful forces are remaking our world." While dealing with the multifaceted crises of his post–Cold War moment in office, he was pushing, in words and in action (including NAFTA and WTO), a U.S.-led effort to harness technology in the service of global prosperity and interdependence, a way of shaping a global social system.

Perhaps, as Talbott observed, he was reluctant to say too much about this while in office, because any President has to celebrate American preeminence and Bill Clinton understood that the future would be a "multilateral" not a "unipolar" time. Unlike the neo-conservatives who attacked him and then dominated foreign/military policy in the administration of his successor, giving us the "Bush doctrine" and the abyss of Iraq, he recognized that "we're not going to be the cock of the roost forever, you know" and that the United States should not aspire to dominate the world. He understood that this would be a futile hope in the future anyway, in an age of expanding Chinese and Indian economic strength. Instead, America must help lead the way in a globalizing world. This was present in his policies and his agenda as President, and certainly in his post–White House career.[2]

In domestic affairs, he faced nothing like the slavery crisis and a war to preserve the Union in Lincoln's time, nothing like the Great Depression, with its implicit fear of political and social upheaval, greeting a newly elected Franklin Roosevelt. But he did confront a wrenching recession, yet one that emerged in a nation still influenced by the libertarian ethos of the Reagan years, in which millions were taught to revile Washington and fear federal government activism. He entered the White House in an age when many supported Republican leaders calling for tax cuts and deregulation as the singular cure-all for economic distress.

This was an enormous challenge. But he responded by reshaping the programs embraced by FDR and LBJ liberals to meet the political realities of this new age. Under Bill Clinton, the government would not, as he put it, "abandon our commitments to equal opportunity and social justice." His White House worked to strengthen the economy, stimulate the job market, expand college aid and after-school programs, provide kids with health insurance and parents with the family leave law, enact gun control, and vastly widen the scope of the Earned Income Tax Credit for those less well off.

His America was a place where, as he would write, "the water got cleaner and more of our national heritage was preserved," where those who were most affluent paid higher taxes to support the national community, despite the frantic efforts of conservatives to preserve all the massive tax cuts of the Reagan years. In his America, efforts to roll back social and economic programs by these same congressional opponents were blocked even as racial, gender, and religious diversity was championed both inside and outside the administration.

He said that he "kept score," and the extraordinary numbers that marked his success in achieving his domestic goals were the reason for his growing popularity across the land. There were startling changes in the critical data: striking increases in employment and real wage growth, declines in poverty levels across every part of the population, and all this happening during a time of budget balancing, with a reduction of the national debt and elimination of yearly deficits.

Bill Clinton wrote that he tried to "build a new vital center for American politics in the twenty-first century." This New Democrat approach was not improvised, it was the product of his evolving vision of what was needed and what was possible in a new political environment. It was present back in the Covenant Speeches in 1991, on display long before he entered the White House. It was a way of using federal resources to strengthen the nation even in a time of deep resistance to Washington authority. It infuriated his critics on the right and did not please many on the left, but the numbers—in the data on the economy and in the approval ratings for this President—speak to his success.

Was Bill Clinton a "great President"? Every citizen, every scholar, every observer will make his or her own decision on that question. But a strong case can be made for "The Man from Hope."

NOTES

1. "Presidential Approval Ratings—Bill Clinton," http://www.gallup.com/poll/116584/Presidential-Approval-Ratings-Bill-Clinton.aspx; "Judging and Ranking U.S. Presidents," *New York Times*, July 29, 2012; "Historical Presidential Approval Ratings—End of Term," http://uspolitics.about.com/od/polls/l/bl_historical_approval.htm; "Is Bill Clinton One of the Best Presidents in History?" *Washington Post*. September 6, 2012.
2. Talbott, *The Great Experiment* (New York: Simon and Schuster, 2008), pp. 324–331; Clinton, *My Life* (New York: Alfred A. Knopf, 2004), pp. 954–956.

PART **II**

DOCUMENTS

THE NEW COVENANT: RESPONSIBILITY AND REBUILDING THE AMERICAN COMMUNITY, OCTOBER 23, 1991

Bill Clinton had grappled with the question of whether to make a run for the White House in 1992 for many months. He made the formal announcement of his candidacy in early October 1991. Later that month, at his alma mater, Georgetown University, he presented a series of extraordinary lectures describing the reasons why he thought he could make a difference as President of the United States. He called these addresses the "covenant speeches." Here is the first one, laying out his views on the state of the nation and the vision he would bring to the office.

I would like to thank all the people who helped me along life's way here at Georgetown, some who are no longer living, some who are no longer here, a few who remain here to teach and help people of your generation move along life's way.

I am profoundly indebted to what this university gave me. I have carried with me to the present day indelible memories of all the things that happened on this campus and in this town, and in our country during the four eventful years in the mid-Sixties when I was here.

I thought those years were eventful years, but the years that you're here, those of you who are students, are truly revolutionary.

When I was here, our country simply sought to contain Communism, not roll it back. Most respected academics held that once a country went Communist, the loss of freedom was permanent and irreversible.

But in the last three years, we've seen the Berlin Wall come down, Germany reunify, all of Eastern Europe abandon Communism, a coup in the

Soviet Union fail, and the Soviet Union itself disintegrate, liberating the Baltics and the other republics.

Now the Soviet foreign minister is trying to help our secretary of state make peace in the Middle East, and in the space of a year Lech Wałęsa and Václav Havel have both come to this city to thank America for supporting their quest for freedom.

For good measure, Nelson Mandela walked out of a jail that he entered even before I entered Georgetown, and now he says he wants his country to have a Bill of Rights just like the one we have here.

America should be celebrating today. All around the world, the American dream is ascendant. Everybody wants political democracy and market economics, and national independence. Everything your grandparents and parents fought for, and stood for, from World War II on, is being rewarded and embraced.

Yet today in America, we're not celebrating. Why? Because all of us fear down deep inside that even as the American dream reigns supreme abroad, it's dying here at home. We're losing jobs and wasting opportunities.

The very fiber of our nation is breaking down: Families are coming apart, kids are dropping out of school, drugs and crime dominate our streets.

And our leaders here in Washington aren't doing much about it. The political system we have now rotates between being the butt of jokes and the object of absolute scorn.

Frustration produces calls for term limits from voters who don't even think they have the power to vote incumbents out, and resentment produces votes for David Duke, not just from racists, but from voters so desperate for change they will support the most anti-establishment message, even if it's delivered by an ex-Klansman who admits it was inspired by Adolf Hitler.

We've got to rebuild our political life before the demagogues and the racists, and those who pander to the worst in us, bring this country down.

People once looked at the President and the Congress to bring us together, to solve problems, to make progress. Now, in the face of massive challenges, our government stands discredited, our people are disillusioned. There's a hole in our politics where our sense of common purpose used to be.

The Reagan–Bush years have exalted private gain over public obligation, special interest over the common good, wealth and fame over work and family.

The 1980s ushered in a gilded age of greed and selfishness, of irresponsibility and excess, and of neglect.

S&L crooks stole billions of dollars in other people's money. Pentagon consultants and HUD contractors stole from the taxpayers.

Many big corporate executives raised their own salaries even when their companies were losing money and their workers were being put into the unemployment lines.

Middle-class families worked longer hours for less money and spent more on health care and housing, and education and taxes.

Poverty rose. Many inner-city streets were taken over by crime and drugs, welfare and despair. Family responsibility became an oxymoron for many deadbeat fathers who were more likely to make their car payments than to pay their child support.

And government, which should have been setting an example, was even worse. Congress raised its pay and guarded its perks while most Americans were working harder for less money.

Two Republican Presidents elected on a promise of fiscal responsibility advanced budget proposals that more than tripled our national debt.

Congress went along with that, too. Taxes were lowered on the wealthiest people whose incomes were rising, and raised on middle-class families as their incomes fell.

Through it all, millions of decent, ordinary people who worked hard, played by the rules, and took responsibility for their own actions were falling more and more behind, living a life of struggle without reward or security.

For twelve years, these forgotten middle-class Americans have watched their economic interest ignored and their values literally ground into the ground. Nothing illustrates this more clearly than the fact that in the 1980s charitable giving among middle-class people went up even as their incomes went down, while charitable giving among the wealthiest Americans went down as their incomes went up. Responsibility went unrewarded and so did hard work.

It's no wonder so many kids growing up on the streets in America today think it really makes more sense to them to join a gang and do drugs and sell drugs than to stay in school and go to work. We have seen a decade in which the fast buck was glorified from Wall Street to Main Street to Mean Street.

To turn America around, we've got to have a new approach, founded on our most sacred principles as a nation, with a vision for the future. We need a new covenant, a solemn agreement between the people and their government to provide opportunity for everybody, inspire responsibility throughout our society, and restore a sense of community to our great nation. A new covenant to take government back from the powerful interests and the bureaucracy and give it back to the ordinary people of our country.

More than 200 years ago, our founding fathers outlined our first social compact between government and the people, not just between lords and kings. More than 100 years ago, Abraham Lincoln gave his life to maintain the Union that compact created. More than 60 years ago, Franklin Roosevelt renewed that promise with a New Deal that offered opportunity in return for hard work.

Today we need to forge a new covenant that will repair the damaged bond between the people and their government, restore our basic values, embed the idea that a country has a responsibility to help people get ahead but that citizens have not only the right but the responsibility to rise as far and fast as their talents and determination can take them, and most important of all, that we're all in this together.

We have to make good on the words of Thomas Jefferson, who once said, "A debt of service is due from every man to his country proportional to the bounties which nature and fortune have measured to him."

Make no mistake. This new covenant means change, change in my party, change in our leadership, change in our country, change in the lives of every American. Far away from Washington and your home towns and mine, most people have lost faith in the ability of government to have a positive impact on their lives.

Out there you can hear the quiet, troubled voices of forgotten middle-class Americans lamenting the fact that government no longer looks out for their interests or honors their values, values like individual responsibility, hard work, family, and community. They believe the government takes more from them than it gives back and looks the other way when special interests only take from our country and give nothing back. And they're right.

So this new covenant can't be between the politicians and the established interests and the political elites. It can't be just another back-room deal in power where the people who have power and the people who keep them there make a decision that looks like something it's not. This new covenant can only be ratified in the election of 1992 and that's why I'm running for President.

Some people think it's old fashioned to talk like this. Some people even think I am naive to suggest that we can restore the American dream through a covenant between people and their government. But I believe with all my heart—after eleven years of work as a governor, working every day to create opportunity and jobs and improve education and deal with all the problems that we all know so much about—that the only way we can hold this country together and move boldly into the future is to do it together with a new covenant.

Over twenty-five years ago my classmates and I all took a class in Western civilization taught by a legendary professor named Carroll Quigley. He taught at the end of the course that the defining idea of Western civilization in general and our country in particular is what he called future preference:

the idea that the future can be better than the present and that each of us has a personal moral responsibility to make it so.

I hope they still teach that lesson here at Georgetown, even though Professor Quigley has been dead for some years. And I hope you believe it because I think it's the only way to save America.

In the weeks to come I will come back to Georgetown and outline my plans to rebuild our economy, regain our competitive leadership in the world, restore the fortunes of the middle class, and reclaim the future for the next generation. I'll give a speech on how we should promote our national security and foreign policy interests after the Cold War and I'll tell you in clear terms what I believe the President and the Congress owe you and all the rest of the American citizens in this new covenant for change.

But I can tell you, based on my long experience in public life, there will never be a government program for every problem. Much of what holds us together and moves us ahead is the daily assumption of personal responsibility by millions and millions of Americans from all walks of life. I can promise to do 100 different things for you as President, but none of them will make any difference unless we all do more as citizens. And today that's what I want to talk about: the responsibilities we owe to ourselves, to each other, and to our country.

It's been thirty years since a Democrat ran for President and asked something of all the American people. I intend to challenge you all to do more and to do better. We simply have to go beyond the competing ideas of the old political establishment, beyond every man for himself on one hand and something for nothing on the other. We need a new covenant that will challenge all of our citizens to be responsible, that will say first to the corporate leaders at the top of the ladder: We will promote economic growth and the free market, but we're not going to help you diminish the middle class and weaken our economy.

We will support your efforts to increase your profits—they're good—and jobs through quality products and services, but we're going to hold you responsible for being good corporate citizens, too.

At the other end of the scale, we'll say to people on welfare: We're going to give you training and education and health care for yourself and your children, but if you can work, you must go to work because we can no longer afford to have you stay on welfare forever.

We will say to hardworking middle-class Americans and those who aspire to the middle class: We're going to guarantee you and your children access to a college education, every one of you, but if you take the help, you have to give something back to your country.

In short, the new covenant must challenge all of us, especially those of us in public service, for we have a solemn responsibility to honor the values and promote the interests of the people who elected us, and if we don't do it, we don't belong in government anymore.

This new covenant should begin in Washington. I want to literally revolutionize the federal government and fundamentally change its relationship to our people. People no longer want a top-down bureaucracy telling them what to do. That's one reason they tore down the Berlin Wall and threw out the Communist regimes in Eastern Europe and the Soviet Union.

Now our new covenant will challenge our own government to change its way of doing business, too. The American people need a government they can afford and a government that works. The Republicans have been in charge of this government for twelve years.

They've brought it to the brink of bankruptcy. But Democrats who want to change the government, who want the government to do more, and I'm one of them, we have a heavy responsibility to show that we're going to spend the taxpayers' money wisely and with discipline, that we can spend more money on the future and control what we spend on the present and the past.

And I want to make government more efficient and effective by following the lead of our best companies: eliminating unnecessary layers of bureaucracy, reducing administrative costs, and most important, giving the American citizens more choices in the services they get, just as we have worked hard to do in Arkansas. We balanced our budget every year, improved services, and treated our citizens like our customers and our bosses, giving them more choices in public schools, child care centers, and services to the elderly, and we can do that in America.

And a new Democratic covenant must also challenge Congress to act responsibly. Democrats must lead the way because they want to use government to help people, and therefore they must restore the credibility of Congress. Congress should live by the laws that apply to other workplaces.

Congressional pay should not go up while the pay of working Americans is going down.

And we should clamp down on campaign spending and open the airwaves in congressional elections to encourage real political debate instead of paid political assassinations.

And finally, there must be no more bounced checks, no more unpaid bills, no more fixed tickets, because service in Congress is itself privilege enough.

We can't go on like this. We've got to honor, reward, and reflect the work ethic, not the power grab, in politics. Responsibility is for everybody and it's got to begin here in the nation's capital.

The new covenant must also challenge the private sector. The most irresponsible people in the 1980s were business leaders who abused their position at the top of the totem pole. This is my message to our business community. As President I'll do everything I can to make it easier for your company to compete in the world with a better trained workforce, cooperation between labor and management, fair and strong trade policies, and incentives to invest here in America in our own economic growth.

But if I do that, I expect the jetsetters and the featherbedders of corporate America to know that if you sell your companies and your workers and your country down the river, you'll be called on the carpet. That's what the President's bully pulpit is for.

All of you who are going into business, it is a noble endeavor. It is the thing which makes this country run. The private sector creates job, not the public sector. But the people with responsibility in the private sector should know it is not enough simply to obey the letter of the law and make as much money as you can. It's simply wrong for executives to do what so many did in the '80s. The biggest companies raised their executive pay four times the percentage their workers' pay went up and three times the percentage their profits went up.

It's wrong to drive a company into the ground and then have the chief executive bail out with a golden parachute to a cushy life.

The average CEO at a major American corporation, according to a recent Senate hearing, is paid about 100 times as much as the average worker. Compare that to two countries doing much better than we are in the world economy. In Germany, it's 23 to 1. In Japan, which just completed 58 months of untrammeled economic growth, it's 17 to 1. And our government today rewards that excess with a tax break for executive pay no matter how high it is. That's wrong. If companies want to overpay their executives and underinvest in their future, that's their business, but they shouldn't get any special treatment from Uncle Sam.

If a company wants to transfer jobs abroad and cut the security of their working people, they may have a legal right to do it but they shouldn't get special treatment from the Treasury, as they do today. That's not right.

In the 1980s we didn't do enough to help our companies to compete and win in the global economy. We didn't. But we did do way too much to transfer wealth away from hardworking middle-class Americans to rich people who got it without good reason and without contributing to production and wealth in this country. There should be no more deductibility for responsibility.

This new covenant must also make some challenges to the hardworking middle class. Their challenge centers around work and education. I know Americans worry about the quality of education in this country and want the best for their children. Under my administration we'll set high national standards for what our children need to know based on the international competition. And we'll develop a national examination system to measure whether they are learning it or not.

It's not enough just to put money in schools. We have to challenge our schools to produce and insist on results.

I just came from Thomas Jefferson Junior High School here in Washington, and the principal of that school, Vera White, is here with me today. She said she was coming and she wanted to approve my speech.

I've been to that school three times in the last five years. That school is almost all black. It's in a building that was built when Grant was President.

They have the plaster models of the Jefferson Memorial in the school auditorium. But every time I've been in that school, you could eat lunch off every floor in the school. There is a spirit of learning that pervades the atmosphere. Almost everyone in the school comes from an ordinary family in Washington— it's almost 100 percent minority. But in several years that school has won the National Math Council's competition, going all the way to the finals for junior high school performance in math. They've been adopted by a company now that has given them excellence in science. And every time I go there I'm just overwhelmed by the spirit that exists from a teacher's and principal's point of view. They know that they're going to produce, and they don't make excuses for the problems that the kids bring to the classroom.

They open those kids to a brighter world. We need more of that. But we also have to recognize that teachers can't do it all. We must challenge parents and children to believe that all children can learn. And here may be the biggest challenge of all, because too many American parents and children really believe that how much children learn in school depends on the IQ God gave them and their family income.

The kids we're competing for the future with are raised to believe that how well they do depends upon how hard they work and how much their parents encourage them to succeed in school. That's the attitude that every American school and parent has to have if we're going to do well.

And we have to challenge our students to stay in school. Students who drop out or fail to learn as much as they can aren't just letting themselves down; they're letting all the rest of us down, because from the point they drop out on, the chances are they'll be subtracting from society instead of adding to it.

We've got to enhance their responsibility. In my state we say, if someone drops out of school for no good reason, they lose the privilege of a driver's license. All over America we have to reexamine this problem and say you have a responsibility to stay in school, you have a responsibility to learn, we have a responsibility to give you a good education.

This new covenant should have challenges for every young person. I want to establish in this country a voluntary system of national service. In a

Clinton administration we will put forth a domestic GI bill that will say to any middle-class or low-income person: We want you to go to college, we'll provide the money for you to go to college, it will be the best money the taxpayers ever spent—but you've got to pay it back, either as a small percentage of your income over time or with two or three years of national service where we need it here at home—as teachers, as policemen, as nurses, as family service workers.

But education doesn't stop in school. Adults have a responsibility to keep learning, too—learning for a lifetime. And all of us are going to have to work smarter in the next century if America is going to compete and win. So all managers and all workers will have to be challenged every year to reorganize the workplace for high performance—a workplace in which workers have more power but can abandon work rules that don't make sense.

And there's a special challenge in this new covenant for the young men and women who live in America's most troubled urban neighborhoods—young men and women like those I've met in Chicago and Los Angeles and many other places in our country. They are kids who live in fear of being shot going to and from school, or being forced to join a gang in order to avoid being beaten.

Many of these young people believe that our country has ignored them for too long—and they're right. They think that America unfairly blames them for everything that is wrong in their neighborhoods, for drugs and crime and poverty and the breakup of the family and the breakdown of the schools—and they're right.

They worry that because by and large their faces are different colors than mine, their only choice in life will be jail or welfare or a dead-end job, and that being a minority in a big city is more or less a guarantee of failure. That's not right. And when I'm President I'm going to do my very best to prove that all those fears are wrong, because I know these young people can overcome these obstacles and become anything they set their minds to. And more importantly for you, I know that America needs their strength, their intelligence, and their humanity.

And because I believe in them and what they can contribute, they can't be let off the responsibility hook either. All society can ever offer them is a chance to develop their God-given capacities. They have to do the rest. Anybody who tells them anything else is lying to them, and they already know that.

As President, I'll see that they get the same deal everyone should have—play by the rules, stay off drugs, stay in school, stay off the streets; don't have children if you're not prepared to support them because governments don't raise children—people do. And if you get in trouble we'll even give you one chance to avoid prison by setting up community boot camps for first-time nonviolent offenders so they can learn discipline and get drug treatment when necessary and continue their education and do useful community work—a second chance to be a first-rate citizen.

But if our new covenant is really pro-work, it must mean that people who work shouldn't be poor. And that's why in our administration we'll do everything we can to break the cycle of working poor by making work pay through expanding the Earned Income Tax Credit for the working poor, creating options for savings accounts, even for people on welfare, and supporting the establishment in the most oppressed areas of America of micro-enterprise businesses.

At the same time, we must assure all Americans that they'll have access to health care when they go to work. That's why so many today maintain themselves on the welfare rolls.

The new covenant can break the cycle of welfare. Welfare should be a second chance, not a way of life. In my administration we're going to put an end to welfare as we have come to know it. I want to erase the stigma of welfare for good by restoring a simple dignified principle: No one who can work can stay on welfare forever. We'll still help people to help themselves. And those who need education and training and child care and medical coverage for their kids—they'll get it. We'll give them all the help they need and we'll keep them on public assistance for up to two years, but after that, people who are able to work will have to go to work, either in the private sector or through a community service job. No more permanent dependence on welfare as a way of life. We can then restore welfare for what it was always meant to be—a way of temporarily helping people who've fallen on hard times.

If the new covenant is pro-work, it must also be pro-family. That means we have to demand the toughest possible child support enforcement. The number of absent parents who run off and leave their children with no financial help, even though they could do it, is a national scandal. We need an administration that will give state agencies that collect child support full law enforcement authority and find new ways of catching deadbeats and collecting the money.

In our state we passed a law this year which says if you owe more than $1,000 in child support, we'll report your name to every credit agency in the state. We don't think people should borrow money until they take care of their children, and that ought to be the law in America.

Finally, the President: The President has the greatest responsibility of all—first to bring us together, not drive us apart. For twelve years this President and his predecessor have divided us against each other, pitting rich against poor, playing for the emotions of the middle class, white against black, women against men, creating a country in which we no longer recognize that we are all in this together. They've profited by fostering an atmosphere of blame and denial instead of building an ethic of responsibility. They had a chance to bring out the best in us and instead they appealed to the worst in us.

Nothing exemplifies this more clearly than the battle over the Civil Rights Act of 1991. You know from what I have already said today that I can't be for quotas. I'm not for a guarantee for anybody. I'm for responsibility at every turn. That bill is not a quota bill. When the Civil Rights Act was in place from 1964 to 1987 I never had a single employer in my state say it's a quota bill.

We need rules of workplace fairness for the 70 percent of new entrants in our workforce who will be women and minorities in the decade of the '90s. That's what that bill is for.

Why does the President refuse to let a civil rights bill pass? Because he knows that the people he is dependent on for his electoral majority—white working-class men and women, mostly men—have had their incomes decline in the 1980s and they may return to their natural home, someone who offers them real economic opportunity. And so he is dredging up the same old tactic that the hard right has employed in my part of the country in the south since I was a child. When everything gets tight and you think you're going to lose those people, you find the most economically insecure white people and you scare the living daylights out of them.

That is wrong. We cannot have a new covenant unless the President assumes the responsibility and insists that every American join in bringing this country back together, fighting against the politics of division and going into tomorrow as one. After all, that's what's special about America.

Don't you want to be part of a country that's coming together instead of coming apart?

Don't you want to be part of a community where people look out for each other and not just for themselves?

Wouldn't it be nice to be part of a Nation again that brings out the best in all of us instead of playing to the worst for personal advantage?

Wouldn't it be nice again to have a leader who really believed that the only limit to what we can do is what our leaders ask of us and what we expect of ourselves?

Nearly sixty years ago, in a very famous speech to the Commonwealth Club, in the final months of his 1932 campaign, President Franklin Roosevelt outlined a new compact that gave hope to a nation mired in the Great Depression. The role of government, he said, was to promise every American the right to make a living. The people's role was to do their best to make the most of that opportunity. He said, and I quote, "Faith in America demands that we recognize the new terms of the old social contract. In the strength of great hope, we must all shoulder the common load."

That's what our hope is today, a new covenant to shoulder the common load.

When people assume responsibility and shoulder that load, they acquire a dignity they never had before. When people go to work, they rediscover a pride in themselves that they had lost.

I'll never forget, once a welfare mother in my state was asked, when she moved from welfare to work, what was the best thing about having a job. And she said: When my boy goes to school and they say, what does your mama do for a living?—he can give an answer.

When fathers pay their child support, they restore a connection that both they and their children need. When students work hard, they find out that they can all learn after all and do as well as any students in Japan or Singapore or Germany or anywhere else.

When corporate managers put their workers and their long-term profits ahead of their own paychecks, their companies do well and so do they.

When the privilege of serving is enough of a perk for people in Congress and when the President finally assumes responsibility for America's problems, we'll not only stop doing wrong, we'll begin to do what's right to move America forward.

That's what this election is really all about—forging a new covenant that will honor middle-class values, restore the public trust, create a new sense of community, and make America work again.

Thank you very much.

SOURCE

William J. Clinton, "The New Covenant: Responsibility and Rebuilding the American Community." Speech given at Georgetown University, October 23, 1991. Online by the William J. Clinton Presidential Center, http://clintonpresidentialcenter.org/georgetown/speech_newcovenant1.php

FIRST INAUGURAL ADDRESS, JANUARY 20, 1993

Following the solemn swearing-in ceremony in January 1993, Bill Clinton, now President of the United States, addressed the huge crowd gathered in front of the Capitol and a vast television audience across the nation and the globe. The inaugural address was a relatively brief but powerful speech focusing on the challenges confronting the nation and the agenda of the new leader in the White House.

My fellow citizens, today we celebrate the mystery of American renewal. This ceremony is held in the depth of winter, but by the words we speak and the faces we show the world, we force the spring, a spring reborn in the world's oldest democracy that brings forth the vision and courage to reinvent America. When our Founders boldly declared America's independence to the world and our purposes to the Almighty, they knew that America, to endure, would have to change; not change for change's sake but change to preserve America's ideals: life, liberty, the pursuit of happiness. Though we marched to the music of our time, our mission is timeless. Each generation of Americans must define what it means to be an American.

On behalf of our Nation, I salute my predecessor, President Bush, for his half-century of service to America. And I thank the millions of men and women whose steadfastness and sacrifice triumphed over depression, fascism, and communism.

Today, a generation raised in the shadows of the Cold War assumes new responsibilities in a world warmed by the sunshine of freedom but threatened still by ancient hatreds and new plagues. Raised in unrivaled prosperity, we inherit an economy that is still the world's strongest but is weakened by business failures, stagnant wages, increasing inequality, and deep divisions among our own people.

When George Washington first took the oath I have just sworn to uphold, news traveled slowly across the land by horseback and across the ocean by boat. Now, the sights and sounds of this ceremony are broadcast instantaneously to billions around the world. Communications and commerce are global. Investment is mobile. Technology is almost magical. And ambition for a better life is now universal.

We earn our livelihood in America today in peaceful competition with people all across the Earth. Profound and powerful forces are shaking and remaking our world. And the urgent question of our time is whether we can make change our friend and not our enemy. This new world has already enriched the lives of millions of Americans who are able to compete and win in it. But when most people are working harder for less; when others cannot work at all; when the cost of health care devastates families and threatens to bankrupt our enterprises, great and small; when the fear of crime robs law-abiding citizens of their freedom; and when millions of poor children cannot even imagine the lives we are calling them to lead, we have not made change our friend.

We know we have to face hard truths and take strong steps, but we have not done so; instead, we have drifted. And that drifting has eroded our resources, fractured our economy, and shaken our confidence. Though our challenges are fearsome, so are our strengths. Americans have ever been a restless, questing, hopeful people. And we must bring to our task today the vision and will of those who came before us. From our Revolution to the Civil War, to the Great Depression, to the civil rights movement, our people have always mustered the determination to construct from these crises the pillars of our history. Thomas Jefferson believed that to preserve the very foundations of our Nation, we would need dramatic change from time to time. Well, my fellow Americans, this is our time. Let us embrace it.

Our democracy must be not only the envy of the world but the engine of our own renewal. There is nothing wrong with America that cannot be cured by what is right with America. And so today we pledge an end to the era of deadlock and drift, and a new season of American renewal has begun.

To renew America, we must be bold. We must do what no generation has had to do before. We must invest more in our own people, in their jobs, and in their future, and at the same time cut our massive debt. And we must do so in a world in which we must compete for every opportunity. It will not be easy. It will require sacrifice, but it can be done and done fairly, not choosing sacrifice for its own sake but for our own sake. We must provide for our Nation the way a family provides for its children.

Our Founders saw themselves in the light of posterity. We can do no less. Anyone who has ever watched a child's eyes wander into sleep knows what posterity is. Posterity is the world to come: the world for whom we hold our ideals, from whom we have borrowed our planet, and to whom we bear sacred responsibility. We must do what America does best: offer more opportunity to all and demand more responsibility from all. It is time to break the bad habit of expecting something for nothing from our government or from each other. Let us all take more responsibility not only for ourselves and our families but for our communities and our country.

To renew America, we must revitalize our democracy. This beautiful Capital, like every capital since the dawn of civilization, is often a place of intrigue and calculation. Powerful people maneuver for position and worry endlessly about who is in and who is out, who is up and who is down, forgetting those people whose toil and sweat sends us here and pays our way. Americans deserve better. And in this city today there are people who want to do better. And so I say to all of you here: Let us resolve to reform our politics so that power and privilege no longer shout down the voice of the people. Let us put aside personal advantage so that we can feel the pain and see the promise of America. Let us resolve to make our government a place for what Franklin Roosevelt called bold, persistent experimentation, a government for our tomorrows, not our yesterdays. Let us give this Capital back to the people to whom it belongs.

To renew America, we must meet challenges abroad as well as at home. There is no longer a clear division between what is foreign and what is domestic. The world economy, the world environment, the world AIDS crisis, the world arms race: They affect us all. Today, as an older order passes, the new world is more free but less stable. Communism's collapse has called forth old animosities and new dangers. Clearly, America must continue to lead the world we did so much to make.

While America rebuilds at home, we will not shrink from the challenges nor fail to seize the opportunities of this new world. Together with our friends and allies, we will work to shape change, lest it engulf us. When our vital interests are challenged or the will and conscience of the international community is defied, we will act, with peaceful diplomacy whenever possible, with force when necessary. The brave Americans serving our Nation today in the Persian Gulf, in Somalia, and wherever else they stand are testament to our resolve. But our greatest strength is the power of our ideas, which are still new in many lands. Across the world we see them embraced, and we rejoice. Our hopes, our hearts, our hands are with those on every continent who are building democracy and freedom. Their cause is America's cause.

The American people have summoned the change we celebrate today. You have raised your voices in an unmistakable chorus. You have cast your votes in historic numbers. And you have changed the face of Congress, the presidency, and the political process itself. Yes, you, my fellow Americans, have forced the spring. Now we must do the work the season demands. To that work I now turn with all the authority of my office. I ask the Congress to join with me. But no President, no Congress, no government can undertake this mission alone.

My fellow Americans, you, too, must play your part in our renewal. I challenge a new generation of young Americans to a season of service: to act on your idealism by helping troubled children, keeping company with those in need, reconnecting our torn communities. There is so much to be done; enough, indeed, for millions of others who are still young in spirit to give of themselves in service, too. In serving, we recognize a simple but powerful truth: We need each other, and we must care for one another.

Today we do more than celebrate America. We rededicate ourselves to the very idea of America, an idea born in revolution and renewed through two centuries of challenge; an idea tempered by the knowledge that, but for fate, we, the fortunate, and the unfortunate might have been each other; an idea ennobled by the faith that our Nation can summon from its myriad diversity the deepest measure of unity; an idea infused with the conviction that America's long, heroic journey must go forever upward.

And so, my fellow Americans, as we stand at the edge of the twenty-first century, let us begin anew with energy and hope, with faith and discipline. And let us work until our work is done. The Scripture says, "And let us not be weary in well doing: for in due season we shall reap, if we faint not." From this joyful mountaintop of celebration we hear a call to service in the valley. We have heard the trumpets. We have changed the guard. And now, each in our own way and with God's help, we must answer the call.

Thank you, and God bless you all.

SOURCE

William J. Clinton: "Inaugural Address," January 20, 1993. Online by Gerhard Peters and John T. Woolley, The American Presidency Project. http://www.presidency.ucsb.edu/ws/?pid=46366

REMARKS AT THE SIGNING OF THE ISRAELI-PALESTINIAN AGREEMENT, SEPTEMBER 13, 1993

September 1993, in the garden outside the White House, Bill Clinton presided at an extraordinary signing ceremony marking a peace agreement negotiated earlier by Prime Minister Yitzhak Rabin of Israel and Palestinian leader Yasir Arafat. President Clinton was deeply involved in efforts to bring a peaceful conclusion to the conflict in the Middle East, right up to the end of his second term in office and the Camp David meetings he organized with Israeli and Palestinian leaders.

———————

Prime Minister Rabin, Chairman Arafat, Foreign Minister Peres, Mr. Abbas, President Carter, President Bush, distinguished guests.

On behalf of the United States and Russia, cosponsors of the Middle East peace process, welcome to this great occasion of history and hope.

Today we bear witness to an extraordinary act in one of history's defining dramas, a drama that began in the time of our ancestors when the word went forth from a sliver of land between the river Jordan and the Mediterranean Sea. That hallowed piece of earth, that land of light and revelation, is the home to the memories and dreams of Jews, Muslims, and Christians throughout the world.

As we all know, devotion to that land has also been the source of conflict and bloodshed for too long. Throughout this century, bitterness between the Palestinian and Jewish people has robbed the entire region of its resources, its potential, and too many of its sons and daughters. The land has been so drenched in warfare and hatred, the conflicting claims of history etched so deeply in the souls of the combatants there that many believed the past would always have the upper hand.

Then, fourteen years ago, the past began to give way when, at this place and upon this desk, three men of great vision signed their names to the Camp David accords. Today we honor the memories of Menachem Begin and Anwar Sadat, and we salute the wise leadership of President Jimmy Carter. Then, as now, we heard from those who said that conflict would come again soon. But the peace between Egypt and Israel has endured. Just so, this bold new venture today, this brave gamble that the future can be better than the past, must endure.

Two years ago in Madrid, another President took a major step on the road to peace by bringing Israel and all her neighbors together to launch direct negotiations. And today we also express our deep thanks for the skillful leadership of President George Bush.

Ever since Harry Truman first recognized Israel, every American President, Democrat and Republican, has worked for peace between Israel and her neighbors. Now the efforts of all who have labored before us bring us to this moment, a moment when we dare to pledge what for so long seemed difficult even to imagine: that the security of the Israeli people will be reconciled with the hopes of the Palestinian people and there will be more security and more hope for all.

Today the leadership of Israel and the Palestine Liberation Organization will sign a declaration of principles on interim Palestinian self-government. It charts a course toward reconciliation between two peoples who have both known the bitterness of exile. Now both pledge to put old sorrows and antagonisms behind them and to work for a shared future shaped by the values of the Torah, the Koran, and the Bible.

Let us salute also today the Government of Norway for its remarkable role in nurturing this agreement. But above all, let us today pay tribute to the leaders who had the courage to lead their people toward peace, away from the scars of battle, the wounds and the losses of the past, toward a brighter tomorrow. The world today thanks Prime Minister Rabin, Foreign Minister Peres, and Chairman Arafat. Their tenacity and vision has given us the promise of a new beginning.

What these leaders have done now must be done by others. Their achievement must be a catalyst for progress in all aspects of the peace process. And those of us who support them must be there to help in all aspects. For the peace must render the people who make it more secure. A peace of the brave is within our reach. Throughout the Middle East, there is a great yearning for the quiet miracle of a normal life.

We know a difficult road lies ahead. Every peace has its enemies, those who still prefer the easy habits of hatred to the hard labors of reconciliation. But Prime Minister Rabin has reminded us that you do not have to make peace with your friends. And the Koran teaches that if the enemy inclines toward peace, do thou also incline toward peace.

Therefore, let us resolve that this new mutual recognition will be a continuing process in which the parties transform the very way they see and understand each other. Let the skeptics of this peace recall what once existed among these people. There was a time when the traffic of ideas and commerce and pilgrims flowed uninterrupted among the cities of the Fertile Crescent. In Spain and the Middle East, Muslims and Jews once worked together to write brilliant chapters in the history of literature and science. All this can come to pass again.

Mr. Prime Minister, Mr. Chairman, I pledge the active support of the United States of America to the difficult work that lies ahead. The United States is committed to ensuring that the people who are affected by this agreement will be made more secure by it and to leading the world in marshaling the resources necessary to implement the difficult details that will make real the principles to which you commit yourselves today.

Together let us imagine what can be accomplished if all the energy and ability the Israelis and the Palestinians have invested into your struggle can now be channeled into cultivating the land and freshening the waters, into ending the boycotts and creating new industry, into building a land as bountiful and peaceful as it is holy. Above all, let us dedicate ourselves today to your region's next generation. In this entire assembly, no one is more important than the group of Israeli and Arab children who are seated here with us today.

Mr. Prime Minister, Mr. Chairman, this day belongs to you. And because of what you have done, tomorrow belongs to them. We must not leave them prey to the politics of extremism and despair, to those who would derail this process because they cannot overcome the fears and hatreds of the past. We must not betray their future. For too long, the young of the Middle East have been caught in a web of hatred not of their own making. For too long, they have been taught from the chronicles of war. Now we can give them the chance to know the season of peace. For them we must realize the prophecy of Isaiah that the cry of violence shall no more be heard in your land, nor wrack nor ruin within your borders. The children of Abraham, the descendants of Isaac and Ishmael, have embarked together on a bold journey. Together today, with all our hearts and all our souls, we bid them shalom, salaam, peace.

SOURCE

William J. Clinton: "Remarks at the Signing of the Israeli-Palestinian Agreement," September 13, 1993. Online at The Miller Center, University of Virginia. http://millercenter.org/president/speeches/detail/3925

TIME FOR HEALING CEREMONY, OKLAHOMA CITY, APRIL 23, 1995

In spring 1995, after a huge terrorist bomb destroyed the Murrah Federal Building in Oklahoma City, taking 168 lives and injuring almost 700 people, Bill Clinton spoke for America.

Thank you very much. Governor Keating and Mrs. Keating, Reverend Graham, to the families of those who have been lost and wounded, to the people of Oklahoma City who have endured so much, and the people of this wonderful State, to all of you who are here as our fellow Americans.

I am honored to be here today to represent the American people. But I have to tell you that Hillary and I also come as parents, as husband and wife, as people who were your neighbors for some of the best years of our lives.

Today our Nation joins with you in grief. We mourn with you. We share your hope against hope that some may still survive. We thank all those who have worked so heroically to save lives and to solve this crime, those here in Oklahoma and those who are all across this great land and many who left their own lives to come here to work hand in hand with you.

We pledge to do all we can to help you heal the injured, to rebuild this city, and to bring to justice those who did this evil.

This terrible sin took the lives of our American family, innocent children in that building only because their parents were trying to be good parents as well as good workers, citizens in the building going about their daily business and many there who served the rest of us, who worked to help the elderly and the disabled, who worked to support our farmers and our veterans, who worked to enforce our laws and to protect us. Let us say clearly, they served us well, and we are grateful. But for so many of you, they were also neighbors and friends. You saw them at church or the PTA meetings, at the civic clubs, at the ball park. You know them in ways that all the rest of America could not.

And to all the members of the families here present who have suffered loss, though we share your grief, your pain is unimaginable, and we know that. We cannot undo it. That is God's work.

Our words seem small beside the loss you have endured. But I found a few I wanted to share today. I've received a lot of letters in these last terrible days. One stood out because it came from a young widow and a mother of three whose own husband was murdered with over 200 other Americans when Pan Am 103 was shot down. Here is what that woman said I should say to you today: "The anger you feel is valid, but you must not allow yourselves to be consumed by it. The hurt you feel must not be allowed to turn into hate but instead into the search for justice. The loss you feel must not paralyze your own lives. Instead, you must try to pay tribute to your loved ones by continuing to do all the things they left undone, thus ensuring they did not die in vain." Wise words from one who also knows.

You have lost too much, but you have not lost everything. And you have certainly not lost America, for we will stand with you for as many tomorrows as it takes.

If ever we needed evidence of that, I could only recall the words of Governor and Mrs. Keating. If anybody thinks that Americans are mostly mean and selfish, they ought to come to Oklahoma. If anybody thinks Americans have lost the capacity for love and caring and courage, they ought to come to Oklahoma.

To all my fellow Americans beyond this hall, I say, one thing we owe those who have sacrificed is the duty to purge ourselves of the dark forces which gave rise to this evil. They are forces that threaten our common peace, our freedom, our way of life.

Let us teach our children that the God of comfort is also the God of righteousness. Those who trouble their own house will inherit the wind. Justice will prevail.

Let us let our own children know that we will stand against the forces of fear. When there is talk of hatred, let us stand up and talk against it. When there is talk of violence, let us stand up and talk against it. In the face of death, let us honor life. As St. Paul admonished us, let us not be overcome by evil, but overcome evil with good.

Yesterday Hillary and I had the privilege of speaking with some children of other Federal employees, children like those who were lost here. And one little girl said something we will never forget. She said, we should all plant a tree in memory of the children. So this morning before we got on the plane to come here, at the White House, we planted that tree in honor of the children of Oklahoma. It was a dogwood with its wonderful spring flower and its deep, enduring roots. It embodies the lesson of the Psalms: that the life of a good person is like a tree whose leaf does not wither.

My fellow Americans, a tree takes a long time to grow, and wounds take a long time to heal. But we must begin. Those who are lost now belong to God. Someday we will be with them. But until that happens, their legacy must be our lives.

Thank you all, and God bless you.

SOURCE

William J. Clinton: "Time for Healing Ceremony," April 23, 1995. Online at The Miller Center, University of Virginia. http://millercenter.org/president/speeches/detail/3441

SECOND INAUGURAL ADDRESS
JANUARY 20, 1997

After his victory in the 1996 presidential election, in a moment of growing optimism about America's future as the strong economic recovery begun in his first term continued to be marked by wage increases for millions and a decline not only in unemployment but the national deficit, President Bill Clinton spoke at his second inauguration. He described the United States, "at the edge of a new century, in a new millennium."

My fellow citizens, at this last presidential inauguration of the twentieth century, let us lift our eyes toward the challenges that await us in the next century. It is our great good fortune that time and chance have put us not only at the edge of a new century, in a new millennium, but on the edge of a bright new prospect in human affairs, a moment that will define our course and our character for decades to come. We must keep our old democracy forever young. Guided by the ancient vision of a promised land, let us set our sights upon a land of new promise.

The promise of America was born in the eighteenth century out of the bold conviction that we are all created equal. It was extended and preserved in the nineteenth century, when our Nation spread across the continent, saved the Union, and abolished the awful scourge of slavery.

Then, in turmoil and triumph, that promise exploded onto the world stage to make this the American Century. And what a century it has been. America became the world's mightiest industrial power, saved the world from tyranny in two world wars and a long cold war, and time and again reached out across the globe to millions who, like us, longed for the blessings of liberty.

Along the way, Americans produced a great middle class and security in old age, built unrivaled centers of learning and opened public schools to all, split the atom and explored the heavens, invented the computer and the microchip, and deepened the wellspring of justice by making a revolution in civil rights for African Americans and all minorities and extending the circle of citizenship, opportunity, and dignity to women.

Now, for the third time, a new century is upon us and another time to choose. We began the nineteenth century with a choice: to spread our Nation from coast to coast. We began the twentieth century with a choice: to harness the Industrial Revolution to our values of free enterprise, conservation, and human decency. Those choices made all the difference. At the dawn of the twenty-first century, a free people must now choose to shape the forces of the information age and the global society, to unleash the limitless potential of all our people, and, yes, to form a more perfect Union.

When last we gathered, our march to this new future seemed less certain than it does today. We vowed then to set a clear course to renew our Nation. In these four years, we have been touched by tragedy, exhilarated by challenge, strengthened by achievement. America stands alone as the world's indispensable nation. Once again, our economy is the strongest on Earth. Once again, we are building stronger families, thriving communities, better educational opportunities, a cleaner environment. Problems that once seemed destined to deepen now bend to our efforts. Our streets are safer, and record numbers of our fellow citizens have moved from welfare to work. And once again, we have resolved for our time a great debate over the role of government. Today we can declare: Government is not the problem, and government is not the solution. We—the American people—we are the solution. Our Founders understood that well and gave us a democracy strong enough to endure for centuries, flexible enough to face our common challenges and advance our common dreams in each new day.

As times change, so government must change. We need a new government for a new century, humble enough not to try to solve all our problems for us but strong enough to give us the tools to solve our problems for ourselves, a government that is smaller, lives within its means, and does more with less. Yet where it can stand up for our values and interests around the world, and where it can give Americans the power to make a real difference in their everyday lives, government should do more, not less. The preeminent mission of our new government is to give all Americans an opportunity, not a guarantee but a real opportunity, to build better lives.

Beyond that, my fellow citizens, the future is up to us. Our Founders taught us that the preservation of our liberty and our Union depends upon responsible citizenship. And we need a new sense of responsibility for a new century. There is work to do, work that government alone cannot do:

teaching children to read, hiring people off welfare rolls, coming out from behind locked doors and shuttered windows to help reclaim our streets from drugs and gangs and crime, taking time out of our own lives to serve others.

Each and every one of us, in our own way, must assume personal responsibility not only for ourselves and our families but for our neighbors and our Nation. Our greatest responsibility is to embrace a new spirit of community for a new century. For any one of us to succeed, we must succeed as one America. The challenge of our past remains the challenge of our future: Will we be one Nation, one people, with one common destiny, or not? Will we all come together, or come apart?

The divide of race has been America's constant curse. And each new wave of immigrants gives new targets to old prejudices. Prejudice and contempt cloaked in the pretense of religious or political conviction are no different. These forces have nearly destroyed our Nation in the past. They plague us still. They fuel the fanaticism of terror. And they torment the lives of millions in fractured nations all around the world.

These obsessions cripple both those who hate and of course those who are hated, robbing both of what they might become. We cannot, we will not, succumb to the dark impulses that lurk in the far regions of the soul everywhere. We shall overcome them. And we shall replace them with the generous spirit of a people who feel at home with one another. Our rich texture of racial, religious, and political diversity will be a godsend in the twenty-first century. Great rewards will come to those who can live together, learn together, work together, forge new ties that bind together.

As this new era approaches, we can already see its broad outlines. Ten years ago, the Internet was the mystical province of physicists; today, it is a commonplace encyclopedia for millions of schoolchildren. Scientists now are decoding the blueprint of human life. Cures for our most feared illnesses seem close at hand. The world is no longer divided into two hostile camps. Instead, now we are building bonds with nations that once were our adversaries. Growing connections of commerce and culture give us a chance to lift the fortunes and spirits of people the world over. And for the very first time in all of history, more people on this planet live under democracy than dictatorship.

My fellow Americans, as we look back at this remarkable century, we may ask, can we hope not just to follow but even to surpass the achievements of the twentieth century in America and to avoid the awful bloodshed that stained its legacy? To that question, every American here and every American in our land today must answer a resounding "Yes!" This is the heart of our task. With a new vision of government, a new sense of responsibility, a new spirit of community, we will sustain America's journey.

The promise we sought in a new land we will find again in a land of new promise. In this new land, education will be every citizen's most prized possession. Our schools will have the highest standards in the world, igniting the spark of possibility in the eyes of every girl and every boy. And the doors of higher education will be open to all. The knowledge and power of the information age will be within reach not just of the few but of every classroom, every library, every child. Parents and children will have time not only to work but to read and play together. And the plans they make at their kitchen table will be those of a better home, a better job, the certain chance to go to college.

Our streets will echo again with the laughter of our children, because no one will try to shoot them or sell them drugs anymore. Everyone who can work, will work, with today's permanent underclass part of tomorrow's growing middle class. New miracles of medicine at last will reach not only those who can claim care now but the children and hardworking families too long denied.

We will stand mighty for peace and freedom and maintain a strong defense against terror and destruction. Our children will sleep free from the threat of nuclear, chemical, or biological weapons. Ports and airports, farms and factories will thrive with trade and innovation and ideas. And the world's greatest democracy will lead a whole world of democracies.

Our land of new promise will be a Nation that meets its obligations, a Nation that balances its budget but never loses the balance of its values, a Nation where our grandparents have secure retirement and health care and their grandchildren know we have made the reforms necessary to sustain those benefits for their time, a Nation that fortifies the world's most productive economy even as it protects the great natural bounty of our water, air, and majestic land. And in this land of new promise, we will have reformed our politics so that the voice of the people will always speak louder than the din of narrow interests, regaining the participation and deserving the trust of all Americans.

Fellow citizens, let us build that America, a Nation ever moving forward toward realizing the full potential of all its citizens. Prosperity and power, yes, they are important, and we must maintain them. But let us never forget: The greatest progress we have made and the greatest progress we have yet to make is in the human heart. In the end, all the world's wealth and a thousand armies are no match for the strength and decency of the human spirit.

Thirty-four years ago, the man whose life we celebrate today spoke to us down there, at the other end of this Mall, in words that moved the conscience of a nation. Like a prophet of old, he told of his dream that one day America would rise up and treat all its citizens as equals before the law and in the heart. Martin Luther King's dream was the American dream.

His quest is our quest: the ceaseless striving to live out our true creed. Our history has been built on such dreams and labors. And by our dreams and labors, we will redeem the promise of America in the twenty-first century.

To that effort I pledge all my strength and every power of my office. I ask the Members of Congress here to join in that pledge. The American people returned to office a President of one party and a Congress of another. Surely they did not do this to advance the politics of petty bickering and extreme partisanship they plainly deplore. No, they call on us instead to be repairers of the breach and to move on with America's mission. America demands and deserves big things from us, and nothing big ever came from being small. Let us remember the timeless wisdom of Cardinal Bernardin, when facing the end of his own life. He said, "It is wrong to waste the precious gift of time on acrimony and division."

Fellow citizens, we must not waste the precious gift of this time. For all of us are on that same journey of our lives, and our journey, too, will come to an end. But the journey of our America must go on.

And so, my fellow Americans, we must be strong, for there is much to dare. The demands of our time are great, and they are different. Let us meet them with faith and courage, with patience and a grateful, happy heart. Let us shape the hope of this day into the noblest chapter in our history. Yes, let us build our bridge, a bridge wide enough and strong enough for every American to cross over to a blessed land of new promise.

May those generations whose faces we cannot yet see, whose names we may never know, say of us here that we led our beloved land into a new century with the American dream alive for all her children, with the American promise of a more perfect Union a reality for all her people, with America's bright flame of freedom spreading throughout all the world.

From the height of this place and the summit of this century, let us go forth. May God strengthen our hands for the good work ahead, and always, always bless our America.

SOURCE

William J. Clinton: "Inaugural Address," January 20, 1997. Online by Gerhard Peters and John T. Woolley, The American Presidency Project. http://www.presidency.ucsb.edu/ws/?pid=54183

SELECTED BIBLIOGRAPHY

Albright, Madeleine. *Madame Secretary*. New York: Hyperion, 2003.

Baker, Peter. *The Breech*. New York: Scribner, 2000.

Begala, Paul, and Carville, James. *Buck Up, Suck Up and Come Back When You Foul Up*. New York: Simon and Schuster, 2002.

Bennett, William J. *The Death of Outrage*. New York: Simon and Schuster, 1998.

Blumenthal, Sidney. *The Clinton Wars*. New York: Penguin, 2004.

Branch, Taylor. *The Clinton Tapes*. New York: Simon and Schuster, 2009.

Brock, David. *Blinded by the Right*. New York: Crown, 2002.

Campbell, Kurt M., and Steinberg, James B. *Difficult Transitions*. Washington: Brookings Institution Press, 2008.

Carville, James, and Matalin, Mary. *All's Fair*. New York: Random House, 1995.

Chafe, William H. *Bill and Hillary*. New York: Farrar, Straus and Giroux, 2012.

Christopher, Warren. *In the Stream of History*. Stanford: Stanford University Press, 1998.

Clark, Wesley. *Waging Modern War*. New York: Public Affairs, 2001.

Clarke, Richard. *Against All Enemies*. New York: Free Press, 2004.

Clinton, Bill. *My Life*. New York: Alfred A. Knopf, 2004.

———. *Back to Work*. New York: Random House, 2011.

———. *Select Remarks, 2001–2011*. Little Rock: William Jefferson Clinton Foundation, 2011.

Clinton, Hillary Rodham. *Living History*. New York: Scribner, 2003.

Conason, Joe, and Lyons, Gene. *The Hunting of the President*. New York: St. Martin's Press, 2000.

Conley, Richard S. *Historical Dictionary of the Clinton Era*. Toronto: Scarecrow Press, 2011.

Daalder, Ivo, and O'Hanlon, Michael E. *Winning Ugly*. Washington: Brookings Institution Press, 2000.

Dershowitz, Alan. *Sexual McCarthyism*. New York: Basic Books, 1998.

Drew, Elizabeth. *On the Edge: The Clinton Presidency*. New York: Simon and Schuster, 1994.

———. *Showdown*. New York: Simon and Schuster, 1996.

Fallows, James. *Breaking the News: How the Media Undermine American Democracy*. New York: Pantheon, 1996.

Gartner, John D. *In Search of Bill Clinton*. New York: St. Martin's Press, 2008.

Gillon, Steven M. *The Pact*. New York: Oxford University Press, 2008.

Gormley, Ken. *The Death of American Virtue: Clinton vs. Starr*. New York: Crown, 2010.

Hamilton, Nigel. *Bill Clinton: Great Expectations*. New York: Random House, 2003.

———. *Bill Clinton: Mastering the Presidency*. New York: Random House, 2006.

Harris, John. *The Survivor*. New York: Random House, 2005.

Holbrooke, Richard. *To End a War*. New York: Modern Library, 1999.

Isikoff, Michael. *Uncovering Clinton*. New York: Three Rivers Press, 2000.

Kalb, Marvin. *One Scandalous Story*. New York: Free Press, 2001.

Kearney, Jaris F., ed. *William Jefferson Clinton: Conversations from Hope to Harlem*. Chicago: Writing Our World Press, 2006.

Klein, Joe. *The Natural*. New York: Random House, 2002.

Lyons, Gene. *Fools for Scandal: How the Media Invented Whitewater*. New York: Franklin Square Press, 1996.

Maraniss, David. *First in His Class*. New York: Simon and Schuster, 1995.

Morton, Andrew. *Monica's Story*. New York: St. Martin's Press, 1999.

Podesta, John. *The Power of Progress*. New York: Crown, 2008.

Rae, Nicol, and Campbell, Colton. *Impeaching Clinton: Partisan Strife on Capitol Hill*. Lawrence: University of Kansas, 2004.

Reich, Robert. *Locked in the Cabinet*. New York: Vintage, 1998.

Sale, Richard. *Clinton's Secret Wars*. New York: St. Martin's Press, 2006.

Sheehy, Gail. *Hillary's Choice*. New York: Random House, 1999.

Shields, Todd; Whayne, Jeannie; and Kelly, Donald, eds., *The Clinton Riddle*. Fayetteville: University of Arkansas Press, 2004.

Starr, Kenneth. *The Starr Report: Findings of Independent Counsel Kenneth W. Starr on President Clinton and the Lewinsky Affair*. Washington: The Washington Post, 1998.

Stephanopoulos, George. *All Too Human*. Boston: Little, Brown, 1999.

Stewart, James. *Blood Sport*. New York: Simon and Schuster, 1996.

Takiff, Michael. *A Complicated Man: The Life of Bill Clinton as Told by Those Who Know Him*. New Haven: Yale University Press, 2010.

Talbott, Strobe. *The Russia Hand*. New York: Random House, 2002.

———. *The Great Experiment*. New York: Simon and Schuster, 2008.

Toobin, Jeffrey. *A Vast Conspiracy*. New York: Touchstone, 1999.

Waldman, Michael. *POTUS Speaks*. New York: Simon and Schuster, 2000.

Wittes, Benjamin. *Starr: A Reassessment*. New Haven: Yale University Press, 2002.

Woodward, Bob. *The Agenda*. New York: Simon and Shuster, 1994.

———. *The Choice*. New York: Simon and Schuster, 1996.

———. *Shadow*. New York: Simon and Schuster, 1999.

INDEX

www.routledge.com/history

Critical Moments in American History

Series Editor: William Thomas Allison,
Georgia Southern University

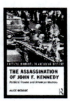

The Battle of the Greasy Grass/Little Bighorn
By Debra Buchholtz
ISBN 13: 978-0-415-89559-0 (pbk)

The Assassination of John F. Kennedy
By Alice L. George
ISBN 13: 978-0-415-89557-6 (pbk)

Freedom to Serve
By Jon E. Taylor
ISBN 13: 978-0-415-89448-7 (pbk)

The Battles of Kings Mountain and Cowpens
By Melissa Walker
ISBN 13: 978-0-415-89561-3 (pbk)

The Nativist Movement in America
By Katie Oxx
ISBN 13: 978-0-415-80748-7 (pbk)

The Cuban Missile Crisis
By Alice L. George
ISBN 13: 978-0-415-89972-7 (pbk)

The 1980 Presidential Election
By Jeffrey D. Howison
ISBN 13: 978-0-415-52193-2 (pbk)

The Fort Pillow Massacre
By Bruce Tap
ISBN 13: 978-0-415-80864-4 (pbk)

The Louisiana Purchase
By Robert D. Bush
ISBN 13: 978-0-415-81457-7 (pbk)

From Selma to Montgomery
By Barbara Harris Combs
ISBN 13: 978-0-415-52960-0 (pbk)

For additional resources visit the series website at:
www.routledge.com/cw/criticalmoments

Available from all good bookshops

Democracy as a Way of Life in America
A History

Richard Schneirov
and **Gaston A. Fernandez**

The United States is a nation whose identity is defined by the idea of democracy. Yet democracy in the U.S. is often taken for granted, narrowly understood, and rarely critically examined. In *Democracy as a Way of Life in America*, Schneirov and Fernandez show that, much more than a static legacy from the past, democracy is a living process that informs all aspects of American life.

The authors trace the story of American democracy from the revolution to the present, showing how democracy has changed over time, and the challenges it has faced. They examine themes including individualism, foreign policy, the economy, and the environment, and reveal how democracy has been deeply involved in these throughout the country's history.

Democracy as a Way of Life in America demonstrates that democracy is not simply a set of institutions or practices such as the right to vote or competing political parties, but a complex, multi-dimensional phenomenon, whose animating spirit can be found in every part of American culture and society. This vital and engaging narrative should be read by students of history, political science, and anyone who wants to understand the nature of American democracy.

978-0-415-83612-8 (pbk)
978-0-415-83611-1 (hbk)
September 2013